Advanced BlackBerry Development

T0225744

▪▪▪

Chris King

apress®

Advanced BlackBerry Development

ISBN-13 (pbk): 978-1-4302-2656-7

ISBN-13 (electronic): 978-1-4302-2657-4

President and Publishing: Paul Manning
Lead Editor: Ewan Buckingham
Technical Reviewer: Levon Dolbakian
Editorial Board: Clay Andres, Steve Anglin, Mark Beckner, Ewan Buckingham, Gary Cornell, Jonathan Gennick, Michelle Lowman, Matthew Moodie, Jeffrey Pepper, Frank Pohlmann, Ben Renow-Clarke, Dominic Shakeshaft, Matt Wade, Tom Welsh
Coordinating Editor: Mary Tobin
Copy Editor: Kari Brooks-Copony and Mary Tobin
Compositor: LaurelTech
Indexer: BIM Indexing and e-Services
Artist: April Milne
Cover Designer: Anna Ishchenko

Distributed to the book trade worldwide by Springer-Verlag New York, Inc., 233 Spring Street, 6th Floor, New York, NY 10013. Phone 1-800-SPRINGER, fax 201-348-4505, e-mail orders-ny@springer-sbm.com, or visit http://www.springeronline.com.

For information on translations, please e-mail info@apress.com, or visit http://www.apress.com.

Apress and friends of ED books may be purchased in bulk for academic, corporate, or promotional use. eBook versions and licenses are also available for most titles. For more information, reference our Special Bulk Sales–eBook Licensing web page at http://www.apress.com/info/bulksales.

The information in this book is distributed on an "as is" basis, without warranty. Although every precaution has been taken in the preparation of this work, neither the author(s) nor Apress shall have any liability to any person or entity with respect to any loss or damage caused or alleged to be caused directly or indirectly by the information contained in this work.

The source code for this book is available to readers at http://www.apress.com. You will need to answer questions pertaining to this book in order to successfully download the code.

For Mom and Dad

Contents at a Glance

Contents

About the Author

 **Chris King** is a software engineer specializing in mobile development. He has written a wide variety of embedded and downloadable libraries and applications, including wireless messaging, lifestyle, shopping, music, and video applications. His software has been pre-loaded on tens of millions of phones in the United States. Chris develops applications for BlackBerry, Android, Java ME, BREW, and Windows Mobile devices. Chris has written articles on mobile development, and was the technical reviewer for the books Android Essentials by Chris Haseman and Beginning Java ME Platform by Ray Rischpater. He currently serves as a Senior Engineer for Gravity Mobile in San Francisco.

Chris graduated summa cum laude from Washington University in St. Louis with majors in Computer Science and English Literature. When he isn't programming or writing for fun or profit, Chris can be found reading, baking, cycling, or hiking throughout the San Francisco Bay Area.

Acknowledgments

First and foremost, I owe Ray Rischpater an enormous debt for the creation of this book. It would be an understatement to say that it couldn't have happened without him. Ray wrote the book that got me started in mobile development; he encouraged me to move to Silicon Valley; he was an excellent mentor and teacher during our years together at Rocket Mobile; he gave me the honor of tech reviewing his Java ME book; and he recommended me to Apress for this current book. I feel fortunate to call Ray a colleague; I feel blessed to call him a friend.

Working with the fine staff at Apress has been a joy. Steve Anglin had the vision for this book and got the project off the ground. My editor Mark Beckner was encouraging and helpful throughout the process, both for the writing and for dealing with unexpected administrative issues. Ewan Buckingham provided thoughtful feedback as the book came together. Mary Tobin masterfully coordinated the sizeable team, and even rolled up her sleeves to help edit chapters as we hurried to reach a deadline. Kari Brooks-Copony did a fantastic job copy-editing the chapters and helped make the words flow. I'm grateful for all their efforts, as well as those from everyone else at Apress who I didn't have the chance to meet.

Levon Dolbakian, my technical reviewer, deserves particular kudos for his contributions to the book. Levon worked extremely hard, plowing through the wide variety of material, and going the extra mile to check the accuracy of all the examples. In the process he uncovered compatibility issues, identified confusing passages, and pointed out where additional explanations would be helpful. The result is a far more accurate book. Any remaining errors are solely my own.

No book or person exists in a vacuum, and I feel extremely grateful for all the people who have supported me throughout my career and made software development such a rewarding field. I'm particularly thankful for Jim Alisago, Erik Browne, Graham Darcey, Cathy Donovan, Dr. Chris Gill, Dr. Ken Goldman, Jonathan Jackson, Craig Kawahara, Mike Ma, Chad Moats, Sasha Parry, Greg Peters, Ian Peters-Campbell, Brian Pridham, Rajiv Ramanasankaran, Dave Robaska, Tom Seago, Charles Stearns, Young Yoon, and Wayne Yurtin. My apologies for anyone whose name I may have forgotten; I consider myself fortunate to have met a surplus of talented and generous people in my career.

A special shout-out goes to the whole gang at Gravity Mobile. Gravity has been one of the most exciting, challenging, and fun places that I have worked, and Noah Hurwitz and Chris Lyon deserve enormous credit for creating such a wonderful environment. I'm especially thankful to work for Sam Trychin, who isn't only one of the smartest people I know, but also one of the nicest. Big thanks as well to Chris Haseman, the ultimate connector. Chris seems to know everyone and everything, and has been instrumental in getting me started at Gravity, lining up writing gigs, and more. Chris seems to succeed at everything he tries, and inspires me to push myself harder. I also appreciate Todd Meyer's approval of this project.

Last but not least, special thanks to Jason Salge. Jason taught me how to be a professional programmer, enabling the transition from academic theory to practical development. Jason has been an invaluable mentor, showing me the ropes in the telecom industry, encouraging my architectural aspirations, helping me learn the questions to ask in a start-up, and above all, demonstrating how to be a good person. Jason provided the opportunities that set my feet on this path, and I will always be grateful.

Introduction

Carrying a BlackBerry used to speak volumes about a person. When you saw someone tapping at that wide keyboard with both thumbs, you could safely assume that the owner was a businessperson, and that their time was so valuable that they couldn't afford to be out of touch from the office. Today, you can no longer make that assumption. BlackBerry devices are carried by teenagers, surfers, knitters, seemingly everyone. The rest of the world has caught on to what initially attracted people to these phones: BlackBerry devices offer the Internet in a pocket-sized block. Anyone who has experienced that large screen, that expansive keyboard, that powerful processor, will not be content to return to a crammed phone with a multi-tap dial pad.

The explosion in the number of BlackBerry devices has raised peoples' expectations, and also created a tempting marketplace for programmers everywhere. BlackBerry applications offer a surprisingly rich and expressive interface for a mobile device, and people are willing to pay for the best apps available. People sell their applications on BlackBerry App World, through off-deck stores like Handango, and through wireless carrier stores. Many more people program for fun and load their applications on their own devices or those of friends. And, because BlackBerry still has a dominant presence in the enterprise marketplace, many programmers write applications particularly for their internal business customers.

This book will show you how to make the most of your BlackBerry applications. It focuses on the most fun, the most impressive, and the most rewarding aspects of development. By the time you finish, you should be able to write professional-quality applications.

The Book's Anatomy

Advanced BlackBerry Development is divided into three parts. Each part concentrates on a particular theme. The book was designed to be read in sequence, as each chapter builds on the chapters that come before, but veteran developers can easily move to the parts that interest them the most.Part 1, "Advanced APIs"

This first part of the book focuses on the rich feature set offered by modern BlackBerry devices. By examining individual topics, you can gain a great depth of knowledge about the material.

- *Chapter 1, "Getting Started"*: Provides a quick introduction to BlackBerry development. You'll see how to set up your programming environment and learn the fundamentals of Java development for BlackBerry.
- *Chapter 2, "Media Capture"*: Shows how to record audio and video from within your application or other applications on the device.
- *Chapter 3, "Media Playback"*: Describes the vast range of media types supported by BlackBerry and how to include each one within an application.

- *Chapter 4, "Wireless Messaging"*: Introduces the technologies used to send and receive various types of messages including SMS, email, and BlackBerry PIN.
- *Chapter 5, "Cryptography"*: Offers a quick primer on security, including how to obscure information, determine authenticity, and prevent tampering. Discusses the various toolkits available for cryptography, their advantages, and how to use each.

Part 2, "Device Integration"

- This part of the book turns towards leveraging the existing functions of the device. Canny programmers will take advantage of the resources built into each BlackBerry, and learn how to make their app indispensible to the user.
- *Chapter 6, "Personal Information"*: Examines the various repositories of personal data on the phone, such as the address book and calendar. Shows how to read, update, and create new records from within your application.
- *Chapter 7, "Browser"*: Explores the rich set of integration possibilities with the built-in browser, including opportunities for embedding your app within the browser or vice versa. Describes the various types of browsers and how they impact your development.
- *Chapter 8, "Digging In Deep"*: Covers a variety of useful techniques such as providing customized icons, communicating between applications, and adding options to the device's native menus.

Part 3, "Going Pro"

- While the first two parts of the book primarily focus on adding features to your applications, this last part focuses on technique: how to improve your software in ways that may not be visible to the user, but that make it more robust and improve your efficiency.
- *Chapter 9, "RIM Security"*: Deciphers the often baffling security model that constraints the behavior of BlackBerry applications. This chapter explains the critical issues that may come up as you develop your application or that emerge only after it has been released. In the process, you'll learn what tools are available to get the permissions you need, and how to deal with cases where your app is forbidden from doing certain things.
- *Chapter 10, "Porting Your App"*: Provides an overview of the many issues to face when you make your application available for multiple devices or multiple countries. By learning these lessons early, you can make the inevitable porting process much quicker and more enjoyable.
- *Chapter 11, "Advanced Build Techniques"*: Shows how to move from a one-person operation to a more professional and organized approach. Introduces the many tools available for use, including build scripts, debug logging, release packages, and more.
- *Chapter 12, "Conclusion"*: Shares some final thoughts on development and offers resources for further education.

How to Read This Book

Depending on your background and goals, you might approach this book in different ways. The chapters are designed to be read in order, as later chapters may reference content from earlier chapters. However, such references are made explicit in the text, and you might find it more useful to approach the book in another order according to your interests or most pressing deadlines.

Novice

If you are new to BlackBerry development, you should start with Chapter 1, which offers an accelerated introduction to the platform. Spend as much time here as you need and continue once you are comfortable with all the material. You can continue reading the remainder of the book in sequence, working through all the examples and reading the notes.

ApprenticeIf you have some familiarity with BlackBerry development, you can skim Chapter 1, reading any topics that are unfamiliar. From here, you can proceed through the book in sequence, focusing on the chapters that offer new material.

Journeyman

Veteran Java ME developers will notice that many of the BlackBerry APIs, particularly those related to media and wireless messaging, are similar or identical to their Java ME counterparts. I point out the important differences within the text. These developers should particularly focus on Chapter 1 for setting up their BlackBerry environment and Chapter 9 to learn about the critical differences between Java ME and BlackBerry security.

Master

Finally, BlackBerry experts can largely skip Chapter 1, and refer to individual chapters to learn about particular topics of interest. Veterans will recognize the importance of BlackBerry device software versions, and will pay particular attention to the tables that show the significant differences between versions.Notes on Conventions

One of my personal pet peeves is that most programming books today are written as if it was still 1990. Thanks to the ubiquitous availability of Javadocs, we can easily look up the details about individual methods. Thanks to modern IDEs, we can easily discover available APIs and find out how to use them properly.

In writing this book, I've focused on the things that you can't easily see in the Javadocs: the meaning behind methods, when to call particular APIs, and the tradeoffs between various solutions. To avoid distraction, I generally omit parameters when I name a method. I generally omit the package name when I name a class. In Eclipse, Ctrl+Space is your friend. Of course, in situations where usage is ambiguous, I provide the details explaining which item is being used.

Similarly, exception handling is a great tool for writing robust software, but tends to muddy even the simplest examples. I generally omit exception handling when introducing a new method unless its exceptions are particularly unusual.

The end of each chapter contains a longer set of sample code that runs as a stand-alone application. Here, I fully handle all exceptions, include full package names, and do everything else to show how a real-world application should perform.

Your Media App

Each chapter contains numerous small snippets of code designed to help illustrate particular points. The end of each chapter is devoted to creating a useful, stand-alone application that incorporates concepts from throughout the chapter. In order to provide the experience of writing a realistic, feature-rich application, you will be building a single media-sharing application throughout the course of the book. Each chapter from Chapter 2 onward will contribute a new section to it, gradually improving it from a skeleton of an app to a robust platform for media communication.

Complete source code for this media app is provided at the Apress web site, http://www.apress.com. You can download the sample for each chapter, along with any other listings provided within the main body of the chapter. I encourage you to use the source code as a reference, not an answer key. You will learn the most by working through the sample yourself, adding sections gradually, then running and observing the code. If you skip chapters while reading, you might want to download the previous chapter's source code solution, and then make the modifications for the current chapter on your own.

The Trailhead

I go hiking in the mountains almost every weekend. I love the sensations you get in a good hike. You feel invigorated by the sense of mystery and possibility. As you climb higher and higher, the ground drops away below you. You start to gain perspective, with your visual range extending to yards and then miles. As you continue to ascend, you see even more of the landscape, but it isn't static: every curve brings an unexpected new sight, every switchback a fresh vista. No matter how challenging a hike is, once you reach the summit you feel that it's all worthwhile, and feel a sense of ownership as you survey the land below you.

I find that learning a new technology is a great deal like that sort of hike. When you start, you can only see the things right in front of you: the editor, the syntax, the tools. As you continue to progress, you begin to catch sight of the wide range of features that the technology offers. You gain more and more mastery, and with that experience comes perspective, as you begin to see how the technology's pieces all work together. But as with a hike, you can always keep going a little further, always learn something new. I've found BlackBerry programming to be a particularly fun trail, and hope you will enjoy the journey too. Keep striving, keep moving upward, and appreciate the view.

Advanced APIs

The best BlackBerry apps take advantage of the rich set of advanced APIs available on this platform. The chapters in Part 1 describe some of the most exciting and compelling features available to you. Chapter 1 provides a crash course in building a variety of RIM applications that can access the local filesystem and the Internet. From there, learn how to use the device to shoot photos, record sound and video, and use the captured data in your app. Next, see the wide variety of options available for playing video, animations, and audio content. Connect the BlackBerry to the rest of the mobile world with wireless messaging and email technologies. Finally, incorporate today's techniques for safeguarding data into your own applications.

Chapter 1

Getting Started

Welcome to the wonderful world of BlackBerry app development! Chapter 1 is intended to get you up to speed as quickly as possible, so you can get right into the good stuff, and it assumes no previous knowledge other than a basic grasp of Java. This chapter will walk you through downloading software, setting up your environment, and then give you a quick tour through the basics of BlackBerry app development. You may linger, skim, or skip ahead as your patience demands.

Initial Setup

As with any new language or platform, you will need to install some new software and set up your computer appropriately. There are many different ways to run a successful BlackBerry project. RIM supports only Windows development, but it has done a good job of releasing tools that enable development on a variety of configurations. This section will focus on what I have found to be the simplest and most effective setup for independent development, with occasional notes for alternative choices you might consider.

Getting Java

You will be developing in Java for the BlackBerry, but before we get that far, we need to make sure Java on your desktop is running properly. RIM uses Java for their *toolchain*—the set of programs that will convert your application source files into a format that can run on the mobile device. Additionally, our Eclipse IDE requires a Java runtime environment.

To see if Java is installed, open a command prompt. You can do this by clicking Start → Run, typing cmd, and pressing enter. A black-and-white command prompt window will appear. Type java -version. You should see something like the following:

```
java version "1.6.0_14"
Java(TM) SE Runtime Environment (build 1.6.0_14-b08)
Java HotSpot(TM) Client VM (build 14.0-b16, mixed mode, sharing)
```

The specific version number isn't important, just getting a response. If Java is not installed or is not configured correctly, you will see an error like the following:

```
'java' is not recognized as an internal or external command,
operable program or batch file.
```

To install Java, go to http://java.sun.com and look for the Java SE download. You only need to install the Java Runtime Environment (JRE). However, if you plan on doing other Java development besides BlackBerry, you can download the full Java Development Kit (JDK), which also includes the JRE.

> **Tip:** When installing any development software, I suggest you pick an install path that has no spaces in it. For example, instead of installing to c:\Program Files\Java, install to c:\dev\java. This will save you time in the future, as some Java programs and other useful utilities have a hard time working with files that have spaces in their name. Follow this rule for all the other downloads in this chapter, as well.

Once you have downloaded and installed the JRE, try opening another command prompt and typing java -version again. If it still doesn't recognize the command, you probably need to add Java to your PATH environment variable. In Windows XP, you can access this by right-clicking on My Computer, selecting Properties, clicking the Advanced tab, and then clicking Environment Variables. Make sure the path to your installed java.exe directory is included in the PATH. This will probably be something like c:\dev\java\jre1.6.0_14\bin.

Goldilocks and the Three IDEs

Once upon a time, a developer was evaluating which IDE to use when writing BlackBerry apps. First she tried the RIM JDE. "Oh my!" she exclaimed. "This IDE is much too ugly!" Then she tried Netbeans. "This IDE doesn't understand BlackBerry," she complained. Finally, she installed Eclipse with the BlackBerry Plug-in. "Ahhh," she smiled. "This IDE is just right!"

The reality is that you can develop in any IDE that you want. The question is how much time and effort you will invest in getting everything to work right. I've found that Eclipse is the best platform for doing serious development, and it has only gotten better and easier since RIM released their official Plug-in. I will be using Eclipse for my examples in the rest of this book, and I recommend installing it unless you are already doing BlackBerry development in another environment.

To get started, go to http://eclipse.org. I suggest you download a recent release of the Eclipse IDE for Java EE Developers. Depending on what other kinds of development you do, you may choose to use another package. This is fine, but Eclipse EE contains the most options and will give you the greatest flexibility.

Caution: As of this writing, there are compatibility issues with Eclipse 3.5 (Galileo) and the BlackBerry JDE Plug-in for Eclipse. If you experience problems, use the older 3.4 (Ganymede) version of Eclipse. This is currently located in the Downloads page of the Eclipse web site, where you can select "Older Versions." You can safely install multiple versions of Eclipse into separate directories on your computer.

Eclipse doesn't have a standard Windows installer. Instead, you simply unzip it to a folder on your computer. You could put it somewhere like `c:\dev\eclipse`. To make it easier to launch, you can right-click and drag the `eclipse.exe` icon to your desktop or task bar in order to create a shortcut.

When you first launch Eclipse, it will ask you to choose a workspace. You can create one wherever you like. Do not check the option for "Use this as the default and do not ask me again." One quirk of BlackBerry development is that each BlackBerry app you develop will require its own separate workspace, so you will be switching workspaces as you go through this book.

Plugged In

I have been a fan of Eclipse for many years now, in large part because of its very flexible and powerful Plug-in system. Plug-ins allow developers to tune their workspace for their specific tasks, without needing the bother of relearning a new tool for each new task.

There are currently two ways to install the Plug-in. The first is to go to BlackBerry's developer web page (currently located at `http://na.blackberry.com/eng/developers/`) and download the Plug-in as an EXE file. This is the simplest approach, as you can simply download the large file, run it, and then restart Eclipse.

The other way to install the Plug-in is directly through Eclipse. I recommend taking this approach, as it allows you more control over what you install and provides a better way to get updates.

In Eclipse, click the Help menu, then Software Updates. Click the Available Software tab, then click Add site. For the location, enter `http://www.blackberry.com/go/eclipseUpdate`. The BlackBerry Update Site will display. Several options are available. At a minimum, you will need to select the BlackBerry JDE Plug-in for Eclipse and at least one BlackBerry Component Pack.

Note: You may be asked to enter a user name and password. You can register for a free developer account on the BlackBerry web site if you have not already done so. This prompt may appear multiple times, so continue entering the account name and password until it goes away. The servers hosting the Plug-in are sometimes temperamental and will fail with unhelpful messages; other times, the installation may appear to hang when it is actually progressing. If you cannot install through Software Updates, you can try again later, or install the EXE file directly as described above.

If you have a particular BlackBerry device in mind, pick the Component Pack that matches the software version of that device. All these files are very large, so you should probably only start with a few even if you know you will eventually want more.

Tip: You can find the software version on your BlackBerry by selecting Options, and then About. It should be a value like "4.5.0.81". When selecting a component pack, only the first two numbers are important. The rest will be used to select an appropriate simulator.

You should restart Eclipse once the install is complete. After it restarts, you will see a new BlackBerry menu option at the top. You will also have access to two new debug configurations: BlackBerry Device and BlackBerry Simulator. Figure 1-1 shows what your Eclipse environment should look like once you have installed the Plug-in and started a new project.

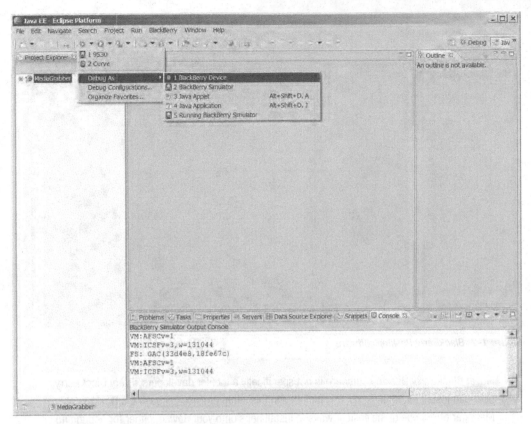

Figure 1-1. Eclipse configured for BlackBerry development

BlackBerry Programs

If you are developing for a personal BlackBerry device, you probably already have the BlackBerry Desktop Manager and the BlackBerry Device Manager installed. If not, installing them is very easy. Go to http://www.blackberry.com and look for the "Desktop Software" download. You may need to select your provider and download the appropriate version for them. You will need to fill out a short form with your name and contact information. Run the downloaded setup file. You may be prompted to install additional software, such as the .NET Framework runtime. Once it's complete, reboot your computer if prompted. The next time you connect your BlackBerry device to the computer, Windows should automatically install the drivers to access it.

You can launch the BlackBerry Desktop Manager by going to your Start menu and looking under BlackBerry. Depending on your installation choices, the manager may automatically start when you log in to Windows. Figure 1-2 shows the BlackBerry Desktop Manager running.

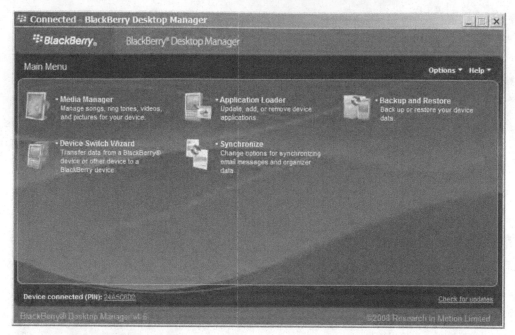

Figure 1-2. BlackBerry Desktop Software

Note: BlackBerry Desktop Software is not specifically a tool for developers. Every BlackBerry user can install it, and most do. It is included in this setup process because the Desktop Manager offers one of the easiest ways to install apps onto your device, either for debugging or to deploy.

Simulator Files

Downloading the proper simulator files for the devices you plan to run on is essential, because different types of devices will have different screen sizes and input modes. Even if you have two devices with the same model number, they will behave differently depending on what software version they are running. Simulators are not just important for testing on the computer, though. They also contain essential information for debugging on the actual device.

If you have the physical device you will be using, find the device software version by visiting Options, then About. You will be looking for a version that matches all parts of the version number. For example, if your device has version 4.5.0.81, only use 4.5.0.81, not another version that starts with 4.5.0. You can download simulator packs from the BlackBerry web site. The exact location will change, so your best bet is to visit the Developers page and look around for the BlackBerry Smartphone Simulators. You will see many, many choices. Pick the one that matches your exact version number and device model and, if applicable, carrier. You'll need to click through another web form—get used to it, as there is no way to save your information. Download the simulator file, then run it to install. You can install to any directory you like.

To switch to using a new simulator in Eclipse, follow these steps, and restart Eclipse if you are ever prompted to do so.

1. Click the Window menu, then Preferences.

2. Expand the BlackBerry JDE menu and select Installed Components.

3. From the drop-down list, select the component pack that corresponds to your device version. For example, pick 4.5 for a device with version 4.5.0.81. If you don't see your component pack listed, install it following the instructions in the section titled "Plugged In" earlier in this chapter.

4. Click the MDS Simulator option and navigate to the MDS directory that matches the component pack from Step 3.

> **Note:** The directory will be located under your Eclipse install folder. The path should look something like `eclipse\plugins\net.rim.eide.componentpack4.x.x_4.6.x.xx\components\MDS`.

5. Click OK. If you already have a project in Eclipse, you will be prompted to rebuild it.

6. Click Run, then Debug Configurations.

7. Create a new BlackBerry Simulator configuration.

8. Click the Simulator tab.

9. From the Profile drop-down, select the item that corresponds to the simulator you installed.

You will now be able to use your device's proper simulator, and you will have access to high-quality on-device debugging.

The Keys to Development

So far, you have installed everything you need to get started writing BlackBerry software. There's a catch, though: RIM has marked some of their APIs as restricted, and if your program uses any of these APIs, it will not run on the device unless it has been code signed.

Code signing is covered in more detail in Chapter 9. For now, just be aware that this is often a necessary step in development. It can take from a few days to a few weeks to receive code signing keys, so start this early.

You apply for the keys from the BlackBerry developer web site. Once again, you will need to fill out a form with information. As part of the form, you will be asked for an email address. Be aware that RIM will send multiple emails to this address every time you sign an application. Also, keep in mind that you must sign an application *every* time you make a change and load it on the device. It isn't unusual for a large RIM app to generate 50 or more emails on a single signing. Therefore, I strongly urge you to enter an unmonitored email address here, or one where you can automatically delete emails from the signing server. If you use your personal email address instead, it will make your life miserable.

The form also includes a question about Certicom cryptography keys. Certicom cryptography is covered in more detail Chapter 5; for now, you can just say "No" here. You should also pick a unique 10-digit PIN. There is a nominal charge for receiving code signing keys, currently $20. You will need one set of keys for each computer you will use for development. The RIM servers sometimes have problems; if you aren't able to complete your order online, you can choose to fax it in instead.

Eventually, you should receive an email from RIM with three key files and instruction on installation. Follow the email instructions. If you run into problems during your installation, follow the links in the email for more support. Once you have installed and registered the keys, you will be all set. You have a limited number of signatures, but the limit is absurdly high, so you don't need to worry about ever running out.

You will initially install the signing keys for a particular version of BlackBerry device software, such as 4.5 or 6.1. At first, you will only be able to sign applications built for that particular device type. There are two fixes for this, though: first, you can safely use an old version of the RIM signing tool on newer versions of device software. In other words, you can use the 4.5 signing tool on builds for 6.1, but not vice versa. Second, you can copy the files SignatureTool.jar, sigtool.db, sigtool.set, and sigtool.csk from one version of the desktop software to another. This also works to sign applications using both the BlackBerry Eclipse Plug-in and another environment on the same computer.

> **Tip:** If you installed the BlackBerry Plug-in, your SignatureTool should be located in a directory like C:\dev\eclipse\plugins\net.rim.eide.componentpack4.5.0_4.5.0.16\ components\bin.

That's it for setup! You now have all the tools you will need to write, debug, and install your own BlackBerry apps.

Application Types

Early in your development cycle, you will face an important decision—what kind of application architecture you should use. BlackBerry supports three very different types of programs, and each offers a unique set of advantages and style of development. This section will provide a quick tour and critique of the available options.

MIDlets

A *MIDlet* is a Java ME application. Java ME, previously known as J2ME, was developed by Sun Microsystem in the 1990s as an early way to write Java applications for extremely limited devices. The ME stands for Micro Edition, and the initial requirements were very micro indeed: devices could have as little as 192 kilobytes of RAM. Over the years, Java ME has expanded and matured along with the mobile market, gradually adding new features and support as they become widely available in handsets.

A collection of optional features for Java ME is called a JSR, or Java Specification Request. You will encounter some of the more popular JSRs later in this book. JSRs cover features like filesystem access, media playback, XML parsing, and more. RIM has been pretty good at adopting the most widespread and useful JSRs. You can find some of a BlackBerry's supported JSRs by visiting the device's Options menu, then selecting About. You will likely see several options such as "Micro Edition File" and "Micro Edition Bluetooth."

Java ME is available on a wide range of handsets, not just BlackBerry devices. Due to different display sizes, supported JSRs, and other discrepancies, MIDlets rarely actually offer "Write once, run everywhere" functions. Still, porting between two Java ME phones is much easier than porting between two different platforms.

MIDlet Behavior

When a user launches a MIDlet, the device will run it in a stripped-down version of the Java Virtual Machine. Unlike a regular Java SE application, which is entered through a `static main()` function and runs until its threads are terminated or it calls `System.exit()`, a MIDlet is a *managed* application. A managed application's methods will be invoked by the managing platform when it needs to respond to something, such as the app pausing or the user selecting a button. This architecture should be familiar to developers of Java servlets and other Java EE applications.

The simplest MIDlets need to reply to only three events: the application starting, pausing, or exiting. An application should handle necessary initialization when starting, release scarce resources when pausing, and perform any remaining cleanup when exiting.

MIDlet UI

MIDlet programming supports several choices for user interface programming. The simplest, but most limited, is using `Screen` objects. Each `Screen` instance corresponds to an application screen. A `Form` is a type of `Screen` that can contain multiple `Item` objects. Examples of items include text entry fields, labels, and images. Using screens allows you to very quickly build up an application UI with your desired functions. Unfortunately, the UI is usually quite limited and unattractive. Screens tend to look better on BlackBerry devices than on most other Java ME devices, but they still do not look nearly as nice as other UI frameworks.

When using a Screen, users will interact with your application through Command objects. Each Command is a specific action the user can take. In an email program, the commands might include choices to compose a new message, save the current message, run a spell checker, or exit the app. You will be notified by the application manager when the user has selected a Command. In BlackBerry apps, commands will display when the user presses the BlackBerry Menu key.

An alternative to Screen is to subclass Canvas. A Canvas allows you to completely control the appearance of your app, down to the level of the pixel. When your app needs to draw, it will be provided with a Graphics context. You can use this to directly draw images, text, rectangles, arcs, and even arbitrary blocks of pixels. This system offers maximum flexibility for creating great looking apps. However, it is also considerably more complex.

A Canvas-based app can continue to use Command objects, but it also gains the ability to directly interact with the user. You will be notified when the user presses a key or interacts with the screen, both for click ball-based BlackBerry devices and touch-based ones. With these capabilities, it becomes possible to write more advanced user interfaces. For example, you could add keyboard shortcuts to your email program or flip between images when the user clicks on them.

Finally, a GameCanvas offers a useful set of behaviors for developers who are writing games or other applications that demand a high degree of interactivity. Screen and Canvas apps are primarily reactive, waiting for notifications and deciding how to respond. GameCanvas allows you to directly query the key states and immediately start painting in response. This gives you maximum control over application speed and responsiveness. Additionally, a GameCanvas offers an offscreen Graphics context that you can progressively draw to before copying it directly to the screen.

A MIDlet Example

Follow these steps to write a simple MIDlet that will be your first BlackBerry app.

1. Start Eclipse and select a fresh workspace.

2. Click File → New, then Project.

3. Expand BlackBerry and select BlackBerry Project. Click Next. Name it HelloWorld. If you hate the idea of writing another Hello World application, call it something else. Click Finish.

4. Right-click the HelloWorld project and select Properties.

5. Click BlackBerry Project Properties in the left pane and fill out the Title, Version, and Vendor fields. You may enter any text you like. To avoid confusion, I like to keep my MIDlet title and project title consistent, so I enter HelloWorld here. Also, check the box for "Always make project active."

6. Click the Application tab and select "MIDlet" from the Project Type drop-down, as shown in Figure 1-3.

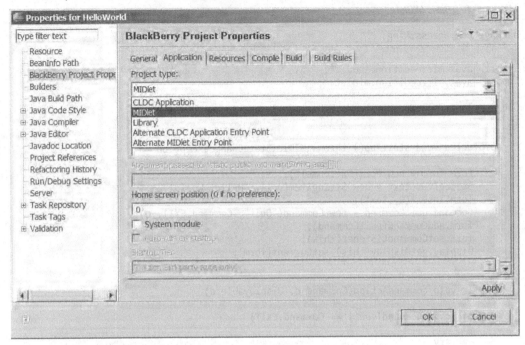

Figure 1-3. *Making a MIDlet*

7. Press OK to exit the properties.

8. Right-click on the src folder in your Project Explorer, then select New, and then Class. (If you can't see your src folder, try expanding the project by pressing the + sign near the project name.)

9. Give this class a name. I chose HelloWorld. Also provide a package name. I will be using packages under com.apress.king throughout this book.

10. Set the superclass to javax.microedition.midlet.MIDlet.

11. Keep "Inherited abstract methods" checked.

12. Click Finish.

You now have an empty MIDlet. If you wanted, you could run it right now. There isn't much point, though, since it doesn't do anything yet.

Listing 1-1 shows how to implement a simple MIDlet. This app uses the screen-based approach to development. It displays a simple message on the screen and offers an option to quit the app. Because the app is so simple, there is nothing to do when the app is paused, and it always destroys itself in a straightforward manner. As you can see, very little boilerplate code is needed to get this running.

Listing 1-1. *A Basic MIDlet*

```
package com.apress.king;

import javax.microedition.lcdui.*;
import javax.microedition.midlet.*;

public class HelloWorld extends MIDlet implements CommandListener
{
    protected void startApp() throws MIDletStateChangeException
    {
        Form form = new Form("Welcome!");
        StringItem text = new StringItem(null, "Hello, World!");
        form.insert(0, text);
        Command quitCommand = new Command("Quit", Command.EXIT, 0);
        form.addCommand(quitCommand);
        form.setCommandListener(this);
        Display.getDisplay(this).setCurrent(form);
    }

    public void commandAction(Command c, Displayable d)
    {
        if (c.getCommandType() == Command.EXIT)
        {
            try
            {
                destroyApp(true);
                notifyDestroyed();
            }
            catch (MIDletStateChangeException e)
            {
                e.printStackTrace();
            }
        }
    }

    protected void destroyApp(boolean arg0) throws MIDletStateChangeException
    {
        notifyDestroyed();
    }

    protected void pauseApp()
    {
        // This method intentionally left blank.
    }

}
```

Running a MIDlet

It's now time to run your first app on the simulator. To do this, select the Run menu in Eclipse, then choose "Debug As," and finally "BlackBerry Simulator". Your default simulator will appear and begin booting.

Note: Later in this chapter, we will see how to start a simulator with networking enabled.

Developers who have previously written for other Java ME phones will be encouraged to hear that RIM's device simulators are very faithful to the actual devices. On the majority of Java phones, simulators provide an overly idealized depiction of the runtime environment. Those simulators are usually fast and bug-free, while the actual mobile device is neither. If you have thoroughly debugged your application on a RIM simulator, though, you can be reasonably confident that it will run well on the actual device. (Of course, there is no way to be completely sure until you actually try it. We'll cover that step at the end of this chapter.)

The downside to this accuracy, though, is that the simulator tends to be rather slow. It takes about as long to boot up as an actual device does. Be patient, and eventually you will see the home screen.

Now, locate the HelloWorld app. On older devices, it will typically be located somewhere on your home screen. On newer devices, it will usually be placed within a Downloads folder, which you can find by pressing the BlackBerry Menu key and then scrolling around. Once you find it, click the icon. It will launch, looking something like Figure 1-4. Note that the exact appearance will vary based on what simulator you are using.

Figure 1-4. *A simple MIDlet running in the simulator*

MIDlet Evaluation

MIDlets should be your first choice if you are planning on writing an application for both BlackBerry and Java ME devices. The consistent programming style will make the whole process much simpler, and you'll minimize the amount of rework.

However, you are giving up the chance to take the fullest advantage of the BlackBerry platform if you go this route. Even the best-looking MIDlets won't integrate cleanly with other applications on the phone, and discerning users will detect that something is different about them.

If you choose to write a MIDlet, I suggest using Screen classes when you are writing a demo or an app where you don't care about the UI. Use a Canvas for commercial applications, and a GameCanvas for games or other high-quality interactive apps.

The rest of this book contains a good amount of information that can be applied to MIDlets. To learn even more, particularly more details about the user interface options, consider reading *Beginning Java ME Platform* by Ray Rischpater (Apress). Most of the content in that book can be applied to writing MIDlets for BlackBerry devices. (Disclaimer: I am the technical reviewer of that book.)

CLDC Applications

MIDlets provide a good bridge of compatibility between Java ME and BlackBerry devices. BlackBerry CLDC, on the other hand, was engineered from the ground up specifically for BlackBerry, and this framework provides the best integration with the native device behavior. Applications written with this platform tend to have a polished feel that is familiar to BlackBerry users.

CLDC stands for Connected Limited Device Configuration. Somewhat confusingly, MIDlets are also technically CLDC applications. Java ME provides support for a wide range of applications; the most popular are the MIDlets, which are defined as part of MIDP, the Mobile Information Device Profile. RIM has taken the CLDC foundation and created their own custom user interface on top of it as a replacement for MIDlets. Within this book, I will use the terms "MIDlet" or "MIDP MIDlet" to refer to a MIDlet app, and the terms "CLDC" or "BlackBerry CLDC" to refer to a BlackBerry CLDC app.

> **Note:** The two types of apps can share almost anything, except for their UI classes. This means that BlackBerry CLDC applications should never import a class under the `javax.microedition.lcdui` or `javax.microedition.midlet` packages, and MIDlets should never import a class under the `net.rim.device.api.ui` package hierarchy. On the other hand, BlackBerry CLDC applications can freely use non-UI Java ME classes under the `javax.microedition` package, and MIDlets running on BlackBerry can use RIM classes under the `net.rim` package.

CLDC Behavior

BlackBerry CLDC apps function like a hybrid between Java SE and MIDlets. They do have a static `main()` function that starts the application and will run until completion. Your main class should extend `UiApplication`. `UiApplication` is the heart of a CLDC app; it provides the following crucial capabilities:

- An event dispatcher that is responsible for managing all user input and updates to the user interface.

- A screen stack that maintains application state.

- Standard controls for menu actions and other commonly used elements.

Once your app starts the event dispatcher, it will behave similarly to a MIDlet: it will be notified when important events occur and can take actions in response.

CLDC UI

Screen objects form the building blocks for CLDC applications. CLDC screens are located in the `net.rim.device.api.ui` package, and they are completely different from the MIDlet screens located in the `javax.microedition.lcdui` package. A `Screen` typically contains one or more displayable items, and also performs specialized logic related to those items. If you were writing a calendar app, you might use one screen to show the entire calendar view, another screen for creating new appointments, and a third screen to view previously entered appointments. Each screen would offer different options depending on its purpose.

An app is composed of screens, and each screen is composed of fields. A CLDC `Field` is roughly analogous to a MIDlet `Item`. RIM offers a rich set of standard fields for things like displaying images and text, and even more advanced fields for displaying things like maps. One specialized type of `Field` is the `Manager`. A `Manager` controls the appearance and behavior for its own children fields. One `Manager` may lay out its children horizontally, another vertically, and another as a grid. By using managers, you can create elaborate and attractive user interfaces.

You can also subclass `Field`, `Manager`, or any other class to add your own desired functions and appearance. For example, you might override `DateField` in your calendar app to create dates that fit in with the visual style of your app, and you might add custom functions to immediately display appointments when the user selects a date.

In the most extreme cases, you may choose to override the `paint()` method for a `Screen` or a `Field`. This will allow you unlimited control over the look of your app. However, the existing `Field` implementations look quite good, and most allow ways that you can easily customize them. You can create attractive apps by sticking to the default toolkit.

A CLDC Example

Now that you've created a MIDlet, making a CLDC app will go more quickly. Switch to a fresh workspace and create a new project called `HelloUniverse`. Follow the instructions in the previous section "A MIDlet Example," but this time keep the Project Type as the default of "CLDC Application." Create a new class called `HelloUniverse` that extends `net.rim.device.api.ui.UiApplication`. Listing 1-2 shows a simple CLDC app that performs the same basic function as the previous MIDlet application. For this example we will be configuring a basic `MainScreen` with some non-interactive elements. Future examples in this book will show how to create more interactive CLDC applications.

Listing 1-2. A Basic BlackBerry CLDC Application

```
package com.apress.king;


import net.rim.device.api.ui.UiApplication;
import net.rim.device.api.ui.component.LabelField;
import net.rim.device.api.ui.container.MainScreen;
```

```
public class HelloUniverse extends UiApplication
{
    public void start()
    {
        MainScreen main = new MainScreen();
        LabelField label = new LabelField("Hello, Universe");
        main.add(label);
        UiApplication app = UiApplication.getUiApplication();
        app.pushScreen(main);
        app.enterEventDispatcher();
    }

    public static void main(String[] args)
    {
        (new HelloUniverse()).start();
    }
}
```

You'll note that this is even less code than was used in the MIDlet. When you build a CLDC app, you get a lot of useful capabilities for free, including automatic state management that allows a user to navigate back through your app and exit. You can override these behaviors if you want, but the default is correct in most cases.

Run your app using the same steps as described in the previous section "Running a MIDlet." Even though the code is different, you build, load, and launch BlackBerry CLDC applications the same way you do MIDlets, and they will be placed in the same location. Figure 1-5 shows the running CLDC application.

Figure 1-5. *A BlackBerry CLDC application running in the simulator*

Note: You'll observe that HelloWorld is still installed, even though you have switched workspaces and started a new project. Although you can only debug one project at a time, any changes you make to the BlackBerry simulator will persist across multiple launches. If you'd like to return to a clean slate, you can do so by clicking on the Eclipse BlackBerry menu, then selecting Erase Simulator File. There are multiple options for deleting everything, deleting the SD card, deleting preferences, and deleting applications.

CLDC Evaluation

Using the BlackBerry CLDC UI is probably the best choice if you are writing an app on your own BlackBerry for fun, if you know that your app is only intended for BlackBerry devices, or if you want to get the highest level of visual integration with the BlackBerry platform. RIM has done a good job at providing attractive, flexible, extensible visual elements. It takes little effort to create a nice-looking app, and you can customize the look as much as you like.

For these reasons, I will be using CLDC applications in my examples for the remainder of the book. Most of the topics can also be used in MIDlet applications, and I will provide occasional directions on how to adapt to MIDlets.

To keep the focus on the advanced topics of this book, I tend to use simple Screen classes that are informative but not flashy. If you'd like to learn more about designing user interfaces for BlackBerry CLDC apps, please consult *Beginning BlackBerry Development* by Anthony Rizk (Apress).

Libraries

The last major type of application is a *library*. "Application" is a misnomer here, since a library is, by definition, headless. A library can provide functions to other applications and can perform tasks, but it cannot be directly launched by a user and does not provide any user interface.

Library Functions

You'll rarely ever distribute a library by itself. Instead, you typically will bundle a library with one or more applications. There are several benefits to doing this. It allows you to encapsulate functions and separate them from the application. If you have multiple apps that need to decode videos, then rather than writing video decoding functions and copying them to both apps, you could just place those functions within a library. When you fix bugs or add new video formats to decode, you only need to update the library.

Libraries can also be useful for performing simple tasks that don't require user interaction. You might use a library that scans for temporary files left behind by your main app and cleans them up, or that tells the device to start your application when the user receives a particular email.

A Library Example

Create a new Eclipse workspace and start a third project, this one called GoodbyeWorld. Follow the instructions in the previous section in this chapter titled "A MIDlet Example," but this time select the Project Type "Library" and check the option for "Auto-run on startup". Create a new class GoodbyeWorld with the default superclass of java.lang.Object.

This particular library will be calling some privileged API methods, so we will notify the build environment that our app has the proper access. Select the Eclipse BlackBerry menu, then choose Configure BlackBerry Workspace. Click Code Signing in the left pane, and verify that all the options are checked. You should have RIM BlackBerry Apps API, RIM Crypto API, and RIM Runtime API selected. If you happen to know that you cannot access one or more of these, for example if you are in a region without permission to use the Crypto API, leave those options unchecked. The compiler will generate a warning if your code attempts to call these restricted methods. You will still be able to call them on the simulator, but they will fail on the device.

Listing 1-3 shows this library's implementation. You'll notice a special entrance function called `libMain()`. Not every library needs one, but if "Auto-run on startup" is selected, then the system will run this method if it is available. In this example, we check to see if the `HelloUniverse` application is installed. If so, we wait for the device to finish booting up, and then launch it.

Listing 1-3. *A Basic Library*

```java
package com.apress.king;

import net.rim.device.api.system.*;

public class GoodbyeWorld
{

    public static void libMain(String[] args)
    {
        System.out.println("GoodbyeWorld launching");
        int handle = CodeModuleManager.getModuleHandle("HelloUniverse");
        ApplicationDescriptor[] descriptors = CodeModuleManager
                .getApplicationDescriptors(handle);
        if (descriptors.length > 0)
        {
            ApplicationDescriptor descriptor = descriptors[0];
            try
            {
                ApplicationManager manager = ApplicationManager
                        .getApplicationManager();
                while (manager.inStartup())
                {
                    try
                    {
                        Thread.sleep(1000);
                    }
                    catch (InterruptedException ie)
                    {
                        // Ignore.
                    }
                }
                manager.runApplication(descriptor);
            }
            catch (ApplicationManagerException e)
            {
                System.out.println("I couldn't launch it!");
                e.printStackTrace();
            }
        }
        else
        {
            System.out.println("HelloUniverse is not installed.");
        }
```

```
        System.out.println("Goodbye, world!");
    }

}
```

When you run this in the simulator, you will see the same screen display as in Figure 1-5, but this time, no action on your part is necessary. Also, if you look in the Console view for the BlackBerry Simulator Output Console in Eclipse, you will see the message GoodbyeWorld launching included within the app startup messages.

Library Evaluation

The possibilities for libraries are practically endless. They can enhance your other applications by providing useful utilities or running common tasks. They are especially useful when you have a portfolio of apps and want to share existing technology between them.

That said, most applications don't use libraries, and most don't need them. Think carefully about what your library is supposed to accomplish, whether it's actually useful, and whether a library is the best place to put those functions. It might be fun to automatically start up an application, but many users would likely be annoyed by that behavior.

Use your best judgment, and you may find situations where libraries are the best solution to a problem. The examples in this book do not use libraries often, but most of the code that does not have a UI component could be placed within a library.

Connecting to Files and Networks

Java ME introduced a new framework to the Java language. The Generic Connection Framework, or GCF, provides a generic mechanism for accessing many different kinds of resources that exist outside your app. The GCF will be used in all but the most trivial applications, whether you are building a MIDlet or a BlackBerry CLDC app.

A GCF Overview

The Connector class provides an entry into the GCF. Connector is a *factory* class—one that is responsible for creating other objects. When you call Connector.open(), you provide a connection string describing the resource you want to access. Connection strings look like URLs, but can describe a wide variety of connection types. Examples include http://apress.com, sms://+14155550100 and file:///SDCard/BlackBerry/Music/.

If the device supports the requested connection type, it will return an object that implements the appropriate subclass of Connection. Figure 1-6 shows the relationship between Connector and Connection, along with a few representative Connection types. If the device does not support a particular type of connection, Connector will throw a

ConnectionNotFoundException. You may encounter an IOException in a variety of situations, such as if networking is disabled when your app requests a network connection.

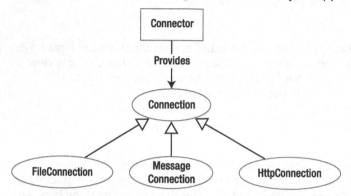

Figure 1-6. *BlackBerry GCF connections*

Because connections represent scarce resources, your app should be prepared to gracefully deal with situations in which they are not available. Depending on the type of resource and the error, you might prompt the user to try again later. Also, because they are scarce, you should take care to clean up Connection objects once you have finished with them by calling their close() method. This will return underlying resources, such as file handles or Internet sockets, to the BlackBerry operating system. The sample code below shows how to open a particular type of connection and clean it up once done.

```
String connectString = "http://www.apress.com";

HttpConnection connection = null;
try
{
    connection = (HttpConnection)Connector.open(connectString);
    // Read from the connection here.
}
catch (ConnectionNotFoundException cnfe)
{
    System.err.println("Couldn't find connection for " + connectString);
}
catch (IOException ioe)
{
    System.err.println("IO exception for " + connectString + ":" + ioe);
}
finally
{
    if (connection != null)
    {
        try
        {
            connection.close();
        }
        catch (IOException ioe) {}
    }
}
```

File Access

File connections are not part of core Java ME, but are specified as part of JSR 75, which all modern BlackBerry devices offer. File connections allow you to read and write files within the BlackBerry device's built-in storage or an SD (Secure Digital) card. This capability allows you to offer extra storage in your app, produce useful files for the user, or communicate with other apps on the phone.

Paths

RIM devices offer two file-system roots. One, located at /store/home/user, corresponds to the device's internal memory. This is limited in size and should be used for small files only. However, it is also fast and responsive and should always be available.

The other root, /SDCard, corresponds to the device's Secure Digital card. This is a removable memory card that is often used for storing large media files. SD cards also offer ways to encrypt files and protect them with Digital Rights Management (DRM). SD cards for BlackBerry devices can be quite large—several gigabytes in size—and users will rarely mind if you use them to store files for your app. However, there is no guarantee that any given user will have an SD card inserted in their device, and you should be prepared to handle situations where it is unavailable.

You indicate a file URL by attaching the file:// prefix. An example of a full path to a local file is file:///SDCard/BlackBerry/Music/song.mp3. Note that there are three slashes after file:, not two.

Access

Each Connection can be opened in one of three modes:

- Connector.READ indicates that your app will only be reading data from this resource.

- Connector.WRITE indicates that your app will only be writing data to this resource.

- Connector.READ_WRITE allows your app to both read from and write to this resource.

By default, connections will open with READ_WRITE access. This is generally desirable, particularly since bugs in some versions of BlackBerry device software cause read operations to fail if a connection is opened with only READ access.

Even when you request these access levels, users still may choose to override your selection. It is reasonable to show an error message to the user asking them to make changes that will allow your app to function properly. Chapter 9 will discuss in more detail how to do this.

Streams

A Connection object by itself represents a resource. In order to interact with a file, you will need to open an appropriate stream by calling one of the following methods:

- openInputStream() returns a raw byte stream for reading.

- openOutputStream() returns a raw byte stream for writing.

- openDataInputStream() allows your app to read basic Java types, such as int and String, from the stream.

- openDataOutputStream() allows your app to write basic Java types to the stream.

Note: BlackBerry does not support many standard Java I/O classes such as BufferedInputStream.

Although you have successfully obtained a FileConnection object, opening the stream may still fail. Security is generally not checked until you attempt to access the file. It is also possible that the file itself does not exist yet, or another app has a lock on it. Be prepared to handle SecurityException, IllegalModeException, and IOException.

Once you have an appropriate stream, you can read or write to it as you would in a standard Java application. Operations on streams are *synchronous* and *blocking*. This means that when you call a stream method like read() or write(), the method will not return until the operation is complete or an error occurs. If you are reading or writing a large file, this may take a long time. Because of this, it is a good practice to perform stream I/O operations in a separate thread.

The following code shows an example of opening a stream from an already opened file connection. As with connections, streams represent scarce resources and should be cleaned up when no longer needed.

```
DataInputStream dis = null;

try
{
   dis = connection.openDataInputStream();
   String bestPlayer = dis.readUTF();
   int highScore = dis.readInt();
   System.out.println(bestPlayer + " scored " + highScore + " points.");
}
catch (IOException ioe)
{
    System.err.println(ioe);
    ioe.printStackTrace();
}
finally
{
    if (dis != null)
    {
```

```
    try
    {
        dis.close();
    }
    catch (IOException ioe) { }
  }
}
```

When you are writing to a stream, be aware that the operating system may be buffering the output. If your app writes individual bytes to a file, it would be highly inefficient to access the filesystem at each byte. All pending bytes will be written out when the close() method is called, or when the program calls flush() on the stream, as demonstrated in the following code snippet.

```
DataOutputStream dos = connection.openDataOutputStream();

dos.writeUTF("Sally Jones");
dos.writeInt(100);
dos.flush();
dos.writeUTF("Joe Smith");
dos.writeInt(98);

dos.close();
```

Other Operations

Although streams are the most important resources provided by a FileConnection, the interface offers several other useful methods, including the following:

- exists() checks to see whether the file or directory is present on the filesystem.
- create() creates a new, empty file at this location.
- mkdir() creates a directory at this location.
- delete() destroys this file or directory.
- list() returns all the files and subdirectories in this directory.
- fileSize() reports how many bytes a file occupies on the filesystem.

Note: Always include the trailing / character when specifying a directory path, such as file:///SDCard/BlackBerry/Music/. If you don't, the BlackBerry operating system cannot determine whether you are referring to a file or to a directory of that name.

The following code snippet checks to see whether a file exists. If it doesn't, it will create it. The create() method does not automatically create directories, so this code first checks to see that the containing directory exists.

```
String directoryPath = "file:///SDCard/BlackBerry/Music/";
```

```
FileConnection connection = (FileConnection)Connector.open(directoryPath);
if (!connection.exists())
{
    connection.mkdir();
}
connection.close();
String filePath = "file:///SDCard/BlackBerry/Music/song.mp3";
connection = (FileConnection)Connector.open(filePath);
if (!connection.exists())
{
    connection.create();
}

connection.close();
```

Networking

Almost every interesting mobile app includes some sort of networking. It might share messages with other users, back up data on a remote server, or download new game levels. The GCF provides access to a variety of network types, and RIM's custom extensions to the GCF allow you to write networking code that takes advantage of BlackBerry device features.

Types of Connections

On BlackBerry devices, a variety of *protocols* are understood by the `Connector.open()` factory method. Table 1-1 lists some of the most useful.

Table 1-1. Network Connection Types

Protocol Name	Returned Interface Type	Comments	Example	Required Permission
http	HttpConnection		http://eff.org	javax.microedition.io.Connector.http
https	HttpsConnection	Secure version of http	https://www.amazon.com	javax.microedition.io.Connector.https
socket	StreamConnection	Raw TCP socket	socket://mysite.com:1066	javax.microedition.io.Connector.socket
udp	DatagramConnection	UDP socket	udp://streamingsite.com:1812	javax.microedition.io.Connector.datagram

The platform also supports more esoteric connections, including to USB ports and raw SSL. This book will use HTTP for examples as this is one of the most common and feature-rich protocols.

HTTP Requests

RIM has defined a set of custom optional parameters that may be included when requesting a network connection. These are used to control features that are not addressed by the standard Java ME interfaces or that apply only to BlackBerry connections. Table 1-2 shows the optional parameters that can be applied to an HTTP connection.

Table 1-2. Optional Parameters for HTTP Connections on BlackBerry

Parameter Name	Meaning	Valid Values
deviceside	Whether to connect via direct TCP or a proxy connection	true or false
interface	Non-cellular connection to use	wifi
WapGatewayAPN	The Access Point name to use as a gateway	Domain name
WapGatewayIP	The gateway to use for a WAP connection	IP address
WayGatewayPort	The port to use for a WAP connection	Integer
WapSourceIP	Local IP address	IP address
WapSourcePort	Local port for this connection	Integer
WapEnableWTLS	Whether to force a secure WAP connection	true or false
TunnelAuthUsername	User name for APN	String
TunnelAuthPassword	Password for APN	String

Of all these parameters, the most important is deviceside. You will generally want to set this to true unless you are specifically developing an app for a BES environment. Otherwise, corporate users may be blocked from accessing the site you attempt to reach.

Optional parameters are appended to your connection string and separated by semicolons. To open a direct TCP connection over Wi-Fi to the CIA's web site, you would use the connection string http://www.cia.com;deviceside=true;interface=wifi.

> **Caution:** If you specify a Wi-Fi connection and no Wi-Fi is available, the connection will throw an exception instead of failing back to a regular cellular connection.

When calling Connector.open() for a network connection, you may choose to specify whether the connection should time out. By default, a connection will wait until the other server replies or an error occurs; however, sometimes no response will come, either because the server is unresponsive or a network connection has quietly dropped. It's a good practice to request the timeout notification so you can display an error to the user. An example of requesting a connection with a timeout follows. The final `true` parameter indicates that we want to receive an exception if the connection is not successfully opened in a timely manner.

```
HttpConnection conn = (HttpConnection) Connector.open(
        "http://www.cia.gov;deviceside=true", Connector.READ, true);
```

Once you have an `HttpConnection`, you can choose to set the request method (`GET`, `POST`, or `HEAD`) by calling `setRequestMethod()`, and specify any custom headers (such as the User-Agent or accepts) by calling `setRequestProperty()`. Once the connection is set up and you are ready to send or receive data, open the corresponding stream type and begin using it. All the same rules that applied to `FileConnection` objects also apply here: run within a separate thread, be prepared for errors, and clean up after yourself when done.

App: Media Grabber

You now know enough essentials to create a functional BlackBerry app. Throughout this book we will be building a media-sharing application through examples at the end of every chapter. This first chapter will concentrate on building up the framework of the app and giving you practice with running and debugging it. In the process, we'll also use some of the features covered in this chapter.

Writing the App

Follow the instructions from earlier in this chapter to start a new Eclipse workspace and create a new BlackBerry CLDC application called MediaGrabber. Within that project, create a class called `MediaGrabber` that extends `UiApplication`. We'll write a static `main()` function that starts running the app, a simple UI to display, and a custom thread that uses the GCF to download a file and compare it to the local filesystem. Listing 1-4 shows the complete class.

Listing 1-4. An App that Grabs and Stores Data from the Internet

```
package com.apress.king;


import java.io.IOException;
import java.io.InputStream;
import java.io.OutputStream;
import java.util.Date;

import javax.microedition.io.Connector;
import javax.microedition.io.HttpConnection;
import javax.microedition.io.file.FileConnection;

import net.rim.device.api.ui.UiApplication;
import net.rim.device.api.ui.component.LabelField;
```

```java
import net.rim.device.api.ui.container.MainScreen;
import net.rim.device.api.util.Arrays;

public class MediaGrabber extends UiApplication
{
    public static void main(String[] args)
    {
        MediaGrabber app = new MediaGrabber();
        app.begin();
    }

    public void begin()
    {
        MainScreen s = new MainScreen();
        LabelField label = new LabelField("Kilroy Was Here");
        s.add(label);
        pushScreen(s);
        (new WebChecker()).start();
        enterEventDispatcher();
    }

    private class WebChecker extends Thread
    {
        public void run()
        {
            HttpConnection http = null;
            FileConnection file = null;
            InputStream is = null;
            OutputStream os = null;
            try
            {
                http = (HttpConnection) Connector.open(
                        "http://www.google.com;deviceside=true",
                        Connector.READ_WRITE, true);
                is = http.openInputStream();
                // Read the first 4 kilobytes.
                byte[] networkBuffer = new byte[4096];
                is.read(networkBuffer);
                is.close();
                http.close();
                file = (FileConnection) Connector
                        .open("file:///store/home/user/last.html");
                if (file.exists())
                {
                    System.out.println("We last checked Google on "
                            + new Date(file.lastModified()));
                    byte[] fileBuffer = new byte[4096];
                    is = file.openInputStream();
                    is.read(fileBuffer);
                    is.close();
                    if (Arrays.equals(networkBuffer, fileBuffer))
                    {
                        System.out.println("Google hasn't changed.");
                    }
                    else
```

```
                {
                    System.out.println("Google's doing something new.");

                }
                file.delete();
            }
            else
            {
                System.out.println("Looks like the first time we've run!");
            }
            file.create();
            os = file.openOutputStream();
            os.write(networkBuffer);
        }
        catch (IOException ioe)
        {
            System.err.println("An I/O error occurred: " + ioe);
        }
        catch (Exception e)
        {
            System.err.println("An unexpected error occurred: " + e);
        }
        finally
        {
            try
            {
                if (os != null)
                    os.close();
                if (file != null)
                    file.close();
                if (is != null)
                    is.close();
                if (http != null)
                    http.close();
            }
            catch (Exception e)
            {
                // Ignore
            }
        }
    }
  }
 }
}
```

Debugging on the Simulator

Because this is the first app to write that requires network support, an extra step is necessary before running. Click on Run, then Debug Configurations. Click on the BlackBerry Simulator entry, and click the new launch configuration icon in the upper left. A new configuration will display. Name it what you like, such as MediaGrabber BlackBerry. Click the Simulator tab and change the Profile from "Default Simulator" to one of the other choices. Mark the checkbox by the message that starts with "Launch

Mobile Data System" as shown in Figure 1-7. Finally, click on the Common tab and check both options under "Display in favorites menu." Click Debug.

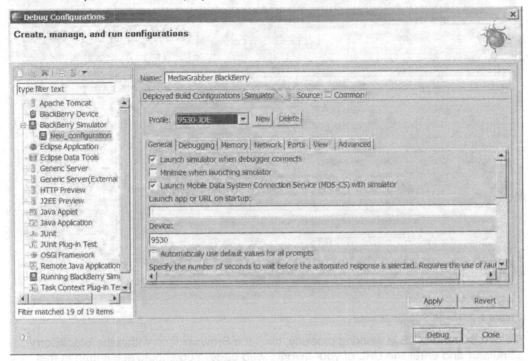

Figure 1-7. Configuring Eclipse to launch the MDS

Caution: Only one copy of the BlackBerry simulator can run at a time. Exit any previous simulator windows you have open before starting a new debug session.

The simulator window will launch again, but this time you will also see a black-and-white terminal window display with a lot of rapidly scrolling text, as shown in Figure 1-8. This is the Mobile Data System terminal. As mentioned before, the BlackBerry Simulator is very accurate to real device behavior, and this accuracy extends to the way BlackBerry devices access the Internet. The simulator cannot directly access the Internet connection on your development computer; instead, it connects to the MDS, which simulates a real wireless connection, and behind the scenes uses your computer's Internet connection to provide data.

Figure 1-8. The MDS status terminal

To test that the MDS is working properly, click the Browser icon within the BlackBerry simulator and enter the URL of your favorite web page. You should see it load in this window, similarly to how it would look on an actual device.

Now you are ready to debug your app. Double-click the side of the Java editing window on line 46, at the line that starts with http = (HttpConnection). A blue breakpoint marker should appear here, as shown in Figure 1-9. Launch your application. The simulator will freeze. You may get a prompt in Eclipse asking if you'd like to open the Debug perspective. Answer Yes here, and check "Remember my decision."

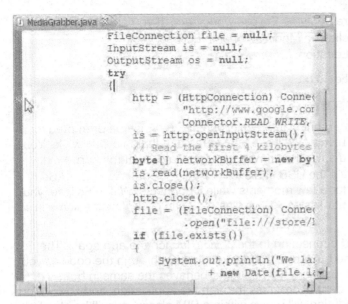

Figure 1-9. Setting a debug breakpoint in Eclipse

You are now in the Eclipse debug view. Even if you have never used Eclipse before, you should recognize its capabilities as similar to other IDEs you may have used such as NetBeans or Visual Studio. You can inspect the values of local variables, add watches to expressions, and control execution of the code. The keyboard commands are F5 to step into a method, F6 to step over the next line, and F7 to step out of a method. Press F8 to continue running until the next breakpoint.

Spend a few moments experimenting. You'll see that you can observe all the data that comes down from the network connection. If there is a problem, you can view the exception that is thrown and determine how to solve it. Launch the app again, noting the different path it takes the second time. Once you're comfortable in the debugger view, you'll be ready to move on to the actual device.

Debugging on the BlackBerry Device

To debug on the BlackBerry, you first must load the application. The simplest way to do this is via the following steps:

1. Right-click on MediaGrabber and select Generate ALX File.

2. Connect a BlackBerry device and open the BlackBerry Desktop Manager.

3. Click Application Loader.

4. Click Start under Add/Remove Applications.

5. Click Browse.

6. Navigate to where you created your Eclipse workspace. If you aren't sure where this is, right-click on MediaGrabber in Eclipse, click Properties, and look for Location.

7. Select the file MediaGrabber.alx.

8. Click Next, then click Finish.

Once your app is loaded, first try running it directly yourself. You may be prompted for permission to access www.google.com; we'll see how to remove that in a little while. You should see the same screen you saw when running the simulator. Exit the app. Next, with the device still connected via the USB cable, click Run → Debug As → BlackBerry Device. Your device will freeze for a few moments while it connects. Within Eclipse, you may see a lot of messages about missing .debug files. You can click "Don't ask me this again."

Once the debugger has finished connecting to the device, launch the app again. The device will freeze when it hits the breakpoint, and you can step through the code as you did with the simulator. For the most part, the debugger behaves the same in both places: you can view variables, control progress through the application, and so on. You may notice that sometimes execution will pause within a RIM class; you will be able to view the entire call stack but not the specific code that is executing. This typically happens when an exception is thrown within RIM code, sometimes due to an action within your code. You can usually step back out of this function or press F8 to continue running and observe what happens; sometimes such exceptions are handled internally before they reach you.

You also may see that sometimes debugger progress stops altogether. This is because the device is waiting for input from the user. This happens most often when a security prompt displays in response to an operation in your program. Answering Yes or No to this prompt will determine whether an exception is thrown in your app.

If you are unable to debug your app on the device, or if you cannot view variable values, please carefully review the steps above. In particular, make sure you are using the simulator that corresponds to the device you are debugging on and double-check the device software version numbers and model numbers.

Finally, sometimes the debugger just detaches while your program is debugging, which can be annoying. Make sure your USB cable is firmly connected; if the problem persists, it may help to carefully set your breakpoints and avoid inspecting certain variables, since certain combinations can result in disconnection.

Working with Devices

On-target debugging is a powerful tool. There is no substitute for running your code on an actual phone and being able to see exactly what is happening. However, running on the phone is more complex than running on the simulator, and there are a few points to keep in mind.

First, make sure that your particular phone is in a good state for running the app. Devices acquired second-hand through eBay or elsewhere can come with configurations that may block certain operations or fail to make connections. Chapter 9 will specifically address the issue of security policies on ex-corporate phones. If your device was originally created for another carrier, you may need to fill out the APN information for the current carrier; this is usually accessed via Options → Advanced → TCP. You can find the proper APN settings on your carrier's web site or in an Internet search.

If you are writing your app for one particular device or for a known configuration, such as devices for a particular company's BES, you just need to set it up to work with those device settings. However, if you want to run on a variety of device types and carriers, you'll need to more carefully think about how to support those differences. You can create a single binary that attempts to detect a user's configuration and uses appropriate settings for them; or, you can create separate versions of the app for each configuration and let users choose which one to install. Chapter 10 addresses this in more detail.

The BlackBerry Desktop Manager is a convenient tool for loading your app, but it can be a little tedious if you are frequently making changes to test on the device. It keeps track of application version numbers, so if you are making a change, either increase the version number (for example, from 1.0.0 to 1.0.1) within Eclipse before building, or delete the old application before attempting to install. Otherwise, the Desktop Manager will see that you have the current version of the app and will not attempt to upgrade. This book will use the Desktop Manager for testing on the device. To learn about alternate ways of deploying your app, consult *Beginning BlackBerry Development* by Anthony Rizk (Apress).

When you are making changes to your code, make sure that the updated COD file is correctly built before you load the ALX with Desktop Manager. The simplest way to do this is to hit the Debug on Simulator option first; you can cancel the simulator before it finishes loading.

BlackBerry devices can take a very long time to reboot after installing an app. To minimize the need to reboot, be sure to exit your app before deleting it or installing an updated version.

Sign Me Up

Hopefully you have received your BlackBerry code signing keys by now. If not, you can skip this part and continue with the later chapters in this book. Return here once you have installed the keys and are ready to start signing.

Caution: Signatures are applied to the most recently built version of the application, which may not include any recent changes you have made in Eclipse. Before starting the signing process, run the application in the simulator to make sure that the updated application was built.

In Eclipse, click the BlackBerry menu, then Request Signatures…. The Signature Tool window will display. Depending on the size of your application and the code you call, there may be many more items shown. You will see some extra SignerID entries that you cannot receive signatures for; this is normal, as these are for advanced cryptography or internal RIM use. Also, you may not see some SignerID entries for keys you do possess. Again, don't be concerned; not all keys will be needed, especially for simple apps.

If you are behind a proxy, click Properties and then fill in your proxy information. Otherwise, just click Request and type in the password you created when you installed the code signing keys, as shown in Figure 1-10. The signing tool will contact the RIM signing servers and download the signature files. You will see a message window describing the status or failure of the signing operation. Click OK and then click Close to dismiss the window.

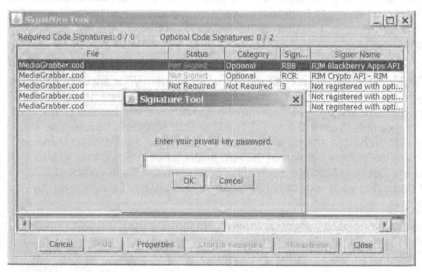

Figure 1-10. *Requesting a signature*

Caution: Whenever you sign an application, you must request a signature from the RIM signing servers. These servers are notorious for their occasional outages of varying lengths that can strike at any time. If you have a deadline for your project, do yourself a favor and plan to finish ahead of time so you aren't stuck if the signing servers happen to be offline right before you need to ship.

Now, replace the old version of your app with the updated signed version. Run MediaGrabber again. Ta-da! No more prompt asking for permission to access Google! (If the prompt persists, see Chapter 9 for more details on eliminating this.) Signed applications gain certain privileges, among them less frequent prompting of users. More importantly, though, only signed applications are allowed to access certain protected RIM APIs. Much of the content in this book requires signing to run.

Once you get the hang of signing, it should become an almost automatic process. It doesn't add as much overhead as some other OEMs' solutions do. Still, it can be tedious to sign when you are frequently making changes that need to be tested on the device. Try to do as much work on the simulator as you can. If you are in a professional environment, consider some of the techniques discussed in the upcoming chapter Advanced Build Techniques. Ideally, though, you should be able to happily develop 95% of your app on the desktop, maybe 5% testing on the device, and then just apply a final set of signatures before distributing it.

WANT MORE?

MediaGrabber isn't actually grabbing any media yet—we'll start doing that in the next chapter. However, this is a good opportunity to play around with the basic app now and get a feel for how development works on the BlackBerry. Here are a few suggestions.

- Spruce up the MainScreen and text. Use a layout Manager to position the text in the center of the screen. Style the LabelField to make it more attractive.

- Try checking multiple web pages in addition to Google. Save each to a separate file. Make sure you are cleaning up your connections after each one. Tip: Create a helper method that can handle any URL.

- If you can, try running the app on different devices from different carriers. Do you need to make any changes for them?

Spend as much time as you like on these or other improvements. Once you feel comfortable with making and testing changes, you are ready to move on.

Excelsior

You have crossed the first threshold for writing advanced BlackBerry apps. Although the treatment in this chapter has been brief, you have learned the essentials for writing useful BlackBerry apps. You now have a functioning environment that allows you to write, test, and deploy your application on the simulator and on BlackBerry devices. You have learned the differences between MIDlets, BlackBerry CLDC applications, and library modules, and when to use each. You have built simple user interfaces. Most importantly, you know how to send and receive data over the wireless network, how to save and read files, and the essential structure of the Generic Connection Framework.

With these tools at your disposal, you can write a variety of useful apps. The remainder of this book will take that core knowledge to the next level by introducing you to the advanced tools and techniques of BlackBerry development. We'll start by examining the advanced features for media capture.

Chapter 2

Media Capture

For several years, manufacturers have been selling phones with promises of increased convenience. They say you shouldn't carry a phone, a camera, and a tape recorder—instead, buy one device that combines all those functions. What was once exotic packaging has now become standard, and even inexpensive phones now usually contain media recording capabilities.

One of the most obvious signs of the BlackBerry phone's evolution from a business-centric tool to a general-purpose device is its embrace of this trend. Most new BlackBerry devices contain a camera and microphone.

While the convenience factor is nice, the fact is that you typically won't get a camera that's as good as a stand-alone camera. A major advantage of having a camera on a phone, though, is that it becomes another tool for software developers. A regular camera just takes pictures, but a camera phone can do much more: display and manipulate those pictures, share them with your friends, detect how bright it is, try to recognize faces, and more. This chapter introduces the media APIs that allow you to consume the information coming from your device and start doing interesting things with it.

BlackBerry vs. Sun APIs

Because RIM's Java ME platform includes the standard set of multimedia APIs (MMAPI), developers already comfortable with Java ME development can immediately use these familiar interfaces in their programs. The Sun concept of media is based around a media `Player` object that plays and records media.

In addition to these standard APIs, BlackBerry has also added its own set of functions that allow access to abilities that are unavailable to most Java phones. Throughout this book you will notice that such packages start with `"net.rim"`. In contrast, Java packages start with `"java"` or `"javax"`. Generally, the RIM APIs will offer more compelling features, but at the price of being more difficult to port to other platforms.

The Sun Standard: A MediaPlayer Connection

Historically, Sun has see-sawed between two extremes when it comes to Java. Their initial release of Java included an enormous set of libraries with a bewildering array of packages, classes, and methods. Each individual component had a very well-defined role, but that meant learning many new components. With Java ME, the pendulum swung the other way with the introduction of the Generic Connection Framework (GCF). Now you had a single component, like a Connector, that was responsible for a wide variety of tasks such as accessing the network or writing a file. The MMAPI is very similar to the GCF in that there are only a few classes to learn, but a great deal of nuance in their use.

Sun broadly defines media to include all audio operations and all visual operations except for the display of still images. In the same way that you access Connection subtypes by making requests to the Connector class, you access Player instances by making requests to the Manager class. Unlike the GCF, though, there are no subclasses of Player; instead, each Player can support an arbitrary number of Control objects. Each Control allows you to manipulate some aspect of the recording/playback operation. For example, playing back a video may provide access to a VideoControl, FramePositioningControl, and VolumeControl, while playing back an audio file will offer only the VolumeControl. Figure 2-1 illustrates two possible configurations of Player objects. This sort of separation allows RIM and other manufacturers to add additional functionality based on new features, and not the specific media type.

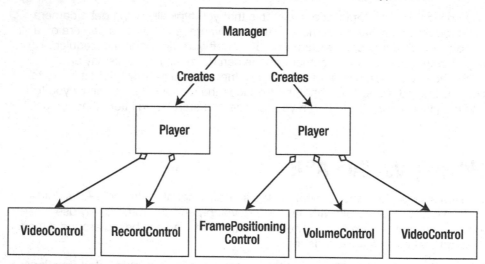

Figure 2-1. *Obtaining different Players from a Manager*

Note: Manager and other media classes can be found under the javax.microedition.media package hierarchy.

Push Me/Pull You

The MMAPI distinguishes between two general tasks involved in any media operation. First comes the data delivery protocol. You can think of this like the TCP/IP stack that you use to download a file over the network. TCP/IP doesn't care whether you're downloading a movie, audio, or text; it's only concerned with how to get the data to you. MMAPI uses the interface DataSource to represent the data delivery protocol. A DataSource might represent a network connection, a file connection, or even a randomized source of data. In the case of media recording, the DataSource will be the piece of hardware used to provide that media.

Once the data has been delivered, the next task is to handle that data content. Content handling involves looking at the raw bytes that have arrived and then performing some task with them. MMAPI's Player class is used as a content handler. Depending on what type of content you've asked for, it might decode an audio stream and direct it to the phone's speakers. When recording media, the Player will generally translate the raw input data into a usable format for you to consume.

It is interesting to note that the same two objects have totally opposite roles when recording or playing. In a recording scenario, the DataSource deals with phone hardware and the Player writes to a representation; in a playback scenario, the DataSource reads a representation and the Player writes to phone hardware. This flexibility can make the MMAPI difficult to understand, but it also accounts for its power. By not tying themselves to the scenarios they could imagine, the MMAPI's authors have created a system that can evolve to accomplish tasks that were not possible at the time the standard was written.

> **Note:** The one aspect of the MMAPI that does not follow this DataSource/Player design is the aspect that appears to have aged badly. At the time of its creation, the majority of phones did not support compressed audio formats, and programs relied on simple tone-based audio playback. Rather than creating a DataSource for those notes and a Player to output them, the authors created a method **Manager.playTone()** that would generate a single note. The widespread adoption of compressed audio has rendered this method largely useless, and its presence in the API feels like an anachronism.

The Life of a Player

Player instances have a standard lifecycle. As handheld devices (even BlackBerry devices) have fewer resources available than desktop computers, the MMAPI strives to keep as light a footprint as possible. Therefore, resources will only be acquired as they are necessary. You can queue up multiple media operations without worrying too much about memory usage, and MMAPI will automatically provide them with appropriate access as needed.

Each step through the lifecycle means you have taken more resources and are closer to actually performing the media operation. The Player will generally advance forward, but in certain cases can return to an earlier state, as shown in Figure 2-2. Details on each state are shown in the following list:

- UNREALIZED: This indicates that you have requested the media operation, nothing more. In a sense, it "isn't real" yet.

- REALIZED: Once a Player enters the Realized state, it knows what it has to do in order to complete the operation. Depending on the request type, it may involve communicating with the filesystem, checking capabilities, or other initial setup. A realized Player should generally be "ready," but not holding on to any scarce resources. For example, if you are going to take a picture, the Player will not be holding an exclusive lock on the camera hardware in this state.

- PREFETCHED: This state must be entered before the operation starts; but for recording tasks, it will likely not do anything. In playback operations, this is generally where data will be downloaded and buffers filled.

- STARTED: A Player that has started continues to operate. When recording, you have exclusive control of the recording hardware while in this state. When playing back, the media is playing during this time.

- CLOSED: Once you have finished with a Player, it enters this state. A closed Player has released nearly all of its resources and cannot be restarted; you must create a new Player if you wish to repeat the operation.

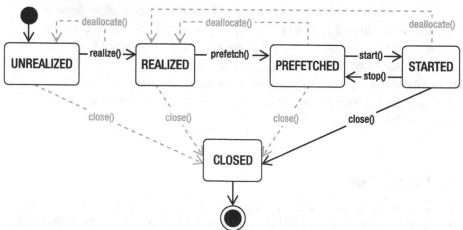

Figure 2-2. The life cycle of a Player object

At any time you have a Player object, you can call close() to shut it down. This will release all scarce resources and make it unavailable for further operations. Alternately, you can call the deallocate() method. This will return it to the REALIZED state unless it hasn't yet been realized, in which case it will keep the Player in the UNREALIZED state. Use deallocate() when you need to give up resources but intend to continue using this Player—for example, if your application contains both an audio and a video recorder, you could create both Player objects, then call deallocate() to share the microphone between them. This would be more efficient than tearing down and recreating the Players from scratch each time you record.

The five states certainly offer a lot of options for managing your Player objects. Fortunately, you don't need to explicitly deal with them unless your app requires it. A Player is smart enough to automatically move through the required states so, for example, if you instruct an UNREALIZED Player to start playing, it will automatically handle any realization and prefetching necessary.

Media operations can be blocking and time-consuming, so you may want to create, configure, and start your Player on a separate thread from the main UI thread. Somewhat confusingly, while most methods on Player are blocking synchronous calls, start() is not. When control returns from the call to start(), the Player is still running. You will generally want this thread to exit or wait until the operation is complete.

Listen to Me

The five states give a big picture of what your media is doing, but sometimes you'll want more granularity than that. It might be nice to know when you have recorded 30 seconds of audio, or when a stream has run out of data and needs to buffer.

RIM supports these use cases by offering a standard listener interface. By implementing PlayerListener, your application can register with a Player instance, as shown in Figure 2-3. PlayerListener defines a single method, playerUpdate(), which will be invoked whenever something interesting happens.

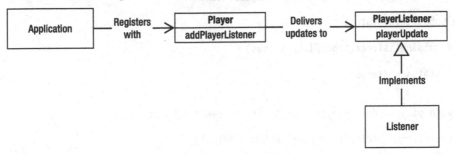

Figure 2-3. *Registering a Listener with a Player*

Updates are tagged as Strings, with additional information optionally provided in an accompanying Object. This flexible design allows manufacturers to define their own event types without requiring changes to the interface. MMAPI defines a broad set of standard event names and makes them available as public fields in the PlayerListener interface. You will need to add references to any RIM-specific event types in your own code. Table 2-1 shows the Player events that can be generated during media capture.

Table 2-1. *Player Events During Recording*

String	Definition	Meaning	EventData Type	EventData Value
recordError	RECORD_ERROR	An error occurred while recording. Call setRecordLocation or setRecordStream on the RecordControl to try again.	String	Detailed error message
recordStarted	RECORD_STARTED	Recording has begun.	Long	Time
recordStopped	RECORD_STOPPED	Recording has stopped.	Long	Time
net.rim.device.internal. media.recordCommitted	N/A	Recording commit completed.	N/A	N/A

Listing 2-1 implements a basic listener class that provides updates about the current status of a recording operation. However, a similar class could perform additional tasks as well, such as automatically restarting capture if an error occurs.

Listing 2-1. *A Status Update PlayerListener*

```
import javax.microedition.media.*;
import net.rim.device.api.ui.component.LabelField;

public class RecordingListener implements PlayerListener
{
    private LabelField status;

    public RecordingListener(LabelField status)
    {
        this.status = status;
    }

    public void playerUpdate(Player source, String event, Object data)
    {
        if (event.equals(PlayerListener.RECORD_STARTED))
        {
            status.setText("Recording started...");
        }
        else if (event.equals(PlayerListener.RECORD_STOPPED))
        {
            status.setText("Recording stopped...");
        }
        else if (event.equals(PlayerListener.RECORD_ERROR))
        {
            status.setText("Uh-oh!  Error:" + data);
```

```
        }
        else if (event.equals("net.rim.device.internal.media.recordCommitted"))
        {
            status.setText("Recorded data saved.");
        }
        else
        {
            status.setText(event + ":" + data);
        }
    }
}
```

Attach the `PlayerListener` to the `Player`, and you will start receiving updates automatically.

```
player.addPlayerListener(new RecordingListener(status));
```

Adding a `PlayerListener` is purely optional. Most advanced applications will want to receive these sorts of notifications so they can update the user and take other actions, but for simple operations, you'll be fine sticking with the basic `Player` API

Have Content, Will Travel

Once the `Player` is finished and your capture is complete, what's next? Depending on the type of capture you're doing, you'll have access to different `Control` objects, each with its own mechanism for accessing the correct data. If you are taking a snapshot, you can call a synchronous method on `VideoControl` that will return you the bytes for that shot. If you are capturing audio, you can obtain a `RecordControl` object and provide it with a file name or output stream that should be used to store the data.

Generally speaking, once you have finished your recording, you should get the data and then close the `Player` as soon as possible. This will make your application and the rest of the phone more responsive, freeing up memory and resources for other tasks.

What Else Is There?

So far, everything described is part of the standard MMAPI. It is a fairly complete solution, and fortunately, RIM has implemented most of their media capabilities within this interface. In some situations, though, you may prefer to use the native RIM applications to perform capture instead of doing it all yourself. There may be advantages to this—the RIM applications will be more familiar to the user and may contain more features than you will implement in your own—but doing so is generally more complicated.

The package `net.rim.blackberry.api.invoke` contains a class, Invoke, which can be used to launch a variety of native applications. For example, to start the camera, you would simply call Invoke with the proper parameters.

```
Invoke.invokeApplication(Invoke.APP_TYPE_CAMERA, null);
```

The second parameter is an optional set of arguments that can be passed to the application. To launch in video record mode, use the appropriate parameter in CameraArguments.

```
Invoke.invokeApplication(Invoke.APP_TYPE_CAMERA, new ↵
  CameraArguments(CameraArguments.ARG_VIDEO_RECORDER));
```

At this point, your application is backgrounded, and you will not be able to interact with the user. However, your application can monitor the filesystem for newly created files, and then use them as if they were created by your application. You'll see an example of this later in the chapter.

Creating a MediaPlayer

As noted earlier, any media operation requires both a DataSource and a Player. In practice, the Manager class is equipped to provide an appropriate DataSource for most request types, so you can request a Player by simply passing in the proper String for the type of capture you want to make.

This raises a very important question: What happens if it fails? On a BlackBerry device that has a built-in camera, such as a Curve 8300, it should work; but on a device without a camera, like an 8800, it will obviously fail. If you are developing for your own personal device, this isn't a problem—you know its capabilities and what will work. However, if you hope to run on many different devices, you will need to be prepared to handle situations where the device doesn't support an operation.

Chapter 10 provides much more detail on strategies to solve this problem. Fortunately, though, there is a clean way to determine at runtime whether the user's device can succeed. MMAPI defines a standard set of system properties, including the media-related properties shown in Table 2-2. By calling System.getProperty() with a given property name, you can determine what the device supports. Based on this, you can show an appropriate message to the user or disable an option entirely instead of waiting for it to fail.

Table 2-2. *MMAPI System Properties*

Key	Description	Returns
supports.audio.capture	Whether audio capture is supported	"true" or "false"
supports.video.capture	Whether video capture is supported	"true" or "false"
supports.recording	Whether recording is supported	"true" or "false"
audio.encodings	Supported audio capture formats	Space-delimited set of audio formats (e.g., "audio/pcm audio/amr"). null if not supported.

Table 2-2. MMAPI System Properties (continued)

Key	Description	Returns
video.encodings	Supported video capture formats	Space-delimited set of video formats (e.g., "video/3gpp video/mp4"). null if not supported.
video.snapshot.encodings	Supported video snapshot formats for the getSnapshot method	Space-delimited set of image formats (e.g., "image/jpeg image/bmp image/png"). The first format is the default. null if not supported.

Once you have checked that this device supports your desired operation, simply issue the request to the Manager.

```
if (System.getProperty("supports.video.capture").equals("true"))
{
    Player player = Manager.createPlayer("capture://video");
}
```

Caution: In order to keep the listings as focused and useful as possible, the short code snippets that you'll see like this will show only the most pertinent parts of an operation. They omit standard boilerplate that actual apps must include (like catching exceptions) or should include (like checking return values for validity). The longer listings at the end of each chapter are designed to show fully functioning programs, and these do include all required exception handling. That being said, it is very important to think about those exceptions. They aren't just there to inconvenience you, but to warn about very likely possibilities. Even if you have verified that your device supports an operation, there is a host of reasons why it might fail. For example, some other application might have an exclusive lock on the resource, or you may have insufficient permissions. You should be prepared to catch a MediaException and IOException from nearly every MMAPI method call, and take a sensible action in response.

Controlling Output

Your Player will contain at least one Control—a RecordControl—which determines what will happen with your recorded audio or video data. Obtain the RecordControl by asking the Player for it.

```
RecordControl recorder = (RecordControl)player.getControl("RecordControl");
```

The RecordControl contains a variety of useful functions. For our purposes, the most interesting are the options for determining where output should be directed. The more generic option is setRecordStream(), which takes an OutputStream. Theoretically, you could use this to directly send the captured data to an HTTP server, an encryption layer, or some other fancy stream. In practice, this method is often used when you're interested in getting the raw bytes of the audio. This capture would require outputting to a proper Stream.

```
ByteArrayOutputStream out = new ByteArrayOutputStream();
recorder.setRecordStream(out);
// Record here
byte[] rawData = out.toByteArray();
```

A very convenient alternative to an OutputStream is the method setRecordLocation(), which takes a URL. This choice will write output directly to the specified location, freeing you from any responsibility for handling the actual recording data.

```
recorder.setRecordLocation("file:///SDCard/BlackBerry/Music/recording.amr");
```

RecordControl offers several other useful operations. You will almost always use the following options:

startRecord() indicates that capture can begin. If necessary, it will wait until the associated Player has entered the STARTED state.

stopRecord() pauses capture. You can call startRecord() later to resume capture again.

commit() will cease capture and deliver the recorded data as earlier directed by setRecordStream() or setRecordLocation(). A commit occurs asynchronously: the data may not actually be saved until some time after the method returns. Your program should not attempt to access the output, whether a stream or a file, until after the "net.rim.device.internal.media.recordCommitted" event has been delivered to a PlayerListener.

For certain apps, the following choices may be useful, as well:

reset() will erase the current recorded contents. If you call reset(), none of the data up to this point will be written out.

setRecordSizeLimit() will set a cap, in bytes, on the amount of data that can be recorded. This is extremely useful if, for example, you are letting the user record video onto internal memory, or if you otherwise wish to cap the size of the output. commit() will automatically be called once the specified limit has been reached.

getContentType() reports the format of the recorded media, such as "audio/amr" or "video/3gp". In practice, you will probably already know this, but it can be informative if using the default unspecified format.

Tip: One item you do *not* have control over is the format of the output. Your format is set to what you specify when creating the Player; you cannot, for example, capture in AMR and output in MP3. If you want such a conversion, you will need to do so yourself by capturing in one format, examining the bytes, and writing out in the other format.

Recording Audio

By now you should have a general idea of how the recording process works. You will request a Player, configure it for your desired capture, start it to begin recording, and then stop it once the recording is complete. At that point you can retrieve the recorded audio data.

Before you start, though, you should ask yourself whether you care what format that data will be in. RIM offers several choices for audio encoding. Your choices are described in Table 2-3. Note that each choice has a required minimum device software version and will not work on versions below this.

Table 2-3. Audio Capture Formats

URL	Recorded Format	Available with Version
capture://audio	AMR	4.2
capture://audio?encoding=amr	AMR	4.2
capture://audio?encoding=audio/amr	AMR	4.2
capture://audio?encoding=pcm	PCM	4.2
capture://audio?encoding=audio/basic	PCM	4.2
capture://audio?encoding=gsm	GSM	4.6
capture://audio?encoding=x-gsm	GSM	4.6
capture://audio?encoding=qcelp	QCELP	4.7

Note: BlackBerry devices currently support AMR narrow band, not the higher quality AMR wide band. PCM recording is mono, 8 kHz, 16-bit.

Compared to what's available for playback, this isn't as rich a set of choices; for example, there is no option to record in MP3 format. However, depending on your application needs, some formats may be better than others. Some are more widely compatible, some are more compressed, and others offer more fidelity. AMR is a very highly compressed format that is optimized for speech, so it would be perfect for applications like a voice memo recorder. On the other hand, PCM is more appropriate for general nonvoice audio capture, and it produces files that are more likely to be compatible with other programs.

You can determine at runtime what formats are supported by calling System.getProperty("audio.encodings"). This is helpful if you prefer to record in a particular format, but can fall back on another format if it is unavailable. This is especially important because even if a device has the appropriate software version number, not every capture mode is necessarily supported. For example, CDMA devices (such as phones on the Sprint or Verizon networks in the United States) may not support PCM regardless of their version.

Capture

At the time you request the Player, you are asking for a particular format. However, you still need to decide where the data will end up. You can use a RecordControl for this purpose. RecordControl.setRecordStream() offers a generic way to output to any desired stream type, such as a byte array or a network connection. For convenience, RecordControl.setRecordLocation() will allow you to write out to a particular file.

The following pseudocode example shows the simplest way to record a 5-second audio clip.

```
Player player = Manager.createPlayer("capture://audio?encoding=amr");
RecordControl recorder = (RecordControl)player.getControl("RecordControl");
recorder.setRecordLocation("file:///SDCard/BlackBerry/Music/recording.amr");
recorder.startRecord();
player.start();
Thread.sleep(5000);
recorder.commit();
player.close();
```

Note: This example assumes that the device has a BlackBerry-formatted SD card inserted. In an actual application, you would want to verify that it is available. If you'd prefer to save to internal memory, you could write to a path under file:///store/home/user. For the best portability, use FileSystemRegistry.listRoots() to obtain a list of all currently mounted filesystems.

Considering everything that takes place, it's rather impressive that this takes only about eight lines of code to write. Real-world applications will be longer, but as you can see, the essential steps are very straightforward.

Using the Camera

Image capture is slightly more complex than audio capture. The MMAPI does not actually provide an interface for grabbing data directly from the camera. Instead, it allows you to capture a screenshot from the device screen. This means you'll need to display the camera viewfinder on the device screen, and then do your capture from that.

> **Tip:** Keep your eyes open. Future versions of BlackBerry may support JSR 234, Advanced Multimedia Supplements (AMMS). AMMS builds on top of MMAPI to provide much finer control over recording operations, including zoom, flash, focus, image and audio effects, and more. Given RIM's track record of adopting successful JSRs that match BlackBerry device capabilities, it seems probable that this may be available in the future.

As with audio capture, you have several choices when it comes to image capture. Unlike with audio, you do not need to make your choice at the time you create the Player. Instead, once you have access to a VideoControl, you can pass your requested format to VideoControl.getSnapShot(). Some supported image types follow:

```
"rgb565"

"encoding=jpeg&width=1600&height=1200&quality=superfine"

"encoding=jpeg&width=1600&height=1200&quality=fine"

"encoding=jpeg&width=1600&height=1200&quality=normal"

"encoding=jpeg&width=1024&height=768&quality=superfine"

"encoding=jpeg&width=1024&height=768&quality=fine"

"encoding=jpeg&width=1024&height=768&quality=normal"

"encoding=jpeg&width=640&height=480&quality=superfine"

"encoding=jpeg&width=640&height=480&quality=fine"

"encoding=jpeg&width=640&height=480&quality=normal"
```

Most options should be self-explanatory: JPEG images are supported for capture, and you have a choice of several different resolutions and three levels of quality. What about that "rgb565" outlier? This is a choice to retrieve raw pixel data instead of a compressed JPEG format. In RGB565, every 2 bytes refer to a single pixel. Within those 16 bytes, the top 5 bits represent the red value, the next 6 bits represent the green, and the final 5 bits represent the blue. You'll want to avoid this format unless you plan on manually manipulating the pixels in memory. Also, confirm that your target device does actually support capture in this format.

Even though RIM offered MMAPI support starting with device software version 4.2, it initially did not implement all aspects of the JSR. This isn't bad—the JSR allows manufacturers to only support parts—but it can be confusing, since the API defines the getSnapShot() method even when it is not supported. As with audio, you should check to make sure that the particular device you are running on supports image capture and that it provides the format you intend to use.

Take a Picture

When taking a picture, you must display the viewfinder within your app screen, as shown in Figure 2-4.

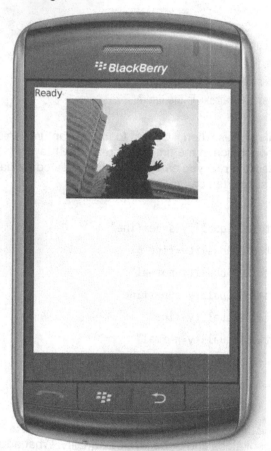

Figure 2-4. A picture-taking app

Capturing an image still requires obtaining a `Player`, but the rest of the process is different, as shown in the following pseudocode.

```
Player player = Manager.createPlayer("capture://video?encoding=video/3gpp");
player.start();
VideoControl control = (VideoControl)player.getControl("VideoControl");
Field cameraView = (Field)control.initDisplayMode↵
    (VideoControl.USE_GUI_PRIMITIVE, "net.rim.device.api.ui.Field");
screen.add(cameraView);
```

```
Thread.sleep(1000);
byte[] snapShot = control.getSnapShot↵
    ("encoding=jpeg&width=640&height=480&quality=normal");
player.close();
```

Several things are worth noting here.

- initDisplayMode() can take one of two arguments. USE_GUI_PRIMITIVE is designed to return a UI element that can be incorporated into your screen. When building a RIM CLDC Application, pass "net.rim.device.api.ui.Field" as the second parameter to retrieve a Field. When building a MIDP MIDlet, pass "javax.microedition.lcdui.Item" to retrieve an Item that can be inserted into your Form.

- If you are building a MIDlet, you also have the option of calling initDisplayMode() with the parameters USE_DIRECT_VIDEO and "javax.microedition.lcdui.Canvas" or "javax.microedition.lcdui.game.GameCanvas". This will return a special Canvas that you can set with Display.setCurrent(), offering a full-screen viewfinder.

- In all cases, the viewfinder must actually be visible on the screen prior to calling getSnapShot().

- Unlike audio recording, once we have obtained a VideoControl, nothing remains to be done with the Player. You can continue to take as many snapshots as you want until you close the Player. If you attempt to take pictures too quickly, however, getSnapShot() may return null. The camera requires time to clear out its buffer and prepare for the next shot.

Video Capture

BlackBerry devices can support video capture starting with device software version 5.0. As you might expect, video capture combines features of audio capture and image capture. Like audio capture, you are recording over a duration instead of at a particular point in time. Like image capture, you must place a viewfinder on the screen. As with both, you should query system properties for "supports.video.capture" and "video.encodings" to determine whether recording is supported and what formats are available for capture.

```
Player player = Manager.createPlayer("capture://video?encoding=video/3gpp");

player.start();
VideoControl control = (VideoControl)player.getControl("VideoControl");
RecordControl recorder = (RecordControl)player.getControl("RecordControl");
Field cameraView = (Field)control.initDisplayMode↵
    (VideoControl.USE_GUI_PRIMITIVE, "net.rim.device.api.ui.Field");
screen.add(cameraView);
```

```
recorder.setRecordLocation("file:///SDCard/BlackBerry/videos/recording.3gp");
recorder.startRecord();
Thread.sleep(5000);
recorder.stopRecord();
recorder.commit();
player.close();
```

Video recording offers the same options as audio recording for controlling where your output data goes. It offers the same options as audio recording for initializing the display mode and placing the viewfinder on the display.

Invoking the RIM Alternative

As discussed earlier, sometimes you may want to launch a native RIM application to handle media capture instead of using MMAPI. Some times this will be your only choice, such as if you need to take a picture on a device without software version 4.6 or take a video on a device without version 5.0. Even if your device supports your desired operation, you may prefer the interface of the native application to what you can provide on your own.

Starting recording in this manner is much simpler than MMAPI: it only takes a single line to start. On the other hand, getting data back out is quite a bit trickier. Because Invoke does not offer a mechanism for passing capture information back to the invoker, your only choice is to observe the filesystem. Once you see that a valid file has been created, you can assume that it was created by the capture application, and then perform whatever processing you want on it.

The listener must implement the FileSystemJournalListener interface. It will receive notifications whenever the filesystem has changed. Listing 2-2 shows a basic listener that will notify via system output when a video has been saved. At the same point, it also could prompt the application to do something with that file.

Listing 2-2. A Class That Listens for Recorded Video Files

```
public class VideoFileListener implements FileSystemJournalListener
{
    private long lastChangeNumber = 0;
    public void fileJournalChanged()
    {
        long nextChangeNumber = FileSystemJournal.getNextUSN();
        for (long change = nextChangeNumber - 1; change >= lastChangeNumber↵
            && change < nextChangeNumber; --change)
        {
            FileSystemJournalEntry entry = FileSystemJournal.getEntry(change);
            if (entry == null)
            {
                break;
            }
```

```
    if (entry.getEvent() == FileSystemJournalEntry.FILE_ADDED)
            {
                String path = entry.getPath();
                if (path != null && path.indexOf(".3gp") != -1)
                {
                    System.out.println("Video saved in " + path);
                    break;
                }
            }
        }
    }
    lastChangeNumber = nextChangeNumber;
  }
}
```

Then, just register your listener before launching the camcorder app. It will launch after a brief delay, as shown in Figure 2-5.

```
VideoFileListener listener = new VideoFileListener();
```

```
UiApplication.getUiApplication().addFileSystemJournalListener(listener);
Invoke.invokeApplication(Invoke.APP_TYPE_CAMERA, new ↵

    CameraArguments(CameraArguments.ARG_VIDEO_RECORDER));
```

Note: If you want to run this code on an actual device, you will need to sign your COD to provide access to the RIM APIs. Read more about this process in Chapter 9, which discusses the RIM security model.

Figure 2-5. *An image captured by the native camera app*

Several items in Listing 2-2 bear closer examination.

- RIM uses a journaled filesystem, where each file operation is assigned a unique number. For performance reasons, you should search backward from the most recent operation to the oldest, as shown earlier in Listing 2-2. Otherwise, it may take a very long time to find the event you're looking for.

- `fileJournalChanged()` will be invoked every time a file is added, deleted, or modified. It's very possible that it will be called for a file other than our video. Keeping track of `lastChangeNumber` ensures that even when it is called multiple times, each entry is checked only once.

- Likewise, because this can be called for any file, we should verify that the correct type of file was added before accepting it. Here we just print it out; in a real application, you would likely pass the file name back to the main application for more processing.

- Don't forget to unregister your listener once you have the data or detect that the user has canceled and returned to your application. Do this with UiApplication.removeFileSystemJournalListener().

- APP_TYPE_CAMERA has been available since software version 4.2 to capture still images. ARG_VIDEO_RECORDER was added in version 4.6 to record videos.

Most developers will likely view the Invoke system as a stop-gap measure. It's good to have available for phones that do not support your desired capture mode in a given software version, but it provides less control and will generally be a poorer user experience. Fortunately, as devices increasingly migrate to more advanced software versions, the need for this alternative will fade away.

App: Media Grabber

It is time to start work on our media sharing application. The end of each chapter will tie together the various topics and examples given so far and provide a complete, functioning application. This first entry is a stand-alone app that, depending on your device capabilities, allows you to record audio, still images, and/or video and save them to a specified location. Listing 2-3 presents the heart of the program: a Screen that will capture media. It is configurable to support all types of capture.

Listing 2-3. A Media Capture Screen Class

```
package com.apress.king.mediagrabber;


import java.io.*;

import javax.microedition.io.Connector;
import javax.microedition.io.file.FileConnection;
import javax.microedition.media.*;
import javax.microedition.media.control.*

import net.rim.device.api.ui.Field;
import net.rim.device.api.ui.MenuItem;
import net.rim.device.api.ui.component.*;
import net.rim.device.api.ui.container.MainScreen;
public class RecordingScreen extends MainScreen implements PlayerListener
{
    public static final int RECORD_AUDIO = 1;
    public static final int RECORD_PICTURE = 2;
    public static final int RECORD_VIDEO = 3;
```

We'll use a simple state machine to keep track of the current operation and guide recording progress. The other instance variables will handle the actual media operations and the visual interface.

```
public static final int STATE_WAITING = 1;
public static final int STATE_READY = 2;
public static final int STATE_RECORDING = 3;

private volatile int state = STATE_WAITING;

private int type;
private String location;

private Player player;
private RecordControl recorder;
private VideoControl video;
private Field cameraView;

private LabelField status;


private ByteArrayOutputStream dataOut;
```

Each MenuItem will display in the BlackBerry menu. To keep these class definitions compact, they call helper methods to perform their actual tasks.

```
private MenuItem goItem = new MenuItem("Go", 0, 0)
{
    public void run()
    {
        go();
    }
};
private MenuItem stopItem = new MenuItem("Stop", 0, 0)
{
    public void run()
    {
        stop();
    }
};
private MenuItem doneItem = new MenuItem("Return", 0, 0)
{
    public void run()
    {
        close();
    }
};

public RecordingScreen(int type, String location)
{
    this.type = type;
    this.location = location;
    status = new LabelField("Waiting");
    add(status);
    dataOut = new ByteArrayOutputStream();
    initMedia();

}
```

We initialize the media objects when first constructing the screen. As a result, the media operations are executed on the main thread and not a separate thread. Some `Player` methods, such as starting and stopping, are asynchronous, so you can safely call them from any thread without delay. Other operations, like the `realize()` and `prefetch()` that implicitly occur when you first call `start()`, block until they complete. This may seem dangerous to astute readers, as blocking operations should be called from a separate thread. Fortunately, BlackBerry devices do not delay long when starting capture, so you can safely fudge the rules here. This is handy, because you need to start your `VideoControl` before you can obtain the `Field`, and you must add your `Field` to the screen from the main UI thread. In other words, doing these tasks synchronously greatly simplifies the code. You'll see examples of handling media on separate threads in Chapter 3.

```
public void initMedia() {
    try
    {
        switch (type)
        {
        case RECORD_AUDIO:
            player = Manager.createPlayer("capture://audio");
            player.start();
            break;
        case RECORD_PICTURE:
        case RECORD_VIDEO:
            player = Manager.createPlayer("capture://video");
            player.start();
            video = (VideoControl)player.getControl("VideoControl");
            cameraView = (Field)video.initDisplayMode(
                VideoControl.USE_GUI_PRIMITIVE, "net.rim.device.api.ui.Field");
            add(cameraView);
            break;
        }
        player.addPlayerListener(this);
        state = STATE_READY;
        status.setText("Ready");
    }
    catch (MediaException me)
    {
        status.setText(me.getMessage());
    }
    catch (IOException ioe)
    {
        status.setText(ioe.getMessage());
    }
}
```

We add the appropriate `MenuItem` objects to the menu based on the current state of the application. For example, "Go" will only display if we are in the READY state.

```
public void makeMenu(Menu menu, int instance)
{
    if (instance == Menu.INSTANCE_DEFAULT)
```

```
    {
        if (state == STATE_READY)
        {
            menu.add(goItem);
        }
        else if (state == STATE_RECORDING)
        {
            menu.add(stopItem);
        }
        menu.add(doneItem);
    }
    super.makeMenu(menu, instance);

}
```

Our actual media operations are quite simple, requiring just a couple method calls. Because image capture is so different from audio/video capture, it uses a separate helper method.

```
private void go()

{
    if (type == RECORD_PICTURE)
    {
        takeSnapShot();
    }
    else
    {
        recorder = (RecordControl)player.getControl("RecordControl");
        if (recorder != null)
        {
            recorder.setRecordStream(dataOut);
            recorder.startRecord();
            state = STATE_RECORDING;
            status.setText("Recording");
        }
    }
}

private void takeSnapShot()
{
    try
    {
        byte[] imageData = video.getSnapshot↩
            ("encoding=jpeg&width=640&height=480&quality=normal");
        if (imageData != null)
        {
            writeToFile(imageData, location + "/image.jpg");
            status.setText("Image taken");
        }
        else
        {
            status.setText("Please try again later.");
        }
    }
    catch (IOException ioe)
```

```
        {
            status.setText(ioe.getMessage());
        }
        catch (MediaException me)
        {
            status.setText(me.getMessage());
        }
    }
```

This helper method moves data from an in-memory buffer to a persistent store. You'll notice that the FileConnection is opened with READ_WRITE access, even though only WRITE is required. This is because of a bug in older versions of BlackBerry device software that caused writes to fail unless READ_WRITE was requested. Newer software versions do not have this problem, but it doesn't hurt to ask for the extra access.

Also, note that the file OutputStream is closed before the FileConnection. Certain versions of BlackBerry device software do not respond well if the FileConnection is closed first, which can leave you unable to reopen the file later.

```
    private void writeToFile(byte[] data, String fileName) throws IOException
    {
        FileConnection file = null;
        OutputStream output = null;
        try
        {
            file = (FileConnection)Connector.open(fileName, Connector.READ_WRITE);
            if (file.exists())
            {
                file.delete();
            }
            file.create();
            output = file.openOutputStream();
            output.write(data);
        }
        finally
        {
            if (output != null) { output.close(); }
            if (file != null) { file.close(); }
        }
    }

    private void stop()
    {
        try
        {
            if (type == RECORD_AUDIO || type == RECORD_VIDEO)
            {
                recorder.commit();
                if (type == RECORD_AUDIO)
                {
                    writeToFile(dataOut.toByteArray(), location + "/audio.amr");
                }
                else
```

```
                    {
                        writeToFile(dataOut.toByteArray(), location + "/video.3gp");
                    }
                    status.setText("Data saved");
                    state = STATE_READY;
                }
            }
        catch (IOException ioe)
        {
            status.setText(ioe.getMessage());
        }
    }

    public void playerUpdate(Player arg0, String arg1, Object arg2) {
        System.out.println("playerUpdate: " + arg1);
    }

}
```

Listing 2-4 presents the RecordingChoiceScreen. This is the first visual element that will display, and offers minimal text as well as menu options for supported forms of media capture.

Listing 2-4. *Examining Device Capabilities and Presenting Options*

```
package com.apress.king.mediagrabber;

import net.rim.device.api.ui.*;
import net.rim.device.api.ui.component.*;
import net.rim.device.api.ui.container.MainScreen;

public class RecordingChoicesScreen extends MainScreen
{
    private BasicEditField location = new BasicEditField↵
        ("Save location:", "file:///SDCard/BlackBerry", 100, ↵
        Field.FIELD_VCENTER | BasicEditField.FILTER_FILENAME);
    private MenuItem audioItem = new MenuItem("Record Sound", 0, 0)
    {
        public void run()
        {
            launchRecorder(RecordingScreen.RECORD_AUDIO);
        }
    };
    private MenuItem pictureItem = new MenuItem("Take a Picture", 0, 0)
    {
        public void run()
        {
            launchRecorder(RecordingScreen.RECORD_PICTURE);
        }
    };
    private MenuItem videoItem = new MenuItem("Record Video", 0, 0)
    {
        public void run()
```

```java
            {
                launchRecorder(RecordingScreen.RECORD_VIDEO);
            }
    };

    public RecordingChoicesScreen()
    {
        setTitle("MediaGrabber");
        add(new LabelField("Please enter a save location, then select⏎
            a recording choice from the menu."));
        add(location);
    }

    public void close()
    {
        location.setDirty(false);
        super.close();
    }

    public void makeMenu(Menu menu, int instance)
    {
        if (instance == Menu.INSTANCE_DEFAULT)
        {
            String property = System.getProperty("supports.audio.capture");
            if (property != null && property.equals("true"))
            {
                menu.add(audioItem);
            }
            property = System.getProperty("video.snapshot.encodings");
            if (property != null && property.length() > 0)
            {
                menu.add(pictureItem);
            }
            property = System.getProperty("supports.video.capture");
            if (property != null && property.equals("true"))
            {
                menu.add(videoItem);
            }
        }

        super.makeMenu(menu, instance);
    }

    private void launchRecorder(int type)
    {
        String directory = location.getText();
        RecordingScreen screen = new RecordingScreen(type, directory);
        UiApplication.getUiApplication().pushScreen(screen);
    }

    public boolean onSavePrompt()
    {
        return true;
    }
}
```

In this class, onSavePrompt() is overridden to suppress a warning about editing the location field. Since we don't actually save this field, the warning isn't necessary.

Finally, Listing 2-5 shows the application's entry point, which creates and starts our RecordingChoicesScreen.

Listing 2-5. *MediaGrabber Application*

```
package com.apress.king.mediagrabber;

import net.rim.device.api.ui.UiApplication;

public class MediaGrabber extends UiApplication
{
    public static void main(String[] args)
    {
        new MediaGrabber().enterEventDispatcher();
    }

    private MediaGrabber()
    {
        pushScreen(new RecordingChoicesScreen());
    }

}
```

Go ahead and try running the application, ideally both in the simulator and on the device. After you successfully run the app, you can find the newly created files by entering the native Media application, then pressing Menu and selecting Explore. Navigate to the directory you selected.

You may notice a few problems at first in the simulator. First of all, because there isn't an actual camera attached, you must provide the camera image. You can do this by opening the native Camera application, or by selecting the Camera Image... option from the simulator menu. Figure 2-6 shows this option in a recent simulator.

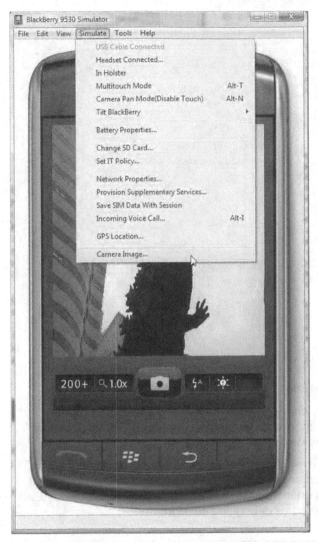

Figure 2-6. *Configuring the simulator with a virtual camera image*

Second, you'll need to insert a virtual SD card for the simulator, which you can do by configuring the simulator. I prefer the option of using a directory on the host PC filesystem, which allows me to easily view files as they are created, modified, and destroyed. In Eclipse, this option is available in the run configuration, as shown in Figure 2-7.

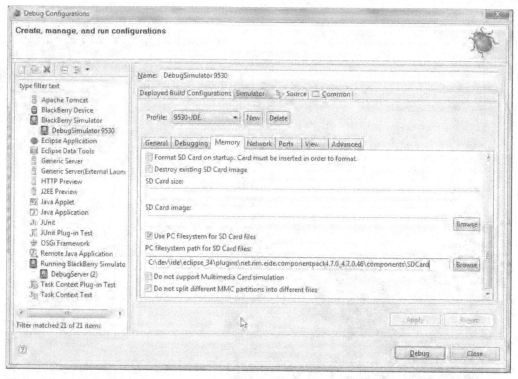

Figure 2-7. Adding a virtual SD card to the simulator

You will probably encounter security prompts when you run the application on the device. Dealing with these prompts is covered in depth in Chapter 9. For now, simply provide all permissions whenever the device asks for them.

How do you debug when things go wrong? Most developers have their favorite techniques. Remember, you can view any information that is printed to the System.out log. When the application is running on the device, never underestimate the usefulness of attaching it to your IDE for an interactive debugging session!

WANT MORE?

If you would like to further enhance the behavior of this app, here are some tasks you can try for extra credit. These go above and beyond the improvements made in later chapters.

- Instead of using hard-coded media formats, parse the supported types provided by System.getProperty() and provide the user with a list of options.

- Let the user choose the file name. Check to make sure they are saving in a valid location.

- Suggest alternatives locations to save the file, such as internal storage.

Touches like this will make an app particularly intuitive and useful.

Excelsior

Congratulations! You have taken a giant step forward in mastering BlackBerry programming. As you have seen, the media capture APIs offered by RIM are quite powerful, providing control over the hardware capabilities of recent devices. You must consider your target market and decide what devices to support, and then check what media capture options are provided on that target. You can use MMAPI to embed media capture functions into your own application, giving you a high level of control over the user experience. Alternately, you can use RIM's Invoke API to pass off control to a native application, and then observe the results on your own.

Media capture can be a compelling application by itself; it's no coincidence that new RIM phones come pre-loaded with a camera app. The most exciting apps, though, are those that use capture to obtain data and then do interesting things with it. In Chapter 3, we'll start looking at ways to display the media you have captured.

Chapter 3

Media Playback

One of the most exciting opportunities modern mobile phones offer is the chance to deliver high-quality media experiences. Entire companies have been founded to provide personal television channel delivery, radio station rebroadcast, or similar repackaging of media. In many other applications, you can use media to enhance the features of your app. You might add background music to your game, a tutorial video to a productivity app, or a slideshow mode to a real estate app.

You must rely on your own judgment to decide whether media is appropriate for your app, and, if it is, to select the appropriate content. Once the time comes to actually present the media, BlackBerry devices offer a set of APIs for locating and playing that content. As with media capture, you can choose between standard MMAPI interfaces that embed playback within your app, or RIM interfaces to use a native app.

Finding Content

Because BlackBerry devices are feature-rich and live on the network, you have a plethora of choices for finding and delivering media files to play. This section discusses the various options and the tradeoffs each offers.

Local Filesystem

You can use the FileConnection API to discover and load content. BlackBerry devices offer both internal memory and external SD card storage. The former is fast and reliable, but limited in size. It is fine for storing app data, but you will annoy your users if you fill it up with large media files. The SD card offers a large amount of storage, but there is no guarantee that the user will have a card inserted at any time.

How to Use

You should first use the FileSystemRegistry to ensure that the file system you want to use is available. You can then use the FileConnection API to look up content, recursing into subdirectories if necessary. Alternately, if you know the absolute path of the media file you're looking for, you can directly test for its existence.

Once you have verified that the media file is present, you can directly create a Player for it by passing the file's URL to Manager.createPlayer(). If you prefer, you can also open the file contents as an InputStream and pass that stream to Manager.createPlayer(). In the latter case, you should also provide the media's MIME type, such as "audio/mpeg". If you omit the MIME type, Manager will attempt to detect it based on the initial contents of the InputStream, which may or may not be possible.

When to Use

A local filesystem offers several advantages

- **Speed.** Your media can load and start playing more quickly than it could when loaded over the network, even on a fast location.

- **Reliability.** Particularly when using internal device memory, you can be relatively sure that the media will be available, assuming the user hasn't manually deleted it.

There are also some drawbacks.

- **Capacity.** The device's internal memory store is limited, and the user may not want you to take up space on their SD card.

- **Authority.** Users may choose to grant or deny your app permission to read files at all, and you will be stuck if they deny it.

An Example

The following code snippet demonstrates how to search for the first available MP3 file.

```
public String getFirstMP3Path() throws IOException
{
    Enumeration roots = FileSystemRegistry.listRoots();
    while (roots.hasMoreElements())
    {
        String root = (String) roots.nextElement();
        String match = getFirstMP3Path(root);
        if (match != null)
        {
            return match;
        }
    }
    return null;
}

public String getFirstMP3Path(String directoryPath) throws IOException
{
    FileConnection directory = (FileConnection) Connector
```

```
            .open(directoryPath);
    Enumeration children = directory.list();
    while (children.hasMoreElements())
    {
        String path = (String) children.nextElement();
        if (path.indexOf(".mp3") != -1)
        {
            return directoryPath + path;
        }
        else if (path.indexOf("/") != -1)
        {
            String match = getFirstMP3Path(directoryPath + path);
            if (match != null)
            {
                return match;
            }
        }
    }
    return null;
}
```

Network Download

The MMAPI is capable of automatically retrieving and playing remote media resources. Therefore, you might want to place media files on an HTTP server and request them when necessary. You won't need to handle the actual network connection and download yourself, although you should still be prepared to handle errors if the file cannot be accessed.

How to Use

Pass the media file location to the Manager using a URL that begins with http:// or https://. If you know at the time you create your application where the file will be located, you can simply hard-code the string. However, if you are creating a networked application, it is better to have the server pass the URL down to the client. This gives you greater flexibility if you later decide that you need to place the files on another server, change their format, or make other changes.

When to Use

Pros:

- **Flexibility.** You can update the media file contents without requiring the user to download a new version of the file. For example, you could offer new music for a game.

- **Size.** Because you are loading off the network, you don't need to place any additional files in your app or in permanent memory. This keeps your users happy.

Cons:

- **Reliability.** You must be prepared to deal with network failures. Depending on your app, you may offer an offline mode if the file cannot be reached; otherwise, your app will not run when there is no connection.

- **Speed.** The file may take quite some time to download, especially if it is large or the user has a slow connection.

- **Memory.** Because the file isn't streaming, the entire contents must be buffered in RAM. Large video files will likely cause you to run out of memory.

An Example

Simply pass a URL to `Manager.createPlayer()`. The URL should contain the complete path to the network resource, such as `"http://myserver.com/files/sample.mp3"`.

Network Stream

One of the most impressive capabilities of the MMAPI is its ability to handle streaming protocols. Streams allow the device to play the media while it is downloading, without requiring you to acquire the entire file first. Not every manufacturer supports this, but RIM handsets do, starting with device software version 4.3. Streaming is a fairly complex process—the player needs to judge how much content to buffer, decide when to start playing, and react properly when the network connection speeds up, slows down, or drops out. Fortunately, these details are hidden from you, and you can simply pass the proper URL and let the `Player` work its magic.

How to Use

Pass the media file location to the Manager using a URL that begins with `rtsp://`. As with media download, you can hard-code the string or obtain it from another resource. Make sure that the RTSP server you are connecting with is properly configured for serving up mobile content. A stream designed for a desktop web browser will likely have far too much data for a mobile device, and trying to access it directly will result in choppiness or other problems.

When to Use

Pros:

- **Speed.** Compared with a regular network download, streams allow you to start playing content much more quickly.

- **Flexibility.** As with network downloads, you have control over a stream's content and can update it without modifying installed apps.

- **Live media.** Unlike regular audio files, which must be of a fixed length, streams can run indefinitely. This allows support for radio stations, live commentary, or other on-the-fly audio delivery.

Cons:

- **Compatibility.** Your users must be using a recent version of RIM device software.

- **Reliability.** While streams have some ability to recover from temporary network problems, they will be of no use if the user is not on the network at all.

- **Speed.** While faster than a network download, streaming will be slower than a locally served file.

- **Quality.** RTSP allows for lossy data transmission—if certain packets cannot be delivered, the player simply won't play them. If the device has a bad connection, the resulting media will seem choppy or worse.

An Example

Create the `Player` as shown above, but use the `rtsp` scheme, as in
`"rtsp://myserver.com/streams/live.m4a"`.

Manual Buffering

What should you do if you want to stream, but you are running on an older version of BlackBerry device software? You could switch to a download, update the phone, or write your own streaming client implementation. This requires an investment in time and effort, but it allows you to have streaming capabilities even when the device doesn't support it.

How to Use

In the previous chapter, we discussed how `DataSource` objects handle the data delivery protocol. When you use a URL that starts with `http://`, `file:///`, or `rtsp://`, the `Manager` is automatically creating an appropriate `DataSource` for that type of protocol. However, you can implement your own version of `DataSource` and `SourceStream` to provide whatever functionality you wanted, including support for streaming. Define this `DataSource`, then pass it to `Manager.createPlayer()`. The `Manager` will then obtain the necessary data from the `DataSource`'s provided streams, as shown in Figure 3-1. Note that you will now be responsible for all the complexity of streaming. You will likely need to experiment and tune your `DataSource`'s behavior to get the best results on different devices.

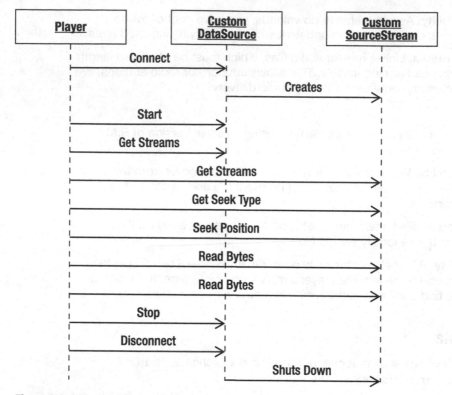

Figure 3-1. *A Player with a user-defined data source*

When to Use

Pros:

- **Compatibility.** Your DataSource can run on any BlackBerry device that supports media playback and network connections.

- **Control.** You will gain a far greater level of control over media playback, beyond what is provided by the standard MMAPI behavior. For example, you could automatically shut off playback when the user's time expires.

Cons:

- **Complexity.** Creating a DataSource is fairly tricky, and it requires tuning to get the best performance.

- **Coordination.** If using a custom protocol, you will need to make sure that the server is set up to provide data in the format you expect.

An Example

This skeleton class shows a DataSource implementation that could be used to create a streaming Player.

```java
public class StreamingDataSource extends DataSource
{

    public StreamingDataSource(String locator)
    {
        super(locator);
    }

    public void connect() throws IOException
    {
        // Connect to the locator and create the stream(s).
    }

    public void disconnect()
    {
        // Close the stream(s).
    }

    public String getContentType()
    {
        // Return content type of underlying stream.
        return null;
    }

    public SourceStream[] getStreams()
    {
        // Return stream(s) created in connect()
        return null;
    }

    public void start() throws IOException
    {
        // Start acquiring content with the stream(s).
    }

    public void stop() throws IOException
    {
        // Stop acquiring content.
    }

    public Control getControl(String controlType)
    {
        // Can return null unless adding custom controls.
        return null;
    }

    public Control[] getControls()
    {
        // Can return null unless adding custom controls.
```

```
        return null;
    }

}
```

The associated SourceStream will do most of the actual work. A skeleton example follows. An implementing class will generally reuse one or more existing InputStream objects, adding any extra logic that is necessary.

```java
public class StreamingSourceStream implements SourceStream
{

    public ContentDescriptor getContentDescriptor()
    {
        // Returns descriptor for content being retrieved.
        return null;
    }

    public long getContentLength()
    {
        // Returns total amount of data to read.
        return 0;
    }

    public int getSeekType()
    {
        // Return one of NOT_SEEKABLE, RANDOM_SEEKABLE, or SEEKABLE_TO_START.
        return 0;
    }

    public int getTransferSize()
    {
        // Return size of a logical chunk to read.
        // Useful to influence the size of requested reads.
        return 0;
    }

    public int read(byte[] dataOut, int offset, int length) throws IOException
    {
        // Retrieve actual data. Can block until sufficient data available.
        return 0;
    }

    public long seek(long position) throws IOException
    {
        // Advance stream to desired position, if supported.
        return 0;
    }
    public long tell()
    {
        // Return current position within the stream.
        return 0;
    }

    public Control getControl(String controlType)
```

```
    {
        // Can return null unless adding custom controls.
        return null;
    }

    public Control[] getControls()
    {
        // Can return null unless adding custom controls.
        return null;
    }

}
```

COD Resource

The most traditional way to deliver media is packaged with your application. When users install your COD file, they will receive all the bundled media files along with it. Because the entire COD is loaded into memory when the application starts, you can be certain that the media is available.

How to Use

Simply include the media file in your BlackBerry project. In Eclipse, right-click the src folder, choose Import, General, File System, Next, Browse, then navigate to and add your resource. It will appear in the src folder, as shown in Figure 3-2, and will be automatically built into the COD. Note that any type of file can be included as a resource. In your application, get an InputStream for that resource, then pass that stream to Manager.createPlayer(). If you know the MIME type, include it here; otherwise, pass null. The Manager will create an appropriate Player for the file.

Figure 3-2. Adding a resource to the COD

When to Use

Pros:

- **Speed.** Because the COD is already loaded in RAM, this is the absolute fastest way to access any media.

- **Reliability.** You know that the media is always there, no matter what the user has done.

Cons:

- **Size.** Every byte of media directly increases the size of your app. Users may not want to even install it if the app seems very large.

- **Inflexible.** You cannot change the media without creating a new version of the app.

An Example

Retrieve the stream and create the player as shown below.

```
InputStream is = getClass().getResourceAsStream("/Lake.wmv");
Player player = Manager.createPlayer(is, "video/wmv");
```

Other

Do you have another source of media that doesn't fit into the above choices? Not to worry! Manager accepts an InputStream, and an InputStream can wrap anything you want. Your underlying data may be stored in a big byte array, be programmatically generated, or spliced together from multiple sources. When you want to hand off arbitrary bytes to the Player, create an InputStream.

How to Use

Java ME defines some useful standard implementations of InputStream. One of the most popular is ByteArrayInputStream, which wraps a block of bytes. You can also create your own subclass of InputStream. There are many methods available to override, but the most important is to provide an implementation of read() that returns the next bytes.

When to Use

The pros and cons of this approach depend on how the underlying data is obtained—whether in memory, from a file, over the network, etc. It will generally perform similarly to one of the above methods. If writing your own InputStream, expect more time required to implement and debug it.

An Example

A fairly common use case is to store media contents in memory, and then wrap it with a valid InputStream.

```
byte[] mediaData;
// Fill in the contents.
InputStream input = new ByteArrayInputStream(mediaData);
```

Playing Audio

After you have identified and prepared the content you want to play, it's time to bring it into your app. Once again, MMAPI hides many of the details from you, but this section will show you what's happening behind the scenes. You'll learn how to choose appropriate formats and encodings and see how to handle problems with playback.

The Player Returns

Playback involves the same classes we saw for capture: Manager, Player, and multiple Controls. You may want to review Figure 2-2 from the previous chapter to observe the states that a Player moves through.

Let's take a look at the particular states a Player might encounter when playing a particular type of media, such as a streaming audio file:

- UNREALIZED. In this state the Player has been created, so it knows that it supports the transport protocol (in this case, RTSP).

- REALIZED. The Player has communicated with the server, verified that the stream exists, and determined that it supports the stream's media type.

- PREFETCHED. The Player has downloaded the initial contents of the stream as an audio buffer. It also has verified that it can direct audio to the output hardware, acquiring an exclusive lock if necessary.

- STARTED. The Player is actively streaming. The Player will usually be producing audio during this time, although if rebuffering is necessary, it will remain in the STARTED state while it fetches more data.

- CLOSED. The Player has finished streaming and released all network and hardware resources.

You can explicitly move a Player through each state by calling realize(), prefetch(), and start(). You can also just call start() to automatically move it through all the states. You should be aware, though, about the underlying operations and what they involve. If you call start() on a video stream from your main UI thread, and the Player is still in the UNREALIZED state, then your app will appear to freeze during the seconds (or minutes!) that it takes to buffer the video. On the other hand, if you call prefetch() in another thread, calling start() will return almost immediately.

The previous chapter discussed the importance of exclusive locks and how you can use deallocate() to surrender those locks. deallocate() is still a useful tool when playing media, but exclusive locks tend not to be as severe of an issue. Only one application can access the microphone or camera at a given time, but more than one application may be able to play sound. However, deallocate() is still important for managing memory. Imagine you are writing a video app with 12 channels, each with its own Player. If the user switches between channels, the nonplaying streams will still hold expensive buffers. However, if you call `deallocate()` on each when it goes away, the overhead for the 11 nonplaying channels will be minimal.

Listening In

As it runs, the `Player` will deliver information about its current status to all registered `PlayerListener` objects. You will almost always want to register at least one `PlayerListener` with each `Player`. At an absolute minimum, this will provide you with useful debugging information about what is happening. In most cases, you will want to take some action based on certain important events. For example, you may show a Loading screen when a stream is buffering, or exit the current screen once a song finishes playing. Figure 3-3 shows the potential sequence of one media play execution.

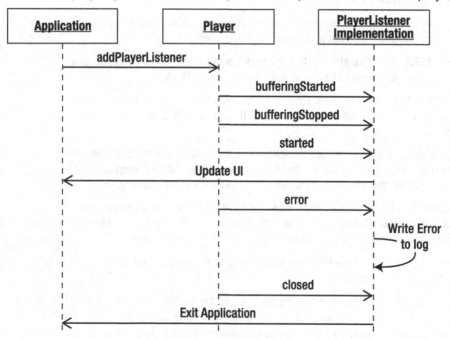

Figure 3-3. A PlayerListener responding to Player events

Many events are defined as part of the MMAPI spec, and RIM can send custom events, as well. Whenever your `PlayerListener` is called, it will be passed a `String` with the event name, and an `Object` containing more information about the event. The most common events are shown in Table 3-1.

Table 3-1. *PlayerListener Events*

String	Definition	Meaning	EventData type	EventData value
bufferingStarted	BUFFERING_ STARTED	Player enters buffering mode.	Long	Media time when buffering starts
bufferingStopped	BUFFERING_ STOPPED	Player exits buffering mode.	Long	Media time when buffering stops
closed	CLOSED	Player closed; end of events.	N/A	null
deviceAvailable	DEVICE_ AVAILABLE	An exclusive device is now available to this Player in the REALIZED state.	String	Name of device
deviceUnavailable	DEVICE_ UNAVAILABLE	This Player has lost access to an exclusive device and placed back in the REALIZED state. The next event must be DEVICE_AVAILABLE or ERROR.	String	Name of device
durationUpdated	DURATION_ UPDATED	The duration for this Player has changed. This generally occurs when the duration cannot be known at start but becomes available later.	Long	Duration of the media.
endOfMedia	END_OF_ MEDIA	The Player has reached the end of the media.	Long	Media time for the end of media.
error	ERROR	The Player encountered an error.	String	Detailed error message (see below).
sizeChanged	SIZE_ CHANGED	A playing video's size has changed; for example, the screen may have changed orientation.	VideoControl	Object with new video dimensions.
started	STARTED	Player has begun to play.	Long	Media time when player started
stopped	STOPPED	Player has received a stop() call and returned to the PREFETCHED state.	Long	Media time when player stopped

Table 3-1. *PlayerListener Events (continued)*

String	Definition	Meaning	EventData type	EventData value
stoppedAtTime	STOPPED_AT_TIME	Player has reached the time specified by a previous call to StopTimeControl.setStopTime and returned to the PREFETCHED state.	Long	Media time when player stopped.
volumeChanged	VOLUME_CHANGED	Volume has changed; for example, user has pressed a volume key.	VolumeControl	Object with new volume level
com.rim.timeUpdate	N/A	Media has advanced. Called about once per second.	Long	Current media time in microseconds.
com.rim.loading	N/A	Media is loading.	N/A	N/A

> **Note:** The MMAPI does not specify what units "media time" correspond to. On BlackBerry devices, each unit of media time is one microsecond. Multiply by 1,000 to convert to milliseconds (useful when comparing to system time), and by 1,000,000 to convert to seconds (useful when showing elapsed play time).

No app will need to respond to all the above events, but every app will likely care about at least a few of them. You should just look for the ones you care about and ignore the rest. Be aware that certain media operations might generate a slew of events—for example, you might receive a "com.rim.timeUpdate" every second while a stream is playing. Because of this, you may want to avoid actions like logging every event that is passed, because doing so would slow down the operation of your app.

Pay particular attention to errors. There is a fundamental difference between transient errors and permanent errors. If media will not play because of a network hiccup or temporary loss of the output device, you may want to retry the operation to save your user the hassle. On the other hand, if the media itself is corrupt or incompatible, you cannot do anything about it. To facilitate more deterministic handling of errors, RIM has decided to use integer values as the ERROR extended message. Table 3-2 shows the currently defined codes and their meaning.

Table 3-2. *RIM Media Error Codes*

Code	Meaning
1	Player is busy.
2	Bad parameter.

Table 3-2. RIM Media Error Codes (continued)

Code	Meaning
3	Out of memory.
4	Stream has exhausted available data.
5	Other error.
6	Media file is corrupt.
7	Server is not responding.
8	Connection is unavailable.
9	Invalid URL.
10	File is unseekable.
11	Streaming server is not responding.
12	Missing DRM rights.
13	Streaming server rejected streaming request.
14	Streaming server error.
15	Payment is required.
16	Streaming server forbids client connection.
17	Item to stream not found.
18	Client must authenticate with a proxy prior to streaming.
19	Request URI too large.
20	Insufficient bandwidth for streaming.
21	Session expired.
22	Unsupported UDP or TCP transport streaming.

As you can see, most of the errors relate to streaming content. Having this level of granularity is extremely helpful when configuring a streaming solution, as it helps you quickly identify whether the problem is client-side or server-side.

A simple `PlayerListener` is shown in Listing 3-1. This `PlayerListener` updates a `Screen` with status information and closes it when playback is complete.

Listing 3-1. *A Custom Listener for Media Playback*

```java
import javax.microedition.media.*;
import net.rim.device.api.ui.Screen;
import net.rim.device.api.ui.component.LabelField;

public class WatchdogListener implements PlayerListener
{
    private LabelField status;
    private Screen screen;

    public WatchdogListener(LabelField status, Screen screen)
    {
        this.status = status;
        this.screen = screen;
    }

    public void playerUpdate(Player player, String event, Object data)
    {
        if (event.equals(PlayerListener.BUFFERING_STARTED))
        {
            status.setText("Buffering, please wait.");
        }
        else if (event.equals(PlayerListener.BUFFERING_STOPPED))
        {
            status.setText("Buffer complete.");
        }
        else if (event.equals(PlayerListener.STARTED))
        {
            status.setText("Playing.");
        }
        else if (event.equals(PlayerListener.STOPPED))
        {
            status.setText("Stopped.");
        }
        else if (event.equals(PlayerListener.ERROR))
        {
            status.setText("Encountered error: " + data);
        }
        else if (event.equals(PlayerListener.END_OF_MEDIA))
        {
            screen.close();
        }
        else
        {
            status.setText (event + ":" + data);
        }
    }
}
```

All About Codecs

Imagine you have an app that plays humorous comedy clips. You find a bit on the Web that you like, add it to the app, and. . .nothing happens! It played just fine on your desktop—what gives?

Welcome to the wonderful world of media codecs. The options available for playback can bewilder, and seem to grow more complicated every year. Investing some time up front in understanding codecs and selecting the appropriate formats for your app can save hours of last-minute scrambling.

Containers and Content

When you receive a media file, it's like a box. Depending on the file format, it will contain various types of things: perhaps the author's name, some metadata about the contents, maybe some DRM. It will also contain one or more smaller locked boxes, which hold the actual audio or video data.

That outer box is a *container*. Containers have names like MP4 and AVI, and refer to the way the media pieces are packaged together. The locked boxes are the actual components. These must be opened with the corresponding key—the *codec*. Codecs have names like MPEG4 or AAC+, and refer to how the actual audio or video bytes should be played. Figure 3-4 shows three of the many possible configurations of codecs and containers.

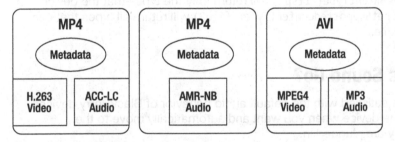

Figure 3-4. *Containers and codecs*

What makes this confusing is that, historically, there often was a 1-1 correspondence between containers and codecs. An MP3 file always used the MPEG1 audio encoding, so all MP3 files are more or less compatible. However, an M4A file may be using H.263, H.264, or MPEG4 encoding, so it isn't enough to say "I need an M4A file," you also need to know what codec it uses. You may have experienced this problem occasionally when using your desktop computer; the problem is far more widespread on mobile devices.

The moral of the story: If you are producing your own content, select a compatible format and use it for everything. If you are acquiring content from others, verify that you support each given piece of content.

Codec Support

Once the device has identified what encoding a piece of content uses, it must decide how to handle playback. Codecs are implemented in one of two ways: in software or in hardware. A software codec analyzes the byte stream, translates it from the compressed format into the device's native format, and then passes the translated bytes to the output device. This can be very time consuming, and on a limited device like a mobile phone, the CPU may not be able to translate fast enough to play at an acceptable rate. A hardware codec is embedded into the graphic or audio chip, and can directly translate the encoded data into sound or video. This is much faster and frees up the CPU for other tasks, but it's also more expensive and therefore rarer.

Software codecs are limited by processor speed. Hardware codecs are limited by hardware design. With this in mind, you shouldn't be surprised that codecs are among the few items in the world of BlackBerry development which are controlled by phone hardware, not just the version of BlackBerry device software installed. Fortunately, RIM has documented their codec support well. Please see the Appendix for a list of currently supported codecs on a range of popular BlackBerry models.

You can also attempt to determine at runtime what types of content are supported on a given device. This can be a good way to future-proof your app, so if a newer device or software version becomes available, the same version of your app will automatically know that it can handle a better codec. Use the method `Manager.getSupportedContentType(null)` to obtain an array of all valid MIME types on this device. You can even pass in a particular protocol to be used for filtering, so `Manager.getSupportedContentType("rtsp")` will return only the types that the device can stream, while `Manager.getSupportedContentType("file")` will return all types that can be played from a local file.

Where Does the Sound Go?

Most often, you will be satisfied with the default audio behavior of BlackBerry devices. Sound will play from the device when you want and automatically move to the headphones when they are plugged in.

However, in certain circumstances you might want to exercise more control over where audio goes. If your app is delivering voice messages, you might prefer the sound to be sent through the earpiece for privacy, rather than through the speakerphone where anyone can hear. Figure 3-5 shows some of the more common audio outputs for a BlackBerry.

Figure 3-5. *Audio connections on a device*

A Player with an audio component will offer an AudioPathControl. You may use this to see where audio is currently being directed, and send it somewhere else if appropriate. The following options are supported.

AUDIO_PATH_BLUETOOTH. Bluetooth SCO, such as a car kit.

AUDIO_PATH_BLUETOOTH_A2DP. Paired A2DP-compatible device, like a stereo Bluetooth headset.

AUDIO_PATH_HANDSET. The earpiece.

AUDIO_PATH_HANDSFREE. The speakerphone.

AUDIO_PATH_HEADSET. Hands-free headset.

AUDIO_PATH_HEADSET_HANDSFREE. The speakerphone and the hands-free headset.

> **Note:** AudioPathControl is available starting with software version 4.2.
> AUDIO_PATH_BLUETOOTH_A2DP was added in version 4.3.

The following code demonstrates how to force audio to be played through the speakerphone.

```
Player player = Manager.createPlayer("file:///SDCard/BlackBerry/Music/Walrus.mp3");
```

```
player.prefetch();
AudioPathControl control = (AudioPathControl)player.getControl("AudioPathControl");
if (control.getAudioPath() != AudioPathControl.AUDIO_PATH_HANDSFREE)
{
    control.setAudioPath(AudioPathControl.AUDIO_PATH_HANDSFREE);
}
```

Mixing Music

There may be times when you would like to play more than one audio file at once. Perhaps you are playing background music for a boxing game, and you also want to play an audio clip of someone landing a punch. How does this work? Well, it depends on the device. MMAPI defines a system property called "supports.mixing". If this is true, the device must support playing at least two audio sources at the same time. If it is false, then only one can be played at a time. In this case the second attempt to play will either fail or interrupt the first player.

Currently, most GSM devices support mixing up to two audio sources. Most CDMA devices do not support any mixing. For the best compatibility, you should check for the system property.

What should you do if mixing is not supported? Your options will generally be limited. If it's two pieces of music, you can try combining them into a single file for playback. If you want to combine music and effects, you will generally need to stop the first Player before starting the second, then restart the first once the second is done. Depending on the application this may sound annoying, and you might prefer to disable either music or effects entirely.

This example demonstrates making a decision whether to start a second Player based on the capabilities of the device. All users will hear the song, but only mixing devices will play the claps.

```
Player music = Manager.createPlayer("file:///SDCard/BlackBerry/Music/ObLaDi.mp3");
Player sound = Manager.createPlayer("file:///SDCard/BlackBerry/Music/clap.amr");
music.realize();
sound.realize();
music.start();
if (System.getProperty("supports.mixing").equals("true"))
{
    for (int i = 0; i < 5; ++i)
    {
        sound.start();
        Thread.sleep(1000);
        sound.stop();
    }
}
```

Bringing It Together

You've found your media and you know what the format is. Now you're ready to create a Player, set it up, and start it going.

With audio, you can create a Player through any of the three createPlayer methods offered by Manager.

- One takes a URL, such as "http://myserver.com/files/clip.mp3"

- Another takes an InputStream and a type, such as myByteStream and "audio/mpeg"

- The last takes a custom DataSource (described earlier in the section titled "Manual Buffering").

You can simply call start() to get it going, or queue it up for later playback. You will likely want to handle media operations in a separate thread for the best performance. You also might want to control other aspects of playback. By calling Player.getControl(), you can obtain a VolumeControl and a StopTimeControl. The VolumeControl allows you to set the volume level (at a value between 0 and 100) and mute/unmute the audio, while StopTimeControl offers a way to specify when the Player should stop. You could combine the two to play a softer 5-second preview of a full audio clip. The code that follows demonstrates how to play audio.

```
InputStream is = getClass().getResourceAsStream("/crowdNoise.mp3");
Player player = Manager.createPlayer(is, "audio/mpeg");
player.realize();
StopTimeControl time = (StopTimeControl)player.getControl("StopTimeControl");
VolumeControl volume = (VolumeControl)player.getControl("VolumeControl");
if (time != null)
{
    time.setStopTime(5000000); // Microseconds
}
if (volume != null)
{
    volume.setLevel(50);
}
player.start();
```

> **Tip:** StopTimeControl may not be available on all platforms. As usual, it's a good idea to check for a nonnull value returned from getControl. If not available, you can work around this by creating a separate Timer and manually stopping playback once it expires.

Other Audio Options: MIDI and Tones

MMAPI defines several options for playing programmatically generated audio. This approach was much more popular when devices were highly limited. As support for playing standard audio formats has improved, these alternatives have fallen out of favor because of their complexity and nonportability. However, they still may be appropriate when porting legacy software, creating sound effects for games or when working on specialized apps such as a virtual piano.

If you look through RIM's documentation, you will notice that it includes references to MIDIControl. This specialized Control offers methods to program MIDI channels and send MIDI events to be played. Theoretically, this would offer a standardized way to play generated music. However, as with much of MMAPI there is no requirement that vendors implement it, and RIM has chosen not to do so. Attempts to create a MIDIControl will result in an "unsupported media type" exception. Note that you can still play existing MIDI files as shown above, just not create low-level MIDI events.

However, RIM does support a similar alternate mechanism, the ToneControl. Unlike other audio playback, you do not need a file or input stream to gain access to this player and control. Instead, Manager offers a custom string, TONE_DEVICE_LOCATOR (with the value "device://tone"), which can be used to retrieve a compatible Player.

Once you have a ToneControl, you can program a monotonic tone sequence. Bytes define the tempo, note pitch, note duration, and volume, and they control progress through the song. The following snippet shows how to play the opening of *Beethoven's Fifth Symphony* using a ToneControl.

```
byte tempo = 30; // 120 bpm
byte eight = 8;      // eighth-note
byte whole = 64;      // whole note
byte C4 = ToneControl.C4; // Middle C
byte eFlat = (byte)(C4 + 3);
byte gMajor = (byte)(C4 + 7);
byte[] beethoven = {
    ToneControl.VERSION, 1,
    ToneControl.TEMPO, tempo,
    gMajor, eight, gMajor, eight, gMajor, eight, eFlat, whole //  Buh-buh-buh BUH!
};
Player player = Manager.createPlayer(Manager.TONE_DEVICE_LOCATOR);
player.realize();
ToneControl control = (ToneControl)player.getControl("ToneControl");
control.setSequence(beethoven);
player.start();
```

If this looks like something you might be interested in, complete documentation is available for the ToneControl class. In practice, ToneControl has too many limitations to be useful to the majority of developers. It can only play a single note at a time, and is cumbersome to program. Unless you need the ability to play arbitrary notes at runtime, look elsewhere.

If you do want to play arbitrary notes, consider using Manager.playTone(). Unlike other methods in Manager, this will directly play sound without going through a Player. You can specify a pitch, length, and volume. As with the ToneControl, it is far too cumbersome to try and play elaborate music with this interface, but it can be useful certain circumstances, such as if you want the device to make a loud noise when it encounters an error condition.

Playing Video

Video playback is similar to audio playback, with the extra wrinkle that you need to display the video somewhere. This process is very similar to the camera viewfinder we created in the last chapter. You will create the Player, obtain a VideoControl, place it somewhere on the Screen, and then start it playing. The most significant difference from video capture is the longer time it will take to start playback, especially if playing a video delivered over the network. The code that follows shows a simple case of playing a video for about 5 seconds and then stopping.

```
Player player = Manager.createPlayer("file:///SDCard/BlackBerry/Video/clip.3gp ");
player.realize();
VideoControl control = (VideoControl)player.getControl("VideoControl");
Field cameraView = (Field)control.initDisplayMode
    (VideoControl.USE_GUI_PRIMITIVE, "net.rim.device.api.ui.Field");
screen.add(cameraView);
player.start();
Thread.sleep(5000);
player.close();
```

The VideoControl offers the following useful options for positioning your playback window:

- getDisplayWidth and getDisplayHeight return the current dimensions of space occupied by the video playback window, in pixels.

- getSourceWidth and getSourceHeight return the dimensions of the actual video file, in pixels.

- getDisplayX and getDisplayY return the coordinates of the upper-left corner of the playing video, relative to the containing GUI object.

- setDisplayLocation allows you to position the video if the display mode is USE_DIRECT_VIDEO.

- setVisible controls whether the video is displayed.

- setDisplaySize will adjust the size of the video image. This may scale the video to fit the requested dimensions, or may just clip the video. You'll need to experiment with your particular videos and devices to determine which happens.

- setDisplayFullScreen attempts to make the video fill the entire screen.

Displaying Images

While audio and video may impress users more, images are the foundation of most apps. Images range from simple bitmaps to animated GIF and SVG files. While you're probably familiar with the simplest ways to display images, more advanced techniques may prove useful in certain cases.

Static Image Display in BlackBerry CLDC Applications

Odds are the first or second BlackBerry program you wrote when first learning the platform included an image. The `Bitmap` class is the foundation of image creation and drawing. Note that *bitmap* refers to any rastered image format, including JPEG and PNG in addition to BMP files. You have a wide variety of options available for creating images.

- Reference a resource in the COD file: `Bitmap.getBitmapResource("clip.png");`

- Create a blank image that you can later draw into: `new Bitmap(300, 300);`

- Obtain a built-in system bitmap: `Bitmap.getBitmapResource(Bitmap.HOURGLASS);`

- Create from raw image data: `Bitmap.createBitmapFromBytes(rawData, 0, -1, 1)` or `Bitmap.createBitmapFromPNG(rawData, 0, -1);`

After you have a `Bitmap` object, you can adjust the raw pixels if necessary by calling `getARGB()` and `setARGB()`. In most cases, though, you can then proceed to display the image by creating a `BitmapField` and then adding it to the screen as you would any other `Field`.

```
screen.add(new BitmapField(bitmap));
```

As an alternative to the `Bitmap` class, you can use the `EncodedImage` class to obtain a drawable image. `EncodedImage` has separate subclasses for each of the supported image types and methods that provide more detail about each than is available for a standard `Bitmap`. For example, a `PNGEncodedImage` offers information about the alpha bit depth for a particular image. However, unlike `Bitmap`s, `EncodedImage`s are not mutable: you cannot alter the images once created. As with `Bitmap`, there are multiple ways to create an `EncodedImage`.

- Reference a resource in the COD file: `EncodedImage.getEncodedImageResource("clip.png");`

- Create from bytes: `EncodedImage.createEncodedImage(rawData, 0, -1);`

You can create a `BitmapField` for an `EncodedImage` in order to display it on the screen.

```
BitmapField imageField = new BitmapField();
imageField.setImage(encodedImage);
```

As with other `Field` objects, you can adjust the size and layout to fit your particular `Screen`.

SVG Image Playback

BlackBerry devices with software version 4.6 or later include support for JSR 226, a standard approach for control and display of SVG animations. SVG images must conform to the W3C SVG Tiny 1.1 profile.

SVG animations rely on classes in the `javax.microedition.m2g` package. If you are just playing existing animations, rather than creating or manipulating them, you will generally only need to use two classes: SVGImage and SVGAnimator. SVGImage contains the data, while SVGAnimator understands how to parse and present it. The following example shows how to create and start an animation.

```
InputStream svgSource = getClass().getResourceAsStream("sample.svg");
SVGImage image = (SVGImage)ScalableImage.createImage(svgSource, null);
SVGAnimator animator = SVGAnimator.createAnimator(image, "net.rim.device.api.ui.Field");
Field field = (Field)animator.getTargetComponent();
screen.add(field);
animator.play();
```

You may notice some similarities between this code and what we did for video capture and playback. In both cases, we needed to specify the full class name for the component that will display the content. "net.rim.device.api.ui.Field" indicates that you wish to display the SVG animation in a CLDC Application. To display animations in a MIDlet, ask for a "javax.microedition.lcdui.Item" instead.

As usual, you can manipulate the Field to control how the content will be displayed within your application. SVGAnimator uses a simplified version of the Player life cycle with only three states: playing, stopped, and paused. Figure 3-6 shows how the methods play(), pause(), and stop() affect playback.

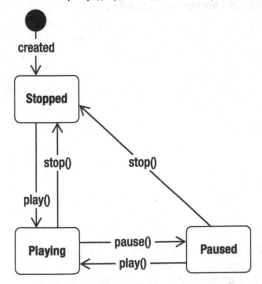

Figure 3-6. SVG animation states

If you are interested in capturing user action on the SVG image and taking some action in response, register an SVGEventListener with the SVGAnimator by calling setSVGEventListener(). You will then be called when the user presses a key, touches the screen, or the visibility of the animation changes.

To learn more about SVG, you can view the official specification online at http://www.w3.org/Graphics/SVG/. Apress publishes a good book on the topic called *SVG Programming: The Graphical Web* by Kurt Cagle.

Getting Plazmic

Long before SVG support became available, RIM offered a semi-custom 2D vector graphics package of its own. Plazmic, a subsidiary of RIM, offers a content creation tool that allow Flash-like authoring, but the generated content is compiled down into a compact binary format that is much more terse than standard SVG. Because of its size, Plazmic usually loads faster over the network. For several years Plazmic was the only choice for adding rich media content to BlackBerry devices. That is changing with the introduction of APIs discussed in this chapter, but because of the compact size and large quantity of existing content out there, you may wish to add Plazmic content to your own app.

Authoring Plazmic is beyond the scope of this book, but it's important to understand how it is created and delivered. An artist creates content using the proprietary Plazmic Content Developer Kit. The kit offers support for importing some elements of SVG and Flash format animations, which may allow for quicker porting of content. The artist's design is compiled into a binary PME, or Plazmic Media Engine, file. This contains the information necessary to describe the animation contents and behavior. Many animations will also include raster graphics or music. Together with the PME, these will be bundled into a PMB, or Plazmic Media Bundle, as shown in Figure 3-7.

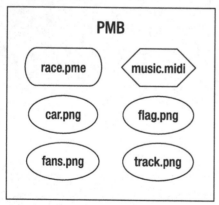

Figure 3-7. A possible PMB configuration

On the client side, Plazmic is often displayed in the browser. It is also the format used to theme BlackBerry devices and make visual changes to native apps. If you'd like to include Plazmic content in your own app, RIM has offered APIs since device software version 3.7—ancient by RIM standards. There are just a few classes involved, all in package `net.rim.plazmic.mediaengine` and `net.rim.plazmic.mediaengine.io`.

> **Caution:** Although Plazmic support exists as far back as 3.7, there are many different versions of the CDK, and not all content will display in all versions. Even if your target phone supports Plazmic playback, check to ensure that you can author content that will display in it.

One crucial difference between Plazmic and SVG is that Plazmic includes logic for handling the download of content. If you are loading a PMB over the network, you will receive regular updates about the status of that operation. This can be useful if you wish to show a loading message, progress bar, or other feedback to the user while loading. You can also bundle Plazmic content directly into your COD, which creates the standard tradeoffs between fast delivery and updateability.

> **Tip:** Due to a limitation in the RIM JDE, you cannot directly include Plazmic PMB files in your COD. Instead, ask for the PME file and all media files separately, then add them to your project. If image files are not in PNG format, configure your project to prevent them from being automatically converted to PNG.

Plazmic's underlying representation is SVG, so it's no surprise that Plazmic playback resembles that of SVG. Plazmic offers three states: UNREALIZED, REALIZED, and STARTED. You move between the states by invoking methods on a `MediaPlayer` object, as shown in Figure 3-8. An UNREALIZED `MediaPlayer` is "blank," with no content assigned to it. A REALIZED player has obtained its content, which can be a time-consuming operation: even once the content file has been loaded, all media resources within that file must be initialized and prepared. A STARTED player is actively playing its content.

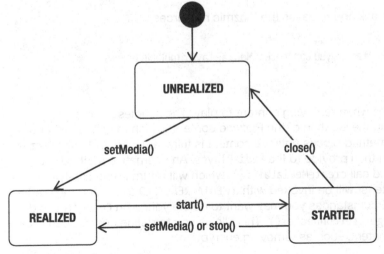

Figure 3-8. Plazmic player states

Plazmic has a single listener interface, MediaListener, which is used by both MediaManager and MediaPlayer. MediaListener defines a single method, mediaEvent(), which delivers messages about content download or playback status. Table 3-3 shows the possible results.

Table 3-3. Plazmic Media Events

Event	Data Type	Data Contents
MEDIA_REQUESTED	String	URI of requested content
MEDIA_IO	LoadingStatus	Current status of the loading operation
MEDIA_LOADING_FAILED	String	URI of requested content
MEDIA_REALIZED	Object	Opaque media data
MEDIA_COMPLETE	Object	Opaque media data

Unfortunately, Plazmic doesn't offer many opportunities for interactive content. Unlike the SVG APIs, there is no mechanism for determining when the user has clicked within the animation, so it is not appropriate for creating simple games. On the other hand, MediaPlayer does include these standard mechanisms for controlling playback:

start() starts playback.

setMediaTime() will instruct a realized player to begin at the specified millisecond time.

getMediaTime() returns the current elapsed media time in milliseconds.

stop() pauses playback.

close() stops playback and releases the Plazmic resources.

> **Note:** Unlike an MMAPI Player, you can reuse a MediaPlayer multiple times after calling close().

You have several options when retrieving content to play. The simplest is to call createMedia(), providing the location of the Plazmic content, which may be a file or a network location. This method blocks until the content is fully retrieved and an Object is returned, which you can then provide to the MediaPlayer. An alternative method is to add a MediaListener and call createMediaLater(), which will return immediately. Sometime later your listener will be invoked with a MEDIA_REALIZED event and the media object. Finally, in rare circumstances you may want to define your own Connector and provide it via MediaManager.setConnector(). This allows you to define custom behavior for retrieving Plazmic content, such as removing encryption.

In its simplest form, creating and starting Plazmic content takes only a few lines of code.

```
MediaManager manager = new MediaManager();
MediaPlayer player = new MediaPlayer();
Object content = manager.createMedia("http://myserver.com/racing.pmb");
player.setMedia(content);
Object ui = player.getUI();
screen.add((Field)ui);
```

Because Plazmic is so strongly associated with native RIM behavior, it cannot be embedded into a MIDlet. Consider using Plazmic if you want a compact animation that will run on a wide number of RIM devices; avoid it if you want to use a more widely supported format or create interactive content.

GIF Animation

Animated GIFs are probably the most widespread form of animation on the Web, and they are often the first choice for simple animation creation. Unfortunately, they are much more complex to deal with on BlackBerry devices. First, if you are including the GIF as a resource in your COD, the program compiler won't have a good way of telling whether a given GIF file will be animated or not. Because PNG files display more efficiently on the device than GIF files, the default behavior is to translate all non-PNG images (including GIF and JPEG) into PNG format. Therefore, all animation information is lost. To avoid this problem, you can either rename the file extension to something else (like .gxx), or instruct your build environment to leave all images alone. If you are using the Eclipse plug-in, right-click your project, select Properties, then modify the BlackBerry Project Properties as shown in Figure 3-9. Note that this last approach is only a good idea if your program only uses PNG files and animated GIF images; otherwise, you will miss out on some valuable optimizations. Also note that this problem is moot if you are loading a GIF file over the network or from a file outside your COD.

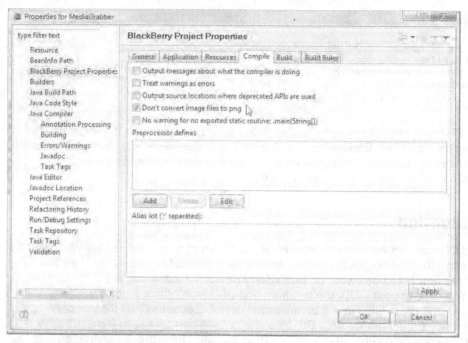

Figure 3-9. Eclipse settings to retain all GIF files

Once you actually have a GIF image, you're faced with another problem. By default, a `BitmapField` will only display the first frame of the image. Fortunately, RIM created `BitmapField` as an extensible class, so you can override it to add animation support. Load the image as a `GIFEncodedImage`, then use the methods exposed by that class to determine how many frames and animation loops are encoded in the image. Create a separate thread that walks through the frames, sleeps for an appropriate time at each frame, then invalidates the `BitmapField`. The custom BitmapField's `paint()` method should retrieve the current frame position, then draw it to the `Graphics` context.

MIDP Images

While this book focuses on RIM CLDC UI, some programmers may be using the MIDP LCDUI for display, so let's briefly touch on how those apps handle images.

If you are using a `Form`, you can directly append an `Image` to your `Form`, or create an `ImageItem` and then add that.

```
Image image = Image.createImage(getClass().loadResourceAsStream("clip.png"));
pmyForm.append(image);
```

However, most MIDlets will probably be using a Canvas or GameCanvas to handle their UI. In these cases, you can draw directly to your graphics context when directed to do so.

```
public class MyCanvas extends Canvas()
{
    public void paint(Graphics g)
    {
        g.drawImage(image, 50, 50, TOP_LEFT);
    }
}
```

Tip: The standard MIDlet API does not provide any support for animated images. If you try to draw an animated GIF, only the first frame will display. You can create simple animations yourself by using a timer to repeatedly call `repaint()` on the canvas and draw the next frame with each invocation.

Invoking Native Apps

On occasion, you may need or want to let a built-in application handle media playback instead of doing it yourself. Perhaps you're running on an older version of device software and the desired APIs aren't available; perhaps you prefer the interface of the native app; or perhaps you just want to simplify the code in your own app. Whatever the reason, RIM has made it relatively simple to communicate your desire to the built-in applications.

Playing Video Through the Browser

Video playback has been supported on BlackBerry devices for a while, but support in Java is fairly recent. If you want to play a video but can't or don't want to do so in your own app, you can pass the location of the video file to the device browser. Note that this works even if the video file is present on the local filesystem.

The following sample code shows how to launch media through the browser on RIM software versions 4.0 and later.

```
BrowserSession browserSession = Browser.getDefaultSession();
browserSession.displayPage("http://myserver.com/video/awards.3gp");
```

This invokes the default browser, which will generally be what you want. In some cases, though, you might need to access a particular browser in order to access the content. For example, the hosting server might only be configured to deliver content over WAP, or it may only be reachable through a BES. If this is the case, you will need to search for the corresponding `ServiceBook` entry and get a `BrowserSession` for that type.

On very old devices with software versions prior to 4.0, gaining access to the browser is trickier. There is no `Browser` object available, so you will need to manually look up the application, then invoke it directly, passing in the URL. To avoid an infinite restart loop, disable auto-restart when invoking the browser this way. The following code demonstrates how to do this.

```
int handle = CodeModuleManager.getModuleHandle("net_rim_bb_browser_daemon");
if (handle > 0)
{
    ApplicationDescriptor[] descriptors =
        CodeModuleManager.getApplicationDescriptors(handle);

    String[] args = {"url", "file:///SDCard/BlackBerry/temp/awards.3gp", null};

    // Turn off auto-restart.
    int flags = descriptors[0].getFlags();
    flags = flags ^ ApplicationDescriptor.FLAG_AUTO_RESTART;
    ApplicationDescriptor newDescriptor = new ApplicationDescriptor (
        descriptors[0], "BrowserPS", args, null, -1, null, -1, flags);
    ApplicationManager.getApplicationManager().runApplication(newDescriptor);
}
```

Note: This method does not allow you to play a video that was bundled within your COD. To play this type of video, first save it out to a temporary file and then invoke the browser.

Using CHAPI to Play Audio

A relatively new but exciting JSR is CHAPI, the Content Handler API. CHAPI finally provides a good generic way of allowing different apps on the same phone to communicate with one another. Certain apps can register as content handlers for particular MIME or URL types. When other apps make a request to handle that type of content, the device AMS (Application Management System) will invoke the registered app and allow it to service the request. When complete, the results are passed to the requesting app. Figure 3-10 illustrates the basic sequence that takes place when requesting content handling through CHAPI.

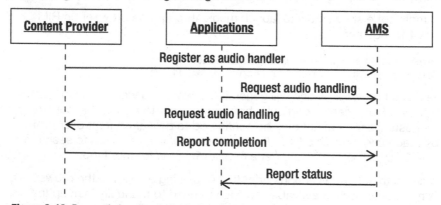

Figure 3-10. Requesting audio playback through CHAPI

> **Note:** If you have programmed for the Android platform, this may sound familiar. A BlackBerry
> CHAPI request is very similar to an Android Intent.

RIM has embraced the CHAPI system for several forms of inter-app communication.
Because the native media application is already registered as a CHAPI handler, all you
need to do is make a request to handle the type of audio, as shown in the code that follows.

```
Invocation request = new Invocation("file:///SDCard/BlackBerry/temp/train.mp3");
Registry registry = Registry.getRegistry
    ("net.rim.device.api.content.BlackBerryContentHandler");
registry.invoke(request);
```

You'll learn more about CHAPI later in this book, including how to register your own
apps to handle special types of content.

App: Media Reviewer

Chapter 2's exercise created an app that could capture media. There's a problem,
though: how do you know if it's any good or not? It would be much more useful if you
could play back what you captured to make sure that your thumb wasn't over the
camera and you can't hear the neighbors in the background.

To get started, copy over your current version of MediaGrabber into a new project. Let's
build on the previous version of the app, adding a media reviewer screen that plays back
captured audio and video content. Listing 3-2 uses a separate class to handle display;
this will allow us to support playing back arbitrary content in the future.

Listing 3-2. A Content Reviewing Screen

```
package com.apress.king.mediagrabber;

import java.io.InputStream;

import javax.microedition.media.*;
import javax.microedition.media.control.VideoControl;

import net.rim.device.api.ui.Field;
import net.rim.device.api.ui.MenuItem;
import net.rim.device.api.ui.UiApplication;
import net.rim.device.api.ui.component.*;
import net.rim.device.api.ui.container.MainScreen;

public class PlayingScreen extends MainScreen implements PlayerListener
{
```

The PlayingScreen uses a state machine similar to what we created in the last chapter
for the RecordingScreen. Many of the same components are present in both screens,
although as we will soon see they are used very differently.

```java
    public static final int STATE_WAITING = 1;

    public static final int STATE_LOADING = 2;
    public static final int STATE_LOADED = 3;

    private int state = STATE_WAITING;

    private UiApplication app;
    private LabelField status;

    private InputStream source;
    private String type;
    private String location;

    private Player player;
    private StatusUpdater updater;

    private MenuItem startItem = new MenuItem("Start", 0, 0)
    {
        public void run()
        {
            start();
        }
    };

    private MenuItem playItem = new MenuItem("Resume", 0, 0)
    {
        public void run()
        {
            try
            {
                player.start();
            }
            catch (MediaException e)
            {
                status.setText("Couldn't resume: " + e);
            }
        }
    };

    private MenuItem pauseItem = new MenuItem("Pause", 0, 0)
    {
        public void run()
        {
            try
            {
                player.stop();
            }
            catch (MediaException e)
            {
                status.setText("Couldn't pause: " + e);
            }
        }
    };

    private MenuItem rewindItem = new MenuItem("Rewind", 0, 0)
```

```
    {
        public void run()
        {
            try
            {
                player.setMediaTime(0);
            }
            catch (MediaException e)
            {
                status.setText("Couldn't rewind: " + e);
            }
        }
    };
```

Superficially, this appears similar to the earlier RecordingScreen; both make heavy use of a Player object to get work done. However, PlayingScreen is much more general purpose. It will accept any type of media, either through a file or an arbitrary stream. There's no guarantee it will play, but it will try. While this class will be used to play back captured local content from a file location, it can also play back networked content or other remote files accessed through an InputStream. Multiple constructors are available for these different uses.

```
    public PlayingScreen(String location, String message)

    {
        this(message);
        this.location = location;
    }
    public PlayingScreen(InputStream in, String type, String message)
    {
        this(message);
        this.source = in;
        this.type = type;
    }

    private PlayingScreen(String message)
    {
        add(new LabelField(message));
        status = new LabelField("Waiting.");
        add(status);
        app = UiApplication.getUiApplication();
        updater = new StatusUpdater();
    }
```

We override the onClose method to call close() on the Player. This is an important step, as Player objects are not automatically unloaded when they can no longer be referenced. If you keep multiple Player instances hanging around, they may still be holding on to scarce resources, making it impossible to play additional media until the garbage collector unloads them some time later.

```
    public boolean onClose()
    {
        if (player != null)
        {
```

```
            player.close();
        }
        return super.onClose();
    }

    public void makeMenu(Menu menu, int instance)
    {
        if (instance == Menu.INSTANCE_DEFAULT)
        {
            if (state == STATE_WAITING)
            {
                menu.add(startItem);
            }
            else if (state == STATE_LOADED)
            {
                if (player.getState() == Player.STARTED)
                {
                    menu.add(pauseItem);
                }
                else
                {
                    menu.add(playItem);
                }
                menu.add(rewindItem);
            }
        }
        super.makeMenu(menu, instance);
    }
```

This class finally introduces extra threads. We could cheat when recording and avoid them because capture starts so quickly, but there's no way a user would accept waiting a minute for an audio file to download over the network. When the user requests the media to start playing, we defer the work of actually initializing the Player to a separate Thread. Doing this allows the UI thread to retake control and provide updates while the media is being retrieved or loaded.

```
    private void start()

    {
        state = STATE_LOADING;
        status.setText("Loading");
        if (player == null)
        {
            (new Thread()
            {
                public void run()
                {
                    try
                    {
                        if (location != null)
                        {
                            player = Manager.createPlayer(location);
                        }
                        else
                        {
                            player = Manager.createPlayer(source, type);
```

```
                }
                player.addPlayerListener(PlayingScreen.this);
                player.realize();
                state = STATE_LOADED;
                VideoControl vc = (VideoControl)player.getControl⏎
                    ("VideoControl");
                if (vc != null)
                {
                    Field video = (Field) vc.initDisplayMode(⏎
                            VideoControl.USE_GUI_PRIMITIVE, ⏎
                            "net.rim.device.api.ui.Field");
                    add(video);
                }
                player.start();
            }
            catch (Exception e)
            {
                status.setText("Error: " + e);
            }
        }
    }).start();
}

}
```

As is often the case with threading, adding a thread complicates the picture. We want to provide updates to the UI about the status of the media, but if we attempt to modify the Screen from outside the main UI thread, something else may also be attempting to modify it at the same time, resulting in corruption. To be safe, we take advantage of UiApplication.invokeLater(), which makes code run on the UI thread. We reuse a single object, updater, for all of the status updates in order to avoid creating tons of garbage objects.

```
public void playerUpdate(Player player, String event, Object eventData)
{
    if (event.equals(PlayerListener.END_OF_MEDIA))
    {
        app.invokeLater(new Runnable()
        {
            public void run()
            {
                close();
            }
        });
    }
    else
    {
        updater.setMessage(event);
        app.invokeLater(updater);
    }
}

private class StatusUpdater implements Runnable
{
```

```
            private String message;
            public void setMessage(String message)
            {
                this.message = message;
            }
            public void run()
            {
                status.setText(message);
            }
        }
    }
```

Now that we have a playback screen available, we can modify the RecordingScreen. Listing 3-3 shows the modifications made to this file. Unchanged portions have been replaced with comments; refer to the previous chapter for the original contents, or download the listing from the Apress web site.

Listing 3-3. *A Recording Screen That Automatically Presents Recorded Content*

```
package com.apress.king.mediagrabber;

// Imports go here.

public class RecordingScreen extends MainScreen implements PlayerListener
{
    // Instance variables here.

    // Constructor and initial methods here.
```

PlayingScreen doesn't make much sense for the camera, since no Player is necessary for showing a static image. In the case of the camera, then, we directly create a new Screen and put the Bitmap on it. This will nicely resize the screen to show the entire image, as shown in Figure 3-11.

```
    private void takeSnapShot()
    {
        try
        {
            byte[] imageData = video↵
                    .getSnapshot("encoding=jpeg&width=640&height=480&quality=normal");
            if (imageData != null)
            {
                writeToFile(imageData, location + "/image.jpg");
                status.setText("Image taken");
                Bitmap taken = Bitmap.createBitmapFromBytes(imageData, 0, ↵
                        imageData.length, 1);
                Screen reviewer = new MainScreen();
                BitmapField bitmap = new BitmapField(taken);
                reviewer.add(bitmap);
                UiApplication.getUiApplication().pushScreen(reviewer);
            }
            else
            {
```

```
                status.setText("Please try again later.");
            }
        }
        catch (IOException ioe)
        {
            status.setText(ioe.getMessage());
        }
        catch (MediaException me)
        {
            status.setText(me.getMessage());
        }
    }

    // File output goes here.
```

`stop()` largely remains the same, except that we automatically start playing back captured data once it has been persisted.

```
    private void stop()
    {
        try
        {
            if (type == RECORD_AUDIO || type == RECORD_VIDEO)
            {
                recorder.commit();
                if (type == RECORD_AUDIO)
                {
                    String file = location + "/audio.amr";
                    writeToFile(dataOut.toByteArray(), file);
                    play(file, "Recorded Audio");
                }
                else
                {
                    String file = location + "/video.3gp";
                    writeToFile(dataOut.toByteArray(), file);
                    play(file, "Recorded Video");
                }
                status.setText("Data saved");
                state = STATE_READY;
            }
        }
        catch (IOException ioe)
        {
            status.setText(ioe.getMessage());
        }
    }
```

The `play()` method creates and displays a `PlayingScreen` for the recorded media.

```
    private void play(String location, String message)
    {
        Screen playback = new PlayingScreen(location, message);
```

```
            UiApplication.getUiApplication().pushScreen(playback);
    }

}
```

Figure 3-11. MediaGrabber displaying a captured image in full-screen mode

To show off the power of the new PlayingScreen, provide a way to directly enter it without going through RecordingScreen. Listing 3-4 shows how you can convert RecordingChoicesScreen from the previous chapter into ChoicesScreen. ChoicesScreen keeps the existing options for starting a record operation, but it also adds the ability to enter a file location or web URL and then select "Play Media" to launch it directly. Note that this will only play MMAPI-compatible media, so it will work for most audio and video, but not SVG, Plazmic, or other unsupported media types.

Listing 3-4. A Screen to Start Recording or Playing a Particular File

```java
package com.apress.king.mediagrabber;

import net.rim.device.api.ui.Field;
import net.rim.device.api.ui.MenuItem;
import net.rim.device.api.ui.UiApplication;
import net.rim.device.api.ui.component.BasicEditField;
import net.rim.device.api.ui.component.LabelField;
import net.rim.device.api.ui.component.Menu;
import net.rim.device.api.ui.container.MainScreen;

public class ChoicesScreen extends MainScreen
{
    private BasicEditField location = new BasicEditField("Location:", ↵
            "file:///SDCard/BlackBerry", 100, Field.FIELD_VCENTER↵
                    | BasicEditField.FILTER_URL);
    private MenuItem audioItem = new MenuItem("Record Sound", 0, 0)
    {
        public void run()
        {
            launchRecorder(RecordingScreen.RECORD_AUDIO);
        }
    };
    private MenuItem pictureItem = new MenuItem("Take a Picture", 0, 0)
    {
        public void run()
        {
            launchRecorder(RecordingScreen.RECORD_PICTURE);
        }
    };
    private MenuItem videoItem = new MenuItem("Record Video", 0, 0)
    {
        public void run()
        {
            launchRecorder(RecordingScreen.RECORD_VIDEO);
        }
    };
    private MenuItem launchVideoItem = new MenuItem("Play Media", 0, 0)
    {
        public void run()
        {
            launchPlayer();
        }
    };

    public ChoicesScreen()
    {
        setTitle("MediaGrabber");
        add(new LabelField(↵
                "Please enter a location, then select a choice from the menu."));
        add(location);
    }

    public void close()
    {
```

```java
                location.setDirty(false);
                super.close();
    }

    public void makeMenu(Menu menu, int instance)
    {
        if (instance == Menu.INSTANCE_DEFAULT)
        {
            String property = System.getProperty("supports.audio.capture");
            if (property != null && property.equals("true"))
            {
                menu.add(audioItem);
            }
            property = System.getProperty("video.snapshot.encodings");
            if (property != null && property.length() > 0)
            {
                menu.add(pictureItem);
            }
            property = System.getProperty("supports.video.capture");
            if (property != null && property.equals("true"))
            {
                menu.add(videoItem);
            }
            menu.add(launchVideoItem);
        }

        super.makeMenu(menu, instance);
    }

    private void launchRecorder(int type)
    {
        String directory = location.getText();
        RecordingScreen screen = new RecordingScreen(type, directory);
        UiApplication.getUiApplication().pushScreen(screen);
    }

    private void launchPlayer()
    {
        String url = location.getText();
        PlayingScreen screen = new PlayingScreen(url, "Playing " + url);
        UiApplication.getUiApplication().pushScreen(screen);
    }

    public boolean onSavePrompt()
    {
        return true;
    }
}
```

Updating MediaGrabber.java is trivial: simply rename RecordingChoicesScreen to ChoicesScreen. At this point, you will be able to build and run the latest incarnation of MediaGrabber. Give it a whirl! You'll want to run this on an actual device to get the best impact; the canned images and audio in the simulator leave a lot to be desired. Try recording whatever media your device supports, and also enter the URL for an external media file.

WANT MORE?

Consider enhancing the app even more by adding these features:

■ Save the most recently entered locations to allow quicker access.

■ Allow the user to choose what audio device is used to play back sound.

■ Write a new Screen that can be used to play back SVG or Plazmic content.

It doesn't make sense to go overboard with this app—after all, BlackBerry devices have a good Media application built in. However, these sorts of enhancements help a great deal when determining how feasible it is to add certain types of content into your own apps.

Excelsior

Phew! You covered a lot of ground in this chapter. As you can see, there's an incredibly wide range of options available for adding compelling media content to your BlackBerry application. Fortunately, no app is expected to use all of them. Depending on your needs, you will likely just choose one or two types of content, a couple of formats, and one or two methods of delivery. You might choose the MMAPI Player interface for maximum compatibility and control, or Plazmic for a high level of integration with BlackBerry, or some other solution that takes advantage of your existing resources and interest. After you have made your decision, you can safely ignore the other media options—at least until it's time to create your next app.

This chapter covered many ways of delivering content to the phone, including in your COD, on the filesystem, or over the Internet. However, there's an entire set of technologies that exist only for mobile phones and offer unparalleled ways to exchange information with other people. The next chapter will dive into the sea of wireless messaging and show you how to create an app that's unlike what you can create on the desktop.

Chapter 4

Wireless Messaging

Nearly every application written today—whether on the server, desktop, or mobile—includes some form of networking component. If you've been programming for any length of time, you probably are familiar with TCP/IP, sending HTTP requests, and other standards of network communication already. When it comes to mobile phones, though, the available technologies quickly multiply. You can tap into the unique systems available to wireless devices and achieve features that are impossible to obtain on other platforms.

This chapter introduces several BlackBerry messaging options, looking at both techniques unique to wireless, such as SMS and MMS messaging, as well as existing technologies that work slightly differently in this environment, such as email. You will learn how to evaluate the different options when each technology makes sense to integrate into your application, and see how to access them from your Java app.

The various techniques share a common characteristic: all are very personal. Remember, whenever you send someone a wireless message, it is likely ending up in his or her pocket. When you need that personal touch, wireless messaging provides the solution.

The Messaging Quiver

BlackBerry devices offer even more messaging options than most other mobile platforms. In addition to the ubiquitous wireless standard of SMS, and the slightly less ubiquitous standard of MMS, they offer a unique form of email integration in addition to a custom form of messaging available only between BlackBerry devices. This section provides a brief, high-altitude look at the available choices for wireless messaging.

SMS

Short Message Service, more often called SMS or simply *text messaging*, is the granddaddy of wireless messaging protocols. It was developed as a lightweight way to provide non-voice communication between mobile devices while not adding extra overhead to carrier networks.

Whenever you receive a call, the mobile tower pushes a packet of data to your phone, notifying it of the incoming call. This packet can be repurposed into a messaging packet, which means that its transmission is essentially free for the carrier to create. (This does not stop them from charging you for it, of course.) When your phone receives this packet, it extracts the content from it and, in most cases, creates a text message that is shown on the screen or stored in the inbox.

When you send a text, it once again is packaged into a single packet and sent to the tower. The tower passes it on to a Message Switching Center (MSC), a kind of junction point for nodes in the carrier's wireless network. The MSC ordinarily routes voice calls, but when it recognizes this as a text message, it will forward that message on to the Short Message Service Center (SMSC). The SMSC will examine the message to determine where it should go. If the recipient is a member of another wireless network, it will look up what carrier that number belongs to and then pass the message on to that network's SMSC. If the recipient is an email address, the SMSC will send the message over the Internet.

Once the SMSC has a message intended for a recipient on its network, it will attempt to find that phone, using the same techniques as it would when placing an incoming call. If the recipient is available, the message is sent. Otherwise, the SMSC will store the message and wait for the subscriber to become available. Depending on the requested configuration of the message, it may be stored for a period of time before it becomes invalid and is removed from the server.

Figure 4-1 shows two users, Patrick and Andrew, sending text messages to Kathryn. Patrick sends his from a mobile phone. In SMS jargon, this is a Mobile Originated (MO) message. When Kathryn receives it, it is a Mobile Terminated (MT) message. Andrew isn't using a mobile phone, but instead connecting through an approved web portal to send his message. Such integration points are common. If you are planning to offer a service that will generate a large number of SMS messages, you will need permission from the wireless carriers to inject these messages into their network. Most often, developers will work with *message aggregators* who have standing deals with the major carriers and can provide you with this sort of access.

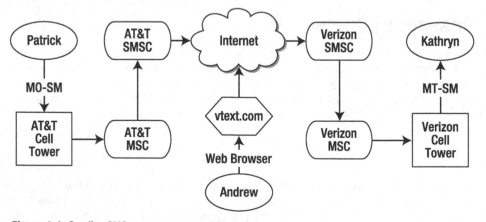

Figure 4-1. Sending SMS messages to a mobile device

So what, exactly, is an SMS? The exact representation can vary depending on the carrier, technology, and message configuration. As shown in Figure 4-2, all SMS messages contain a section of SMS headers and a 140-octet payload. The headers control things like the recipient address, delivery confirmation settings, validity intervals, and so on; other than the recipient, third-party developers usually cannot access these. The payload, however, is very standard. If it was not, then messages between carriers would not be compatible. An *octet* is a collection of 8 bits—most humans would call this a "byte." Using the word "octet" emphasizes that these bits can be arranged in nonstandard configurations. SMS messages are often encoded using US-ASCII or GSM 7-bit character schemes, which allows 160 characters to fit within the 140 octets. If sending binary data, 140 bytes are available. If recipients use Eastern or Arabic languages, messages can be sent in 16-bit Unicode, allowing 70 characters. Sometimes, extra routing or metadata that is not part of the SMS headers must be added to the SMS payload. For example, if sending to an email address, that address must be included in the payload, reducing the available number of characters.

Message Headers	140 Octet Payload

Figure 4-2. SMS message structure

Interoperability is usually quite good between different wireless carriers in the same country. As long as you will be operating primarily within a single region, you can be fairly confident in sending messages to any wireless number. However, it's important to note that SMS does not include any delivery guarantees. The SMSC will make an effort to send the message, but there are many technical reasons why it may fail to do so. If you ask for and receive a delivery confirmation, you can be certain it was delivered. Because of the lack of a strong service guarantee, you should use SMS in ways that supplement your apps functions and not make it a required component.

SMS tends to be a good choice when you need to send a signal or provide an extremely short piece of data. Theoretically, you could send or receive multiple SMS messages and build them up into a larger binary message. Carrier support for such bundled messages is much less reliable, though, and if you try to implement such a system yourself, you are multiplying the risks of a lost message and incomplete data.

Pros

- Very quick transmission time.

- Sent and received over carrier networks, so it will be available even if Internet service is unavailable.

- Strong interoperability between carriers.

Cons

- Most users are charged for each message sent or received, or have a limited number of free messages.

- Not available over Wi-Fi.
- Extremely limited payload size.

> **Note:** You may occasionally hear references to EMS, the Extended Message Service. EMS is a standardized extension of SMS that works by concatenating multiple SMS packets together into a single larger message. EMS was invented to allow sending longer messages, and especially to send small binary data files such as sounds and images. The technology is widely available on handsets, but it has never really taken off in popularity. Given the increasing usage of standard Internet technologies such as email, it seems unlikely that this situation will change anytime soon.

MMS

SMS has proven extremely popular, but, over time, its architecture has not allowed it to adapt to more data-intensive applications. Binary data delivery in SMS has always been a bit of a kludge, and ever-increasing data usage has eliminated it as a feasible delivery channel for large files. The rise of camera phones caused a corresponding increase in the desire to share photos with others, and the Multimedia Messaging Service (MMS) was created in order to provide this kind of data transfer.

MMS was born in the mobile world, but it was born in the Internet age. While SMS uses existing carrier technologies to deliver messages, MMS operates along an Internet backbone. Phones send and receive messages over an IP connection, meaning that MMS is unavailable to phones without a data connection. On the other hand, MMS is a service controlled by the carriers, and they do not allow just anyone access to their servers. Mobile subscribers with a data plan can send and receive messages almost without restriction; as with SMS, carriers require outsiders to be vetted before allowing them to send messages into their network.

The core of the MMS system is the Multimedia Messaging Service Center, or MMSC. Each carrier will have one of these centers, which is responsible for routing all MMS messages to and from their subscribers. The WAP standard for MMS defines a set of standard interfaces that an MMSC must provide.

MM1: Connection to mobile devices over the carrier's network.

MM3: Connection to other servers for this carrier, most importantly an SMTP email gateway.

MM4: Connection to other MMSCs for message routing.

MM7: Connection to Value Added Service Provider (VASP) offered by third parties.

Figure 4-3 illustrates three ways in which an MMS message could be created and sent to a mobile handset.

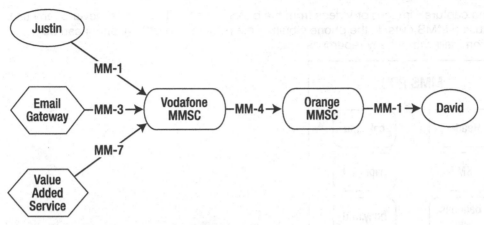

Figure 4-3. *Generating and delivering MMS messages*

You can generally send a few messages to MMS via email, but for large-scale message distribution, you will need to get an agreement with the carriers or go through a message aggregator. When this happens, you become a Value Added Service Provider. You can use MMS messages to communicate directly with your users, or to carry multimedia data to an application on their phone.

SMS messages were tightly constrained by existing carrier infrastructure and had to conform to those limits. In contrast, MMS messages were designed to be flexible and expandable. A single MMS message is transmitted in a Protocol Data Unit, or PDU. The PDU contains a set of message headers that include data such as the recipients, the size of the message, delivery confirmation requests, and other factors. After the headers come one or more attachments. Each carrier can mandate what media formats a phone must accept, and OEMs can choose to add additional formats, so you should check with your target carrier to see if they support your desired media on your targeted devices. However, all major MMSCs include *transcoders*, which are specialized services that translate attachments into compatible formats. For example, if you attempt to send a 640×480 resolution BMP to a device that only supports JPEG format up to 320×240, the MMSC will automatically convert the message attachment before it reaches the recipient. An MMSC can even split up a video file into a slideshow of still images. This can be very useful for ordinary use, but is a fact you should be aware of when sending messages: you cannot assume that the file you send will be binary equivalent to the file the phone receives. Again, support varies, but nearly all picture phones support JPEG and PNG images and MIDI and AMR audio, and nearly all video phones support 3GP video.

One important, extra piece of information in an MMS message is a Synchronized Multimedia Integration Language, or SMIL, attachment. This is a special type of attachment that describes how the other components within the message should be presented. The SMIL defines a series of *slides*, each of which will display for a specified length of time, and it can include some combination of text, image, and video. It's possible, therefore, to construct fairly elaborate messages with synchronized sound for an impressive impact. Figure 4-4 shows one possible configuration of such an MMS message. In practice, however, MMS messages are rarely used for anything more than sending captured images or videos from the phone. The SMIL is almost never of any use when using MMS outside the phone's built-in messaging application, and it can be safely omitted without any repercussions.

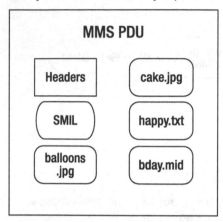

Figure 4-4. *A user-created MMS message*

MMS is an interesting technology with some useful applications, but has never really taken off in popularity the way SMS has. A variety of factors have played into this. Carrier interoperability is not as strong for MMS as for SMS, with some carriers eschewing support altogether or offering different solutions. MMS is usually only available for camera phones with data plans, which includes most BlackBerry devices but not a lot of ordinary low-level phones. A user must also explicitly sign up for MMS messaging, which may or may not be bundled with SMS messaging, and which has the same sorts of costs associated with it. Finally, the increasing availability of email clients on smartphones and high-level feature phones has made it easier than ever to attach and send media off the device, which provides an alternative to the reason for MMS's existence.

From an application developer's viewpoint, MMS can be a compelling choice when you want to send or receive multimedia content from a compatible phone, and you are sure the users' service plans include MMS. If you plan to run on a wide variety of devices across multiple countries and regions, though, you would be better off finding another solution. As with SMS, it is generally a good idea to view MMS as a channel to enhance the value of your app rather than a requirement for the app to function properly.

Pros

- Native support for sending and receiving multimedia content.

- Based on an open standard that allows communication with nonBlackBerry devices.

- Supports large message payloads.

- Can generate attractive messages when sent directly to other users.

Cons

- Most users are charged for each message sent or received, or have a limited number of free messages.

- Lower level of interoperability between carriers.

- Requires connection to the carrier network; cannot send over Wi-Fi.

- Many users have devices that do not support MMS or do not include MMS in their subscription plans.

- Transcoder can modify message contents without your knowledge.

Email

If people know one thing about BlackBerry devices, it's that they are great for email. Since their inception people have praised the combination of keyboard and network connection that, for better and worse, always makes it feasible to stay connected via email.

Most BlackBerry devices have access to the public Internet, and depending on how the device is configured, most users will be able to add personal email accounts to the device. This requires configuring the mail client for the device, a process similar to configuring a desktop email program such as Outlook.

In the majority of situations, email is configured so outgoing messages are sent through an SMTP server. When the user composes and sends mail from their private account, it is routed through the BlackBerry infrastructure and sent to the configured SMTP server. After it enters the SMTP server, it is treated exactly the same as if you sent from your desktop computer. Unlike SMS or MMS, there is no carrier-specific step in here; as long as you can reach the Internet, whether over the mobile network or through a Wi-Fi access point, you can send email. Figure 4-5 shows how a BlackBerry device can access email services over the network.

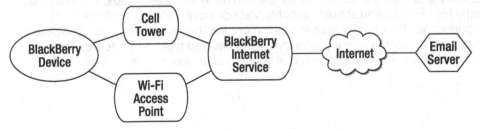

Figure 4-5. A BlackBerry client sends an SMTP message

Similarly, devices are often configured to retrieve email from POP3 or IMAP servers. The BlackBerry Internet Service will check for new messages periodically or when prompted by the user, and it can automatically download new messages that it finds. Such incoming messages will be directed to the user's inbox. Depending on the device software version and user configuration, all email may be dumped into a single inbox, or each account may have its own separate inbox.

When sending or receiving messages this way, synchronization inconsistencies may appear. For example, if you send a message from your BlackBerry device, you probably will not be able to view it on your Outlook client later. Certain web-based email providers, such as Gmail, do a better job at providing a unified view of all messaging activity on a given account. In all cases, though, the details will depend on how a given user has set up their particular accounts.

In the real world, email is ubiquitous. Everyone has at least one address, and most users will not mind giving you an email address to contact them. In the mobile world, email is very common on smartphones, but still quite rare on feature phones and low-end consumer phones. Many users can be expected to have access to email on BlackBerry devices or similar phones, but do not make this assumption for mobile users in general.

Email is a convenient way to exchange data, and sharing information via attachments is rather common. In some cases you can attach arbitrary blocks of binary data to a message and pass it straight through to an application. However, given the constant threat of email viruses, email providers increasingly block attachments that they do not recognize, both on incoming and outgoing mail. These filters vary in quality. Sometimes you can simply rename to a well-known extension type such as .bmp, but most modern filters will scan the actual content of attachments and reject those that are unknown or not approved.

Email is almost always free to send and receive, but the data usage and time on the network may not be. Be sure to warn users if you will be transmitting large messages over email (or really any type of connection). Otherwise, you will be blamed when their large monthly service bill arrives. Additionally, individual email providers' policies vary widely on the details of maximum message size, attachment size, and total traffic allowed.

Consider using email when you need a message-based way to transmit data to and from the device, are mainly targeting BlackBerry and similar platforms, and do not mind the possibility that your application's data will end up in the user's inbox. In most cases where email is feasible, you should probably first consider using a traditional HTTP server connection. That architecture is much more traditional, reliable, and controllable. Email may be a better solution if you're looking to develop a peer-to-peer application without a central server infrastructure, or if you intend to generate human-readable emails.

Pros

- Available over Wi-Fi and mobile networks.
- Stored delivery: messages will be delivered even if the recipient is not currently connected to the network.
- Large messages can be sent and received.
- Good support for text and binary attachments.

- Excellent interoperability with all other email addresses and nearly all other email clients.

Cons

- No guarantee any individual user will have a private email account on his or her BlackBerry device.

- Inconsistent policies on allowable attachments, message sizes, and so on.

- Very visible to the user.

- Cannot be applied for many platforms other than BlackBerry.

BES Email

Internet-based email is no longer as rare as it once was on mobile phones, thanks to the increasing proliferation of well-designed smartphones. However, BlackBerry continues to hold the edge in email thanks to its BlackBerry Enterprise Server (BES) service. BES, used by corporate users around the world, allows people immediate access to their business email accounts, no matter where they are. BES continues to evolve, and its details can be difficult to pin down, but you can think of it as being a little like a Virtual Private Network (VPN). When users connect through their BES, they gain access to their company's secure infrastructure, including the email accounts.

BES users are almost always corporate users. They likely were given the phone by their employer, and their service bills may be subsidized, as well. In exchange, they are expected to play by the company's rules. Keep this profile in mind when developing apps that depend on a BES email account. However, it is possible for individual users to gain access to a personal BES through subscription. This generally involves a monthly subscription fee in exchange for receiving the benefits of a BES.

A BES has several interesting features. First, enterprise email is synchronized. Unlike regular email accounts, which may have messages scattered across multiple desktop and mobile devices, a BES email account resides in a single canonical location, and all clients accessing it share a unified view into its contents. Changes made at any terminal will be reflected in all of them, so deleting or reading a message on your phone means you won't need to deal with it again at work the next day.

The second, and most striking, feature of BES email is that it is a true push email service. Unlike other mail programs that require you to push a button to check for mail, or that check for mail on an interval, your BES will notify you the instant a new message comes available. In this respect, BES is closer to SMS than to traditional email. This also helps account for BlackBerry devices' infamous addictive properties. When people are instantly notified of new messages, they are more inclined to respond quickly.

Figure 4-6 depicts a simplified view of the BES environment. As shown in this figure, a BES involves a level of integration between the company network, the wireless carrier network, and RIM's own custom infrastructure. All these pieces work together to provide a high degree of reliability and access. Recent versions of the BES environment support providing access to BES email over Wi-Fi even if the wireless carrier network is not available.

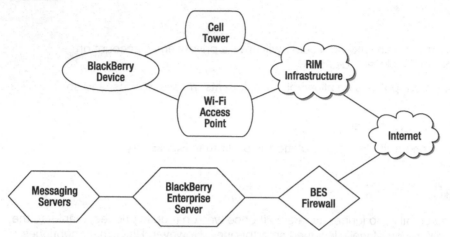

Figure 4-6. *Communicating from a remote BlackBerry device to a corporate email account*

While the delivery mechanism for a BES is more interesting than that of a regular email account, the actual message contents themselves are identical. You can still create fairly large, long messages, and add attachments. However, BES administrators can be quite strict in how they administer their users' accounts. This may involve actions such as blocking certain types of attachments or only allowing communication to certain other email addresses. In all cases, you should avoid hijacking a user's BES email account for a private application. At best you are increasing load on their servers; at worst, you may be gaining access to confidential information. On the other hand, if you are writing an app for one or more businesses, a BES can be a great data transport mechanism: all of your users are guaranteed to have access to it, and you know in advance what the email policies are. Just be sure to clear your plans with the appropriate administrator before getting too far, or they may cut you off.

Pros

- Push email offers near-instant delivery, provided the device is available.

- Stored delivery: messages will be delivered even if the recipient is not currently connected to the network.

- Large messages can be sent and received.

- Good support for text and binary attachments.

- Available over Wi-Fi and mobile networks.

- Consistent environment for corporate users.

Cons

- Not available to most private users.
- Not available if porting to devices other than BlackBerry.
- May involve restrictive security settings.
- May be inappropriate to mix application messages with business emails.

BlackBerry PIN Messaging

The previous section described how RIM's custom infrastructure—separate from, but integrated with, the wireless carrier network and private business network—is used to provide push email and other useful features to BES users. That infrastructure can be used even apart from email to provide a truly unique form of messaging.

Any given mobile device will have several numbers attached to it. These include the Mobile Device Number (MDN), which you dial to ring the device; the Mobile Equipment Identifier (MEID), which uniquely identifies the physical phone, and possibly others as well. In addition to these numbers, every BlackBerry device has a BlackBerry Personal Identification Number (PIN). This number allows RIM's infrastructure to recognize every device that connects with it, even if it has been resold or changed wireless carriers.

Any BlackBerry connected to the Internet and the RIM infrastructure can be located, so if you know another user's PIN, you can directly message them through the network, as shown in Figure 4-7. Note that this is possible even if you do not know the other user's email address or phone number. PIN messages are sent over the data channel, through the network, and are available even if the user cannot access the wireless network or is using the voice channel.

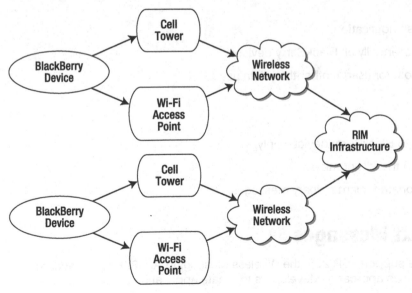

Figure 4-7. A BlackBerry PIN-routed message

Recent BlackBerry devices take advantage of this capability to offer a form of instant messenger, similar to AOL Instant Messenger or Skype. Once you receive a PIN message, you can immediately reply to the recipient. If they are in your contacts, you will be able to see their full name and not just the PIN.

PIN messages are interesting for several reasons. First of all, they are truly peer-to-peer. You cannot generate them outside a BlackBerry device, and they are not dependent on any other server to store and forward. They also have an extremely high level of integration with BlackBerry devices. You cannot assume that every BlackBerry device uses a BES, and you cannot assume that every user has a text messaging plan, but by definition every device has a PIN.

Note: In certain cases, such as a device being reported stolen, the PIN may be unavailable for messaging.

There are limits on the size of a PIN message. They are quite generous for text, but may be too small for large sections of binary data. Devices with software versions 4.2 or later currently can send messages with a subject of up to 255 Unicode characters and a body of up to 30,835 Unicode characters. On software version 4.1, the limit was still 255 characters for the subject, and only 16,385 for the body. These same limits apply to the text portion of a sent or received email.

If you are planning on targeting *only* BlackBerry devices and have access to your users' PIN numbers, this form of messaging may be an appropriate platform. It can certainly make for a compelling technology demo.

Pros

- Instant push notification.
- Available to virtually all BlackBerry devices.
- No extra cost for usage, other than data used.

Cons

- Restricted to BlackBerry devices only.
- Must obtain the PIN number.
- Not appropriate for large binary messages.

Sending Text Messages

BlackBerry devices support JSR 205, the Wireless Messaging API 2.0. This standard Java framework allows application developers to create applications that run on a variety of platforms and carriers, leveraging well-known techniques to easily integrate wireless messaging into their apps.

WMA is an extension of the GCF, the Generic Connection Framework that is the basis for nearly all forms of resource access on mobile Java devices. As with other GCF interfaces, you obtain a MessageConnection by issuing a request to the general `Connector.open()` method. When sending SMS messaging, the protocol is `sms://`. The contents after the protocol part should show the address where the messages will be delivered. One possible address would be `"sms://+14155550100"`. In this case, we are sending a message to a number in America (+1), in the city of San Francisco (415), with a seven-digit phone number (5550100). As when sending SMS messages using the phone's built-in messaging application, the phone will not know at the time you create the message whether the recipient can receive texts or even exists.

> **Note:** SMS and MMS classes are located in the `javax.wireless.messaging` package. Many classes have generic names like `Message` that match the names of classes in other RIM packages. Therefore, you may need to selectively import the classes you use or use fully qualified class names within your code. From the context of code examples it should generally be clear what classes to import, but I will point out the package names in cases where it may seem ambiguous.

Creating Texts

Once you have obtained a `MessageConnection`, you can create the specific type of message that you intend to send by calling `MessageConnection.newMessage()`. You must provide the type of message to be sent, which can be one of `MessageConnection.TEXT_MESSAGE`, `MessageConnection.BINARY_MESSAGE`, or `MessageConnection.MULTIPART_MESSAGE`. You may also specify an address, although this is superfluous since messages will be sent to the address provided to `Connector.open()`. Figure 4-8 shows the interface hierarchy for objects returned from `newMessage()`.

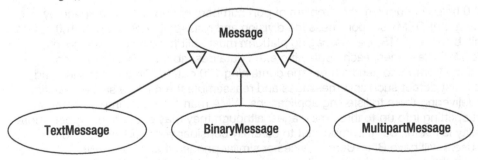

Figure 4-8. Available message types on BlackBerry devices

Both TextMessage and BinaryMessage objects will be sent over SMS. As discussed in the previous section, the size of an SMS message payload is fixed, but it can be encoded in different ways. A TextMessage can set its body with the setPayloadText() method, which allows up to 160 ASCII characters in a single message. The following code shows how to create and send a basic text message from your program.

```
MessageConnection smsConnection = (MessageConnection)Connector.open⏎
    ("sms://+14155550100");
TextMessage bottle = (TextMessage)smsConnection.newMessage⏎
    (MessageConnection.TEXT_MESSAGE);
bottle.setPayloadText("Sending out an SMS");
smsConnection.send(bottle);
```

Note: send() is a blocking synchronous method, so this method will not return until after the message has finished transmission or an error occurs. As such, you will always want to send your messages from a separate thread.

Sending Data

WMA provides a powerful tool for application developers by allowing you to specify a destination port number for your message. Regular messages like the one shown above will be delivered to the recipient's built-in inbox, but messages sent to a particular port will be delivered to applications that are listening on that port. This allows you to easily use messages to deliver data to and from applications. Note, though, that there are some complications to this process. First, under the hood, port numbers are included in the payload of the sent SMS message, and thus take away from the available space. Second, wireless carriers have only inconsistently implemented SMS ports. Most GSM (Global System for Mobile) carriers make ports available, but support in CDMA (Code Division Multiple Access)is rarer. Even when CDMA phones do support text message ports, they may use custom and incompatible methods for embedding the port number. This makes interoperability between carriers extremely difficult, particularly if you do not know what carrier a recipient is using.

WMA 2.0 helps circumvent the problem of port numbers occupying extra space by mandating that OEMs support message division and reassembly. Since only 160 octets are available in an SMS, the messaging platform must split the single message into multiple SMS messages, each containing extra data describing reassembly, if an application attempts to send a message containing 180 octets. On the receiving end, phones must detect such split messages and reassemble them into a single message before delivering them to listening applications. WMA mandates that implementation support splitting into up to three messages, although they may choose to support more. This ability is useful, but it is important to carefully consider your audience. If you know that all users will have BlackBerry devices or similar phones that support WMA 2.0, you can rely on this behavior; however, if messages are sent to other phones that do not implement message reassembly, the received messages will appear garbled.

The combination of binary message support and the ability to direct messages to particular applications can make text messages an attractive data delivery vehicle. Consider, for example, writing a play-by-SMS chess game. Both players would have a copy of the app on their phone showing the board. Whenever a move is made, the game sends the details of that move to the opponent's phone number. When that phone receives the move, it notifies the user and updates their local view of the board. This game takes advantage of the store-and-forward design of existing SMS infrastructure, so if one player's phone is turned off, the message will wait until the phone becomes available. The following code demonstrates how to construct and send such a binary SMS message.

```
MessageConnection smsConnection = (MessageConnection)Connector.open⏎
    ("sms://+14155550100:5000");
BinaryMessage chessMove = (BinaryMessage)smsConnection.newMessage⏎
    (MessageConnection.BINARY_MESSAGE);
byte[] move = new byte[]{1, 3, 4, 'k', 3, 5};
chessMove.setPayloadData(move);
smsConnection.send(chessMove);
```

When Things Go Wrong

The previous code examples omit exception handling for clarity. However, it's critical for real applications to recognize and respond to errors. Wireless messaging is fraught with connectivity issues, and other problems can arise, as well. You should be prepared to deal with the following exceptions:

- IOException can be thrown in a variety of situations, including when the network is unreachable or the message is rejected by the carrier.

- A SecurityException occurs if the application has not secured the necessary permissions.

- ConnectionNotFoundException is thrown if the protocol type is not known.

- An InterruptedIOException means that the message could not complete sending or receiving. This happens if a timeout occurs or another thread shuts the MessageConnection during transmission.

- IllegalArgumentException generally indicates a programming bug and means that the parameter is invalid.

Whenever exceptions occur, try to recover and continue gracefully. You will generally want to notify the user with a message such as "Unable to connect. Please confirm that your device has service and try again." If you are allowing the user to directly set the phone number or message payload, then suggest that they check those, as well.

In all cases, be sure to clean up your connections in all exit situations. This is a good programming practice in general, and is especially important on limited-resource mobile devices. If you fail to clean up a MessageConnection, future attempts to send messages may fail. You can usually accomplish this best through use of a finally block, as shown below.

```java
public void sendMessage() throws IOException
{
    MessageConnection conn = null;
    try
    {
        conn = (MessageConnection)Connector.open("sms://+14155550100");
        // Use the connection to create and send a message.
    }
    finally
    {
        if (conn != null)
        {
            conn.close();
        }
    }
}
```

The `finally` block ensures that whether or not an exception occurs, the connection is cleaned up.

> **Caution:** Robust exception handling is usually omitted from the small samples of code within a chapter. The resulting code is usually easier to read, but certainly not appropriate for production-quality code. Keep this in mind as you work through a chapter.

System Setup

In order to send messages, your application will need to declare appropriate permissions within its JAD or manifest. Application permissions are covered in more detail in Chapter 9. For now, just be aware that in order for your code to run on the device, you will need to include the following permissions.

javax.microedition.io.Connector.sms: Required to open an SMS connection.

`javax.wireless.messaging.sms.send`: Required to send the actual SMS message.

The full permissions directive will look like the following, with any other required permissions also added.

```
MIDlet-Permissions: javax.microedition.io.Connector.sms,
javax.wireless.messaging.sms.send
```

If you fail to declare these permissions, users will still be able to install and run your app, but a `SecurityException` will be thrown when you try to use SMS.

WMA also defines a system property for the SMSC. As discussed in the first section, the SMSC is the piece of equipment that handles the actual delivery of SMS messages. You can retrieve the SMSC by retrieving the wireless.messaging.sms.smsc system property as follows.

```
String smscAddress = System.getProperty("wireless.messaging.sms.smsc");
```

The SMSC is generally provided as a phone number on the carrier network, such as +15555550100. You won't access this number directly, but it is a great way to determine what SMS provider a given user has. Once you learn the SMSC addresses for carriers in your desired regions, you can use this information to make decisions about any special handling that a given carrier may require.

Sending SMS on CDMA

Speaking of special handling, one of the most significant workarounds you're likely to face is the difference between GSM and CDMA carriers. WMA was specifically designed to be carrier-agnostic, and on most other platforms you can happily reuse code for both GSM and CDMA. On most BlackBerry devices, though, SMS messages will fail to send from CDMA devices. This is a known issue that affects the 7130, 7250, 8703e, 8830, Curve 8330, and Pearl 8130 phones. It appears to have been fixed for more recent CDMA models including the Storm 9530 and beyond.

> **Note:** Code Division Multiple Access (CDMA) and the Global System for Mobile (GSM) are the two most widely used wireless technologies. They use fundamentally different methods for wireless communication, so a GSM phone cannot be used on a CDMA carrier or vice versa. For the vast majority of applications, it makes absolutely no difference which type of phone you are running on. However, RIM and other OEMs must use different CPUs and architectures for the different types of devices, so in certain edge cases such as this, discrepancies will crop up. These can be frustrating, but the issues are generally fairly well documented. To determine what type of network you are using, call `RadioInfo.getNetworkType()`.

Fortunately, RIM has a work-around available for affected phones. Instead of using the WMA `MessageConnection` and Message interfaces, send a UDP packet via a `DatagramConnection`. This does make a certain amount of sense—SMS messages do appear somewhat similar to UDP in structure and purpose. You should still use the existing SMS protocol when addressing the recipient of the message. A short example follows.

```
if (RadioInfo.getNetworkType() == RadioInfo.NETWORK_CDMA)
{
    DatagramConnection backDoor = (DatagramConnection)Connector.open↵
        ("sms://+14155550100");
    byte[] data = "You cannot stop me".getBytes();
    Datagram dg = backDoor.newDatagram(backDoor.getMaximumLength());
    dg.setData(data, 0, data.length);
    backDoor.send(dg);
    backDoor.close();
}
```

Note that there is no distinction here between a regular text message and a binary message; you simply send bytes in both cases. Other BlackBerry devices will detect and interpret these messages correctly, but other phones may interpret them as binary data and not be able to display as regular text. In addition, note that this method generally does not work for GSM devices. If you plan to run on both types of network and intend to use SMS messaging, you will need to create separate versions for each network or detect the current network and use one strategy or the other.

Sending Multimedia Messages

SMS is a good go-to technology for compact messages—either bits of human-readable text or small custom binary messages. When considering how to move large pieces of multimedia data on and off the device, think about MMS as an option. MMS messages can be built using the same WMA framework used by SMS messages, but offer much more capacity and more flexibility in message construction.

> **Caution:** MMS support in BlackBerry is still relatively new, having only become available with device software version 4.6. There were several bugs with RIM's initial implementation of MMS. These problems have been fixed starting with device software version 5.0, but to be safe, be sure to test on actual devices early in your development cycle. Also, because carrier MMSCs are closed to traffic from outside their wireless network, you will not be able to test MMS messages from the BlackBerry Simulator.

Talk to the World

MMS messages can be addressed to mobile phone numbers, but also to short codes, email addresses, even IP addresses. This offers a great deal of flexibility when designing your application architecture. Instead of a peer-to-peer app design, you might choose to send data over MMS to an email address and have a server component that receives those messages and acts on them. Therefore, while the general form of constructing a MessageConnection is similar to that for SMS messages, you have more options available.

```
MessageConnection mms = (MessageConnection)Connector.open↵
      ("mms://+14155550100");
MessageConnection mms = (MessageConnection)Connector.open↵
      ("mms://sally@email.com");
MessageConnection mms = (MessageConnection)Connector.open↵
      ("mms://127.66.0.255");
```

Because MMS messages are more closely aligned with the Internet world than the telephonic world, you also have the option of directing messages directly to an application ID. Similar to the port in an SMS message, this allows you to send a message directly to an application that has registered for to handle those messages. To avoid conflicts, you should use a unique namespace when selecting an application ID. If you do not specify an application ID, the message will be delivered to the phone's default message client.

```
MessageConnection mms = (MessageConnection)Connector.open
        ("mms://+114155550100:com.apress.king.mms");
```

Constructing Parts

An MMS message can contain one or more pieces of content. Each piece is represented as a separate `MessagePart`. A `MessagePart`'s primary job is to contain data, such as the actual sound, image, or text. You can set binary data directly on the `MessagePart`, or assign an `InputStream` to it to make it read in the data. In addition to the data, you can set the following pieces of metadata on the `MessagePart`:

- A MIME type describes the format of the data, such as `"image/jpeg"` or `"audio/amr"`.

- The Content ID uniquely identifies this message part.

- The Content Location provides a filename.

The following code demonstrates how to create `MessageParts`. For convenience, the text data is set directly from bytes and the image data is loaded through an InputStream, but both could be set in either way.

```
String captionContent = "It's a boy!";
String captionContentId = "text_boy";
String captionContentLocation = "/boy.txt";
MessagePart textMessagePart = new MessagePart(captionContent.getBytes(), 0,
    captionContent.length(), "text/plain", captionContentId,
    captionContentLocation, null);
InputStream imageContent;
String imageContentId = "img_boy";
String imageContentLocation = "/photo.png";
imageContent = getClass().getResourceAsStream(imageContentLocation);
MessagePart imageMessagePart = new MessagePart(imageContent, "image/png",
    imageContentId, imageContentLocation, null);
```

If sending to another MMS-capable phone, you might consider adding a SMIL as well. This is a special type of `MessagePart` that is used to control the display of other attachments in the message. It allows you to divide a message into multiple slides, specify how long each should display, group together audio, image, and text elements, and set up repeating loops. A full discussion of SMIL is beyond the scope of this book; for more details, you can view the specification defined by the W3C, available online at `http://www.w3.org/TR/REC-smil/`. An example of creating a simple SMIL follows.

```
String smilContent =
    "<smil>" +
        "<body>" +
          "<par dur='15000ms'>" +
              "<img src='photo.png'/>" +
              "<text src='boy.txt' />" +
          "</seq>" +
        "</body>" +
    "</smil>";
```

```
String smilContentId = "start";
String smilContentLocation = "/first.sml";
MessagePart smilMessagePart = new MessagePart(smilContent.getBytes(), 0, ↵
        smilContent.length(), "application/smil", smilContentId, ↵
        smilContentLocation, null);
```

SMILs will almost always be omitted if your MMS message is intended to transmit data to an application or a server, as presentation is not generally important.

Making the Message

Apart from the addition of attachments, MMS messages also add additional options to the message itself. We have already discussed the different addresses an MMS message can include, such as phone numbers and email addresses. Unlike an SMS, which is sent to only a single recipient, an MMS message can have multiple recipients. In addition, MMS messages support the email-style address types of "to" (main recipients), "cc" (carbon copy, secondary recipients), and "bcc" (blind carbon copy). "bcc" recipients will receive the message, but their addresses will not appear in the message, so other recipients will not see those addresses. "bcc" may be a good choice if you want to send a single message to many recipients while protecting their privacy.

MMS messages offer several other fields that may be useful:

- You can set the subject, which may be presented to the recipient before they choose to download the message.

- The start content ID refers to the SMIL attachment, if one exists, and directs the MMS transport to place it appropriately in the final message.

- You can set message headers. Two are defined and available for direct use.

- X-Mms-Delivery-Time specifies when the message may be delivered to the recipient. It may be delivered later than this, but not earlier, and is appropriate for sending holiday greetings or similar timed messages in advance. The value should be the number of milliseconds since the Unix epoch.

- X-Mms-Priority may be set to one of "high", "normal", or "low". This does not affect message delivery, but it may result in different presentation to the recipient.

The most important aspect of an MMS message, though, is the assembly of its attachment parts into the final message. You may add attachments in any order. As noted earlier, the start content ID should be set to indicate the SMIL if it is present; the SMIL information will control how the other parts are presented.

MMS messages can be large, but not unlimited. Carriers will generally set message limits on individual phones within their networks. You can expect to be able to send at least a few hundred kilobytes in a single MMS, and possibly as much as a megabyte or above for phones with high-quality cameras. In addition to the carrier limits when sending a message, you may run into limits when simply composing your message. If an attachment causes the message to exceed the size limit, or run out of memory, the operation will fail with a `SizeExceededException`.

The following code demonstrates how to create an MMS message, configure it, and attach the previously created media files.

```
MessageConnection mms = (MessageConnection)Connector.open
    ("mms://+14155550100");
MultipartMessage birthMessage = (MultipartMessage)mms.newMessage
    (MessageConnection.MULTIPART_MESSAGE);
birthMessage.addAddress("to", "+14155550101");
birthMessage.addAddress("to", "aunt.dotty@server.com");
birthMessage.addAddress("bcc", "my_email@work.com");
birthMessage.setSubject("The moment you've been waiting for...");
birthMessage.setStartContentId("start");
birthMessage.addMessagePart(textMessagePart);
birthMessage.addMessagePart(imageMessagePart);
birthMessage.addMessagePart(smilMessagePart);
```

Get Out Of Here

Configuring an MMS requires a fair amount of work, but once you are ready, it is sent using the exact same technique as an SMS. Again, the method will block until the message is sent or an error occurs. Keep in mind that long messages take even longer to send than short messages, and handle message sending in a separate thread.

```
mms.send(birthMessage);
```

Plugging In to Email

If SMS is the dominant form of messaging on wireless devices, email is certainly the dominant form in the rest of the world. Everybody has an email address, and people are increasingly sending and receiving emails while on the go. BlackBerry devices have always had a strong level of integration with email, and you can take advantage of this affinity when moving data off the handset. Turn toward email when you want to move a relatively large amount of data off the device in a standard format.

Taking Account

Email is so popular on BlackBerry devices that a given device may have many accounts registered. These may range from highly encrypted push email accounts delivered over a BES to a basic free Gmail or Hotmail account. To support specialized network behaviors, RIM uses the concept of a *service book* to describe the configuration of each given account.

Service books are a unique property of BlackBerry devices that you will not find on other mobile operating systems. They perform several functions, but most importantly each book directs how an account connects to BlackBerry infrastructure, uses the mobile radio, handles encryption, and directs traffic. Even a basic user's device will contain multiple service books—perhaps one for handling WAP traffic through the carrier's wireless network, another for unencrypted Wi-Fi browsing, two for email accounts, and several more for essential device functions. Figure 4-9 depicts some possible service book configuration.

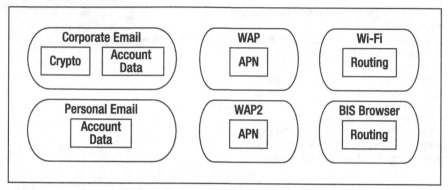

Figure 4-9. *Representation of BlackBerry service books*

Note: Most documentation uses the term *service book* to describe these types of accounts. However, the RIM API uses the term *service record* to describe each individual account, and service book to describe the sum collection of all device accounts. I will use the term service book in this section due to its more common usage.

Any given device will contain many service books, but few of interest when sending email. Once you have retrieved the appropriate service book, you can create an email session for that account. The session is used to associate your email activity with the proper account and ensures that "Sent From" and other information appears correctly in outgoing messages. You can easily retrieve a session for the default email account as follows.

```
Session defaultSession = Session.getDefaultInstance();
```

Caution: While rare, it's possible that a user will not have any email account configured on their phone, in which case attempts to retrieve the default session will return null. Additionally, service book information may not be available immediately if the device has recently powered on, in which case you can try again later and retrieve the account.

You may want to send from another email account. For example, a business BlackBerry device probably has a corporate email address configured as the default, which is not appropriate for sending messages from a game. You can query the device for all email service books. Each service book has a content ID describing the general function of the book. The content ID for email accounts is CMIME (Compressed Multipurpose Internet

Mail Extension). Once you have access to the accounts, you can select an appropriate one for your application to use—or, better, present your user with the choice of which to use. The following code shows how to scan through the available accounts on a device.

```
ServiceBook book = ServiceBook.getSB();
ServiceRecord[] records = book.findRecordsByCid("CMIME");
if (records != null)
{
    for (int i = 0; i < records.length; ++i)
    {
        ServiceRecord record = records[i];
        String name = record.getName();
        int type = record.getType();
        String description = record.getDescription();
        // Check to see whether to use this account. If so...
        ServiceConfiguration config = new ServiceConfiguration(record);
        Session emailSession = Session.getInstance(config);
    }
}
```

If you already know the account you wish to use, you can retrieve it via `ServiceBook.getRecordById()`, `ServiceBook.getRecordByCidAndUserId()`, and similar methods.

Creating the Message

Once you have obtained an email session for the account you wish to use, you can construct and configure the message. The BlackBerry API exposes a message *store* that holds all messages, both incoming and outgoing. The store, in turn, contains multiple folders. You cannot create a stand-alone message; instead, you must create a message within an existing folder. Create outgoing messages within the sent folder, as shown next.

```
Store msgs = Session.getDefaultInstance().getStore();
Folder[] sentFolders = msgs.list(Folder.SENT);
Folder sentfolder = sentFolders[0];
Message msg = new Message(sentfolder);
```

Note: The BlackBerry mail classes are located in the `net.rim.blackberry.api.mail` package.

Observe that the `list()` method returns an array of folders. This allows greater flexibility with different mailbox configurations, but users are very unlikely to ever have more than one sent folder. You can safely use the first sent folder that is returned.

Once you have constructed a `Message`, you can invoke appropriate methods on it to configure the message. These include all the options you would expect in a standard email client, including choosing recipients, setting priority, and picking a subject. Be prepared to handle an `AddressException` if the recipient address is malformed. You also have access to fields that are usually not accessible in other clients, such as configuring the date a message was sent, or requesting a read acknowledgement via a flag. The following code shows how you can programmatically write a message to a famous BlackBerry user.

```
Address to[] = new Address[1];
to[0] = new Address("obama@whitehouse.gov", "Barack Obama");
msg.addRecipients(Message.RecipientType.TO, to);
msg.setPriority(Message.Priority.HIGH);
msg.setSubject("Mission complete");
msg.setContent("The job is done. Awaiting further instructions.");
```

Once your message has been composed, you can send it using the Transport. A Transport handles the sending and receiving activities of a given email session. This operation may fail with a MessagingException, which can occur if the message could not be sent due to being rejected or encountering other problems.

```
Transport.send(msg);
```

Adding Attachments

Making the basic message is straightforward, but what if you want to add attachments? Most of the message construction will still happen in the same way, but instead of setting the content directly as shown above, you will need to construct a multipart message. Much like multipart MMS messages, with email you can combine a series of BodyPart objects into a Multipart container. Each BodyPart consists of a chunk of binary data and a content type. For convenience, RIM offers several Part classes to use:

- TextBodyPart provides a simple way to set the text in a message that also contains attachments. The content can be set with a String, and it automatically has type text/plain.

- SupportedAttachmentPart is a more generic kind of Part that can contain any type of content. You are responsible for setting the binary data and content type appropriately. You should also declare the file name used by the binary data.

> **Caution:** You will see several more Part subclasses in the Java API. Be aware that some of these classes are only used for incoming messages and cannot be applied when constructing an outgoing email.

The following example shows how to construct and add attachments to a message. The rest of the message can be configured in the same way as in the previous example.

```
Multipart multipart = new Multipart();
TextBodyPart text = new TextBodyPart(multipart, "The job is done.");
SupportedAttachmentPart image = new SupportedAttachmentPart(multipart,
                "image/jpeg", "plans.jpg", imageData);
byte[] secretKey = new byte[]{17, 33, 0, 127};
```

```
SupportedAttachmentPart key = new SupportedAttachmentPart
    (multipart, "application/octet-stream", "key.dat", secretKey);
multipart.addBodyPart(text);
multipart.addBodyPart(image);
multipart.addBodyPart(key);
msg.setContent(multipart);
```

Testing Sending

If you try to run an app that sends email from your device, the message will be sent properly (assuming your email account is configured correctly and you have appropriate permissions). However, if you attempt to send from the device simulator on your desktop, the message will not be sent. What's going on?

You cannot configure an email account on the desktop device simulator. This is sensible, since the simulator connects through a simulated MDS connection that does not actually connect to the real BlackBerry infrastructure. When you try to send a message from the default messaging client, it will appear to be sent properly, but no message is actually generated.

To work around this issue, RIM has developed a separate stand-alone application. Much like the MDS, which simulates a BlackBerry network connection, the Email Server Simulator (ESS) simulates a BlackBerry-supported email connection. The ESS provides a bridge between the MDS and outside email, allowing you to test sending and receiving email messages. If you plan on spending much time working with email in your app, I highly recommend configuring the ESS early on. It will save you a great deal of time and allow you to complete most of your development on the desktop.

> **Caution:** The ESS is a local server, and you may need to modify your development machine to allow it to run properly. If you run into problems while setting it up, try disabling your firewall, turning off other local servers such as Apache, and running the ESS as an administrator.

The Email Server Simulator is not currently accessible directly through the BlackBerry Eclipse plug-in, but you can locate it under your Eclipse plugins folder. The full path should be something like c:\eclipse\plugins\net.rim.eide.componentpack4.7.0_4.7.0.46\ components\ESS. Run the load.bat file to launch the ESS. ESS is also available as part of the standard RIM JDE install, which you can find on the BlackBerry web site. Once you have installed the JDE, you will be able to find the Email Server Simulator in your Start menu under the Research In Motion folder, as shown in Figure 4-10. Both methods of installing and launching ESS work equally well. Running from the command line does give the advantage of displaying debug output from the ESS, which can help when tracking down issues.

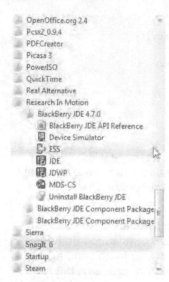

Figure 4-10. *Locating the Email Server Simulator*

The Email Server Simulator offers two different modes. The Connected mode will connect to a third-party email account. If using connected mode, outgoing messages from the BlackBerry simulator will create actual email messages from the configured account. Unfortunately, Connected mode doesn't work for several versions of the MDS/ESS combination. Even when it does work, it is extremely limited: it can only send through nonauthenticated, nonencrypted SMTP connections. There are very few of those left today, due to spammers and other abusers.

The best mode to use, then, is Standalone mode. Instead of sending to an external email account, this mode causes the ESS to behave like a simple POP3/SMTP email server. It will store outgoing messages, and you can connect a third-party desktop email application, such as Outlook Express, to retrieve and send messages. Figure 4-11 shows one possible configuration of Standalone mode. You can pick any port numbers you want, which may be useful if the defaults are already in use on your machine. After you have set up the simulator, click "Launch" to start running. You won't see any log information about what the ESS is doing.

Figure 4-11. *Configured Email Server Simulator*

Now, download a standalone email client or open an existing one. Create a new account and set both the POP3 and SMTP server addresses to "localhost". This directs the email client to access your local machine instead of an external mail server. Consult your email client's documentation to learn how to add an account. Figure 4-12 depicts adding an account using Windows Live Mail.

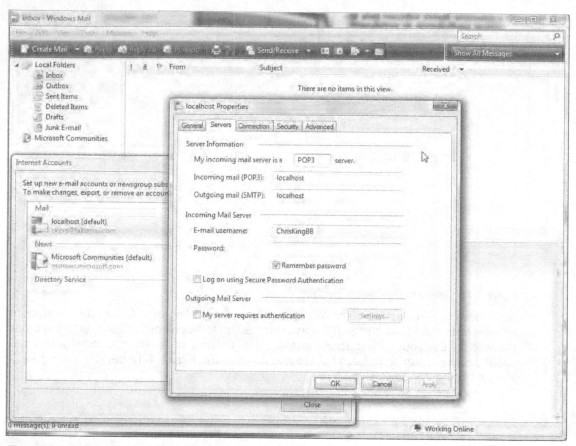

Figure 4-12. *Adding a dummy localhost email account*

Be sure to set the port numbers that you configured in the Email Server Simulator window on the new account. This will usually be available under the advanced options, as shown in Figure 4-13. Without the correct port numbers, the client will not be able to connect with the ESS.

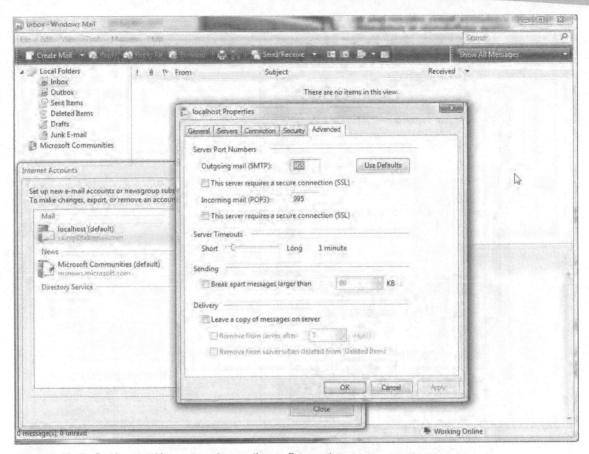

Figure 4-13. Configuring matching port numbers on the email account

Before testing with your app, I highly recommend you send a test message from the default BlackBerry message application. It doesn't matter what address you use, as all outgoing messages will be sent to the ESS. Compose the message like you would on an actual device, as shown in Figure 4-14.

Figure 4-14. *Creating a test email message*

After you send, the message should shortly become available in your desktop email client. Figure 4-15 shows a properly received message. Check your spam folder if you do not see it right away.

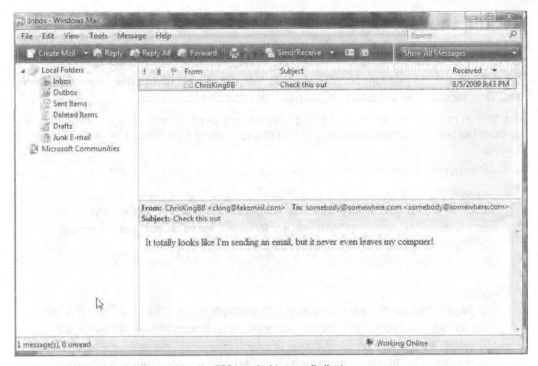

Figure 4-15. *A message delivered from the ESS to a desktop email client*

Once your ESS is configured, you should be able to test sending messages from your app when running in the simulator. These will be delivered to the desktop client, where you can confirm that they contain the settings and attachments you expect to see.

> **Caution:** If the ESS is not running, outgoing email messages will not be sent. This can prevent other networking operations, such as HTTP connections, from working properly.

Receiving Text Messages

The earlier part of this chapter dealt with sending messages. Now we will look at how to receive messages. Not every app will need both kinds of functions. You may just send messages to share information about what your app is doing, or just receive messages in order to activate functions within your app. Some peer-to-peer apps will do both. The classes used to receive messages are usually the same as those used to send them, but they are used in different ways.

Getting the Message

The simplest case to handle is when your app is already running, and you want to be notified of an incoming message. To do this, you will open a special kind of `MessageConnection` that functions as a server instead of a client. In other words, you are declaring an intention to handle messages that others send to you.

The format of a server connection string resembles that of a client string, but the phone number portion is omitted, and instead you display only the port number. An example follows.

```
MessageConnection receiver = (MessageConnection)Connector.open("sms://:4000");
```

> **Tip:** On most BlackBerry devices, a connection string of "sms://:0" indicates that this app wants to receive ALL incoming SMS messages. This should not be abused, as it will prevent messages from being delivered to other apps.

> **Tip:** As described above, if you wish to send SMS messages to your app from a server, you will need to make an agreement with the wireless carriers or go through an SMS aggregator. SMS aggregators are generally more accustomed to sending regular SMS messages and not port-directed messages. To indicate that a message should be delivered to a particular GSM port, use the TP-User-Data/User-Data-Header header when sending your server request to generate the outgoing SMS message.

Once you have a `MessageConnection`, you have two choices. The method `MessageConnection.receive()` blocks until a message is available. If you are running in a separate message-handling thread, you may choose to just call `receive()` within a loop to handle all incoming messages. Alternately, you may choose to register a listener with the connection. By implementing the `MessageListener` class and calling `setMessageListener()`, your main thread can continue running normally. Your `MessageListener` class will later be invoked whenever a message becomes available. Note that the invocation may run on your app's main thread, so you should still spawn a separate thread in this situation. A simple anonymous `MessageListener` may look like the following:

```
receiver.setMessageListener(new javax.wireless.messaging.MessageListener()
{
    public void notifyIncomingMessage(MessageConnection connection)
    {
        Message incoming = connection.receive();
        // Handle the message here.
    }
});
```

Notice that we have declared the `notifyIncomingMessage` method to process the message. Again, a real application should receive the message on a separate thread.

Waking Up

So far, this all works well as long as our app is running. But what if it isn't running? If we expect to receive messages on port 4000, and the phone receives a message for that port while the app isn't running, the message is simply discarded. It will not be presented to the user, and the app will not be notified.

For BlackBerry CLDC applications, the simplest way to handle this is to have your application automatically start on boot-up. It can then use the above approaches to open a `MessageConnection` and either register as a listener or create a thread that calls `receive()`. Once a message arrives, you can process it, calling `UiApplication.requestForeground()` to bring up your UI if so desired.

MIDlets, however, cannot automatically start on boot-up. If you are writing a MIDlet, you must register with the *push registry*. The push registry is a component of the device AMS that is responsible for starting up apps when certain circumstances occur. In our particular case, we want to register to handle incoming messages.

Push registry can take one of two forms: dynamic or static. Dynamic registration is done through application code. Imagine that someone is playing a mobile version of chess. They will start the game and start playing. The game notifies the push registry that it wants to handle incoming messages to port 6060. During a particularly long wait, the player exits the app so they can listen to some music. When the other player finally moves, their device sends your player a message to port 6060. The AMS notices the port number and automatically starts your chess game app back up again. At this point you can retrieve the incoming message and show the latest move.

When registering with the push registry, you provide these three pieces of data:

- The connection URL describes the protocol and address of incoming connections; this is equivalent to the string that will be passed to `Connector.open()`.

- The MIDlet class name is the fully qualified MIDlet class that should be started when the message is received.

- The allowed sender indicates that the app should be started only if the connection came from this source.

To register for all incoming SMS messages to a particular port, use something like this:

```
PushRegistry.registerConnection↵
    ("sms://:4000", "com.apress.king.chess.ChessGame", "*");
```

If you only want to receive from one specific sender, specify it in the last parameter.

```
PushRegistry.registerConnection("sms://:4000", "com.apress.king.chess.ChessGame",
    "+14155550133");
```

This method will throw a `ClassNotFoundException` if the class cannot be found, and an `IOException` if these is some other problem, such as another application already reserving the same port. You can call this method from a different class than the one that will be invoked.

Dynamic registration can be handy. Among other advantages, it allows you to decide on the fly what port you want to use, perhaps based on what's available and what a server wants to use. It's also tougher for hackers to exploit a known port number and send your app data it isn't expecting. On the other hand, you cannot dynamically register an app until it is already running. That works fine for a chess game, but it means your app will no longer be started after the user reboots their phone, until they remember to start the app themselves.

To get around this issue, consider using static registration. A static registration is declared in your application JAD or `MANIFEST.MF` file, and is registered with the AMS at the time the app is first installed. From that time on, your app will always be invoked whenever a matching message is received, even if it has never run before. As the example below shows, you provide the same information in static registration that you would use in dynamic registration, just as a standard name-value pair.

```
MIDlet-Push-1: sms://:4000, com.apress.king.chess.ChessGame, *
```

If your app registers for multiple types of incoming messages, or for other types of push notification, just keep incrementing the number after `MIDlet-Push` to `MIDlet-Push-2`, `MIDlet-Push-3`, and so on.

> **Caution:** Using static registration carries its own pitfalls. Your app must be guaranteed to start when an appropriate message is sent, so it can be installed only if the user has not already installed another app that registers for the same port number. To be as safe as possible, pick a random number that is high in the available range, and stay away from well-known port numbers.

We've Got Incoming

The push registry doesn't use any special interfaces when launching your MIDlet for an incoming message: it uses the same `startApp()` method that is used when the user manually launches the app. To determine whether your app was launched by the AMS, you should query the pending connections from the `PushRegistry`. If your app has registered for multiple push types, there may be more than one push pending. Search to find the proper one. Once you have located it, you can open the `MessageConnection` and proceed as usual. The code that follows shows an example of retrieving the message that launched this MIDlet.

```
String[] pendingConnections = PushRegistry.listConnections(true);
if (pendingConnections != null && pendingConnections.length > 0)
{
    for (int i=0; i<pendingConnections.length; i++)
```

```
{
    String url = pendingConnections[i];
    if (url.startsWith("sms"))
    {
        MessageConnection messageConnection =
            (MessageConnection)Connector.open(url);
        Message incoming = messageConnection.receive();
    }
}
}
```

> **Caution:** RIM devices generally require a full phone reboot when you install an application with static push registry. This is because the static push registry is initialized when the phone boots up. This will be only a minor inconvenience to your users, but it can be frustrating for developers and testers who may be loading an app hundreds of times. Consider omitting the push registry entry on debug builds.

What Is It?

You now have a Message. That isn't the end of the story, though. Remember that there are two types of SMS messages: TextMessage and BinaryMessage. If you are certain which kind of message you are expecting, you can cast directly to the form you want. Otherwise, test for the specific type in order to determine how to access its parts.

> **Tip:** BlackBerry CDMA phones may receive incoming plain text messages as type BinaryMessage. To reconstruct the original text, just create a String from the byte payload.

TextMessage and BinaryMessage are the same classes used to create and send messages, and you can retrieve the same type of information from both. In certain cases the meaning changes. For example, the address in an outgoing message refers to the recipient address, whereas the address of an incoming message refers to the sender address. The following code shows how to retrieve information from a retrieved SMS message.

```
String sender = incoming.getAddress();
if (incoming instanceof TextMessage)
{
    TextMessage text = (TextMessage)incoming;
    String body = text.getPayloadText();
}
else if (incoming instanceof BinaryMessage)
{
    BinaryMessage binary = (BinaryMessage)incoming;
    byte[] payload = binary.getPayloadData();
}
```

Testing SMS in the Simulator

The BlackBerry simulator will cheerfully send outgoing SMS messages. However, it is quite difficult to receive incoming messages. RIM has released a Java application named smsdemo that echoes back SMS messages from a specialized client. At present, there isn't a convenient way to inject an arbitrary SMS message into the simulator.

One possibility is to configure two simulators to connect with each other. Within Eclipse, you can set the SMS source port and SMS destination port under the debug configuration's Simulator Network tab. When launching from the command line, you can specify the ports via the /sms-source-port=[value] and /sms-destination-port=[value] arguments. You should be able to start two simulators at the same time—one from within Eclipse and the other from the command line—provided both simulators are not in the same directory. The second simulator will complain about not being able to open all its ports; you can ignore this message.

In theory, you should now be able to send from one simulator to the other. In practice, this doesn't currently work very well. The second simulator to start will be crippled. Hopefully RIM will soon offer better tooling for SMS messages similar to what they offer for email messages. Until then, it may be simplest to just run on the device.

Receiving MMS Messages

Once you are comfortable with the process of receiving SMS messages, you'll find receiving MMS to be very familiar. It uses the same MessageConnection interface to retrieve messages, just with the mms protocol instead of the sms one. As with sending, you can register a class name instead of a port number. You can use the push registry for MMS in the same way you would for SMS. Once you are ready to receive, simply retrieve the message as shown below.

```
MessageConnection receiver = (MessageConnection)Connector.open
    ("mms://:com.apress.king.mms");
MultipartMessage mms = (MultipartMessage)receiver.receive();
```

> **Caution:** MMS messages can be quite large and take a long time to fully receive. Be sure to receive in a separate thread from your main app. Consider showing some sort of progress indicator to let your user know that the app is retrieving data.

Observe that the mms protocol will retrieve only MultipartMessage messages, so unlike with SMS, there is no need to test for the class type before casting.

Reading MMS

The incoming MMS message will have the same fields available that you could set for outgoing messages. Simply call the accessors to pull out whatever information you are interested in, as shown here:

```
String sender = mms.getAddress();
String subject = mms.getSubject();
```

Of course, you wouldn't be using MMS if all you wanted were the sender and the subject. To get at the attachment data for the message, retrieve the message parts. Each part will contain a content ID, a content location, a MIME type, and data. If you control the incoming messages to this app, you may know exactly what you will be receiving and can directly get the attachments you need; otherwise, you may want to scan all the attachments, and take appropriate behavior on each. The sample that follows shows how to look for JPEG image and text attachments.

```
MessagePart[] parts = mms.getMessageParts();
for (int i = 0; i < parts.length; ++i)
{
    MessagePart part = parts[i];
    String name = part.getContentID();
    String type = part.getMIMEType();
    String file = part.getContentLocation();
    if (type.equals("image/jpeg"))
    {
        InputStream is = part.getContentAsStream();
        // Could set this picture on the UI or save it.
    }
    else if (type.equals("text/plain"))
    {
        byte[] messageBytes = part.getContent();
        String text = new String(messageBytes);
        // Could display this text.
    }
}
```

Testing MMS

Unfortunately, it is not currently possible to test sending or receiving MMS messages within the simulator. MMS relies on a combination of SMS message delivery, a cooperative MMSC, and data delivery to send messages. The simulator cannot easily recreate this complicated environment.

Your best option will be to test on the actual device. Your phone will need to be able to send and receive MMS messages through the native Message application in order for it to be able to send or receive MMS messages within your app. If it can not, contact your wireless carrier or IT administrator to properly set up your wireless data plan and IT policy.

If your app uses MMS heavily, deploying to the device every time you make a change may be too labor-intensive. Consider writing a local test harness for the simulator instead. Test to see whether or not you are running on the simulator; if you are, you can omit the outgoing messages and invoke appropriate incoming methods. For example, you might programmatically construct a `MultipartMessage` and proceed as if it had been delivered from the `MessageConnection.receive()` method.

Reading Email

Email can be a great way to move data off your BlackBerry app. It also might be a good way to receive data, but there are more complications to deal with. Because email isn't exclusively a wireless technology, its policies and standards tend to be more complex. If you can clear those hurdles, though, email is usually the fattest message-oriented pipe at your disposal.

Listening

The previous two sections discussed how your app could directly receive incoming SMS and MMS messages. These capabilities allow an app to use wireless messaging as a pure data channel, meaning the user will never see the actual messages. However, email doesn't have this sort of exclusive relationship. Your app cannot intercept incoming email—if it could, just imagine the potential for abusive programs to wreak havoc with business email accounts.

What you can do is listen for messages. After a message has been delivered to the handset, the BlackBerry device will check to see if anyone has registered to be notified of changes in a particular folder. You can join this notification list by implementing the `FolderListener` interface. The following code shows the skeleton of a listener class.

```
public class ArrivingListener implements FolderListener
{
    public void messagesAdded(FolderEvent event)
    {
        if (event.getType() == FolderEvent.MESSAGE_ADDED)
        {
            // Handle arrived messages here.
        }
    }
    public void messagesRemoved(FolderEvent event)
    {
        // This method intentionally left blank.
    }
}
```

You must attach your `FolderListener` to a particular message store. The previous section on sending email described how to find and retrieve an appropriate store. The next example sets a store on the user's default email account.

```
Session session = Session.getDefaultInstance();
Store store = session.getStore();
ArrivingListener listener = new ArrivingListener();
store.addFolderListener(listener);
```

Note: You may want to use a dedicated email folder for your app. Because the user will see incoming email messages, it will probably annoy them to have a large number of app-directed messages delivered to their inbox. Depending on the user and the type of email account, you may need the cooperation of an IT administrator to set up folders correctly.

Reading Messages

Incoming email messages contain all the same fields that you can provide to outgoing messages. Once you have obtained the message, you can read those fields in directly, as shown in this example:

```
net.rim.blackberry.api.mail.Message arrived = event.getMessage();
Address sender = arrived.getFrom();
String senderAddress = sender.getAddr();
String senderName = sender.getName();
String subject = arrived.getSubject();
int size = arrived.getSize();
byte priority = arrived.getPriority();
```

Note that the Address object contains multiple pieces of information about the sender. Depending on your app design, you may care about the sending email address, the associated name, both, or neither. The priority will correspond to one of Message.Priority.HIGH, Message.Priority.MEDIUM, or Message.Priority.LOW.

For basic email messages with just a text component, you can retrieve the body text directly as shown below.

```
String text = arrived.getBodyText();
```

This will return null if there is no body text in the message.

Reading Attachments

If the message contains attachments, they will be collected in a multipart message part. Once you retrieve the multipart, you can iterate through the constituent parts and pull out the individual attachments.

If you are building a general-purpose app that handles messages in a variety of formats, this will require a fair amount of introspection. Individual parts might contain MIME data, a downloaded attachment, plain text, and other pieces of content. You may need to scan all the attachments to find what you are interested in, as shown in the following example. On the other hand, if you know exactly what attachments you are expecting, you can retrieve them directly.

```
Object contents = arrived.getContent();
if (contents instanceof BodyPart)
{
    // Read body
}
else if (contents instanceof Multipart)
{
    Multipart attachments = (Multipart)contents;
    int num = attachments.getCount();
    for (int i = 0; i < num; ++i)
    {
        Part part = attachments.getBodyPart(i);
        if (part instanceof SupportedAttachmentPart)
        {
            SupportedAttachmentPart attachment = ↩
                (SupportedAttachmentPart)part;
            String type = attachment.getContentType();
            if (type.equals("image/png"))
            {
                InputStream image = attachment.getInputStream();
            }
        }
        else if (part instanceof TextBodyPart)
        {
            TextBodyPart body = (TextBodyPart)part;
            String message = (String)body.getContent();
        }
        else if (part instanceof MimeBodyPart)
        {
            MimeBodyPart attachment = (MimeBodyPart)part;
            String type = attachment.getContentType();
            if (type.equals("image/png"))
            {
                InputStream image = attachment.getInputStream();
                // Could display or save the image here.
            }
        }
    }
}
```

If a message is large, the device may initially download only the first portion of the message. The user will be able to view important information like the sender and subject, and possibly the first few lines of the message. The user can then decide whether to download the entire message. To detect whether a particular part has been fully downloaded, call hasMore() on the part. If additional data is available, your app can request it to be downloaded by calling Transport.more(). Provide the BodyPart and true if you want the entire part to be downloaded, or false to download the next available chunk. The following snippet provides an example. Note that this method is not synchronous. If you want to be notified when the body part has been retrieved, attach a MessageListener to the message prior to calling Transport.more().

```
if (attachment.hasMore())
{
    Transport.more(attachment, true);
}
```

> **Caution:** It bears repeating that you should use extreme care when listening for email messages. Don't put yourself in a position where you could be accused of eavesdropping on confidential messages. Be sure to clearly state to the user how your app will be accessing email, and ask for their permission when doing so.

PIN Messaging

All of the messaging technologies described so far exist on multiple platforms. PIN messaging is the one form truly unique to BlackBerry devices. Each BlackBerry has a unique PIN, and only BlackBerry devices have PINs. If your app is exclusively aimed at BlackBerry users, PIN messaging offers an interesting way to exchange information.

Getting Pinned

The PIN number is exclusive to this particular device. You may be interested in using the PIN even if not using PIN messaging, as it provides a way to uniquely identify each of your users. You can access the PIN by retrieving it from the device info by calling DeviceInfo.getDeviceId().

If you know the PIN number for another BlackBerry, you can send it a message. RIM uses the same interfaces for constructing PIN messages as it does for constructing emails: you will retrieve a store to an email session, then construct a message within that store and send it. Once the message hits the network, though, it will be intercepted by the RIM infrastructure and routed to the corresponding device.

You flag an outgoing message as a PIN message by adding a PIN recipient. PINAddress takes the same form as a regular Address, but should be populated with the recipient's PIN number (represented as a String) and name. The rest of the message can be configured as you would a regular plain-text email. You cannot add attachments to a PIN message.

The following code shows how to construct, configure, and send a PIN message.

```
Store store = Session.getDefaultInstance().getStore();
Folder[] folders = store.list(Folder.SENT);
Folder sentFolder = folders[0];
Message msg = new Message(sentFolder);
PINAddress recipients[] = new PINAddress[1];
recipients[0]= new PINAddress("10000000", "Chris King");
msg.addRecipients(Message.RecipientType.TO, recipients);
msg.setSubject("Poke");
```

```
msg.setContent("You've been pinned!");
Transport.send(msg);
```

Receiving PINs

Receiving a PIN is also similar to the process for an email. You should add a listener to the user's email folder, which will be notified when an incoming message arrives. The listener will receive *all* incoming notifications, for both email and PIN messages, so if you are only interested in PIN messages, you should check the message type as shown in the example below. Use the standard email access methods to pull out the PIN message contents you are interested in.

```
public class PINListener implements FolderListener
{
    public void messagesAdded(FolderEvent event)
    {
        Message message = event.getMessage();
        if (message.getMessageType() == Message.PIN_MESSAGE)
        {
            String pinSubject = message.getSubject();
            String pinContent = message.getBodyText();
        }
    }
}
```

Caution: The message type functions are broken on several versions of the device software. If the previous example doesn't work on your particular platform, print out the value returned by getMessageType() for an incoming PIN message, and then change the code to test for that integer instead of for PIN_MESSAGE.

Unfortunately, PIN messaging is not supported on the BlackBerry device simulator. I recommend using the Email Server Simulator and email messages for development on the simulator, then switch to PIN messages when running on the actual device. Most of your app logic should be able to remain the same, you will just switch between sending to a PINAddress instead of an Address, or switch whether you test for a PIN_MESSAGE type.

App: Sending and Receiving Media Messages

So far, our MediaGrabber is able to record media, save it to the local filesystem, and play media back to us. That's cool, but isn't it a bit of a shame that we're the only ones who can enjoy it? Let's enhance the app and come up with a way to pass media off the device so we can share it with friends and family.

First, let's take care of a little housekeeping. In Chapter 3 we saw how time-consuming operations should run in a separate thread to keep the UI responsive. We also saw that we needed to use a separate class to handle updates to our Screen that originated from a new thread. We will have the same issue with sending media as we did with playing it, so rather than reimplementing that special class again, let's create a general-purpose stand-alone class that is capable of handling asynchronous UI updates.

Listing 4-1 shows the implementation of StatusUpdater. Feel free to use this in any of your own projects, as this is a fairly common task. You may also want to adapt it for other types of Field objects other than simple text labels.

Listing 4-1. *A General Class for Updating Label Elements Asynchronously*

```
package com.apress.king.mediagrabber;

import net.rim.device.api.ui.UiApplication;
import net.rim.device.api.ui.component.LabelField;

public class StatusUpdater implements Runnable
{
    private LabelField status;
    private String message;
    private UiApplication app;

    public StatusUpdater(LabelField status)
    {
        this.status = status;
        app = UiApplication.getUiApplication();
    }

    public void sendDelayedMessage(String message)
    {
        this.message = message;
        app.invokeLater(this);
    }

    public void run()
    {
        status.setText(message);
    }

}
```

Next, let's look at the main task of sending an outgoing message. To keep things nice and organized, we'll create a new class, SendingScreen. This Screen will allow the user to enter an email address. Once the user selects send, the screen will compose a new email message to that user, attach the media data, and then send it out. Listing 4-2 provides all the details.

Listing 4-2. *Sending Media from the Device to an Email Address*

```
package com.apress.king.mediagrabber;

import net.rim.blackberry.api.mail.*;
import net.rim.device.api.ui.*;
import net.rim.device.api.ui.component.*;
import net.rim.device.api.ui.container.MainScreen;
```

```java
public class SendingScreen extends MainScreen
{
    private static final int STATE_INPUT = 0;
    private static final int STATE_SENDING = 1;
    private static final int STATE_SENT = 2;

    private int state = STATE_INPUT;

    private String contentType;
    private String filename;
    private String message;
    private byte[] data;

    private BasicEditField receiver;
    private LabelField status;

    private StatusUpdater updater;

    private MenuItem sendItem = new MenuItem("Send", 0, 0)
    {
        public void run()
        {
            send();
        }
    };

    public SendingScreen(String contentType, String filename, String message, ↩
                  byte[] data)
    {
        this.contentType = contentType;
        this.filename = filename;
        this.message = message;
        this.data = data;
        status = new LabelField("Please enter an email address.");
        receiver = new BasicEditField("Recipient:", "", 100, ↩
                     BasicEditField.FILTER_EMAIL | Field.USE_ALL_WIDTH);
        add(status);
        add(receiver);
        updater = new StatusUpdater(status);
    }

    public void makeMenu(Menu menu, int instance)
    {
        if (instance == Menu.INSTANCE_DEFAULT)
        {
            if (state == STATE_INPUT)
            {
                menu.add(sendItem);
            }
        }
        super.makeMenu(menu, instance);
    }

    private Message createMessage(String recipient, String type, ↩
                  String filename, String message) throws MessagingException
```

```
    {
        Store defaultStore = Session.getDefaultInstance().getStore();
        Folder sentFolder = defaultStore.getFolder(Folder.SENT);
        Message outgoing = new Message(sentFolder);
        Address friend = new Address(recipient, "");
        outgoing.addRecipient(Message.RecipientType.TO, friend);
        outgoing.setSubject(message);
        Multipart multipart = new Multipart();
        SupportedAttachmentPart file = new SupportedAttachmentPart(multipart, ↵
                        type, filename, data);
        multipart.addBodyPart(file);
        TextBodyPart text = new TextBodyPart(multipart);
        text.setContent("Check this out!");
        multipart.addBodyPart(text);
        outgoing.setContent(multipart);
        return outgoing;
    }

    private void send()
    {
        status.setText("Sending, please wait.");
        state = STATE_SENDING;
        receiver.setEditable(false);
        (new Thread(new MessageSender())).start();
    }

    private class MessageSender implements Runnable
    {
        public void run()
        {
            String address = receiver.getText();
            try
            {
                Message outgoing = createMessage(address, contentType, ↵
                                filename, message);
                Transport.send(outgoing);
                updater.sendDelayedMessage("Message sent");
                state = STATE_SENT;
            }
            catch (Exception e)
            {
                updater.sendDelayedMessage("Problem sending: "↵
                                        + e.getMessage());
                e.printStackTrace();
            }
        }
    }

    public boolean onSavePrompt()
    {
        return true;
    }
}
```

The rest of the changes are minor. We must update the RecordingScreen to use the SendingScreen once media has been recorded. The code that follows shows a new method to initiate the send, along with an example of updating the previous code to use the new functions. Most of the class is identical to the Chapter 3 version; you can download the complete updated RecordingScreen from the Apress web site.

```
private void send(String location, String contentType, String message, ↵
                byte[] data)
{
    SendingScreen sending = new SendingScreen(contentType, location, ↵
                message, data);
    UiApplication.getUiApplication().pushScreen(sending);
}
// Within the stop() method, use the following:
if (type == RECORD_AUDIO)
{
    String file = location + "/audio.amr";
    writeToFile(dataOut.toByteArray(), file);
    send("audio.amr", "audio/amr", "Here's some sound!", ↵
                dataOut.toByteArray());
}
```

Finally, update PlayerScreen to use the new version of StatusUpdater we created. In the constructor, use the following code.

```
updater = new StatusUpdater(status);
```

In PlayerUpdate, substitute the following code for the old updater reference.

```
updater.sendDelayedMessage(event);
```

This app is difficult to test on the desktop. First, the simulator configuration puts a low limit on attachment sizes, meaning that you'll get an "Attachment too big" error for all but the smallest captured files. Second, the ESS does not handle attachments well and will not deliver them to your mail client, so focus on running on the device. If you haven't already, test sending email from the built-in Messaging application. Include an attachment to make sure you can send those files properly. Then launch and run MediaGrabber. Record as before, enter any email address you like, and select Send. The outgoing message should shortly arrive in your inbox.

Note: The native Messaging application can automatically resize attachments if they are larger than the maximum size. Your own application does not automatically get this capability. Depending on your own app purpose, you can experiment with splitting an attachment into multiple parts, performing custom resizing, or setting limits on attachment sizes.

WANT MORE?

As you've seen in this chapter, there's a bewildering range of technologies available for wireless messaging. The current version of MediaGrabber works fine, so long as the user has a compatible email account, but you could expand it to provide even more features to your users.

- Attach a MessageListener to your outgoing email. When the message status is updated, check to see whether it was sent successfully or if there was an error. Report the final message status to the user. Be sure to remove the MessageListener when the SendingScreen is dismissed.

- If your device and plan support it, try sending MMS messages instead of email.

- Listen for incoming email messages. If the message contains one of the strings our app uses (like "Here's some sound!"), notify the user that a friend has sent them a MediaGrabber file.

You can decide whether to add these new capabilities to the existing SendingScreen, or create new classes to handle those expanded functions. You can also polish the presentation by allowing people to enter their own custom messages on outgoing media.

Excelsior

This chapter has shown the many wireless messaging choices that you can use when developing an app. Each option has its own unique profile and advantages, so there is no one-size-fits-all solution. Depending on your app's needs, you may be drawn to the ubiquity of SMS, the presentation options of MMS, the desktop integration and wide capacity of email, or the unique BlackBerry aspect of PIN messaging. Each has its own quirks, and now that you are aware of them, you will be able to take full advantage of each to its fullest.

Many successful BlackBerry apps will stick with conventional networking technologies, such as HTTP or socket programming. Those are great choices if you want to reuse existing server components, run on any device with a data connection, or require more continuous communication. Wireless messaging, on the other hand, is perfect for connecting with existing platforms of message delivery with very little extra effort on your part. Decide early in your project which is the best approach.

Your app is now capturing information on the device and sending it over the network. Wouldn't it be bad, though, if your boss ended up seeing the pictures you took at that wild party? Chapter 5 will examine ways to protect the data we send from the device, keeping it secure and making sure that the intended recipient has access.

Cryptography

Next to their email capabilities, BlackBerry devices are probably most famous for their security. Corporations love them because data sent over a BlackBerry Enterprise Server is automatically encrypted, because they can remotely wipe stolen devices, and because of their integration with corporate security policies. With this strong legacy, many BlackBerry users are naturally interested in the strength of security offered by applications they run.

Cryptography is a broad topic that can and does fill many books. This chapter focuses on some of the tools available to an application developer like you when writing for the BlackBerry platform. We will look at some of the most common goals when writing secure apps, and the various APIs you can use to implement those goals. Keep in mind that security is a serious, multi-faceted issue. You should view this chapter's contents as a useful starting point that will continue with further education, security audits, and real-world testing.

Is It Secret? Is It Safe?

Suppose that you write a business expense-tracking app. This app allows users to enter their receipts onto the BlackBerry, then uploads the data to a server or sends the user an email. So far, so good. Now, imagine that while the app is transmitting that data, a hacker uses a *packet sniffer* to observe the message being sent. Now, someone else has access to personal financial information from your users, which they may use to steal their identity or crack bank accounts.

To be sure, not every app will need to worry about this sort of thing. Who cares if a hacker eavesdrops on a weather-predicting app? Early on in development, you should consider and discuss the security profile of your app.

1. Does the app have access to sensitive data?
2. Does the app store such data? Transmit it?
3. What are the risks associated with loss or interception of that data?

4. What would it take to protect the data?

5. How hard will it be to protect the data? How long will it take? Will it inconvenience the user?

If, after a thorough analysis, you decide that the app needs to protect its data, you can proceed to a consideration of the best method to do so.

Data Encryption

When most people hear the word *cryptography*, they may first think of cipher encryption—that is, transforming a *plaintext*, such as "hello," into seeming gibberish called a *ciphertext*, such as "ifmmp." Ciphers have existed for millennia, and modern ones have grown to be incredibly sophisticated.

All but the most trivial ciphers rely on use of a *key*. The key is a secret piece of data that is used to encrypt a message. For example, consider a cipher that adds the key value to the plaintext value. We might have a plain text of "hello" and a key of "world." We can convert those letters into numeric values, starting with 1 for "A" and 26 for "Z". Then, for each letter, we add the value of the plain text to the value of the key. If the total is greater than 26, we subtract 26 so we end up with a value between 1 and 26. Finally, we convert the number back to the numeric value. In this example, "h" has a value of 8 since H is the 8th letter in the English alphabet; "w" has a value of 23 since it is the 23rd letter. 8 + 23 = 31. We subtract 26 to get a value of 5, which corresponds to the letter "e". Table 5-1 shows how to apply these steps to the entire words.

Table 5-1. *Applying a Simple Cipher*

Plaintext Letter	Key Letter	Plaintext Number	Key Number	Sum	Cipher Letter
h	w	8	23	5	e
e	o	5	15	20	t
l	r	12	18	4	d
l	l	12	12	24	x
o	d	15	4	19	n

Without any other context, the word "etdxn" doesn't seem to mean anything, and any would-be attackers are left frustrated. Even if they know how the cipher works, without the extra information supplied by the key, they will be stuck.

What happens if someone figured out your key, though? When this happens, the cipher becomes useless, and attackers will be able to decrypt any ciphertext that they come across later. It is imperative to keep your keys secret. Some modern systems generate keys on the fly based on secret processes, such as the time of day or the motion of a lava lamp. Apart from the keys, modern ciphers are, of course, far more complex than the example shown above, and often involve scrambling the order of letters in addition to performing various permutations on each byte of data.

There are many types of ciphers available for use in software applications. Most fall into one of two major categories. A *block-based* cipher encrypts data in certain chunk sizes. In our previous example, since our key is 5 letters long, we would want to process plaintext in sets of 5 letters. If the incoming plaintext has only 13 letters, then we can substitute random characters for the last 2 letters and discard them when we decode the message. Alternately, a *stream-based* cipher can process plaintexts of arbitrary length. Neither type is inherently more secure than the other.

Data Decryption

If a server sends your app encrypted data, you will need to write code to decrypt that data so you can process it. Similarly, if you encrypt your user's data and store it on the local filesystem, you'll decrypt that data when you need to access it. Decryption is the reverse of encryption, and transforms a ciphertext back into a plaintext, as shown in Figure 5-1.

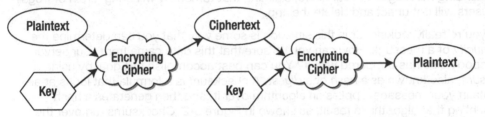

Figure 5-1. *Using a key to encrypt and decrypt a message*

We can easily decrypt the sample cipher from the previous section. For each cipher letter, convert to a number, then subtract the key's value. If the result is a negative value, count back from 26 to arrive at the plaintext. Table 5-2 shows the decryption stage.

Table 5-2. *Reversing a Simple Cipher*

Ciphertext Letter	Key Letter	Ciphertext Number	Key Number	Sum	Plaintext Letter
e	w	5	23	(26–18=)8	h
t	o	20	15	5	e
d	r	4	18	(26–14=)12	l
x	l	24	12	12	l
n	d	19	4	15	o

The most common ciphers rely on a *shared secret*, also known as a *symmetric key*, when performing decryption. This means that both the encoder and decoder must have access to the same key, which each uses to perform its operation. The past half-century has also witnessed the development of *public key* encryption, also known as an *asymmetric key* system. In this crypto system, the encryptor and the decryptor use two separate keys. This is very useful in applications like internet commerce where you want many strangers to be able to send you encrypted data, but you do not want to allow any of those strangers to decrypt each others' messages. However, the private key for an asymmetric key system is still a critical secret that must be preserved.

Validation

Encryption and decryption are useful when you want to protect an entire chunk of data so nobody else can read it. Sometimes, however, that's more protection than you really need. Suppose your weather-predicting server sent messages to the BlackBerry telling it whether or not it will rain tomorrow. You don't really care if someone else intercepts that message; however, you still worry about another situation. What if a rival programmer starts sending messages to your users, claiming that tomorrow will bring a rain of frogs? Your users will get upset and delete the app.

What you're really looking for in this situation is some way that you can determine the *authenticity* of a message. How can you be sure that this data came from your server and nobody else has tampered with it? You can best accomplish this goal by using a *checksum*, also known as a *hash* or a *digest*. A checksum is a formula that looks at all the data in your message, applies an algorithm over it, and then generates a hash representing that algorithm's result, as shown in Figure 5-2. Checksums run over the plain messages protect against inadvertent errors that may occur during transmission. To protect against intentional attacks, you can add a secret key to the end of the message, and then find the hash value generated by the combination of the message and the key. Using this method, you can pass the entire message through in unencrypted format, which allows for faster processing, and still protect against tampering. This process is sometimes referred to as *cryptographic signature*, or more informally, *signing*. The signature is proof of authorship without the overhead and inconvenience of full encryption.

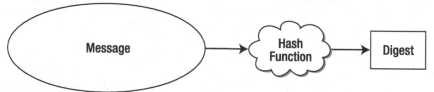

Figure 5-2. *A hash function generates a cryptographic digest for a message*

When your app receives the message, it can add the same secret key and then run that same algorithm and compare the calculated result to the received hash. If the two are the same, it can be reasonably sure that the message is authentic.

A trivial checksum might first convert every letter to a numeric value, as in our examples before, and then add the values together. It will then divide the sum by 26 and take the remainder (for a value between 0 and 25) plus 1 (for a value between 1 and 26). This final letter is then appended to the end of the string prior to submission.

Suppose we want to send the message "hello" and our secret key is "j". So, the message "helloj" is transformed to $8 + 5 + 12 + 12 + 15 + 10$, which equals 62. Dividing by 26 yields a remainder of 10, so the hash value is 11, or "k". We transmit the value "hellok," keeping the secret key out of the message. If an attacker tries to send the message "aloha" to our app, but doesn't know the key, he may send "alohak". When the app receives this message, it will add the secret "j" to the text "aloha", then transform "alohaj" to $1 + 12 + 15 + 8 + 1 + 10$, which equals 47. We divide by 26, take the remainder of 21, add 1 to get 22, and end up with "v". However, we can see that the checksum value was "k". Therefore, we know this message is not authentic, and we discard it.

You may choose to combine a checksum and a cipher for a transmitted message. This is slower than just cryptographically signing, but helps ensure both that nobody else can read the message and that the message was not modified in transit. To do this, calculate a digest for your entire message, combine the two, and then run the entire result through a cipher before sending.

There are a variety of well-known checksum algorithms available. While on the Web you have probably encountered MD5 hashes, which are used to verify that a file has not been tampered with. Some potential weaknesses have been discovered in MD5, and today most new apps should use SHA or the more secure SHA-1. If you prefer, you can roll your own checksum algorithm. However, keep in mind that anything you come up with will likely be far less secure than the more widely used technologies.

SATSA

Java ME has introduced JSR 177, the Security and Trust Services API (also known as SATSA), to address some common security concerns. Like several other JSRs, SATSA ended up being a bit of a grab bag with several disparate elements thrown in together. It defines some standard Java classes to use for cryptography, ported over from the Java SE versions. It also defines interfaces for interacting with SIM cards and managing security certificates. Individual manufacturers can decide which components of SATSA they wish to implement and which they do not.

Thus, even though RIM has technically supported SATSA since device software version 4.2.1, they have adopted only the SIM card–related functions. They have also taken some, but not all, of the certificate-management classes. None of the cryptography classes were adopted.

As you will shortly see, there are still plenty of options available. RIM has offered their own security classes since long before they adopted SATSA, and it makes sense that they would not have imported the duplicate functionality of the SATSA crypto packages. The downside, of course, is that you cannot easily port Java ME applications written using SATSA crypto to run on BlackBerry.

Bouncy Castle

While SATSA can be very useful, it implements only a subset of the many available cryptographic systems. Additionally, RIM and many other manufacturers have not added SATSA support to their devices. To make up for these deficiencies, an open source project called Bouncy Castle has gained a lot of attention and support. Bouncy Castle provides free access to a wide variety of crypto functions.

An Introduction

Most security algorithms are well-documented in academic literature. However, the actual implementations of those algorithms tend to be written by for-profit companies who make money by licensing their use. Bouncy Castle started when two programmers grew tired of needing to reimplement standard security classes every time they switched projects. There is no great secret behind how each algorithm works—the real secret is the key—but such ad-hoc rewrites are not only tedious and time-consuming, they also increases the risk of writing a flaw that may allow the code to be exploited. The programmers decided to start a new project that would allow them and other developers to reuse a stable, proven base of cryptographic classes.

Bouncy Castle contains a *clean room* implementation of major crypto classes, meaning that they were written based on documentation and not by looking at any pre-existing code. Therefore, no other company's patents or copyrights are applied to Bouncy Castle. The code is open source and made available under a version of the MIT X Consortium license, which is widely considered quite reasonable. The license is also quite short, so you should read it and understand it before using the code in your own project.

Adding Bouncy Castle to Your Project

Because Bouncy Castle is not part of the standard RIM environment, you must manually add the classes to your project. You can download the entire Bouncy Castle source from the website at www.bouncycastle.org. Bouncy Castle exists for many different versions of Java; you will want to download the latest release of the lightweight J2ME implementation, a .zip file that contains the compiled classes, source code, tests, and documentation. When you see it, you may gulp—it is several megabytes. Needless to say, this could have a significant impact on your binary size.

Fortunately, because you have access to the source, you can simply add the classes you need to your project and ignore the rest. Alternately, you can add everything at once, and later go back to trim it out. Pulling in all the code except for the tests and examples will increase the size of your program by about 600 kb; the impact is far less if you import only the classes you need.

To import the classes in Eclipse, right-click on your projects source folder and select Import. Expand the General window and select File System, then click Next. Browse to the location on your hard drive where you unzipped the Bouncy Castle .zip file, and select the src folder. You can check src to import everything, or expand it and select only the files you need. When done, click Finish.

> **Note:** If building outside of Eclipse, you might consider using an *obfuscator*—a third-party program that can be used to automatically remove unused code from your program. The most widely used obfuscator for Java ME is Proguard.

When you import the source files, note that some of them are included in the java.* package tree. Java ME is missing some common Java SE classes that are needed for Bouncy Castle to function properly, such as BigInteger. The download contains reimplementations of these classes. On some versions of the RIM software, you may need to rename the packages because the classloader does not approve of loading user-created code in the java namespace. The easiest way to rename is to right-click on a package in the Package Explorer, select Refactor and then Rename…, change the name to something like xjava.io, and finally click OK. Eclipse will work its magic, searching for and automatically converting all references to the affected files. Repeat for any remaining packages.

Using Bouncy Castle in Encryption

Bouncy Castle is too vast to completely cover here. This section focuses on the essentials for encoding or decoding messages. Consult the API documents to learn more details on how specific ciphers work.

The two most important types of classes in the package are *ciphers* and *engines*. A cipher describes a generic interface for how encryption or decryption operations behave. The root cipher classes include BufferedBlockCipher and StreamCipher. Each defines the core operations of a cipher: initializing with a key, processing blocks of bytes and returning results. Subclasses of each can define custom behavior, such as how to pad extra bytes in a block cipher.

Any given cipher class can be initialized with a variety of compatible engines. The engine takes care of the actual process of converting bytes into ciphertext, while the cipher takes care of passing around input and output. Engines implement one of two main interfaces. BlockCipher is used for a variety of symmetric key cipher engines, including AES. AsymmetricBlockCipher is used for asymmetric key cipher engines, including RSA. Each individual engine is usually initialized with a CipherParameters object, which provides the key or other data needed by the engine.

In many cases, your app will be working within an existing crypto system. For example, you may already have a server that accepts data in Blowfish, in which case you can simply start using the BlowfishEngine class. If you are responsible for setting up a new crypto system, then read about each cipher to determine which ones best fit your needs. Most often you will need to decide between speed and protection. Of course, the strongest cipher won't help if you fail to keep your keys secure.

Once you have set up your cipher appropriately, you just need to feed it data. All ciphers work on arrays of bytes, so if your input is some other format, like a String or an InputStream, you will need to access the underlying bytes first. After encryption is complete, you will have access to the encoded byte stream. The following code example demonstrates a sample encryption from a plaintext string into an encoded version. This sample uses the Twofish cipher, a very secure algorithm with pretty good performance. The cipher is initialized with a preshared secret string, and true to indicate that the cipher should perform encryption. Next, the input bytes are encoded. Note that the doFinal() method call is necessary for a block-based cipher like Twofish in order to fill out the remainder of the last block. At the end of the process we have the raw bytes. Here we construct a string to display, but this step often doesn't make sense, since the encrypted ciphertext contains many nonprintable characters.

```
String plaintextString = "Five Tons of Flax";
byte[] plaintextBytes = plaintextString.getBytes();
String keyString = "illuminati";
byte[] keyBytes = keyString.getBytes();
KeyParameter key = new KeyParameter(keyBytes);

TwofishEngine twofish = new TwofishEngine();
BufferedBlockCipher cipher = new PaddedBufferedBlockCipher(twofish);
cipher.init(true, key);

byte[] cipherBytes = new byte[cipher.getOutputSize(plaintextBytes.length)];

int cipherLength = cipher.processBytes(plaintextBytes, 0, ↩
        plaintextBytes.length, cipherBytes, 0);
cipher.doFinal(cipherBytes, cipherLength);
String cipherString = new String(cipherBytes);
System.out.println("Encrypted cipher is [" + cipherString + "]");
```

> **Tip:** Notice that we allocate a byte buffer large enough to hold the entire ciphertext. This is fine for short messages like this one, but if we were encrypting a 10 MB data file, we might not be able to allocate that much contiguous memory. Later in this chapter you'll see an example of how to allocate a smaller buffer that can be reused to progressively encrypt or decrypt a larger message.

You should prepare to catch a CryptoException, which will occur if any problems happen during the process. When you run the code, you should see the encrypted message.

> **Caution:** In an actual application, you should use a randomly generated binary key for maximum security. Using a dictionary word, or even a combination of printable characters, makes your key easier to guess.

Using Bouncy Castle in Decryption

The exact same classes can be used for decryption as for encryption. Typically, all you need to do is substitute false for true in your cipher's init() method. The overall process is the same: after initialization, you feed the ciphertext bytes into the cipher, finalize if necessary, and then use the output decoded bytes. The following example continues the previous one, taking the encrypted cipherBytes and restoring them to their original state. Note that we can reuse the existing crypto classes here.

```
cipher.init(false, key);
byte[] decryptedBytes = new byte[cipher.getOutputSize(cipherBytes.length)];
int decryptedLength = cipher.processBytes(cipherBytes, 0, ↵
        cipherBytes.length, decryptedBytes, 0);
cipher.doFinal(decryptedBytes, decryptedLength);
String decryptedString = new String(decryptedBytes);
System.out.println("Decrypted message is [" + decryptedString + "]");
```

Using Bouncy Castle to Create Digests

You can find classes for the most popular message digest algorithms in Bouncy Castle, including SHA1Digest and MD5Digest. Unlike ciphers, no initialization is necessary for digests, and you only interact with one class to make the digest. If you just wish to create a simple checksum to ensure that the message was not corrupted, you can feed bytes directly to the digest. To cryptographically sign the message as discussed earlier, you should add a secret key to the beginning or the end of your message, generate the digest, and then attach the digest to the message. Digests typically follow the message body. The following code generates an SHA-1 hash for a message/key combination.

```
String message = "Yond Cassius has a lean and hungry look";
String postfix = "caesar";
byte[] messageBytes = message.getBytes();
byte[] postfixBytes = postfix.getBytes();
SHA1Digest digest = new SHA1Digest();
digest.update(messageBytes, 0, messageBytes.length);
digest.update(postfixBytes, 0, postfixBytes.length);
byte[] hash = new byte[digest.getDigestSize()];
digest.doFinal(hash, 0);
```

As with ciphers, digests generate their output as raw byte data. This poses a problem if your app transmits plain text, such as XML or JSON, because it cannot transmit the non-printable characters. The customary solution to this problem is to encode hash values in Base64. Base64 converts raw byte values to a 64-character alphabet of printable characters, including A–Z, a–z, 0–9, "+" and "/". This will slightly expand the number of characters, but ensures that they can be transmitted. Bouncy Castle includes a useful Base64Encoder class that converts between binary and Base64. Despite the name, the class can be used for both encoding and decoding. The next example uses this class to convert the previous hash into a regular String, and then attaches it to the message for transmission. Depending on your message format, the final hash may be placed in an XML tag or similar element.

```
Base64Encoder base64 = new Base64Encoder();
ByteArrayOutputStream out = new ByteArrayOutputStream();
base64.encode(hash, 0, hash.length, out);
byte[] base64Bytes = out.toByteArray();
String hashString = new String(base64Bytes);
String transmitted = message + "\n" + hashString;
System.out.println("Transmitted message is [" + transmitted + "]");
```

Using Bouncy Castle to Verify Digests

As you would expect, verification of a digest is the reverse of creating one. Once you
receive the complete message, separate the digest from the message body. If the
message is cryptographically signed, attach the key to the body. Use the same digest
algorithm to calculate a hash. If the received hash used Base64 encoding, either decode
the received hash or encode your calculated one. Finally, confirm whether the two
hashes are identical. If they are, you know that the message sender possessed the
proper key. The next example shows how to verify the message generated by the
previous example.

```
String received;
int separation = received.indexOf('\n');
String receivedHash = received.substring(separation + 1);
String message = received.substring(0, separation);
byte[] messageBytes = message.getBytes();
String postfix = "caesar";
byte[] postfixBytes = postfix.getBytes();
SHA1Digest digest = new SHA1Digest();
digest.update(messageBytes, 0, messageBytes.length);
digest.update(postfixBytes, 0, postfixBytes.length);
byte[] calculatedHash = new byte[digest.getDigestSize()];
digest.doFinal(calculatedHash, 0);
ByteArrayOutputStream output = new ByteArrayOutputStream();
Base64Encoder base64 = new Base64Encoder();
base64.decode(receivedHash, output);
byte[] receivedHashBytes = output.toByteArray();
if (Arrays.equals(calculatedHash, receivedHashBytes))
{
    System.out.println("Message is valid.");
}
else
{
    System.out.println("Et tu, Internet?");
}
```

Bouncy Castle Analysis

Bouncy Castle offers several advantages that make it worth serious consideration:

- You can easily port your code to Java ME devices.

- Because it is widely used, it has received a lot of scrutiny and is widely
  considered to be quite secure.

- It provides classes for most major cryptographic algorithms.

You should look elsewhere if any of the following issues concern you:

- You must follow the terms of the open-source license.

- No commercial support is available.

- Using Bouncy Castle will increase your application size.

RIM Crypto Classes

BlackBerry devices use a host of security options as part of their ordinary operations, and many of those algorithms are available for you to use as a developer. Most of these algorithms are the same as those available in Bouncy Castle, but these have been implemented specifically for Research In Motion and are available exclusively for development on BlackBerry devices.

> **Caution:** Depending on your geographic location, agreement with RIM, and other factors, you may not have access to the RIM Crypto API code signing keys required for these classes. If this is the case, consider using Bouncy Castle or another crypto solution.

An Introduction

While the RIM crypto classes are not quite as complete as those in Bouncy Castle, they do contain a wide range of available algorithms. You can start using them immediately as you would any other RIM-specific classes. The available items are located in the `net.rim.device.api.crypto` package. Encryption and decryption are handled through a set of standard elements:

- A key, implementing the Key interface, is used to initialize a cipher with the secret or public key. The major types are `PublicKey`, `PrivateKey`, and `SymmetricKey`. Each cipher has its own particular implementing key class.

- Stream-based ciphers are provided as subclasses of `StreamEncryptor` or `SteamDecryptor`. Note that, unlike Bouncy Castle, the RIM API uses separate classes to handle decryption than are used for encryption.

- Block-based ciphers implement `BlockEncryptorEngine` or `BlockDecryptorEngine`. Subinterfaces define the type of key used, such as `PublicKeyEncryptorEngine` and `SymmetricKeyEncryptorEngine`.

- Block-based ciphers can use implementations of the `BlockFormatterEngine` interface to provide padding to their crypto tasks.

Tip: Make use of Eclipse's auto-complete feature by typing the start of a class name, then holding down Ctrl while pressing Space. A list of valid selections will display. As a bonus, Eclipse automatically adds the required import statements to your `java` class. For example, if you wish to use RC5 encryption, you can type RC5 and press auto-complete, and you will see `RC5Key`, `RC5EncryptorEngine`, and `RC5DecryptorEngine`.

The actual classes are very well named, with all relevant classes sharing a common prefix. RIM divides their classes into a set of libraries. For space considerations, only a limited subset may be available on a given device. All devices are guaranteed to, at a minimum, include classes for SHA-1 checksums. Devices may optionally also include classes for WTLS, Wireless Transport Layer Security. This will be delivered in the file `net_rim_crypto_1.cod`, and includes support for additional digest and encryption algorithms, as shown in Table 5-3.

Table 5-3. Crypto Resources in `net_rim_crypto_1`

Digests	Encryptions
SHA256	AES
SHA384	ARC4
SHA512	DES
MD5	TripleDES
	RC4
	RC5
	RSA PKCS v1.5

To see if your device includes crypto1, select Options from the main menu, click Advanced Options and then Applications. Press the menu key and select Modules. This will bring up the list of every COD file loaded on the device. Scroll down and see if `net_rim_crypto_1` is included. Most modern devices appear to include this library, along with its companions `net_rim_crypto_2` and `net_rim_crypto_3`.

`net_rim_crypto_2` will only be present if the first one is. This library adds support for SSL/TLS (Secure Sockets Layer/Transport Layer Security), which introduces support for RSA PKCS (Public Key Cryptography Standard) version 2.0.

Finally, `net_rim_crypto_3` may also be present if the first two are. It adds a somewhat random assortment of additional, less commonly used crypto resources, as shown in Table 5-4.

Table 5-4. *Crypto Resources in* `net_rim_crypto_3`

Digests	Encryptions
MD2	CAST-128(CAST5)
MD4	RC2
RIPEMD-128	Skipjack
RIPEMD-160	ECIES
	ElGamal
	RSA-PSS
	RSA ANSI X9.31

In practice, unless you know that your users are likely to be on limited devices, it is reasonable to write your app assuming all these algorithms are available, and to instruct users to acquire them if they happen to not be installed.

Encryption with the RIM Crypto Classes

While the general process of encryption proceeds similarly whether you are using Bouncy Castle or the RIM libraries, the actual details vary. You start by creating the secret key for the operation. Next, create either a stream encryptor or a block encryptor engine. If using a block cipher and your messages are not already padded, create a formatter engine. The RIM BlockEncryptor class plays a similar role to the Bouncy Castle Cipher classes: it manages the details of passing around the input plaintext, running the engine appropriately, and generating the output ciphertext. Unlike Bouncy Castle, which outputs directly to a byte array, RIM will write the ciphertext into an OutputStream. This can be convenient if you wish to direct the encoded message to a file or network connection, without managing the actual bytes. The code that follows shows how to encrypt a message using the RIM RC5 classes.

```
String messageString = "The falcon cannot hear the falconer.";
byte[] messageBytes = messageString.getBytes();
String keyString = "beast";
byte[] keyBytes = keyString.getBytes();
RC5Key key = new RC5Key(keyBytes);
RC5EncryptorEngine engine = new RC5EncryptorEngine(key);
PKCS5FormatterEngine padder = new PKCS5FormatterEngine(engine);
ByteArrayOutputStream output = new ByteArrayOutputStream();
BlockEncryptor encryptor = new BlockEncryptor(padder, output);
encryptor.write(messageBytes);
encryptor.close();
output.flush();
byte[] cipherBytes = output.toByteArray();
String cipherString = new String(cipherBytes);
```

```
System.out.println("Encoded message is [" + cipherString + "]");
```

You can adapt this example for any other type of block cipher. For stream encryption, you will provide the OutputStream directly to the StreamEncryptor subclass's constructor and omit the padder.

Several exceptions may occur during encryption and decryption operations. CryptoUnsupportedOperationException indicates that this particular algorithm is not supported. CryptoTokenException occurs when the operation is associated with a physical token, such as a smart card, that is not present or has a problem. Finally, a generic IOException may occur due to problems writing to the requested OutputStream.

Decryption with the RIM Crypto Classes

As mentioned before, the RIM libraries include separate classes to handle the decryption step. For example, the RC5DecryptorEngine is the counterpart of RC5EncryptorEngine, and a BlockUnformatterEngine matches a BlockFormatterEngine. The most significant difference between encryption and decryption is that decryption writes its output into a provided byte array, not an OutputStream. If you do not know in advance how large a message will be, you will need to progressively build up the decrypted message yourself. The example below illustrates how to do this, decrypting the ciphertext that was generated above. You'll notice the loop that repeatedly reads data in small chunks. This is a common pattern that is used in many I/O operations other than crypto.

```
byte[] cipherBytes;
String keyString = "beast";
byte[] keyBytes = keyString.getBytes();
RC5Key key = new RC5Key(keyBytes);
RC5DecryptorEngine engine = new RC5DecryptorEngine(key);
PKCS5UnformatterEngine unpadder = new PKCS5UnformatterEngine(engine);
ByteArrayInputStream input = new ByteArrayInputStream(cipherBytes);
BlockDecryptor decryptor = new BlockDecryptor(unpadder, input);
ByteArrayOutputStream decryptedStream = new ByteArrayOutputStream();
byte[] buffer = new byte[1024];
int bytesRead = 0;
do
{
    bytesRead = decryptor.read(buffer);
    if (bytesRead != -1)
    {
```

```
        decryptedStream.write(buffer, 0, bytesRead);
    }
} while (bytesRead != -1);
byte[] decryptedBytes = decryptedStream.toByteArray();
String decodedMessage = new String(decryptedBytes);
System.out.println("Original message was [" + decodedMessage + "]");
```

Using RIM Crypto with Digests

The RIM crypto packages include several popular hash algorithms, including multiple versions of SHA and MD. As when creating digests for Bouncy Castle, you may run a digest over an entire message and obtain a hash. For this section's examples, we'll create unsigned digests to simply verify message integrity, but you can apply the exact same principles as before to cryptographically sign your messages.

RIM does add some convenient classes to use in digest operations. Unlike Bouncy Castle digests, which are more focused on byte arrays for operations, RIM digests can work with streams. You may choose to wrap several streams together to obtain a desired result. The following code example demonstrates how to use two useful utility stream, Base64OutputStream and DigestOutputStream, to automatically Base64 encode the digest value. Data flows from the input bytes, through the digest algorithm, out to the digest stream, then through Base64 encoding, and finally to the destination bytes.

```
String message = "Not all who wander are lost.";
byte[] messageBytes = message.getBytes();
MD5Digest digest = new MD5Digest();
ByteArrayOutputStream bytesOut = new ByteArrayOutputStream();
Base64OutputStream base64 = new Base64OutputStream(bytesOut);
DigestOutputStream digestOut = new DigestOutputStream(digest, base64);
digest.update(messageBytes);
digestOut.flush();
byte[] base64Checksum = bytesOut.toByteArray();
String base64String = new String(base64Checksum);
```

If you wish to verify the checksum for data you have received, follow the exact same code as before, comparing the calculated base64Checksum with the version you received. If they are identical, the message was not corrupted since it was sent. You may also use a cryptographic signing strategy if you wish to verify the authenticity of the sender.

RIM Crypto Analysis

Turn to the built-in RIM solution in the following situations:

- You want to minimize the size of your application.
- You cannot accept the conditions of an open-source library.
- You expect to only run on BlackBerry devices.
- You control the BlackBerry devices that will be running your app.

Consider another solution if the following are high priorities for you:

- There is a chance that users have removed support for advanced crypto from their devices.

- Certain crypto algorithms are not supported.

Using the Certicom Classes

Several classes in the `net.rim.device.api.crypto` package are not available for use in most applications. However, if you are developing commercial applications with needs such as secure electronic commerce, you may find them very useful.

An Introduction

You can safely write all RIM crypto classes into your code and even run with them in the simulator, but when you try to run your app on the device, you may face an error message like `Uncaught exception: Missing RCC signature. Not allowed to access Certicom functionality`. To access these classes, you must contact Certicom, a subsidiary of Research In Motion that owns the rights to these functions. You can do this by accessing their website at `http://certicom.com/rim`, where you can contact a member of their sales team. Once you receive approval, you will receive additional code signing keys that permit access to these restricted APIs. Certicom classes will be of greatest interest to "serious" applications with strong business aspects, particularly mobile commerce. Most applications can consider using other forms of encryption instead, including the RSA classes included in Bouncy Castle.

You can determine which classes require the use of a Certicom license by consulting the API javadocs. The most interesting ones are the public-key systems, including the Elliptic Curve Integrated Encryption Scheme (ECIES), the Digital Signature Algorithm (DSA), Diffie-Hellman (DH), Key Exchange Algorithm (KEA), and RSA.

Public key encryption tackles the difficult problem of how to establish secure communication with another party if you have not previously agreed upon a secret key to use. Our previous encryption example required both the sender and the receiver to use the same key, which is reasonable if we are writing the code for both parties, but would not work in situations where we expect to receive messages from other applications or senders. Public Key Infrastructure (PKI) is based upon some interesting modern mathematics that shows how you can create a system with multiple keys that allows for one-way encryption. In other words, everyone can know a public key that allows them to encrypt a message, but only one person knows the secret private key. Public key encryption is most often thought of as encoding and decoding messages, but it also plays a useful role in determining another party's authenticity. If you receive a message from someone else, and can decrypt it using their public key, then you know that it was signed by the actual sender's private key. RSA, the most famous and widely used public key system, relies on modulus operations and the difficulty of finding very large prime numbers. If you're interested in learning more about the history and mathematics behind public key encryption, I highly recommend *The Code Book* by

Simon Singh (Anchor), the most intelligent and approachable book I've found yet on the topic of cryptography.

Encryption with Certicom Public Keys

RIM's asymmetric ciphers are based around the CryptoSystem interface. Each also includes a PublicKey, a PrivateKey, and several other classes relating to that crypto system's operation. The issue of key distribution is outside the scope of this chapter. If your app only needs to encrypt outgoing messages, it can be configured with the recipient's public key, but if the app needs to decrypt incoming messages, you must decide how best to give senders access to the client's public key. With that in mind, the following code demonstrates how you can use Certicom's implementation of RSA cryptography to encrypt a message. Here, we construct a random pair of public and private keys; in real applications, these would likely be generated from known key values. Because the underlying cipher is a block cipher, we wrap and pad it as before, then run the input through the cipher to generate the encrypted message.

```
String message = "Purple monkey dishwasher";
byte[] messageBytes = message.getBytes();
RSACryptoSystem rsa = new RSACryptoSystem(1024);
RSAKeyPair keyPair = new RSAKeyPair(rsa);
RSAEncryptorEngine rsaEncryption = new RSAEncryptorEngine(↵
        keyPair.getRSAPublicKey());
PKCS5FormatterEngine padder = new PKCS5FormatterEngine(rsaEncryption);
ByteArrayOutputStream output = new ByteArrayOutputStream();
BlockEncryptor encryptor = new BlockEncryptor(padder, output);
encryptor.write(messageBytes);
encryptor.close();
output.flush();
byte[] ciphertextBytes = output.toByteArray();
```

Decryption with Certicom Public Keys

To decrypt this message, the receiver will use a private key part of the pair, and then run the received message through the decrypting system. The BlockDecryptor class operates on a byte array, so the following example builds up a total output array through repeated operations on a byte buffer.

```
RSADecryptorEngine rsaDecryption = new RSADecryptorEngine(↵
        keyPair.getRSAPrivateKey());
PKCS5UnformatterEngine unpadder = new PKCS5UnformatterEngine(rsaDecryption);
ByteArrayInputStream input = new ByteArrayInputStream(ciphertextBytes);
BlockDecryptor decryptor = new BlockDecryptor(unpadder, input);
byte[] buffer = new byte[1024];
ByteArrayOutputStream out = new ByteArrayOutputStream();
int bytesRead = 0;
do
{
    bytesRead = decryptor.read(buffer);
    if (bytesRead != -1)
```

```
    {
        out.write(buffer, 0, bytesRead);
    }
} while (bytesRead != -1);
byte[] decryptedBytes = out.toByteArray();
String decryptedMessage = new String(decryptedBytes);
System.out.println("Decrypted message is " + decryptedMessage);
```

As with the regular RIM crypto package, you will need to catch `CryptoException` and `IOException`. Even if your application has received Certicom signatures, there's still a small chance that the required crypto libraries will not be loaded on the device, in which case your app may choose to present an error message.

> **Caution:** Several class names in the RIM crypto package clash with those found in the standard Java libraries and other packages. For example, `RSAPrivateKey` is used both in `net.rim.device.api.crypto` and in `java.security.interfaces`. Double-check the package names of your imports.

If you wish to store keys for crypto operations, consider using the keystore classes located in the `net.device.api.crypto.keystore` package. You can choose from a variety of keystore types, including stores that only persist until the device is reset and stores that can be synced to the user's computer via the desktop manager. Also available under the crypto package are classes for certificate management, useful to help control and determine the authority that backs keys you receive.

Certicom Analysis

For the most part, use of Certicom requires the same choices considered for RIM Crypto. Specifically, you keep your code size small and avoid potential licensing issues, but are restricted to a particular set of ciphers and locked in to RIM's API. The significant extra detriment for Certicom is the extra cost involved in acquiring the keys. Balanced against this is the confidence many institutions and individuals have in dealing with a business as a provider of strong encryption.

Other Encryption Choices

So far, this chapter has examined how to implement cryptographic systems within your app. You have seen how this requires making appropriate choices about the specific crypto algorithm you will use, how to create and distribute keys, and other issues. However, it is possible to get cryptographic security through existing systems without inventing your own. Consider the options covered in this section if you want more passive protection.

HTTPS Encryption

If your app communicates with a server that already supports HTTPS, you can omit additional encryption in your messages. BlackBerry devices support HTTPS out of the box, and a connection between your app and an HTTPS server will be as secure as the connection between your web browser and an HTTPS website. You can create an HTTPS connection by using the proper protocol string, as in the example that follows:

```
HttpsConnection https = (HttpsConnection) Connector↵
    .open("https://www.amazon.com");
```

HTTPS encryption is applied through the use of public key encryption. When your app first issues a request to a server using the https:// protocol, the TLS/SSL will take over. A handshake begins between the client and the server. The client will notify the server what types of encryption it supports (DES, DSA, etc.) and provide a random string to the server. The server will respond with its own random string, along with a certificate and its public key. The client will inspect the certificate to see whether or not it is valid; if it is, it can trust that it is dealing with the actual server. The client then creates a random *premaster secret* that will be used as the basis for an encryption key, encrypts that premaster secret with the server's public key, and then transmits it to the server.

Even if an attacker intercepts this transmission, he will not be able to decrypt the premaster secret without the server's private key. The server can decrypt the premaster secret. Both the client and the server then use that premaster secret to generate a master secret, and finally create *session keys* from the master secret. The session key is a symmetric key that will be used to encrypt all future traffic between the client and the server during this session (that is, until it times out).

The initial handshake can be a little slow. Once the symmetric key is determined and encrypted traffic begins, transmission will be a little slower and take a little more space than it would be in regular HTTP communication due to the overhead of encryption. The difference tends not to be very noticeable.

If your application uses lower-level socket programming instead of higher-level HTTP communication, you can use the ssl:// or tls:// protocols, which will generate an SSL or TLS session. These perform handshakes similarly to HTTPS, but subsequent traffic is carried over a low-level socket instead of higher-level HTTP. The following code demonstrates how to create each type of connection.

```
SecureConnection ssl = (SecureConnection) Connector↵
        .open("ssl://myserver.com:5555");
SecureConnection tls = (SecureConnection) Connector↵
        .open("tls://myserver.com:5556");
```

After the connection is established, you can use each SecureConnection as you would an ordinary SocketConnection. You can also call getSecurityInfo() to obtain additional details about the negotiated security, such as the server's certificate and the cipher being used for crypto.

> **Note:** After establishing a secure connection, encryption is applied in both directions, on both outgoing and incoming data.

MDS Encryption

All traffic between the BlackBerry device and the Mobile Data System is automatically encrypted. As a result, if you make sure that outgoing traffic is sent to a server on your corporate BES environment and travels over the BES network, no extra encryption is necessary. However, traffic sent between the MDS and the ultimate destination server is not encrypted. You still may need to use encryption if the receiving server expects encrypted traffic, or if you are concerned about eavesdropping from other entities within the corporate network.

File Encryption

In addition to manual file encryption using Bouncy Castle or the RIM Crypto APIs, you may also choose to apply built-in support for file encryption. RIM offers a custom interface called `ExtendedFileConnection` that extends the standard `FileConnection` interface. Any `FileConnection` can be cast to an `ExtendedFileConnection` and provides access to several additional features for encryption.

- `enableDRMForwardLock()` will allow other applications on the device to read this file, but prevents it from being read when transferred off the device. If the user copies the file to their computer, it will be copied in an encrypted format. This method works on both the /store and the /SDCard roots.

- `setControlledAccess()` controls access to this file so that only your application can read or write it. You must obtain a `CodeSigningKey` for your module and then set it on the `ExtendedFileConnection`. When the file is accessed in the future, the OS will verify that the request comes from the module that signed it. This method works on the SD card but not on the internal memory store.

In both cases, you must set any protection before you create the file. You can access standard file encryption as shown in the following example.

```
ExtendedFileConnection file = (ExtendedFileConnection)Connector.open⏎
    ("file:///SDCard/BlackBerry/purchase.mp3");
file.enableDRMForwardLock();
file.create();
```

Once the file has been created, you can open streams to read and write data as you normally would. The encryption is automatically applied and removed by the operating system, with no extra intervention needed.

App: Securing MediaGrabber

MediaGrabber provides a convenient way to record your thoughts, take pictures of your surroundings, and send such info off to a place where you can review it later. Occasionally, though, you might be a little nervous about what happens to your media once it leaves your phone. Perhaps your musings about pursuing another job will be overheard by a bored IT worker monitoring your business email account. Or maybe you don't want your father or son to accidentally open pictures from your Vegas trip sent to your shared home computer. Let's add an extra layer of security by providing the ability to encrypt the media we sent out.

Adding Encryption

We will be using the DES encryption algorithm for this enhancement, using the version provided in the RIM crypto packages. DES actually is not a great algorithm; modern computers can use brute force to crack it. I chose it here because the key size is nice and short. You may choose to use AES-128 or a similar block cipher for added security at the cost of greater complexity.

To add an extra layer of security, we will also be using an *initialization vector*. The vector, known as IV, is a bit of random information that is combined with the key in the encryption. This helps protect the secrecy of the key. If you encrypt two messages with the same key, then attackers can more easily decrypt the messages; using a random IV is one of several ways to help avoid this problem. The IV protects the key but is not itself secret, so we will send it along with the message so the recipient can decrypt it.

The actual changes to add encryption are rather brief. We will add the following two new instance variables to the SendingScreen to manage the crypto operations.

```
private boolean encrypt;
private String iv;
```

The constructor will be updated to accept encryption as an additional parameter. Then we can write a new method encryptData() that applies our secret DES key to binary data. I find it's easiest to represent key values in hexadecimal strings. Each character in a hex string can represent 16 characters, and so it holds 4 bits of data. We can write simple utility functions that will translate hex string values to and from the byte arrays that the crypto classes prefer to work with.

The only other piece to update is the createMessage() method, which will check to see whether encryption was requested. If so, it will call our new method to encrypt the attachment data and include the initialization vector information in the plaintext of the message. The rest of the send operation runs the same as before. The modified methods are shown in Listing 5-1.

Listing 5-1. *Optionally Encrypting Attachments Prior to Sending*

```
private byte[] bytesFromHexString(String input)
{
    int length = input.length();
```

```java
        // Each hex character represents 4 bits, so 1
        // byte is 2 characters.
        byte[] bytes = new byte[length / 2];
        for (int i = 0; i < length; i += 2)
        {
            bytes[i / 2] = (byte) Integer.parseInt(input.substring(i, i + 2),
                    16);
        }
        return bytes;
    }

    private String hexFromBytes(byte[] input)
    {
        int length = input.length;
        StringBuffer builder = new StringBuffer(length * 2);
        for (int i = 0; i < length; ++i)
        {
            byte value = (byte) input[i];
            String hex = Integer.toHexString(value);
            if (hex.length() == 8)
            {
                // Integer.toHexString assumes "negative" 4-byte inputs yield an
                // 8-character string, so trim off all but the last 2
                // characters.
                hex = hex.substring(6);
            }
            builder.append(hex);
        }
        return builder.toString();
    }

    private byte[] encryptData(byte[] in) throws CryptoException, IOException
    {
        ByteArrayOutputStream out = new ByteArrayOutputStream();
        String hexKey = "2BEAFABBABE4AFAD";
        byte[] binaryKey = bytesFromHexString(hexKey);
        DESKey key = new DESKey(binaryKey);
        DESEncryptorEngine encryptor = new DESEncryptorEngine(key);
        InitializationVector vector = new InitializationVector(8);
        byte[] ivValue = vector.getData();
        iv = hexFromBytes(ivValue);
        CFBEncryptor cfb = new CFBEncryptor(encryptor, vector, out, true);
        cfb.write(in);
        out.flush();
        return out.toByteArray();
    }
    private Message createMessage(String recipient, String type,
            String filename, String message) throws MessagingException,
            CryptoException, IOException
    {
        if (encrypt)
            data = encryptData(data);
        Store defaultStore = Session.getDefaultInstance().getStore();
        Folder sentFolder = defaultStore.getFolder(Folder.SENT);
        Message outgoing = new Message(sentFolder);
```

```
    Address friend = new Address(recipient, "");
    outgoing.addRecipient(Message.RecipientType.TO, friend);
    outgoing.setSubject(message);
    Multipart multipart = new Multipart();
    SupportedAttachmentPart file = new SupportedAttachmentPart(multipart,
            type, filename, data);
    multipart.addBodyPart(file);
    TextBodyPart text = new TextBodyPart(multipart);
    if (encrypt)
    {
        text.setContent("The attached file is encrypted, the vector is "
                + iv);
    }
    else
    {
        text.setContent("Check this out!");
    }
    multipart.addBodyPart(text);
    outgoing.setContent(multipart);
    return outgoing;
}
```

Better Choices

Our little app is getting quite feature-rich. Let's allow our users to easily decide what operation they want to take on each piece of media they record. We can easily do this by adding additional menu items in the recording screen: rather than automatically perform a particular operation once they have acquired the media, we will allow them to make a selection from a menu. We will add two new states, STATE_RECORDED and STATE_RECORDED_IMAGE, to represent the condition where the user has finished media capture. We also will store information about the captured media. Based on these states, additional options will be presented in the menu. Best of all, the user can now perform multiple operations on the same media; for example, she can first view it, and then send two encrypted copies. Listing 5-2 shows the modifications to our improved recording screen.

Listing 5-2. A Better Recording Screen

```
package com.apress.king.mediagrabber;
// Imports here

public class RecordingScreen extends MainScreen implements PlayerListener
{
    public static final int STATE_WAITING = 1;
    public static final int STATE_READY = 2;
    public static final int STATE_RECORDING = 3;
    public static final int STATE_RECORDED = 4;
    public static final int STATE_RECORDED_IMAGE = 5;

    // Additional member variables
    private String filename;
    private String contentType;
    private String message;
```

```java
        private byte[] data;

        // New menu items
        private MenuItem playItem = new MenuItem("Play", 0, 0)
        {
            public void run()
            {
                play();
            }
        };
        private MenuItem showItem = new MenuItem("Show", 0, 0)
        {
            public void run()
            {
                showPicture();
            }
        };
        private MenuItem sendItem = new MenuItem("Send", 0, 0)
        {
            public void run()
            {
                send(false);
            }
        };
        private MenuItem sendEncryptedItem = new MenuItem("Send Encrypted", 0, 0)
        {
            public void run()
            {
                send(true);
            }
        };

        // New menu options
        public void makeMenu(Menu menu, int instance)
        {
            if (instance == Menu.INSTANCE_DEFAULT)
            {
                if (state == STATE_READY)
                {
                    menu.add(goItem);
                }
                else if (state == STATE_RECORDING)
                {
                    menu.add(stopItem);
                }
                else if (state == STATE_RECORDED)
                {
                    menu.add(playItem);
                    menu.add(sendItem);
                    menu.add(sendEncryptedItem);
                }
                else if (state == STATE_RECORDED_IMAGE)
                {
                    menu.add(showItem);
                    menu.add(sendItem);
```

```
                menu.add(sendEncryptedItem);
            }
            menu.add(doneItem);
        }
        super.makeMenu(menu, instance);
    }

    // Modified capture
    private void takeSnapShot()
    {
        try
        {
            data = video
                    .getSnapshot("encoding=jpeg&width=640&height=480&quality=normal");
            if (data != null)
            {
                String file = location + "/image.jpg";
                writeToFile(data, file);
                status.setText("Image taken");
                filename = "image.jpg";
                contentType = "image/jpeg";
                message = "Here's a picture!";
                state = STATE_RECORDED_IMAGE;
            }
            else
            {
                status.setText("Please try again later.");
            }
        }
        catch (IOException ioe)
        {
            status.setText(ioe.getMessage());
        }
        catch (MediaException me)
        {
            status.setText(me.getMessage());
        }
    }

    private void stop()
    {
        try
        {
            if (type == RECORD_AUDIO || type == RECORD_VIDEO)
            {
                recorder.commit();
                data = dataOut.toByteArray();
                if (type == RECORD_AUDIO)
                {
                    String file = location + "/audio.amr";
                    writeToFile(data, file);
                    contentType = "audio/amr";
                    message = "Here's some sound!";
                    filename = "audio.amr";
                }
```

```
                        else
                        {
                            String file = location + "/video.3gp";
                            writeToFile(data, file);
                            contentType = "video/3gp";
                            message = "Here's a video!";
                            filename = "video.3gp";
                        }
                        status.setText("Data saved");
                        state = STATE_RECORDED;
                    }
                }
                catch (IOException ioe)
                {
                    status.setText(ioe.getMessage());
                }
                finally
                {
                    if (dataOut != null)
                    {
                        try
                        {
                            dataOut.close();
                        }
                        catch (Exception e)
                        {

                        }
                    }
                    dataOut = new ByteArrayOutputStream();
                }
            }

            // New option implementations
            private void play()
            {
                Screen playback = new PlayingScreen(location + "/" + filename, message);
                UiApplication.getUiApplication().pushScreen(playback);
            }

            private void send(boolean encrypt)
            {
                SendingScreen sending = new SendingScreen(contentType, filename,
                        message, data, encrypt);
                UiApplication.getUiApplication().pushScreen(sending);
            }

            private void showPicture()
            {
                Bitmap taken = Bitmap.createBitmapFromBytes(data, 0, data.length, 1);
                Screen reviewer = new MainScreen();
                BitmapField bitmap = new BitmapField(taken);
                reviewer.add(bitmap);
                UiApplication.getUiApplication().pushScreen(reviewer);
            }
        }
```

Decryption

Run the app in the simulator first. You should be able to send both encrypted and decrypted versions. Now, load it on the phone and send yourself an encrypted message.

When you try to open the attached file, at best you'll get an error message. In the worst case, you may crash your player application. Looks like the encryption works—now, how to reverse it? Unless you already have a tool in place, I recommend using the popular openssl program. openssl is installed by default on modern Linux and OS X machines, and is also included as part of the Cygwin package for Windows, available at http://www.cygwin.com/. openssl is mainly used for secure connections, but also contains a very useful and powerful set of tools for encryption and decryption.

Save your encrypted file to your local disk, then navigate there in a command line. You can perform the decryption with a single step that should look like the following:

```
openssl enc -d -des-cfb8 -K 2BEAFABBABE4AFAD -iv 36bd3018c8116220 ↵
    -in audio.amr -out decrypted.amr
```

Breaking this apart:

- enc tells openssl to run in crypto mode.

- -d is used for decryption; use -e to encrypt instead.

- -des-cfb8 corresponds to the encryption we used, a DES key and a CFB encryptor with an 8-byte IV. You can type openssl enc --help to see a complete list of supported ciphers.

- -K provides the secret key.

- -iv is the random initialization vector. You should substitute the value received in the email.

- -in and -out control input and output respectively. Substitute the actual file names here.

The operation should run without any errors. If it doesn't, please double-check your encryption code and the arguments to openssl. Now, open your attachment again. Huzzah! It should now be safe to view. Congratulations on creating a secure application.

Paranoia

Or is it secure? At a minimum, you'll want to change the key value; otherwise, anyone reading this book will be able to easily crack your security. Even that may not be enough, though. Let's perform a quick audit of the app.

In the same directory as your .project and MediaGrabber.alx file, you will see a MediaGrabber.cod file. This contains the code that is actually loaded onto the BlackBerry device. Open this file with a hex editor. On Windows, I prefer XVI32, a freeware hex editor that you can find with a simple web search. You will see the program data, much of which is unreadable. Now, search in this file for our secret key, 2BEAFABBABE4AFAD or whatever you have substituted for it. Eep! There it is, plain as day.

This is a habitual problem in computer security. In order to perform crypto, the program must contain crypto keys. It must keep those keys secret. And yet, those keys must be distributed within, generated by, or sent to the app. How can you keep attackers from discovering these keys?

There are several strategies available. The more obfuscation you use, the more casual attackers you will deter. You can split up the key into multiple parts and then recombine the pieces. You can generate the key in memory—for example, by shifting every letter one position down the alphabet. You can encrypt a key with another key, although this leads to a chicken-and-egg problem. Ultimately, a sufficiently determined hacker with unlimited time and resources can theoretically decompile and reverse engineer your program to discover your keys. Depending on your app design, you may be able to use public key encryption where it does not matter if an attacker discovers the public key.

WANT MORE?

Cryptography is a fascinating area, and, if it interests you, you can easily spend hours, days, or years reading about different options and experimenting with them. There are a few extra items you can pursue in MediaGrabber to make it more secure for your users.

- Allow the user to enter her own key that will be used for encryption instead of using a hard-coded one. *Extra credit:* Generate a strong key based on text that she enters (e.g., generate a value like 0x42FAAB783C10CE77 from the password tristero.) *Super extra credit:* Securely store the user's key so she doesn't need to type it in every time she sends an encrypted message.

- Add support for multiple ciphers to the app, such as AES, TripleDES, and RC5. Allow the user to select which encryption method to use when sending. Keep in mind that this also will require support for multiple key sizes.

- Make your app as secure against hackers as you can. Conceal your key within the .cod file. Experiment with ways to generate key values that also allow the receiver to figure out the key.

Program security requires constant vigilance, so completing these exercises will help you develop the mindset of constant paranoia and inquisitiveness that will help you discover flaws before they can be exploited.

Excelsior

Choices abound in the world of security. The rich resources of the built-in RIM crypto libraries and the free offerings of Bouncy Castle make it very unlikely that you will ever find yourself lacking crypto options. The bigger challenge is to make sense of what's out there and pick what makes the most sense for your app. If your app is for personal use or you just want to discourage potential hackers, very little is needed. Applying even the simplest cipher will deter the vast majority of abusers, who will move on to easier targets. However, if you are responsible for crafting a system that manages people's money, personal information, or sensitive data, you must fulfill the mission of protecting that trust. Involve others, consult experts, and make sure your app is reviewed and tested.

Please keep in mind that the examples in this chapter included hard-coded keys for maximum readability, but this will rarely be used in true applications. Consider whether each user will need their own key, and if so, how to distribute them. Think about whether you can algorithmically generate a key, and if you can, how to ensure both parties stay in sync.

"Security through obscurity" is a persistent enemy of good design. Too many people convince themselves that, by not talking about how their app works, they are protecting against intrusion. You will know your app is secure if you can tell someone every detail about how it works and still know that they will not be able to crack it.

Fortunately, simply by thinking about these issues, you already have a head start on many other developers. Not to mention, you have more than a head start on using advanced BlackBerry APIs—you have completed the race!

Part 1 of this book has provided you with the tools for creating feature-rich applications that exploit the best built-in capabilities of BlackBerry devices. Up until this point, our apps have been growing upward, gaining new functionality. Next, we will turn out focus inward and start exploring ways to more tightly integrate with other systems on the device.

Part 2

Device Integration

You now have the tools to make a useful and interesting mobile BlackBerry app. If you're lucky, lots of people will get it… and it will sit in the Downloads folder or at the bottom of their home screen. It may be great while people are using it, but even the best app becomes forgettable if people don't see it often.

This next section focuses on *integration*, the process of connecting your app with other powerful apps and features on the device. You will gain access to the user's personal address book, calendar, and more, so that you can access information and provide new updates. You will learn how to use the BlackBerry web browser in your app, and use your app in the BlackBerry web browser. Finally, you will learn how to elevate your app to the level of a first-class application, capable of providing services to other apps on the phone and displaying custom icons from the BlackBerry menus.

By the end of this part, your apps won't just have more features: they'll also be irresistible. Obtaining this level of polish and mutual cooperation with built-in device applications can turn your app from something you download into a part of your daily routine.

Chapter 6

Personal Information

If you work for a large company, your boss probably has a large Rolodex with all his business contacts' information in it. The boss may have a secretary who manages scheduling and appointment reminders. If you're like most programmers, you likely don't have either of those. What you do have is a computer in your pocket that has the capability of storing all sorts of personal information: your friends' names, their phone numbers and email addresses, your plans for the weekend, a grocery list, and more. Our mobile phones have become intensely personal devices, one of the few things that are with us almost all day long. We trust the phone with a great deal of information, and, if users are willing to share that information, your apps can become far more useful, immediate, and personal.

This chapter looks at the various options offered by the BlackBerry API for integrating with the user's personal information. Their friends will be your friends, their calendar an open book, their notes a reminder to you. Of course, not every app will need to connect in these ways, but almost everything can benefit from a little personal touch.

Address Book

It's easy to overlook the fact that mobile phones are ultimately about communication. Specifically, communication with other people through voice calls or messaging. The built-in address book app (sometimes labeled Contacts) is usually one of the first items a user will see when they turn on their BlackBerry, and even the most die-hard luddites take the time to enter their friends' information for easier calls. RIM exposes every piece of information about those contacts through the Personal Information Management (PIM) interface, which also forms the basis for other types of information.

An Overview of PIM

The PIM API was first deployed as part of JSR 75, the same standard that brought us the FileConnection API. It has proven extremely successful, and is now present on the vast majority of Java ME phones as well as all BlackBerry devices with software version

4.0 or higher. This common basis makes it much easier to port applications between BlackBerry and other types of devices.

PIM and Lists

PIM took a different approach from FileConnection, eschewing the GCF in favor of a more specialized interface. Rather than allowing for arbitrary types of personal information stores, it defined a particular set of the most common. These stores include a user's address-book, calendar, and to-do list. Each type of store is presented as a list—conceptually, an ordered sequence of records, whether those records are contacts or appointments. Because the lists were predefined, RIM was not able to add specialized classes directly; however, because the lists are presented as interfaces, RIM was able to derive from those interfaces to add their own specialized behavior. Figure 6-1 illustrates the current class hierarchy for list management on BlackBerry devices.

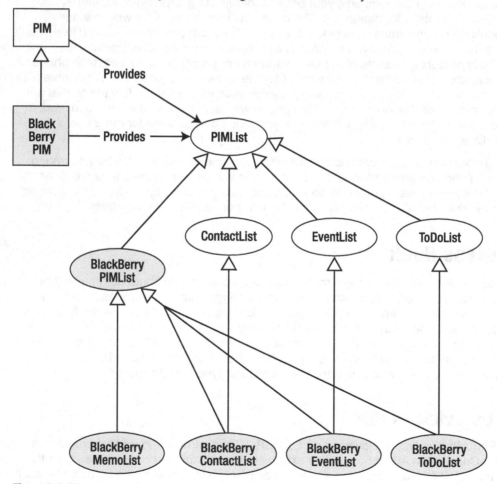

Figure 6-1. *PIM access to information lists*

PIM and BlackBerryPIM are factory classes that provide access to the lists, as well as methods for serializing or deserializing individual list items. These two classes actually refer to the same singleton object, and can safely be cast back and forth. BlackBerryPIM defines access to RIM-exclusive lists and capabilities. Each PIMList comes in both a standard and a BlackBerry-specific flavor. The BlackBerry versions of these classes offer additional useful features that were not included in the original JSR specification. For example, a ContactList presents ways to look up contacts by searching for certain criteria, while a BlackBerryContactList adds the ability to search for contact groups, or to directly retrieve a contact by their unique ID. As with PIM and BlackBerryPIM, each PIMList and BlackBerryPIMList are singleton objects, so each can be cast into the other version.

> **Tip:** If you need the extra abilities offered by the BlackBerry version of a list, go ahead and use it. Otherwise, stick with the plain version to ease porting to other platforms.

A special type of list, BlackBerryMemoList, was created for BlackBerry devices and does not have a standard counterpart. As you might expect, this provides access to the Memos application.

You cannot add your own type of list to the PIM structure. For example, if your application provides voice memos, you cannot use PIM to store or look up that data because voice memos are not one of the existing PIMList implementations. However, among the existing lists, your app has complete control. Any changes you make will appear in other PIM-related apps and vice versa. So, if you add a ToDo list item within your app, it will appear the next time the user opens their Tasks application.

You open a list by providing the enumerated type to the PIM singleton and casting to the appropriate type. The returned lists share many characteristics with I/O connections: lists can be opened in read-only, write-only, or read-write modes, and should be closed when finished, as shown below. Keeping PIMList instances open may block others from being able to access the associated data.

```
PIM pim = PIM.getInstance();
ContactList contacts = (ContactList)pim.openPIMList(
        PIM.CONTACT_LIST, PIM.READ_ONLY);
// Use the contacts here.
contacts.close();
```

> **Note:** The PIM classes can be located in the javax.microedition.pim package.

Almost every PIM-related operation can fail with a PIMException. The exact reason for the exception will vary from operation to operation; when opening a PIMList, it may fail if the requested list isn't available. SecurityException can also be thrown on a variety of methods, usually because the user hasn't authorized the app to read or modify personal data.

Certain device configurations may support multiple lists of each type. One ContactList may be provided for contacts stored on a SIM card, while another ContactList represents the contacts on a Microsoft Exchange server. The PIM class provides methods to determine what list names are available and to grab those particular lists, as shown in the example below.

```
PIM pim = PIM.getInstance();
String[] listNames = pim.listPIMLists(PIM.EVENT_LIST);
for (int i = 0; i < listNames.length; ++i)
{
    EventList contacts = (EventList)pim.openPIMList(
            PIM.EVENT_LIST, PIM.READ_WRITE, listNames[i]);
    // Use the list
    contacts.close();
}
```

Each list is maintained separately from other lists. It is not possible to combine all lists of one type into one master list.

Categories

Each type of PIMList can contain an arbitrary number of categories. Categories logically group together groups of items. In a ToDo list, you might have separate categories for Sales, Research, Projects, and Personal. Then, when adding a new ToDo item, you could choose to assign it to an appropriate category.

Note: Preloaded BlackBerry applications sometimes refer to a category as a Filter.

Categories are entirely optional. PIMList includes a special type of category called UNCATEGORIZED that is associated with every item in the list that does not belong to any category. If you do choose to assign a category to an item, that category must already exist. You can determine this by querying the associated list as shown below.

```
String[] categories = contacts.getCategories();
```

Categories in PIM are more like tags than folders. Each individual item might belong to zero, one, or many categories. If you need to pick up flowers for a co-worker's birthday party, you might file that in your ToDo list under both Projects and Personal. Later, when you filter by Projects, Personal, or all, you will see that reminder. Figure 6-2 shows a theoretical user's address book as organized by categories.

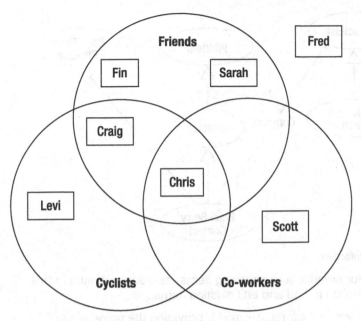

Figure 6-2. Contacts shown by category

Items

Up until now, all the classes in this chapter have offered organization and access. However, items are the heart of PIM. They provide the actual data that users care about: a person's name, the time of an appointment, and the priority of a task.

Each `PIMList` provides access to a set of `PIMItem` objects. Every item in a `PIMList` has the same class type: an `EventList` will only contain `Event` objects, a `ContactList` contains `Contact` objects, and so on. As with the `PIMList` class, each `PIMItem` subclass has an associated BlackBerry version as well. Figure 6-3 shows the complete hierarchy for `Contact` items; the same structure applies to all other types of items as well. Once again, you can always downcast from a `PIMItem` to its BlackBerry counterpart, such as from a `Contact` to a `BlackBerryContact`.

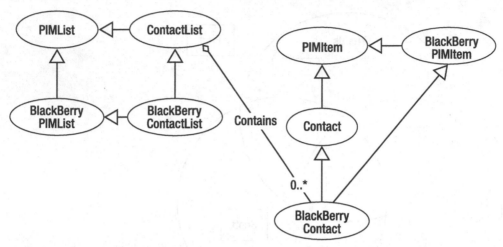

Figure 6-3. *Items contained in a ContactList*

Each list contains methods for creating and removing items, as discussed later in this chapter. You can also search lists to find and edit existing items.

To manage an item's categories, call addToCategory(), providing the name of the desired category. Conversely, call removeFromCategory() to detach a category from this item. The method maxCategories() indicates how many categories an item can belong to, with -1 indicating that there is no limit.

Fields

If you have completely filled out a contact's information in the address book, you have seen the wide variety of data types that are included. Some things, such as the name and phone number, are simply text. Others are collections of text items; for example, an address contains separate entries for the street, city, and so on. You can enter the birthday or anniversary through a special date control. All of these pieces of information are referred to as *fields*, and together they tell you everything there is to know about a particular item.

To support the many different kinds of information that items require, fields are fairly complex. They can theoretically support many data types, so each individual field must declare what particular type it provides. Examples include strings, arrays of strings, Date objects, and binary data. Each field may have zero or more values with that data type. For example, if you enter three email addresses for the same contact, all three entries will be provided by one field. Certain fields support *attributes*. An attribute provides more detailed information about the data it contains, such as distinguishing between a home and a work phone number. Finally, the field also has a human-readable label that describes what information it provides.

> **Caution:** Depending on your application's internationalization language needs, the human-readable label may not be in the language you wish to display.

Contacts usually have the most complex data structure, and are the only type of item that uses attributes. Use `PIMItem.ATTR_NONE` whenever you work with fields that do not support attributes.

At runtime, you can query a `PIMList` about the fields it supports. `getSupportedFields()` returns an array of integers, with each integer corresponding to an enumerated field value, such as `Event.START` or `ToDo.PRIORITY`. You can use this to determine whether to provide or display values for particular fields. BlackBerry offers consistent support for particular sets of fields, so it is less important to check for fields if your app will only run on BlackBerry devices. However, you should do this if you plan to run it on other devices as well. You can also look up the data type, label, maximum number of values, and attributes for a field, as shown in the following code.

```
int[] supportedFields = contacts.getSupportedFields();
for (int i = 0; i < supportedFields.length; ++i)
{
    int field = supportedFields[i];
    String label = contacts.getFieldLabel(field);
    int type = contacts.getFieldDataType(field);
    int[] attributes = contacts.getSupportedAttributes(field);
    for (int j = 0; j < attributes.length; ++j)
    {
        int attribute = attributes[j];
        String attrLabel = contacts.getAttributeLabel(attribute);
    }
}
```

Support for fields is consistent across all the items in a given list. You will never have one Contact that supports a birthday and another that doesn't. However, not every field will necessarily have a value. In some cases, a field may be mandatory, meaning it cannot be stored without having some value. When this happens, an initial default is usually provided that your app can choose to overwrite.

Contacts

Contacts are probably the most complex item in the PIM database. They certainly have the greatest number of fields, and are the only items that support field attributes. Contacts are also likely to be the most widely used piece of personal information. Access to contacts can greatly enhance the usefulness of your app, so understanding their structure is important.

Hello, Stranger

A contact is an entity with whom you can communicate. Contacts are most often people, but may also include companies, automated response lines, or other things. At a minimum, we are likely to assign a name to each contact, whether it is "Bob" or "Apress" or "That one weird guy who's always in the coffee shop." Around that name, we attach a lot of associations and information.

In the world of PIM, we can quantify a lot of that information into data. People have phone numbers, so we enter that into the contact record. We further distinguish between a person's fax number, their work number, and their mobile number. Any individual contact may have multiple versions of the same type of data, and be missing other types of data entirely. Figure 6-4 shows the set of fields included for a hypothetical item in the address book.

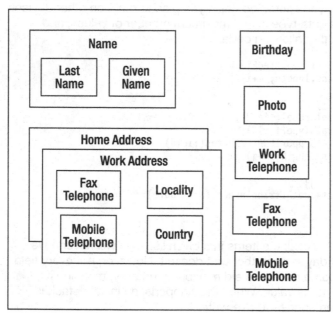

Figure 6-4. Data fields provided by a contact

This data is extremely malleable. People might change their address when they move, change their name when they marry, and change their photo when they grow a beard. The contact record remains the same, because it refers to the same entity, but the fields within it may change entirely.

Representing a Contact

Prior to the creation of the PIM API, a consortium of technology companies defined a standard format for contact data. This standard is called vCard, and you might have seen them attached to emails or included in web pages. A vCard stores information about a particular entity in a well-structured format that can be parsed by any application. The most widely used format is vCard 2.1, created in 1996, while the most advanced version is vCard 3.0. A sample vCard is shown below.

```
BEGIN:VCARD
VERSION:2.1
N:Maas;Oedipa
FN: Oedipa Maas
ORG:Inverarity Estate
TITLE:Executor
TEL;WORK;VOICE:(818) 555-0144
TEL;HOME;VOICE:(707) 555-0135
ADR;WORK;;;400 Inverarity Drive;San Narciso;CA; 91340;United States of America
LABEL;WORK;ENCODING=QUOTED-PRINTABLE: 400 Inverarity Drive =0D= San Narciso,
   CA 91340=0D=0AUnited States of America
ADR;HOME;;;303 Palm Avenue; Kinneret;CA; 95418;United States of America
LABEL;HOME;ENCODING=QUOTED-PRINTABLE: 303 Palm Avenue =0D= Kinneret, CA 95418
   =0D=0AUnited States of AmericaStates of America
EMAIL;PREF;INTERNET:oedipa@waste.example.net
END:VCARD
```

Although a vCard is a useful standard for data interchange, the actual storage will hopefully not look anything like this. Each contact will most likely be broken apart and stored in a compact database. The vCard specification includes a large number of fields that are highly unlikely to actually be used on a mobile device, such as LOGO and AGENT fields. The standard also allows anyone to create additional fields by prefixing them with an X-. Some nonstandard fields that have gained widespread adoption include X-ANNIVERSARY and X-SKYPE-USERNAME. Some of these fields might be useful on a mobile phone, while others won't. The PIM Contact API was derived from vCard 3, and selected a subset of fields from the standard that were believed to be the most useful. However, each individual manufacturer could decide which of those fields to implement. There is usually a 1–1 correlation between the fields exposed in the Java PIM API and what is shown by a device's native contacts app. If there is no Assistant entry in the address book, the API doesn't need to bother supporting Contact.ASSISTANT. This allows for far better efficiency in storing contact information in the device's native format.

A BlackBerry Contact

Fortunately, RIM has standardized the fields they make available. Besides selecting a subset of the standard PIM fields listed in the Contact class, they have added several additional fields as well in BlackBerryContact. Table 6-1 shows the available fields along with their supported attributes and the total allowed quantity.

Table 6-1. Supported BlackBerryContact Fields

Name	Field	Type	Attributes	Total Allowed
Address	Contact.ADDR	PIMItem.STRING_ARRAY	Contact.ATTR_WORK Contact.ATTR_HOME	1
Anniversary	BlackBerryContact.ANNIVERSARY	PIMItem.DATE		1
Birthday	Contact.BIRTHDAY	PIMItem.DATE		1
Direct Connect ID	BlackBerryContact.DCID	PIMItem.STRING		1
Email	Contact.EMAIL	PIMItem.STRING		3
Notes	Contact.NOTE	PIMItem.STRING		1
Organization	Contact.ORG	PIMItem.STRING		1
Photo	Contact.PHOTO	PIMItem.BINARY		1
PIN	BlackBerryContact.PIN	PIMItem.STRING		1
Telephone	Contact.TEL	PIMItem.STRING	Contact.ATTR_FAX, Contact.ATTR_HOME, BlackBerryContact.ATTR_HOME2, Contact.ATTR_MOBILE, Contact.ATTR_OTHER, Contact.ATTR_PAGER, Contact.ATTR_WORK, BlackBerryContact.ATTR_WORK2	8
Title	Contact.TITLE	PIMItem.STRING		1
Unique ID	Contact.UID	PIMItem.STRING		1
User 1	BlackBerryContact.USER1	PIMItem.STRING		1
User 2	BlackBerryContact.USER2	PIMItem.STRING		1
User 3	BlackBerryContact.USER3	PIMItem.STRING		1
User 4	BlackBerryContact.USER4	PIMItem.STRING		1

Note: The Direct Connect ID is only supported on iDEN devices. (iDEN is most often used for push-to-talk mobile phones.) `BlackBerryContact.PIN` must be a hex number represented as a string.

As Figure 6-5 shows, this list precisely corresponds to the native BlackBerry address book app. Any changes you make to a contact within your app will be reflected when the user next views their address book.

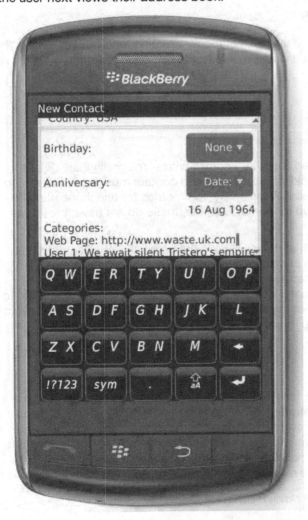

Figure 6-5. A native BlackBerry contact

Adding Contacts

There might be some occasions when you want your app to introduce the user to someone new. You might include contact information for technical support, or perhaps allow them to import friends from a social networking app into their address book. PIM allows two options for adding new items: creating a blank item from scratch, or importing an existing item from an outside source.

Creating Blank Contacts

Each `PIMList` subinterface includes a factory method for creating a new, blank item within that list. For a new contact you would use `ContactList.createContact()`, as shown here.

```
PIM pim = PIM.getInstance();
ContactList contacts = (ContactList) pim.openPIMList(PIM.CONTACT_LIST,↩
        PIM.READ_WRITE);
Contact contact = contacts.createContact();
```

When your blank contact is initialized, it actually comes with some preliminary default values. This is a minimal set on BlackBerry devices. Each contact must have a name, so by default this will be "Empty Contact." Additionally, four entries for telephone numbers will be created, two for work and two for home; however, these do not have any values set by default.

If you create multiple contacts, each of them will have the name "Empty Contact." It is perfectly valid to have two separate contacts with the exact same name—otherwise, it wouldn't be possible to have two friends named "John Smith." If your app is going to create contacts, such as a tech-support contact for your product, it should check first to make sure that those contacts do not already exist in the address book in order to avoid duplicates. Later in the chapter, you'll see how to search for existing contacts.

Importing a Contact

The PIM class provides the method `fromSerialFormat()` for importing an item from a stream. The following code demonstrates how to do this from an array of UTF-8 bytes. You can just as easily load a vCard over the network, from a file, or through any other type of input stream source. However, keep in mind that `fromSerialFormat()` expects to receive plain characters; if the data has been received over an HTTP or email connection, any encoding should be removed prior to deserializing.

```
ByteArrayInputStream input = new ByteArrayInputStream(cardData);
PIM pim = PIM.getInstance();
PIMItem[] items = pim.fromSerialFormat(input, "UTF-8");
if (items.length > 0 && items[0] instanceof Contact)
{
    Contact imported = (Contact) items[0];
}
```

When importing a contact, the first byte in the input stream should be the "B" character of the "BEGIN:VCARD" or "begin:vcard" tag. (vCard tags are not case-sensitive.) The vCard must be in the 2.1 or 3.0 format. PIM will continue processing all characters until it reaches the "end:vcard" tag or an error occurs. As it reads in tags, it will import any compatible tags (such as name, email, mobile, etc.) into the Contact object's data fields. If it comes across any incompatible tags (such as nickname, public key, or photo URL), those fields are silently dropped. If the card is missing the mandatory name field, "Empty Contact" is provided as a default.

Even though this method returns an array of PIMItem objects, it will only read in a single Contact. The method returns an array because sometimes a single data entry can result in multiple PIMItem instances. For example, a calendar appointment can be represented as both a ToDo and an Event. If multiple vCards are located within this stream, you must call fromSerialFormat() multiple times.

> **Caution:** Versions of BlackBerry device software prior to 4.6.1 have flawed implementations of fromSerialFormat() that may result in exceptions when you try to import vCards. In some cases, you might be able to avoid this by restricting the set of fields in the vCard; be sure to test it on your target devices if you plan on using this method.

Editing Contacts

After you have created, imported, or looked up an existing Contact, you can start making changes to it. This might involve adding new fields, editing existing fields, or removing fields. Keep in mind that you can only edit items from a list that was opened with WRITE_ONLY or READ_WRITE access.

Modifying Basic Fields

Most of the fields in the Contact class have only a single value associated with them. To edit them, provide a new value of the appropriate type, as previously shown in Table 6-1.

Editing Strings

Strings can be directly added to a contact record, as shown here.

```
contact.addString(Contact.ORG, PIMItem.ATTR_NONE, "Engineering");
```

You can modify an existing string value by calling the setString() method with an appropriate index.

```
contact.setString(Contact.TITLE, 0, PIMItem.ATTR_NONE, "Senior Engineer");
```

How can you know which version to call? Most string fields can only accept a single entry. If you try to add a new entry when one already exists, a `FieldFullException` will be thrown. Conversely, if you try to set a field and no value is currently set, you'll get an `IndexOutOfBoundsException`. If you have just created a blank new contact, you can safely call `addString()` since no fields currently exist. Otherwise, you should check to see whether the field already has any values, and then set or update it appropriately as in the following example.

```
if (contact.countValues(Contact.NOTE) > 0)
{
    contact.setString(Contact.NOTE, 0, PIMItem.ATTR_NONE, "Next victim");
}
else
{
    contact.addString(Contact.NOTE, PIMItem.ATTR_NONE, "Next victim");
}
```

If you have previously added a string, and then later call `setString()` with an index of 0, the previously added value will be overwritten. This occurs even if the `Field` supports multiple entries.

Finally, for maximum portability, you can check to see whether a field is supported before you attempt to access it. This will protect you if you ever run on devices that do not support the given field.

```
if (contacts.isSupportedField(BlackBerryContact.USER1))
{
    contact.addString(BlackBerryContact.USER1, PIMItem.ATTR_NONE, "BB user");
}
```

Editing Dates

A date in a Contact item is provided as a long 64-bit integer in Unix epoch time—that is, the number of milliseconds since midnight on January 1, 1970 GMT. If you wish to use the current time, you can call `System.currentTimeMillis()`. You can also calculate the time value yourself. However, I find it easiest to use the `Calendar` class, which provides useful methods for converting a calendar date and time into a suitable `long` value. The following example assigns an anniversary value to a contact.

```
Calendar calendar = Calendar.getInstance();
calendar.set(Calendar.YEAR, 2008);
calendar.set(Calendar.MONTH, Calendar.JULY);
calendar.set(Calendar.DATE, 21);
long time = calendar.getTime().getTime();
contact.addDate(BlackBerryContact.ANNIVERSARY, PIMItem.ATTR_NONE, time);
```

> **Note:** The getTime().getTime() call is not a typo. The first method converts a Calendar into a Date, the second from a Date into a primitive time value. The BlackBerry version of java.util.Calendar is missing some useful functions from the Java SE version, including getTimeInMillis() and overloaded set() functions that specify multiple fields at once.

Editing Binary

A BlackBerry contact supports a single binary field, the photo. You can use any image type supported by EncodedImage, including PNG, BMP, WBMP, GIF, JPEG, and TIFF. However, there are some quirks. First, not all specific images will be supported. I've noticed that most PNG files can be added successfully, while others generate an "Image type is not supported" error. Second, the binary data may either be Base64 encoded or provided in raw byte format; however, the length of the data must be given as the number of bytes in the unencoded format. On recent devices, you may directly set image bytes for the photo as shown here.

```
EncodedImage image = EncodedImage.getEncodedImageResource("silhouette.png");
byte[] data = image.getData();
contact.addBinary(Contact.PHOTO, PIMItem.ATTR_NONE, data, 0, data.length);
```

On devices with older software versions, you may need to Base64 encode the data first. Fortunately, a convenient class provides a quick way to do this, as shown in the following code.

```
EncodedImage image = EncodedImage.getEncodedImageResource("silhouette.png");
byte[] data = image.getData();
byte[] encoded = Base64OutputStream.encode(data, 0, data.length, false, false);
contact.addBinary(Contact.PHOTO, PIMItem.ATTR_NONE, encoded, 0, data.length);
```

Of course, you can obtain the image bytes any way you like. This example shows how to use a resource in your application, but you can also download an image from the Internet or select something from the local filesystem.

Modifying Email Addresses

The basic fields shown in the previous section all support a single entry. An email address is a String, but any given user may have multiple addresses. BlackBerry devices support up to three addresses for any given contact. You may simply call addField() multiple times, as in the following example.

```
contact.addString(Contact.EMAIL, PIMItem.ATTR_NONE, "westley@example.com");
contact.addString(Contact.EMAIL, PIMItem.ATTR_NONE, "farmboy@example.com");
contact.addString(Contact.EMAIL, PIMItem.ATTR_NONE, "dread.pirate@example.com");
```

Should you ever need to add another address once the maximum has been reached, you must remove one of the existing ones first. You can remove any field, not just email addresses, by calling the removeValue() method. The example below will remove the second item; if run after the preceding code, the two remaining addresses will be westley@example.com at index 0 and dread.pirate@example.com at index 1.

```
contact.removeValue(Contact.EMAIL, 1);
```

New email addresses will always be added to the end of the list. You can call setString() with the appropriate index to modify an existing email address slot.

Modifying Names

Contact.NAME has the type PIMItem.STRING_ARRAY. It is helpful to be able to access individual components of a name; for example, "John Smith" can be easily sorted by first name, but you'd like individual access to the "Smith" part in order to sort by the last name. PIM defines five potential elements that make up the name array. BlackBerry supports a subset of these, as shown in Table 6-2.

Table 6-2. *Elements in the Name Array*

Name	Meaning	Example	Supported?
Contact.NAME_FAMILY	Last name	House	Yes
Contact.NAME_GIVEN	First name	Gregory	Yes
Contact.NAME_OTHER	Middle name, nick name, etc.	Greg	No
Contact.NAME_PREFIX	Honorific or title placed before name	Dr.	Yes
Contact.NAME_SUFFIX	Honors, offices, or generational information	M.D.	No

You cannot directly set an individual name element; instead, you must add or remove the entire string array at once. You can build up and apply the array as shown in the following example.

```
int nameCount = contacts.stringArraySize(Contact.NAME);
String[] names = new String[nameCount];
names[Contact.NAME_PREFIX] = "Dr.";
names[Contact.NAME_GIVEN] = "Nick";
names[Contact.NAME_FAMILY] = "Riviera";
names[Contact.NAME_SUFFIX] = "M.D.";
contact.addStringArray(Contact.NAME, PIMItem.ATTR_NONE, names);
```

You can include as few name parts as you like, although, if neither a given nor a family name is included, BlackBerry will apply a default of "Empty" and "Contact" respectively. It is safe to include unsupported name parts such as NAME_SUFFIX. These will be silently discarded. If you'd prefer to check at runtime whether a name is supported, use the method isSupportedArrayElement().

```
if (contacts.isSupportedArrayElement(Contact.NAME, Contact.NAME_SUFFIX))
    names[Contact.NAME_SUFFIX] = "M.D.";
```

Modifying Phone Numbers

The phone number field is the first that supports attributes. As described previously, an attribute provides more detailed information about the data it contains. When you add multiple email addresses, there is no way to distinguish whether one email address will be more appropriate than another to use. For phone numbers, however, you can attach an attribute to each number describing its purpose, as the following code demonstrates.

```
contact.addString(Contact.TEL, Contact.ATTR_HOME, "5555550100");
contact.addString(Contact.TEL, Contact.ATTR_WORK, "5555550103");
contact.addString(Contact.TEL, BlackBerryContact.ATTR_WORK2, "5555550104");
```

As long as you stick to the defined attributes and don't repeat yourself, everything will work as expected. However, BlackBerry follows some unusual rules in other cases. If you try to add an attribute that isn't supported (such as Contact.AUTO), or one that already has a value assigned to it, then, rather than discarding the value or throwing an error, the number will be assigned to the next available slot. Therefore, it is possible for your code to add a mobile number to a contact, and have that number stored as a pager number. There is a limit of eight numbers per contact, and adding any more after that will result in a FieldFullException.

To avoid this problem, you can use the countValues() method to determine how many entries are already stored in a field, and then a getAttributes() call to retrieve the attributes. Attributes are bit flags, so you can use a bitwise "AND" operator to determine whether a given attribute is set, as shown in the next example. This code will scan through all the telephone numbers already set on a contact and, if it finds a mobile number, update it.

```
int telCount = contact.countValues(Contact.TEL);
for (int i = 0; i < telCount; ++i)
{
    int telAttrs = contact.getAttributes(Contact.TEL, i);
    if ((telAttrs & Contact.ATTR_MOBILE) != 0)
    {
        contact.setString(Contact.TEL, i, Contact.ATTR_MOBILE, "5555550109");
        break;
    }
}
```

Modifying Addresses

The address field is the most complex field in a Contact, as it combines both the array elements we saw in the name field and the attributes found in telephone numbers. Now that you have mastered both of these concepts, addresses should be relatively straightforward. First you will build up an array of address elements, and then assign that array to a specific address attribute. The address array elements are shown in table 6-3.

Table 6-3. *Elements in the Address Array*

Name	Meaning	Example	Supported?
Contact.ADDR_COUNTRY	Country	Canada	Yes
Contact.ADDR_EXTRA	Any other information	Head office	Yes
Contact.ADDR_LOCALITY	City, town, rural area	Waterloo	Yes
Contact.ADDR_POBOX	Post office box	54321	No
Contact.ADDR_POSTALCODE	ZIP or other postal code	N2L 3W8	Yes
Contact.ADDR_REGION	Province, territory, or state	Ontario	Yes
Contact.ADDR_STREET	Street number and name	295 Philip Street	Yes

As with phone numbers, if you try to add an address that isn't supported or that already has a value, it will be assigned to the next available slot. However, with just two supported attributes, this is less of a problem. You may reuse an existing array to add multiple addresses, as the next example shows.

```
int addrCount = contacts.stringArraySize(Contact.ADDR);
String[] address = new String[addrCount];
address[Contact.ADDR_STREET] = "1600 Pennsylvania Ave NW";
address[Contact.ADDR_LOCALITY] = "Washington";
address[Contact.ADDR_REGION] = "D.C.";
address[Contact.ADDR_POSTALCODE] = "20500-0004";
address[Contact.ADDR_COUNTRY] = "USA";
contact.addStringArray(Contact.ADDR, Contact.ATTR_HOME, address);
address[Contact.ADDR_STREET] = "One First Street N.E.";
address[Contact.ADDR_LOCALITY] = "Washington";
address[Contact.ADDR_REGION] = "D.C.";
address[Contact.ADDR_POSTALCODE] = "20543";
address[Contact.ADDR_COUNTRY] = "USA";
contact.addStringArray(Contact.ADDR, Contact.ATTR_WORK, address);
```

You may remove or update individual address entries as discussed previously.

Saving Contacts

All modifications to a contact happen entirely in memory. In order to persist those changes to the device's long-term storage, you must commit them by calling Contact.commit(). Even if no errors have occurred when you add and modify fields, an exception still may be thrown on the call to commit(). For example, if you try to add an invalid image to a contact via the Contact.PHOTO field, the problem may not be detected until you try to save the contact.

After you call `commit()`, you can continue using this Contact object, but additional changes won't be saved unless you call `commit()` again.

Besides a local save, you might be interested in exporting contact data so you can send it to a server or other application. You can do this yourself by iterating through a contact's fields and writing the information to a custom format, but it's much easier to use PIM's built-in vCard support, assuming the receiving party is capable of reading that format.

You can serialize a Contact by calling `PIM.toSerialFormat()`. You provide the `Contact` and the output stream. Additionally, you must specify a character encoding; UTF-8 is assumed if this is `null`. Finally, you must specify the data format. BlackBerry devices offer two: `VCARD/2.1` and `VCARD/3.0`. If you'd like to dynamically check what formats are supported, you can call `PIM.supportedSerialFormats(PIM.CONTACT_LIST)`. This returns an array of all supported formats. The following is an example of exporting a contact to an in-memory array.

```
ByteArrayOutputStream out = new ByteArrayOutputStream();
String[] formats = pim.supportedSerialFormats(PIM.CONTACT_LIST);
pim.toSerialFormat(contact, out, "UTF-8", formats[0]);
byte[] vCardData = out.toByteArray();
```

Searching for Contacts

A few users might never get around to creating any contacts in their address book, while others might have hundreds or thousands. The number of contacts is limited only by the available memory on the device. How do you go about finding the contacts you want? There are a variety of tools at your disposal, including both standard PIM APIs and special searches that are only available for BlackBerry devices.

I Want It All

If you need the entire haystack and not just the needle, `ContactList.items()` is the method for you. This method returns an `Enumeration` filled with `Contact` items. Why would you want to use this? It would be handy if you wanted to present the user with a list of all available contacts to pick one, or for a spam app that sent emails to everyone you know.

> **Caution:** Remember that some users will have a *lot* of contacts. You should never write an app that does something like create a new `LabelField` for every contact they have; this will thrash the memory and be unrunnable on certain power users' devices. It's safe to call `items()`, just be cautious about when and how you allocate new objects based on what it returns. Similarly, don't do a linear search through the enumeration, since it will take a long time if there are many contacts.

BlackBerryContactList offers an extra method and two more fields that provide a little more refinement to the raw items() call. BlackBerryContactList.SEARCH_CONTACTS will return only Contact entries, while BlackBerryContactList.SEARCH_GROUPS will return only BlackBerryContactGroup objects. The default behavior is to return both. Most of the other lookup methods described later in this chapter also have alternate versions that accept these two search types. The following code will first process all of the contacts in a user's address book, and then operate on all the groups.

```
PIM pim = PIM.getInstance();
BlackBerryContactList contacts = (BlackBerryContactList) pim↵
        .openPIMList(PIM.CONTACT_LIST, PIM.READ_WRITE);
Enumeration items = contacts.items(BlackBerryContactList.SEARCH_CONTACTS);
while (items.hasMoreElements())
{
    BlackBerryContact contact = (BlackBerryContact) items.nextElement();
    // Process contact here.
}
items = contacts.items(BlackBerryContactList.SEARCH_GROUPS);
while (items.hasMoreElements())
{
    BlackBerryContactGroup group = (BlackBerryContactGroup) items.nextElement();
    // Process group here.
}
```

Note: A BlackBerryContactGroup is a special type of address-book entry that represents an address list, such as an email distribution or a working group. These can be read by your application but cannot be modified or removed. A BlackBerryContactGroup is not compatible with a Contact, so do not attempt to cast between the two.

BlackBerryContactList provides a useful method, getSortOrder(), that tells you how returned items will be sorted. Depending on the device configuration, this can be BlackBerryContactList.SORT_ORDER_FIRST_NAME, BlackBerryContactList.SORT_ORDER_LAST_NAME, or BlackBerryContactList.SORT_ORDER_COMPANY. Unfortunately, there is no way to modify the sort order yourself, but this can be helpful for displaying a message to the user or to determine whether you need to sort the results yourself.

Particular Retrieval

If you're fortunate enough to know the unique ID for a contact, you can look up your contact directly by calling BlackBerryContactList.getByUID(). This presumes that you have previously stored the UID in RMS or another suitable medium. The UID is a String only available to developers; it is not visible when users view their address book. Each Contact has its own unique ID, but IDs may be reused if a contact is deleted, so you may want to check for validity after retrieving a Contact through this method.

If you happen to know the name of a contact, you can try to retrieve it by using the itemsByName() method. This comes in several versions, including one where you provide a simple search string, like "Jon," and another version where you provide a Contact object. If using the string, PIM will run a case-insensitive search of the list for a contact whose first name or last name starts with that string. So "Jon" will match "Jonathan Myers" and "Ben Jonson" but not "Longjon Silver." If you provide a Contact, the family and given names will be searched, and contacts will only be returned if both names start with the provided strings.

Keep in mind that these methods can return multiple results. You might hope that searching for "Horatio Xavier" will only return one result, but someone might know two people of that name. A search for "A" will almost certainly return multiple results. The next example demonstrates how to search for a particular name, and then act on the first result.

```
Contact nameTemplate = contacts.createContact();
String[] name = new String[contacts.stringArraySize(Contact.NAME)];
name[Contact.NAME_GIVEN] = "Daniel";
name[Contact.NAME_FAMILY] = "Waterhouse";
nameTemplate.addStringArray(Contact.NAME, PIMItem.ATTR_NONE, name);
Enumeration matches = contacts.itemsByName(nameTemplate);
if (matches.hasMoreElements())
{
    Contact daniel = (Contact)matches.nextElement();
}
```

Note: Even though a new Contact is created here, commit() is never called, so it will not be saved to the address book.

Broader Searches

Another version of items() accepts a String. This behaves somewhat similarly to itemsByName(), except that all fields in an item are checked, and the matching string can occur anywhere within them. Searching for "stan" would match "Stanley," "Pakistan," and "instant@example.com". As with itemsByName(), this method returns an Enumeration of all matches. This method tends to be slow, because it must search every character of every field, and of limited use, because rarely would you want all possible matches.

You might also choose to call itemsByCategory() to retrieve all contacts belonging to a particular category. As mentioned previously, some items might belong to multiple categories while others don't belong to any. You can pass the field PIMList.UNCATEGORIZED to this method to retrieve all items without any associated categories.

Once you have retrieved an Enumeration by either method, you can walk it and downcast to Contact objects as shown previously.

Template Matching

The most powerful type of search available is the use of a Contact object as a template. This performs similarly to the specialized version of itemsByName() used previously, but this time all fields are matched. You can use this to narrow in on a particular Contact, such as the entry with a particular email address, or to find a set of related items, such as all your contacts who belong to a given organization.

Template matching follows several well-defined rules.

- Two STRING fields match if the template item's string is contained anywhere within the item's string value. So, "key" would match "Turkey."

- If the template item uses the empty string "" for a field, all items with any value for that field match.

- For items with multiple values in a field, the position of the value is not important. So, if your template has an email address of "bob@example.com", it will match "bob@example.com" whether it is in slot 0, 1, or 2.

- If PIMItem.ATTR_NONE is supplied, any matching item will be accepted regardless of attribute type.

- Otherwise, the attribute type in the item must match the attribute in the template.

- Any type other than a STRING must match exactly. Keep in mind that DATE fields may not share the exact same millisecond value, even if they fall on the same calendar date.

Your templates can be as broad or as focused as you need. The following example shows how to locate all of your contacts who belong to the Guild of Calamitous Intent and have a San Francisco area code.

```
Contact template = contacts.createContact();
template.addString(Contact.ORG, PIMItem.ATTR_NONE, "Guild of Calamitous Intent");
template.addString(Contact.TEL, Contact.ATTR_WORK, "415");
Enumeration henchmen = contacts.items(template);
```

Remote Lookup

Corporate BlackBerry users usually access a BES that is attached to a large enterprise database with access to extended contact information, such as a Microsoft Exchange server. Even though an individual user may only have 100 contacts saved on their SIM card, they might be able to access thousands more through the remote address server.

Since device software version 4.0.0, developers have been able to access this data through the BlackBerryContactList.lookup() method. Two versions are provided: one takes a String, the other takes a Contact. These perform searches in the same way as ContactList.items(). However, because the data is not immediately accessible, the interface behaves differently. Instead of blocking until the search is complete, calling lookup() will start an asynchronous search through the network for contacts. You must pass in an instance of RemoteLookupListener. The provided object will be notified through its items() callback function once the search is complete.

lookup() can safely be called even on devices that are not on a BES; they will simply never receive the callback. Once the items are available, you can access them as you would items returned through the other searches. Because the items reside on an external server, you cannot update them. However, you can import the items into your own local contact list by calling ContactList.importContact(). The following code demonstrates how to kick off a remote search for root email addresses, and then import the results into your address book.

```
final BlackBerryContactList localContacts = (BlackBerryContactList) pim↵
    .openPIMList(PIM.CONTACT_LIST, PIM.READ_WRITE);
Contact remoteSearch = contacts.createContact();
remoteSearch.addString(Contact.EMAIL, PIMItem.ATTR_NONE, "root");
contacts.lookup(template, new RemoteLookupListener() {
    public void items(Enumeration results)
    {
        while (results.hasMoreElements())
        {
            Contact contact = (Contact)results.nextElement();
            Contact imported = localContacts.importContact(contact);
            try
            {
                imported.commit();
            }
            catch (PIMException pime) {}
        }
    }
});
```

Reading Contact Data

Once you have found a contact, you can access its information through the defined fields. If you are confident that the certain fields have assigned values, such as if you have done a search for those fields, you can access them directly. Otherwise, you should use Contact.countValues() first to ensure that there is something there to read. For maximum portability, you can initially call ContactList.isSupportedField() to check that the field is safe to access.

The following code shows how to unpack certain information from a retrieved contact. We retrieve the contact's organization, create a readable version of their birthday, and then grab all email addresses. Finally, we look through all the addresses in the record and, if we find a work address, pull out some relevant fields from it.

```
String org = contact.getString(Contact.ORG, 0);
long birthdayTime = contact.getDate(Contact.BIRTHDAY, 0);
Calendar birthday = Calendar.getInstance();
birthday.setTime(new Date(birthdayTime));
```

```
int emailCount = contact.countValues(Contact.EMAIL);
for (int i = 0; i < emailCount; ++i)
{
    String email = contact.getString(Contact.EMAIL, i);
}
int addrCount = contact.countValues(Contact.ADDR);
for (int i = 0; i < addrCount; ++i)
{
    String[] address = contact.getStringArray(Contact.ADDR, i);
    int attribute = contact.getAttributes(Contact.ADDR, i);
    if ((attribute & contact.ATTR_WORK) != 0)
    {
        String street = address[Contact.ADDR_STREET];
        String city = address[Contact.ADDR_LOCALITY];
        String state = address[Contact.ADDR_REGION];
    }
}
```

This technique works well when you want to find specific fields. Sometimes you might want to show all of a contact's fields that have data, or look for a set of fields. Rather than call countValues() for every single field you are interested in, you can use the method getFields(), which tells you what fields have data. Fields are returned as an array of integers, which you can then use to directly access the data. The following debugging code looks at every field defined on a particular contact and writes the information to standard out.

```
int[] fields = contact.getFields();
for (int i = 0; i < fields.length; ++i)
{
    int field = fields[i];
    String fieldLabel = contacts.getFieldLabel(field);
    int dataType = contacts.getFieldDataType(field);
    if (dataType == PIMItem.STRING)
    {
        int dataCount = contact.countValues(field);
        for (int j = 0; j < dataCount; ++j)
        {
            String fieldValue = contact.getString(field, j);
            System.out.println(fieldLabel + ":" + j + ":" + fieldValue);
        }
    }
    else
    {
        System.out.println(fieldLabel);
    }
}
```

Deleting Contacts

PIM has the ability to delete contact entries. Obviously, this should be used with great caution. You will infuriate people if you eliminate their friends. However, it is entirely appropriate to remove a contact that your app created itself, or to perform a deletion at the request of your user. You can only delete a contact from a list that was opened with WRITE_ONLY or READ_WRITE permissions.

To perform a deletion, first locate a Contact using one of the techniques described above. Then you can call ContactList.removeContact(). As with other PIM operations, be prepared to deal with PIMException and possibly SecurityException as well if the user refuses to allow you to delete the contact.

Invoking the Native Address Book

Probably the most common use of PIM in third-party apps is allowing the user to select one or more contacts from her address book and then extracting some information from those selections. On most platforms, developers need to write custom screens using the PIM APIs that read in all of the user's contacts and then present a list of options. Fortunately, RIM has a better solution: BlackBerryContactList.choose() allows your app to directly launch into a customized version of the built-in address book. As shown in Figure 6-6, this option displays a familiar UI that lets the user scroll to find a contact, or type to narrow down the available field.

Figure 6-6. Choosing a contact from the native address book

The choose() method will block until the user has finished with the address book. One of three outcomes may result.

- The user might have selected an existing entry that will be provided as the return value.

- The user might have created a new Contact, also provided as the return value.

- The user might have dismissed the address book without making any selection, in which case null is returned.

The choose() method is very useful, but you should keep a few caveats in mind.

- You cannot control the sort order that is used to display the choices.

- You cannot filter the contacts. For example, if you wish to select an email address, contacts without email will also be displayed, and may be chosen.

- There is no option to select multiple contacts. If you wish to pick more than one, you must call choose() multiple times, and handle cases where the same contact is selected more than once.

- Only local contacts may be selected this way, not contacts stored on a remote server.

- Both Contact and BlackBerryContactGroup items are shown, and either may be returned. If you are looking for contacts only, you should check to see that you are getting one.

The next example shows how to launch the native address book and check that the user selected a contact with an email address. In a full application, you can repeatedly invoke this code, displaying "Please select an email contact" until one is provided.

```
PIM pim = PIM.getInstance();
BlackBerryContactList contacts = (BlackBerryContactList) pim↵
        .openPIMList(PIM.CONTACT_LIST, PIM.READ_WRITE);
PIMItem selected = contacts.choose();
if (selected != null)
{
    if (selected instanceof Contact)
    {
        Contact selectedContact = (Contact)selected;
        if (selectedContact.countValues(Contact.EMAIL) > 0)
        {
            // Process the selection here.
        }
    }
}
```

The BlackBerry Calendar

Some users go for years without ever opening the calendar app on their mobile phone. Others depend on it to drive their day. Your app can integrate with the calendar to provide your users with reminders, set up appointments, or perform other tasks to help schedule their time.

BlackBerry allows you to access calendar information through the `EventList` class. This class behaves similarly to the `ContactList` class, except that it provides `Event` items in place of `Contact` items. You can obtain an instance as shown below.

```
PIM pim = PIM.getInstance();
EventList events = (EventList)pim.openPIMList(PIM.EVENT_LIST, PIM.READ_WRITE);
```

For the most part, events behave like contacts. An event list contains multiple events, and each event supports a certain collection of fields, any one of which may have no, one, or more items. The following sections focus on the unique aspects of events.

Calendar Syncing

Users with a full-featured desktop email client such as Microsoft Outlook can set up their BlackBerry Desktop Manager program to automatically sync between their desktop and mobile calendars. This means that, when a user accepts a meeting invitation on Outlook and then leaves the office, his BlackBerry can vibrate to remind him that the meeting time is approaching. Keep in mind that events you create or manipulate on the phone might be propagated to other devices. Conversely, even if no events are modified on the phone, the calendar may change the next time the device connects to the desktop.

In order to support this kind of syncing, a standard interchange format is necessary. The original PIM Event implementation was derived from vCalendar 1.0, also known as vCal. This is a standardized format created by the Internet Mail Consortium, the same organization responsible for vCard. vCalendar has since been supplanted by the newer iCalendar standard, developed by the Internet Engineering Task Force. BlackBerry PIM supports import from and export to both formats. The following shows a simple iCalendar event.

```
BEGIN:VCALENDAR
VERSION:2.0
BEGIN:VEVENT
SUMMARY:Mom's Birthday Breakfast
DTSTART:20100610T060000Z
DTEND:20100610T070000Z
END:VEVENT
END:VCALENDAR
```

Different calendaring programs have long had trouble with importing and exporting each other's calendar events, although the situation has improved in recent years. Despite the existence of a standard, different programs have added their own quirks, and some are better at dealing with those quirks than others. If your app is going to share calendar data with a server or another program, you should check to make sure both parties can share data successfully.

Repeat After Me

For the most part, Event objects are simpler than Contact. There are no string arrays, attributes, or binary data. However, events do add one significant new characteristic: the idea of repetition. Imagine that you have a daily appointment to walk your dog at 7pm. You'd like to create an appointment so you don't forget this duty. If your calendar program created an event for every single day, that would be 365 events in a single year—quite a lot of data, and far too much space to take up on a mobile device.

Repeating events offer a way for you to create a single event within your calendar, and then specify rules about how often it repeats. Repeating events can be defined very flexibly; you can specify repetition on calendar days (such as every June 10), weekdays (every Tuesday), or more complex constructions (the first and fourth Saturday of every month). You can even specify exceptions—for example, if you're going on vacation next week, you can hire a dog-walker and remove those pesky reminders during the time you'll be gone. Figure 6-7 shows how a single repeating event can be virtually represented multiple times within an event list.

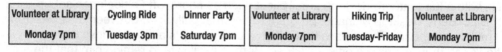

| Volunteer at Library | Cycling Ride | Dinner Party | Volunteer at Library | Hiking Trip | Volunteer at Library |
| Monday 7pm | Tuesday 3pm | Saturday 7pm | Monday 7pm | Tuesday-Friday | Monday 7pm |

Figure 6-7. A repeating calendar event

PIM events support four fundamental types of repetition: RepeatRule.DAILY, RepeatRule.WEEKLY, RepeatRule.MONTHLY, and RepeatRule.YEARLY. Each of these can be set alone on a RepeatRule to create a simple repetition. For example, to have an event repeat at the same time each week, you would define the FREQUENCY as shown below.

```
RepeatRule repeat = new RepeatRule();
repeat.setInt(RepeatRule.FREQUENCY, RepeatRule.WEEKLY);
```

You can control when an event stops repeating by also applying a COUNT or an END value. The former states that the event will recur a certain number of times at the provided frequency and then stop. The latter means that the event will keep recurring until a certain calendar time, at which point it will cease. COUNT must be provided as an int, while END is a date. To make this event repeat for the next eight weeks, we would use the COUNT as shown below.

```
repeat.setInt(RepeatRule.COUNT, 8);
```

You can also specify multiple times at which an event will fire. To repeat an event on Monday, Wednesday, and Friday, you specify the DAY_IN_WEEK rule and provide a bitwise OR for those dates.

```
repeat.setInt(RepeatRule.DAY_IN_WEEK, RepeatRule.MONDAY | RepeatRule.WEDNESDAY
        | RepeatRule.FRIDAY);
```

The available repetition modifiers are shown in Table 6-4. All the constants are defined in the RepeatRule class.

Table 6-4. *Repetition Modifiers*

Field	Values Allowed
DAY_IN_WEEK	SUNDAY, MONDAY, TUESDAY, WEDNESDAY, THURSDAY, FRIDAY, SATURDAY
DAY_IN_MONTH	1-31
DAY_IN_YEAR	1-365
WEEK_IN_MONTH	FIRST, SECOND, THIRD, FOURTH, FIFTH, LAST, SECONDLAST, THIRDLAST, FOURTHLAST, FIFTHLAST
MONTH_IN_YEAR	JANUARY, FEBRUARY, MARCH, APRIL, MAY, JUNE, JULY, AUGUST, SEPTEMBER, OCTOBER, NOVEMBER, DECEMBER

For certain frequencies, you can combine multiple modifiers to create a more fine-grained event time. If you want to celebrate American Thanksgiving, create a yearly event that occurs the fourth Thursday of every November.

```
repeat.setInt(RepeatRule.FREQUENCY, RepeatRule.YEARLY);
repeat.setInt(RepeatRule.MONTH_IN_YEAR, RepeatRule.NOVEMBER);
repeat.setInt(RepeatRule.WEEK_IN_MONTH, RepeatRule.FOURTH);
```

Not every modifier is available for every frequency; for instance, DAY_IN_YEAR doesn't make sense when applied to a WEEKLY recurrence. Frequencies can be controlled on a handset-by-handset basis depending on what the underlying calendar supports. To determine whether a certain modifier or set of modifiers is supported, you can query EventList.getSupportedRepeatRuleFields(). If a combination of modifiers is accepted, the set will be returned in a bitwise AND. The next example checks to see how yearly recurring events are supported.

```
int[] supported = events.getSupportedRepeatRuleFields(RepeatRule.YEARLY);
for (int i = 0; i < supported.length; ++i)
{
    int rules = supported[i];
    if (rules == (RepeatRule.DAY_IN_MONTH & RepeatRule.MONTH_IN_YEAR))
        System.out.println("Can specify by month.");
    else if (rules == RepeatRule.DAY_IN_YEAR)
        System.out.println("Can specify by absolute date.");
}
```

Finally, you can specify exceptions to a repetition. You would add one exception for each time that the event should not occur. Exceptions are implemented as long time values. If you decide to cancel next month's appointment but keep all future appointments, you could use the following code.

```
Calendar exceptionTime = Calendar.getInstance();
exceptionTime.set(Calendar.MONTH, 1);
repeat.addExceptDate(exceptionTime.getTime().getTime ());
```

You can check to see what exceptions have already been added by calling getExceptDates() and remove an existing exception by calling removeExceptDate(long date).

To query a previously created repeat rule, use the following methods.

- getFields() returns an array of all the fields that have been set.

- getInt(int field) retrieves a previously set field, such as the FREQUENCY or the DAY_IN_YEAR.

- getDate(RepeatRule.END) retrieves the specified end time.

- dates(long startdate, long subsetBeginning, long subsetEnding) allows you to provide a time window, and will return all of the repetitions that would occur within that window, excluding any exceptions.

Once you have a RepeatRule configured the way you want it, call Event.setRepeat(RepeatRule repeat). This will replace any previously configured repeat rule. You can query an event's current repetition by calling Event.getRepeat(); this will return null if no repetition has been provided.

Eventful Data

As with contacts, there are a variety of fields at your disposal when editing or reading event data. Table 6-5 displays all the fields supported on BlackBerry. Most of these are very simple, with a single nonarray nonattribute value provided. LOCATION is a single string, which is easier than providing a structured address but also makes it more difficult to parse an event's location. The special ATTENDEES field can have multiple values, one for each attendee. ALLDAY is a special convenience field that will convert the event into an all-day event, running from midnight GMT of the start date through midnight GMT of the end date.

Table 6-5. *Supported BlackBerry Event Fields*

Field	Meaning	Type	Example
Event.SUMMARY	Title of this event	PIMItem.STRING	"Quarterly food strategy meeting"
Event.START	Date and time that this event begins	PIMItem.DATE	1207042400000
Event.END	Date and time that this event ends	PIMItem.DATE	1207042500000

Table 6-5. *Supported BlackBerry Event Fields (continued)*

Field	Meaning	Type	Example
BlackBerryEvent.ALLDAY	All day event	PIMItem.BOOLEAN	true
Event.ALARM	Time to display or sound a reminder, given in seconds before the time specified in START	PIMItem.INT	900 for an alarm 15 minutes before the event
BlackBerryEvent.FREE_BUSY	Status of the event	PIMItem.INT	BlackBerryEvent.FB_FREE, BlackBerryEvent.TENTATIVE, BlackBerryEvent.FB_BUSY, or BlackBerryEvent.OUT_OF_OFFICE
BlackBerryEvent.ATTENDEES	Email addresses of event attendees	PIMItem.STRING	bob@example.com
Event.LOCATION	Place where the event occurs	PIMItem.STRING	"Floor 13 Kitchen"
Event.CLASS	Visibility of this event	PIMItem.INT	Event.CLASS_PUBLIC, Event.CLASS_PRIVATE, Event.CLASS_CONFIDENTIAL
Event.NOTE	Additional information about this event	PIMItem.STRING	"Donuts will be served"
Event.UID	Unique identifier of this Event	PIMItem.STRING	"1234567890"

As with contact fields, the fields on an event correspond to what is available in the BlackBerry Calendar app. The ALARM field corresponds to the "Reminder" in an appointment. Both PRIVATE and CONFIDENTIAL classes will display as "Private."

The BlackBerry applies a few special rules for the standard event fields.

- Events have a minimum duration of one minute. If the END is less than one minute later than START, its duration will automatically be extended.

- Setting a NOTE to a value of "" will remove it from the event.

The Event and BlackBerryEvent interfaces both apply to the same objects; similarly, EventList and BlackBerryEventList can be interchangeably cast. Unlike with contacts, there are no special methods available in the specialized subinterfaces; they are primarily used to define additional fields like those shown in Table 6-5.

Using BlackBerry Calendar Events

Once you have gotten the hang of the Contact class, you are probably ready to work with Event objects. The specific data values you will work with are different, but the overall structure of building and accessing fields remains the same.

Creating and Editing Events

You can construct, import, and modify Event objects in the same way that you would Contact objects. The next example demonstrates how to create an Event from scratch. Here we assume that the app will be running on a BlackBerry device, so we freely use BlackBerry-specific event fields and do not check for supported fields. This code will create a new five-hour-long event, set a reminder for 30 minutes before, include 3 attendees, and specify a location and a busy status before saving the event.

```
PIM pim = PIM.getInstance();
EventList events = (EventList) pim.openPIMList(PIM.EVENT_LIST, PIM.READ_WRITE);
Event event = events.createEvent();
event.addString(Event.SUMMARY, PIMItem.ATTR_NONE, "Radiohead Concert");
Calendar cal = Calendar.getInstance();
cal.set(Calendar.YEAR, 2001);
cal.set(Calendar.MONTH, Calendar.AUGUST);
cal.set(Calendar.DATE, 2);
cal.set(Calendar.HOUR_OF_DAY, 18);
event.addDate(Event.START, PIMItem.ATTR_NONE, cal.getTime().getTime());
cal.set(Calendar.HOUR_OF_DAY, 23);
event.addDate(Event.END, PIMItem.ATTR_NONE, cal.getTime().getTime());
event.addInt(Event.ALARM, PIMItem.ATTR_NONE, 1800);
event.addString(BlackBerryEvent.ATTENDEES, PIMItem.ATTR_NONE,
        "pat@example.com");
event.addString(BlackBerryEvent.ATTENDEES, PIMItem.ATTR_NONE,
        "chris@example.com");
event.addString(BlackBerryEvent.ATTENDEES, PIMItem.ATTR_NONE,
        "scott@example.com");
event.addString(BlackBerryEvent.LOCATION, PIMItem.ATTR_NONE, "Grant Park");
event.addInt(BlackBerryEvent.FREE_BUSY, PIMItem.ATTR_NONE,
        BlackBerryEvent.FB_OUT_OF_OFFICE);
event.commit();
```

Later, we might check to see if a repeat rule has already been set on the event. If not, we can say that this is a biennial event that will recur on the first Wednesday of every other August for the next decade.

```
if (event.getRepeat() == null)
{
    RepeatRule repeat = new RepeatRule();
    repeat.setInt(RepeatRule.FREQUENCY, RepeatRule.YEARLY);
    repeat.setDate(RepeatRule.MONTH_IN_YEAR, RepeatRule.AUGUST);
    repeat.setInt(RepeatRule.WEEK_IN_MONTH, RepeatRule.FIRST);
    repeat.setInt(RepeatRule.DAY_IN_WEEK, RepeatRule.WEDNESDAY);
    repeat.setInt(RepeatRule.INTERVAL, 2);
```

```
        repeat.setInt(RepeatRule.COUNT, 5);
        event.setRepeat(repeat);
}
```

And, as a reminder, you can check for existing fields before setting or adding them. You also can remove values from previously set fields. The following code does both.

```
if (event.countValues(Event.NOTE) == 0)
        event.addString(Event.NOTE, PIMItem.ATTR_NONE, "Bring a sweater");
else
        event.setString(Event.NOTE, 0, PIMItem.ATTR_NONE, "Bring a sweater");
event.removeValue(BlackBerryEvent.ATTENDEES, 1);
event.commit();
```

Searching and Reading Events

EventList offers the same set of items() methods as found in ContactList for retrieving all or a subset of items. You can also look up an event by its UID. The next example shows how you can use a template to discover all of a user's public busy events.

```
Event template = events.createEvent();
template.addInt(Event.CLASS, PIMItem.ATTR_NONE, Event.CLASS_PUBLIC);
template.addInt(BlackBerryEvent.FREE_BUSY, PIMItem.ATTR_NONE, BlackBerryEvent.FB_BUSY);
Enumeration matches = events.items();
```

EventList also defines a new items() method that searches for all events that occur within a given timeframe. You can specify whether to look for events beginning, ending, or occurring at any point during that time. You also can control whether all occurrences of a repeating event are returned or just the initial instance. The next example retrieves all events occurring in November, counts them, and writes their names to standard out. The events will be returned from oldest start date to newest start date; you can resort if you like.

```
Calendar calendar = Calendar.getInstance();
calendar.set(Calendar.YEAR, 2010);
calendar.set(Calendar.MONTH, Calendar.NOVEMBER);
calendar.set(Calendar.DAY_OF_MONTH, 1);
long startTime = calendar.getTime().getTime();
calendar.set(Calendar.DAY_OF_MONTH, 30);
long endTime = calendar.getTime().getTime();
int eventCount = 0;
Enumeration matches = events.items(EventList.OCCURRING, startTime, endTime, true);
while (matches.hasMoreElements())
{
        ++eventCount;
        Event match = (Event)matches.nextElement();
        if (match.countValues(Event.SUMMARY) > 0)
        {
                String summary = match.getString(Event.SUMMARY, 0);
                System.out.println(summary);
        }
}
```

Exporting and Deleting Events

Events can be written out in a standard vCal or iCal format using PIM, as in the following example.

```
FileConnection saveCal = (FileConnection)Connector.open(↵
        "file:///store/home/user/app/schedule.ical");
OutputStream out = saveCal.openOutputStream();
PIM.getInstance().toSerialFormat(event, out, "UTF-8", "VCALENDAR/2.0");
```

This will write the iCal data to the specified file, where it can later be opened from this or another app, or copied to another device.

Once you have finished with an event, or wish to cancel one, you can delete it from the list by calling removeEvent.

Showing Calendars

While there is no EventList equivalent of BlackBerryContactList.choose(), you do have some options for accessing nice built-in views of the calendar without needing a lot of extra work.

Invoking the Native Calendar

If you want to display a particular event or a period of time within the built-in Calendar app, you can do so using the Invoke class. You specify that you wish to open APP_TYPE_CALENDAR and then provide suitable CalendarArguments. You can choose one of the following time arguments.

- Provide a Calendar to open to a specific date and time.

- Open on a particular Event.

- If neither is specified, open to the default calendar.

You can also specify one of several view arguments.

- ARG_NEW brings up the "New Appointment" screen, where the user can create an event. If an Event was provided, the initial fields will be set accordingly.

- ARG_VIEW_AGENDA will open in the agenda view, with upcoming events stacked vertically on top of one another.

- ARG_VIEW_DAY brings up the daily view, divided by hours.

- ARG_VIEW_WEEK brings up the weekly view, with dates as rows and hours as columns.

- ARG_VIEW_MONTH displays a month grid.

- ARG_VIEW_DEFAULT displays the calendar in the current default format.

Unlike with `choose()`, no return value is provided from the Invoke call. You can check to see if the user has added or modified an event by adding a `PIMListListener`, as discussed later in this chapter.

Using Invoke is useful when you want to display event information to your user or show him a chunk of his schedule without writing your own user interface. The following example searches for a particular event and then shows the entire week in which it occurs, which may be handy for planning purposes.

```
PIM pim = PIM.getInstance();
EventList events = (EventList)pim.openPIMList(PIM.EVENT_LIST, PIM.READ_ONLY);
Enumeration matches = events.items("Hootenanny");
if (matches.hasMoreElements())
{
    Event event = (Event)matches.nextElement();
    CalendarArguments args = new CalendarArguments(↵
            CalendarArguments.ARG_VIEW_WEEK, event);
    Invoke.invokeApplication(Invoke.APP_TYPE_CALENDAR, args);
}
```

Although your app can create events directly, you might prefer to give your user a chance to review and approve the event before saving it to the address book herself. The next example does just that, setting up an event but presenting it in the native calendar instead of committing it.

```
Event proposed = events.createEvent();
Calendar time = Calendar.getInstance();
time.set(Calendar.YEAR, 2010);
time.set(Calendar.MONTH, Calendar.SEPTEMBER);
time.set(Calendar.DATE, 19);
proposed.addDate(Event.START, PIMItem.ATTR_NONE, time.getTime().getTime());
proposed.addString(Event.SUMMARY, PIMItem.ATTR_NONE, "Talk Like A Pirate Day");
proposed.addString(Event.NOTE, PIMItem.ATTR_NONE, "Arrrr...");
CalendarArguments view = new CalendarArguments(↵
        CalendarArguments.ARG_NEW, proposed);
Invoke.invokeApplication(Invoke.APP_TYPE_CALENDAR, view);
```

Picking a Date

You can use built-in UI components for date and time selection instead of creating them yourself. If building a BlackBerry CLDC app, use the `DateField` class in the `net.rim.device.api.ui.component` package. You can style this as you would any other `Field`, and can also specify one of `DateField`'s special style constants to indicate whether to show the DATE, TIME, or both with DATE_TIME. You can optionally provide a `DateFormat` to give suggestions about how to display the date prompt; these may or may not be honored. You can construct the field and add it from within a Screen by using the following code.

```
Calendar initial = Calendar.getInstance();
initial.set(Calendar.MONTH, Calendar.JANUARY);
initial.set(Calendar.DATE, 1);
initial.set(Calendar.YEAR, 1980);
```

```
DateField birthday = new DateField(
    "Birthday", initial.getTime().getTime(),DateField.DATE);
add(birthday);
```

A representation of the currently selected time will display on the screen. When the user accesses the control, a special view that allows fairly easy modifications will be displayed, as shown in Figure 6-8.

Figure 6-8. *Activating a BlackBerry DateField control*

Assuming you save the DateField in an instance variable, you can query it later to discover what time the user has selected. If you'd like to immediately update your UI when a change is made, you can call setChangeListener() to receive notifications of updates. The following code shows how you can read the selected Unix time into a more accessible Calendar object.

```
long selectedTime = birthday.getDate();
Calendar selected = Calendar.getInstance();
selected.setTime(new Date(selectedTime));
```

If you are building a MIDP MIDlet, you have access to another class called `DateField`, this version in the `javax.microedition.lcdui` package. Its interface is simpler than the CLDC version, and not quite as customizable, but it is very simple to use: it is an Item that can be inserted into a `Form`. You can provide the label and specify whether the user can select the date, the time, or both. Time is provided up to a granularity of one minute. You can set an initial default time to suggest via `setDate()` and read the final result via `getDate()`. The actual display of the MIDlet `DateField` is identical to that of the CLDC `DateField`. You can set up a `DateField` with no initial time as follows.

```
Form form = new Form("Date Selection");
DateField wedding = new DateField("Wedding", DateField.DATE_TIME);
form.insert(0, wedding);
Display.getDisplay(this).setCurrent(form);
```

I Have A ToDo List?

The PIM concept of ToDo corresponds to the BlackBerry Tasks application. This is an area where you can provide yourself with lists of things to be done. With access to the `ToDoList` interface, your app can chime in on what's important.

Each ToDo encapsulates a specific task. ToDo is based on the VTODO spec that is included as a subset of the vCalendar specification. There is a close relationship between calendar events and todo tasks, but they are not the same. An Event should have a time associated; ToDos may have due dates, but can also simply be reminders of outstanding tasks. The following is an example of a simple VTODO.

```
BEGIN:VCALENDAR
VERSION:2.0
BEGIN:VTODO
DUE:20100401T235959
STATUS:NEEDS-ACTION
SUMMARY:Research practical jokes
END:VTODO
END:VCALENDAR
```

ToDo shares many of the same features as Event, as shown in Table 6-6. They are not interchangeable, so do not attempt to cast one to the other or use a field locator like `Event.SUMMARY` to read a ToDo summary.

Table 6-6. *ToDo Fields*

Field	Meaning	Type	Example	Supported
ToDo.SUMMARY	Title for this task	STRING	"Bring Goodies"	Yes
ToDo.NOTE	Complete details on this task	STRING	"Bring in enough cookies for 30 people"	Yes
ToDo.PRIORITY	Importance of this task	INT	0 for unspecified, 1 for highest, 9 for lowest	Yes
ToDo.CLASS	Visibility of this ToDo	INT	ToDo.CLASS_PUBLIC, ToDo.CLASS_PRIVATE, ToDo.CLASS_CONFIDENTIAL	No
BlackBerryToDo. STATUS	Current completion of this task	INT	BlackBerryToDo.STATUS_NOT_STARTED, BlackBerryToDo.STATUS_IN_PROGRESS, BlackBerryToDo.STATUS_DEFERRED, BlackBerryToDo.STATUS_WAITING, BlackBerryToDo.STATUS_COMPLETED	Yes
BlackBerryToDo. REMINDER	Day and time to sound or display a reminder alarm	DATE	1207042400000	Yes
ToDo.DUE	When this task should be done	DATE	1207050400000	Yes
ToDo.COMPLETED	Whether the task is finished	BOOLEAN	true	Yes
ToDo.COMPLETION_ DATE	When this task was finished	DATE	1207045400000	No
ToDo.REVISION	Last time this task was modified	DATE	1207032700000	No
ToDo.UID	Unique identifier	STRING	"5678901234"	Yes

> **Note:** Although PRIORITY can be provided in a range from 0 to 9, BlackBerry devices only support 3 levels of task priority. 1-3 will be stored as 1 and displayed as "High," 7-9 will be stored as 9 and displayed as "Low," and everything else is stored as 5 and displayed as "Normal."

Other than the different fields, ToDo objects behave like Event objects. You access fields in the same way, and have access to the same kind of time-ranged search. You can use the extended BlackBerryToDo to access custom fields. The following sample demonstrates creating a new task for the user.

```
PIM pim = PIM.getInstance();
ToDoList todos = (ToDoList)pim.openPIMList(PIM.TODO_LIST, PIM.READ_WRITE);
ToDo todo = todos.createToDo();
todo.addString(ToDo.SUMMARY, PIMItem.ATTR_NONE, "Buy a new BlackBerry");
if (todos.isSupportedField(ToDo.CLASS))
{
    if (todo.countValues(ToDo.CLASS) == 0)
    {
        todo.addInt(ToDo.CLASS, PIMItem.ATTR_NONE, ToDo.CLASS_PUBLIC);
    }
}
todo.addInt(BlackBerryToDo.STATUS,
        PIMItem.ATTR_NONE, BlackBerryToDo.STATUS_IN_PROGRESS);
Calendar time = Calendar.getInstance();
time.set(Calendar.YEAR, 2010);
time.set(Calendar.MONTH, Calendar.NOVEMBER);
time.set(Calendar.DATE, 15);
time.set(Calendar.HOUR, 8);
todo.addDate(ToDo.DUE, PIMItem.ATTR_NONE, time.getTime().getTime());
time.set(Calendar.DATE, 8);
todo.addDate(
        BlackBerryToDo.REMINDER, PIMItem.ATTR_NONE, time.getTime().getTime());
todo.commit();
```

Take a Memo

The BlackBerryMemoList and its contained BlackBerryMemo objects are the easiest
PIMItem classes to work with. These allow you to access the user's saved memos or
add memos of your own. A BlackBerryMemo contains only three fields, all of which have
the STRING data type.

- TITLE provides the name of the memo, which will be viewable from a
  list perspective.

- NOTE is the memo's contained text.

- UID is the standard unique identifier.

You can create, edit, search, read, and delete memo objects just as you would other
PIMItem objects. The next example shows a grocery list app that will look for a shopping
list memo in the user's existing memos. If it finds one, it will add items to the list;
otherwise, it will create a new memo. This is a way for your app to integrate with other
parts of the phone that the user can interact with even when your app is not running.

```
String ingredients = "Butter\nEggs\nChocolate Chips\nFlour";
PIM pim = PIM.getInstance();
BlackBerryMemoList memos = (BlackBerryMemoList)pim.openPIMList(
        BlackBerryPIM.MEMO_LIST, PIM.READ_WRITE);
BlackBerryMemo template = memos.createMemo();
template.addString(BlackBerryMemo.TITLE, PIMItem.ATTR_NONE, "Shopping List");
Enumeration matches = memos.items(template);
if (matches.hasMoreElements())
{
```

```
    BlackBerryMemo existing = (BlackBerryMemo)matches.nextElement();
    if (existing.countValues(BlackBerryMemo.NOTE) > 0)
    {
        String text = existing.getString(BlackBerryMemo.NOTE, 0);
        ingredients = text + "\n" + ingredients;
        existing.setString(
                BlackBerryMemo.NOTE, 0, PIMItem.ATTR_NONE, ingredients);
    }
    else
    {
        existing.addString(BlackBerryMemo.NOTE, PIMItem.ATTR_NONE, ingredients);
    }
    existing.commit();
}
else
{
    template.addString(BlackBerryMemo.NOTE, PIMItem.ATTR_NONE, ingredients);
    template.commit();
}
```

It is very important to set the TITLE before saving a note; if you fail to specify one, a PIMException will be thrown. This is different from required fields in other PIMItem objects, which provide a default value if none is specified.

Personal Changes

Every BlackBerryPIMList allows you to add and remove listeners. The listener will inform you when a change has come to the list: an item has been created, modified, or removed. You only need to respond to the events that interest you, and will continue to receive notifications until you remove the listener.

Listing 6-1 shows how to write a simple screen that instructs the user to delete a contact. It does not directly offer a UI for the deletion, but, if the user switches to the address book application and makes the deletion, this screen will be notified, and will update some text using the same StatusUpdater we created for the MediaGrabber app. You can apply the same type of listener to any of the PIMList implementations.

Listing 6-1. *Listening for Contact Deletion*

```
import javax.microedition.pim.Contact;
import javax.microedition.pim.PIM;
import javax.microedition.pim.PIMItem;

import net.rim.blackberry.api.pdap.BlackBerryContactList;
import net.rim.blackberry.api.pdap.PIMListListener;
import net.rim.device.api.ui.UiApplication;
import net.rim.device.api.ui.component.LabelField;
import net.rim.device.api.ui.container.MainScreen;

public class RemoveContactListener extends MainScreen implements PIMListListener
{
```

```
        LabelField instructions;
        StatusUpdater status;

        public RemoveContactListener()
        {
            instructions = new LabelField();
            instructions.setText("It's time to vote someone off the island!");
            add(instructions);
            status = new StatusUpdater(instructions);
            try
            {
                BlackBerryContactList contacts = (BlackBerryContactList)PIM.
                    getInstance().openPIMList(PIM.CONTACT_LIST, PIM.READ_ONLY);
                contacts.addListener(this);
                contacts.close();
            }
            catch (Exception e)
            {
                System.err.println(e);
                e.printStackTrace();
            }
        }

        public void itemAdded(PIMItem added)
        {
            status.sendDelayedMessage("No!  You're supposed to get RID of people!");
        }

        public void itemRemoved(PIMItem removed)
        {
            if (removed instanceof Contact)
            {
                if (removed.countValues(Contact.NAME) > 0)
                {
                    String[] name = removed.getStringArray(Contact.NAME, 0);
                    String message = "Goodbye, " + name[Contact.NAME_GIVEN] + "!";
                    status.sendDelayedMessage(message);
                }
            }
        }

        public void itemUpdated(PIMItem oldContent, PIMItem newContent)
        {
            status.sendDelayedMessage("Something changed, but they're still here.");
        }
    }
```

After you start the app and view the message, press the red end key on your BlackBerry to background the app. Open the address book and delete a contact. When you switch back to the app, you'll see the updated farewell message.

App: Selecting Recipients

BlackBerry devices have great keyboards, but it can still be cumbersome to enter a long email address. If you know a lot of people, the odds of remembering everyone's address is fairly small. The rest of the world has had access to integrated contacts for a long while, so your users should be able to do so as well.

The next iteration of MediaGrabber will allow you to select your recipient directly from the address book. For fun, after you send the message, use one of the extended BlackBerry user fields to keep track of how many messages you've sent. This could form the basis for later enhancements, like automatically suggesting the most frequently emailed contacts. All of your changes will occur within the SendingScreen class. Two new methods, selectRecipient() and updateContact(), do the bulk of the work. Listing 6-2 shows the sections of SendingScreen that have been modified to support your new features.

Listing 6-2. Integrating Media Sending with a User's Contacts

```
package com.apress.king.mediagrabber;

// Newly imported packages.
import javax.microedition.pim.*;
import net.rim.blackberry.api.pdap.*;

public class SendingScreen extends MainScreen
{
    private MenuItem selectItem = new MenuItem("Select Recipient", 0, 0)
    {
        public void run()
        {
            selectRecipient();
        }
    };
    private void selectRecipient()
    {
        BlackBerryContactList contacts = null;
        try
        {
            PIM pim = PIM.getInstance();
            contacts = (BlackBerryContactList) pim.openPIMList(
                    PIM.CONTACT_LIST, PIM.READ_ONLY);
            PIMItem item = contacts.choose();
            if (item == null || !(item instanceof Contact))
                return;
            Contact contact = (Contact) item;
            if (contact.countValues(Contact.EMAIL) > 0)
            {
                String email = contact.getString(Contact.EMAIL, 0);
                receiver.setText(email);
            }
        }
        catch (Throwable t)
        {
```

```
                    updater.sendDelayedMessage(t.getMessage());
            }
            finally
            {
                if (contacts != null)
                {
                    try
                    {
                        contacts.close();
                    }
                    catch (PIMException pime)
                    {
                        // Empty
                    }
                }
            }
        }

        private void updateContact(String address)
        {
            BlackBerryContactList contacts = null;
            try
            {
                PIM pim = PIM.getInstance();
                contacts = (BlackBerryContactList) pim.openPIMList(
                        PIM.CONTACT_LIST, PIM.READ_WRITE);
                Contact template = contacts.createContact();
                template.addString(Contact.EMAIL, PIMItem.ATTR_NONE, address);
                Enumeration matches = contacts.items(template);
                while (matches.hasMoreElements())
                {
                    Contact match = (Contact) matches.nextElement();
                    if (match.countValues(BlackBerryContact.USER4) == 0)
                    {
                        // First time sending to them.
                        match.addString(BlackBerryContact.USER4, PIMItem.ATTR_NONE,
                                "1");
                    }
                    else
                    {
                        // Increment our counter.
                        String oldString = match.getString(BlackBerryContact.USER4,
                                0);
                        // If this isn't a number, will fall into the catch below.
                        int oldNumber = Integer.parseInt(oldString);
                        String newString = Integer.toString(oldNumber + 1);
                        match.setString(BlackBerryContact.USER4, 0,
                                PIMItem.ATTR_NONE, newString);
                    }
                    match.commit();
                }
            }
            catch (Throwable t)
            {
                updater.sendDelayedMessage(t.getMessage());
```

```
        }
        finally
        {
            if (contacts != null)
            {
                try
                {
                    contacts.close();
                }
                catch (PIMException pime)
                {
                    // Empty
                }
            }
        }
    }

    private class MessageSender implements Runnable
    {
        public void run()
        {
            String address = receiver.getText();
            try
            {
                Message outgoing = createMessage(address, contentType,
                        filename, message);
                Transport.send(outgoing);
                updateContact(address);
                updater.sendDelayedMessage("Message sent");
                state = STATE_SENT;
            }
            catch (Exception e)
            {
                updater
                        .sendDelayedMessage("Problem sending: "
                                + e.getMessage());
                e.printStackTrace();
            }
        }
    }
}
```

WANT MORE?

PIM is one of the more entertaining areas of the BlackBerry API to play with, and there are several ways you can enhance almost any application with a little extra integration. Here are a few other things you might consider adding to MediaGrabber.

- Allow the user to select multiple recipients so they can send one file to many people at once.

- Show the recipients' names instead of their email addresses. Note that you will still need to store the addresses somewhere.

■ Create a rolling ToDo that provides a random challenge for the user. For example, "Take 10 pictures in the next 5 days." Update their progress in the task, and provide a new one once it is complete.

While it's easy to go overboard, it's also a great way to learn things. You can always remove features later if they seem cumbersome or aren't popular… and who knows, you may stumble across a really interesting combination.

Excelsior

You might know more about your users now than their own mothers do. With access to their daily schedule, circle of friends and business associates, and lists of what's important to them, your app has a great shot at making itself more useful and interesting. With this level of trust comes an enormous responsibility. Many users are leery of sharing their private information, and you will quickly lose their trust if you start mining that data for your own purposes.

With that warning in mind, users are more amenable than ever before to sharing information about themselves so long as they are rewarded for doing so, whether it's in the form of entertainment, convenience, or winning achievements. Most successful apps that use PIM will fall into one of two categories. Either they are fundamentally about personal information, or they use PIM to supplement their main purpose. If your app falls into the first category, you can use the information with confidence, so long as you disclose it; simply by installing your app, a user has indicated her interest in sharing data with you. In the latter case, in order for your app to be popular it's important that it degrades gracefully in the absence of permission. If your app provides a carpooling service, and lets users upload their address books to find other carpoolers, it should continue to run even if the users don't feel comfortable sharing that data; people can still search and see who else wants to carpool. Once you have established a sufficient level of trust, most users will eventually choose to share their data for their own convenience. The key is to be forthright in what data you collect, how you will use that data, and what will happen if the data isn't shared.

In Chapter 7, you'll continue your tour through the powerful set of built-in applications by examining the browser. The few BlackBerry users who don't use the device's PIM features will almost certainly pop open a browser from time to time, and you will soon learn how to take advantage of it.

Chapter 7

Browser

BlackBerry devices have long offered the benefit of putting the Internet in your pocket. With strong data features, access to corporate intranets, a relatively large screen and high-quality keyboard, it's little surprise that the browser gets so much use. As we continue our tour through ways to integrate more deeply with BlackBerry devices, we will look at how to effectively tap the browser as a portal to rich content on the Web.

Browser Types

Even though there might only be a single Browser icon on your BlackBerry, behind the scenes there are several different browsing standards and technologies supported. Before digging into code, it will be helpful to consider the various options available for mobile web sites.

WAP

When web browsing first came to mobile devices, it did not look anything like the desktop browsing experience. Screens were small, resolution was low, and data transfer rates abysmal. Even if you wanted to, loading a full-featured web page would take minutes and be unreadable once complete.

That said, there has been a steady demand for web access ever since mobile phones gained data capabilities. In order to support the extremely limited capabilities on a handheld, the Wireless Application Protocol (WAP) Forum developed a set of specifications in the late 1990s describing how to deliver mobile web content and how that content should be displayed.

The first crack at the mobile Web was the development of the Wireless Markup Language (WML). It assumed that most phones could not display images, and made other assumptions about device capabilities in an effort to guide design and improve performance. WML used the metaphor of a deck of cards, with each WML document defining a single deck and each viewable screen a single card. A sample WML document is shown here.

```
<?xml version="1.0"?>
<!DOCTYPE wml PUBLIC "-//WAPFORUM//DTD WML 1.1//EN"
   "http://www.wapforum.org/DTD/wml_1.1.xml" >
<wml>
  <card id="index" title="Welcome">
    <p mode="wrap">Movie tickets on sale this weekend</p>
    <p>
      <b>Call Our Operators</b><br />
      <a href="wtai://wp/mc;14155550188">415-555-0188</a>
    </p>
  </card>
</wml>
```

Note: You can find the entire specification for WML online at www.wapforum.org/what/ technical/wml-30-apr-98.pdf. However, be aware that no mobile browser completely implements the spec. Look on the BlackBerry web site for the BlackBerry Browser Development Guide for a complete list of supported WML tags.

Aside from the oddness of the "card" element, this probably looks familiar if you've worked with HTML before. The most interesting innovation of WML comes in that href link. Instead of a standard web-style "http://" reference, it uses the protocol "wtai://", Wireless Telephone Application Interface, which provides a powerful way for mobile web content to gain access to phone hardware features: select a link in your browser, and the phone automatically makes a call without your needing to remember and dial the number yourself.

So how is WML created? You can write and serve it up yourself as a document with the MIME type text/vnd.wap.wml. More often, though, WML documents are created by a WAP *gateway*. As Figure 7-1 illustrates, a WAP gateway handles traffic from a mobile web browser, retrieves the requested content (which may be full HTML), and then *transcodes* that content into WML. In other words, the WAP gateway rewrites the document into a format appropriate for the browser. This may include stripping out large images, removing styling information, flattening frames, and otherwise making the content more accessible.

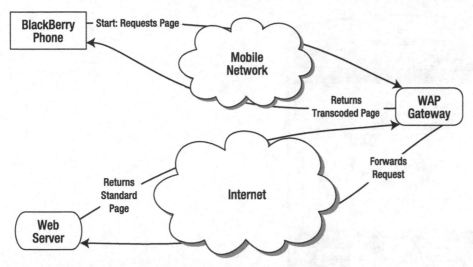

Figure 7-1. A WAP gateway generates WML content from a regular web site

WML is on the way out for multiple reasons. Modern mobile phones have far greater capabilities, larger and more detailed screens, access to faster wireless networks, and often unlimited data plans. Even lower-capability phones are increasingly migrating towards WML's successor languages. Still, there are a large number of legacy WAP sites available, and these will continue to exist for a long time. The oldest BlackBerry phones with device software version older than 4.0 may only be able to browse WAP sites without using a third-party browsing application, and newer BlackBerry phones are capable of rendering WAP content well.

Figure 7-2 shows a sample mobile web page. You'll notice the numbered links; these would be unusual in a regular desktop web browser, but they allow very easy navigation for people using basic 12-key phone keyboards.

Figure 7-2. *Accessing a web site formatted for mobile content*

HTML and XHTML

The BlackBerry browser started adding support for full HTML with software version 4.0, and support has gradually improved with every new release. HTML is by far the most popular markup language on the Web, and you can use your BlackBerry to visit any site you would on your desktop computer. Still, the handheld HTML browsing experience on a mobile device is not as pleasant. While data speeds have gotten better, browsing can still be painfully slow, especially if on an older non-Wi-Fi connection. If pages are not specifically designed for mobile devices, they can be hard to navigate and view. The BlackBerry browser is infamous for having trouble rendering certain common HTML elements such as tables. Additionally, a lot of content that requires special Plug-ins simply will not display. As a result, while you can open just about any web page in your BlackBerry browser, only some of them will look good and be usable. If you choose to use HTML when deploying a mobile web site, you should view the pages with every version of the BlackBerry that you wish to support. If you have an existing page that looks good, no extra work may be necessary. Figure 7-3 shows a full-featured HTML web page displaying within the BlackBerry browser.

Figure 7-3. *Full web content in a mobile browser*

The current best practice for deploying mobile web sites is to use XHTML mobile profile. This is a fully conforming document that contains a specialized set of XHTML page elements, selected with a mobile browsing experience in mind. The most recent version is XHTML-MP2, and pages written in this language may load faster and render better than ordinary HTML. Best of all, XHTML-MP2 is very close in design to HTML, making it much easier to support both mobile and desktop views of the same type of content. XHTML-MP2 should be provided with a MIME type of `application/xhtml+xml` or `application/vnd.wap.xhtml+xml`. The following is a sample of a XHTML-MP2 document.

```
<?xml version="1.0" encoding="UTF-8"?>
<!DOCTYPE html PUBLIC "-//WAPFORUM//DTD XHTML Mobile 1.2//EN"
  "http://www.openmobilealliance.org/tech/DTD/xhtml-mobile12.dtd">
<html xmlns="http://www.w3.org/1999/xhtml" xml:lang="en">
  <head>
    <title>Progressive Dinner</title>
```

```
    </head>
    <body>
      <p>Details on our <a href="http://example.net/may/">next dinner</a>.</p>
    </body>
</html>
```

> **Note:** You can see a specification for XHTML-MP at `http://www.openmobilealliance.org/` `tech/affiliates/wap/wap-277-xhtmlmp-20011029-a.pdf`. The document is short and mainly references other resources.

You will occasionally run across the term WAP2. Mobile carriers and developers have realized that today's phones are far more capable than those that motivated the original WAP system, and WAP2 removes many of the limitations present in WAP. When your phone uses a WAP2 connection, it is still connecting through a gateway, but in the case of WAP2 no special transcoding or transformation is done. The gateway may add some extra identifiers to your outgoing request that help identify the device or the mobile network, which can help your web server determine the appropriate content to provide.

BlackBerry devices do a good job at rendering this type of content. When dealing with full-featured pages like HTML or XHTML-MP, you should be aware that the user has a great deal of control over the behavior of her browser. People may enable or disable Javascript, HTML tables, even images. Your application won't know how the browser is configured, so, if your app uses the browser and relies on certain features being enabled, it should provide instructions on how to configure the browser properly.

Embedding Content

HTML and XHTML documents support embedded content. You often see examples of this on the Web for special items such as Java applets or Flash video. BlackBerry devices have had supported embedding since device software version 4.0, and their support is considered complete as of version 4.6. You can embed a variety of content including midi files, Plazmic animations, and other HTML documents.

> **Note:** If serving Plazmic content, your server must be configured to associate the .pme file extension with MIME type `application/x-vnd.rim.pme` and .pmb with `application/` `x-vnd.rim.pme.b`.

You can embed content by using the <object> tag, as in the following example. Use embedded objects when you want to present something within a larger context, or if you want to show something else if the browser cannot display the main content.

```
<OBJECT border=0 type="application/x-vnd.rim.pme" width="50" height="50"↵
data="spinner.pme">
```

Other Browser Options

Third-party installable browsers have been popular on BlackBerry devices for years. They started making inroads when the official browser lagged behind in capabilities; a smaller portion of users install them now, but thanks to the increase in BlackBerry owners a growing number are turning to these alternative options. One of the most popular is Opera Mini, available at http://www.opera.com/mini/.

Unfortunately, you cannot integrate your app with third-party browser apps as you can with the native browser. You can't be sure that all your users will have a particular browser, and, even if they do, they do not offer as rich a set of APIs for interaction as you can find with the built-in browser. Still, it helps to be aware of the possibility for other browsers, especially if you are building a mobile web site and want to make sure all your visitors can view it properly.

BES administrators and users may be interested in BlackBerry push content. This is a very specialized application of the browser that allows corporations to send web content directly to their users' BlackBerry devices, where they can later view and use it. Pushing content requires some specialized server coding but no special support from the client. If you are interested in learning more, you can find a useful document on the BlackBerry web site called the "BlackBerry Browser Content Developer's Guide." This includes sample code, information on the necessary headers, and how to configure your MDS environment.

Web Development or App Development?

Since you've read this far into the book, you have probably already decided to write a "real" client app. Still, it's good to periodically take stock of the situation and see whether that is still the best way to deliver your app. You also might need to justify your decision to someone else, or provide advice on future projects. Therefore, consider the following tradeoffs before proceeding too far in BlackBerry development.

Lightweight Web

Browsers and browser-like applications are sometimes described as *thin clients*. Their only job is to send data, receive data, and format the results. They do not come with code describing how to play a game, read a patient's medical chart, or draw a map. They might seem to do all those things, but only because the *content* delivered to the client can do so.

Thin clients can have many advantages over their thicker counterparts.

- ■ Easy Updates: Assuming you have access to the web server, making changes is almost unbelievably easy. Whether you have one user or one million, everyone will see the change the next time their browser launches.

- Familiarity: People are very comfortable using their browsers, and may trust a browser more than a random app they have installed.

- Cost: You don't need to pay RIM for signature keys.

- Security: The user won't see security prompts or other warnings when they visit your site.

- Consistency across Apps: Users appreciate how pressing Back will always take them back one page, pressing the BlackBerry Menu key will always bring up options for bookmarking and entering a URL, etc.

- Potentially Faster Startup Time: If your app contains a lot of content, it will take a while to load it all into memory. On the Web with a fast data connection, users can start using the app as soon as the first page loads.

You should keep some caveats in mind, especially if you are new to mobile web development.

- Browser Differences: If you develop a web site for the desktop, you'll probably be in good shape if it runs well in Firefox and Internet Explorer. If you're developing a general mobile web site, you need to be prepared to support dozens of different browsers, each with different versions and problems. Supporting all this can be a nightmare, especially if you use unusual features or want a good-looking site.

- Lack of Control: The user drives the browser configuration, and many do choose to speed things up by disabling images or otherwise lowering their capabilities.

- Limited Capabilities: Web sites simply don't have access to many of a phone's capabilities, such as the microphone or the file system.

- Slow Connections: Many users are still using slower data networks, and others may be stuck with a weak signal. Don't assume that everyone is connecting over a fat pipe. Make the pages as small as possible, and consider offering a link to an even more limited version for very slow connections.

- No Connections: If the phone goes into a tunnel, deep into an office building, or out in the woods, the user will be totally cut off from your web site. Consider when and how people will want to use your app to determine if this is acceptable. Note that users can choose to make certain bookmarked pages available in offline mode; this is a good solution if you just present text or use Javascript on a single page, but not if you use multiple pages or AJAX-style dynamic content loading.

Heavy-duty Apps

Besides being a lot of fun to write, applications bring many improvements to the table. Often referred to as *rich clients*, apps arrive with knowledge about how to perform their tasks. An app actually understands how to play a game or read a medical chart, and doesn't need to include information on tasks it will never perform. Apps are specialized, and because of that they can deliver a much more satisfying experience to the user.

Rich clients offer quite a few improvements over the flatter web browser.

- Faster Performance: If your app is written well, it will run circles around a web site doing the same task.

- Full Capabilities: A signed app with the proper permissions can do practically anything at all on the phone.

- Offline Support: If your app doesn't contain networking components, it will be fully functional even if the phone's radio is turned off or the user doesn't subscribe to a data plan. Even if it does use networking, you have more options than on the browser: you can cache old data, offer a reduced-functionality mode, and so on.

- Monetization: You can use existing storefronts to distribute and get paid for your app. With mobile web sites, you'll need to manage billing and charges on your own.

- Consistency across Devices: Although it takes effort, you can construct a consistent look and feel that runs the same on a variety of mobile devices, both BlackBerry and others.

Do consider the following caveats before embarking on a mobile app, especially if you are new to mobile development.

- Testing: The process of signing and loading your app is much slower than simply hitting refresh, and can significantly slow down your development speed.

- Porting: A web page will at least render on most phones, even if it doesn't look good. A BlackBerry-compiled app won't even run on other phones.

- Distribution: You must work with a mobile storefront (and share your revenue) or be prepared to manage updates and distributions yourself.

Launching the Browser

In many circumstances, you will want to offload some of your app's functions to a separate web browser. Perhaps you have a privacy policy that might be updated; rather than needing to release a new client every time it changes, you can instruct them to check it out and then direct the browser to a page with the updated policy. Or you might connect them to enhanced content, like leader boards or photo galleries, which can be quickly developed and deployed over the Web. Whatever the reason, opening the browser is a perfectly reasonable portal into online content.

Starting the Browser

In Chapter 3, we saw how easy it can be to open the web browser, requiring only two lines of code on device software version 4 and later.

```
BrowserSession browserSession = Browser.getDefaultSession();
browserSession.displayPage("http://www.sfgate.com");
```

Note: See the section in Chapter 3 for information on launching a web browser on very old devices with software versions prior to 4.0.

However, this is only part of the story. While most users perceive a single "browser" application on their phone, the reality is that most commercial BlackBerry devices contain multiple browsers. This is because of the different underlying radio technologies that may be used (such as cellular or Wi-Fi antennae), the different gateways that can be accessed (such as a BES gateway to corporate content or a WAP gateway to a carrier's subscriber page), and different rules configured on each account (the user may be charged for the mobile network but not for Wi-Fi).

In many cases, this need not concern you. If you are writing an app for your personal use, and know that the site is accessible from every gateway, then you can use the above code. However, if you need to open the browser content over a particular channel or wish to let the user decide, then you will have to dig a little deeper.

Service Options

You may remember service books from previous chapters. A service book describes a particular set of network configuration settings. By inspecting the available service books, you can find what connection types are available, and get the information necessary to open the correct browser.

Service books can be freely examined by signed apps, but aren't terribly well documented in the API. Records contain a set of application data, which is a raw array of bytes that provide connection information. These bytes are in a format that allows the device to exchange information with the BlackBerry Desktop Manager over a serial or USB interface. The information is a sequence of tagged fields: each starts with a 2-byte size, followed by a 1-byte type indicator, followed by the actual data payload.

Fortunately, RIM has provided a couple of classes to help in extracting the necessary information from this opaque block. ConverterUtilities lets you scan through the types in the service book data to locate a particular type. ConverterUtilities in turn uses a DataBuffer, a general-purpose utility class that wraps a byte array and allows you to read and write basic types from that array, similar to the functions provided by DataInputStream and DataOutputStream.

Next comes the deep voodoo—the specific configuration type of the service book is stored in a record field with type 12. Once you retrieve that value, you must match it against the proper browser configuration, as shown in Table 7-1. You should also check to make sure that the record is active and valid; there's no sense in launching a browser that is disabled.

Table 7-1. *Browser Configuration Types*

Number	Browser
0	WAP
1	BES
3	Wi-Fi
4	BIS
7	WAP2

Listing 7-1 shows a general-purpose class you can use to retrieve a desired type of browser session. You can call this repeatedly with different parameters in order to find your most preferred available browser. For convenience, the browser config types are provided as constants.

Listing 7-1. *A Convenient Wrapper Class for Retrieving a Specific Type of Browser*

```
import java.io.EOFException;
import net.rim.blackberry.api.browser.*;
import net.rim.device.api.servicebook.*;
import net.rim.device.api.synchronization.ConverterUtilities;
import net.rim.device.api.util.DataBuffer;

public class BrowserLocator
{
    public static final int BROWSER_TYPE_WAP = 0;
    public static final int BROWSER_TYPE_BES = 1;
    public static final int BROWSER_TYPE_WIFI = 3;
    public static final int BROWSER_TYPE_BIS = 4;
    public static final int BROWSER_TYPE_WAP2 = 7;

    public static BrowserSession createBrowserSession(int browserType)
    {
        ServiceBook book = ServiceBook.getSB();
        ServiceRecord[] records = book.findRecordsByCid("BrowserConfig");
        int recordCount = records.length;
        for (int i = 0; i < recordCount; i++)
        {
            ServiceRecord record = records[i];
            if (record.isValid() && !record.isDisabled()
                    && getConfigurationType(record) == browserType)
            {
                return Browser.getSession(record.getUid());
            }
        }
        return null;
    }
```

```
    private static int getConfigurationType(ServiceRecord record)
    {
        try
        {
            byte[] appData = record.getApplicationData();
            if (appData != null)
            {
                DataBuffer buffer = new DataBuffer(appData, 0, appData.length,
                        true);
                // Skip past the first entry.
                buffer.readByte();
                // 12 is the magic field that holds the service
                // record's configuration type.
                if (ConverterUtilities.findType(buffer, 12))
                {
                    // Buffer is now pointing at the value.
                    return ConverterUtilities.readInt(buffer);
                }
            }
        }
        catch (EOFException eofe)
        {
        }
        return -1;
    }
}
```

> **Tip:** Just because a browser is available doesn't necessarily mean that it is usable; poor signal or other problems may prevent you from connecting. In the case of the Wi-Fi browser, you can at least check to see if the user has a valid access point by checking whether WLANInfo.getWLANState() returns WLANInfo.WLAN_STATE_CONNECTED. Otherwise, Wi-Fi may be on but disconnected.

With this class, you can retrieve an appropriate browser and display a page with very little code. The example below shows how to open a browser through a BES connection to view an online comic.

```
BrowserSession session = BrowserLocator.createBrowserSession(
        BrowserLocator.BROWSER_TYPE_BES);
if (session != null)
{
    session.displayPage("http://www.xkcd.com");
}
```

Launching with HTML

So far, we have focused on using the browser as a portal to dynamic, regularly updated external content. However, sometimes the browser can be helpful purely as a presentation tool. If your app is capable of generating HTML, and running on a device with software version 4.2 or later, it can use the browser to display it. This may be more efficient than developing a custom UI framework within your own app. This is also a great option for applications that ordinarily do not contain any UI, such as libraries, but that occasionally want to show an error screen or other visual element.

To show your own HTML you use the same `BrowserSession.displayPage()` method that's used to show web sites, but, instead of prefixing with a protocol like `"http:"`, use the protocol `"data:"`. This instructs the browser that it should load the remaining content as its own page. Because there is no web server to provide the MIME type of the following content, you must supply it yourself with a string such as `"text/html"` or `"application/xhtml+xml"`.

> **Note:** Because `BrowserSession.displayPage()` takes a regular String, it cannot handle binary data or other special characters. If your document will contain these, you should first Base64-encode the data using Base64OutputStream. Append `";base64"` to the end of your MIME type to indicate that the remaining content is Base64-encoded.

The next code sample demonstrates how to create a simple HTML document in memory and then display it using the default browser.

```
String content = "data:text/html,";
content += "<html>" +
    "<head><title>Party Alert</title></head>" +
    "<body>" +
        "<p>Only 243 days left until National Hangover Awareness Day!</p>" +
    "</body></html>";
Browser.getDefaultSession().displayPage(content);
```

This technique clearly has some limitations. You can't easily link to other local content, and handling images is also hard. Some users may be confused when they see the browser and not realize that it is connected to your app; you should clearly communicate where the content is coming from. Still, it is another handy tool to have in your toolbox, and can be the perfect solution to certain problems.

Embedding a Browser in Your App

After you've gone to the bother of writing an app and getting people to run it, it seems like a shame to send them packing when you want to display some Web content. You are implicitly admitting that your app can't handle displaying that sort of content, and once they hit the browser you have no idea what they are doing. They may pop open their bookmarks and forget what they were doing before.

There is an alternative: instead of going into a separate app, bring the browser into your own. This is a somewhat involved process, but it can pay big dividends. You get to keep the user's attention within your app longer, and you get a great deal of insight into their actions: where they go, what they see, what they do. You can make the embedded browser as simple or as complex as you like.

An Overview

Bringing browser content into your app requires a fair amount of coordination. It isn't like displaying a simple image; the content needs to be loaded over the network, translated into a format that the RIM browser can display, and then positioned appropriately on the screen. And that's just the beginning: the process grows more complicated if the page includes embedded content, or if you want to allow navigation within the browser.

Ultimately, the content will be rendered out to a `Field` like other visual elements in the CLDC UI, but be prepared for more interaction with this `Field` than with others we have worked with before.

The Major Players

Four classes provide most of the important interaction when populating an embedded browser field.

RenderingSession

This is your entrance point to browser content. A rendering session can create multiple page views, each based at a particular URL or similar content source. The session also maintains information about what types of media and data formats are supported. Additionally, it provides access to the RenderingOptions, another class that controls the display behavior of browser content.

BrowserContent

BrowserContent handles the bulk of the heavy lifting. It contains the logic for retrieving data over the input connection, translating that retrieved data, parsing HTML/XHTML/WML/etc., keeping track of additional resources that need to be fetched, and so on. It owns, provides, and updates the `Field` that contains all the rendered content.

RenderingApplication

While BrowserContent is very capable, it is not a full-fledged application. Because of this, it requires occasional assistance from your program to do things like start new threads, open additional network connections, and so on. RenderingApplication is an interface that defines all the things BrowserContent might need from you. You do not need to fulfill every request it makes unless you want to make a fully featured browsing field. Table 7-2 displays the various contracts available in this interface.

Table 7-2. *RenderingApplication Methods*

Method name	Description	Required?
eventOccurred	Can respond to a variety of status events or user actions	No, can return null
getAvailableHeight	Determine browser height in pixels for layout purposes	Yes
getAvailableWidth	Determine browser width in pixels for layout purposes	Yes
getHistoryPosition	Find position in the history state stack	No, can return 0
getHTTPCookie	Provide JavaScript with a cookie	No, can return null
getResource	Open an HTTP connection to retrieve the requested resource	No, can return null
invokeRunnable	Start a new thread	Yes

Event

The most interesting RenderingApplication method is eventOccurred(). This is called frequently as the BrowserContent proceeds to fetch, process, and lay out content. By examining the Event passed to this method, you can determine what is happening and whether you need to take any action. Certain user-initiated actions will be reported within this method, so it is helpful to recognize them. Table 7-3 introduces the various types of events that can occur.

Table 7-3. *Browser Field Events*

Event identifier	Class	Description
EVENT_BROWSER_CONTENT_CHANGED	BrowserContentChangedEvent	The content within the browser field has changed
EVENT_CANCEL_REQUEST_RESOURCE	Event	Previously requested resource is no longer needed; can cancel the resource fetch
EVENT_CLOSE	CloseEvent	Browser requested to close

Table 7-3. Browser Field Events (continued)

Event identifier	Class	Description
EVENT_ERROR_DISPLAY	ErrorEvent	Display error message to user
EVENT_EXECUTING_SCRIPT	ExecutingScriptEvent	Javascript or WMLscript is running
EVENT_FULL_WINDOW	FullWindowEvent	Browser requested full window
EVENT_HISTORY	HistoryEvent	Request to add, remove, or navigate to a point in the browser history state stack
EVENT_REDIRECT	RedirectEvent	Request to move to another URL
EVENT_SET_HEADER	SetHeaderEvent	Header request
EVENT_SET_HTTP_COOKIE	SetHttpCookieEvent	JavaScript requested to set an HTTP cookie
EVENT_STOP	StopEvent	No longer need to load; can cancel previous URL request
EVENT_TICK_CONTENT_READ	ContentReadEvent	Progress of content loading
EVENT_UI_DIRECTION_REQUEST	Event	UI direction was set and scrollbars should be updated
EVENT_URL_REQUESTED	UrlRequestedEvent	Initialize a new BrowserContent for the requested URL

Fortunately, most apps will only need to handle a few of these, and some can ignore them altogether. It can be helpful to log these to help track down errors.

Flow of Events

As you have seen, properly rendering embedded browser content requires a high degree of cooperation between your app and the rendering engine. Figure 7-4 illustrates one possible sequence of events when you request a page to display. Note that most of the communication occurs between the application and the BrowserContent. Once the initial connection is provided, the remaining events largely occur asynchronously: you do not know exactly when they will occur, and should respond as you can. The BrowserContent drives most of the operations, issuing requests when it needs additional network or processing resources.

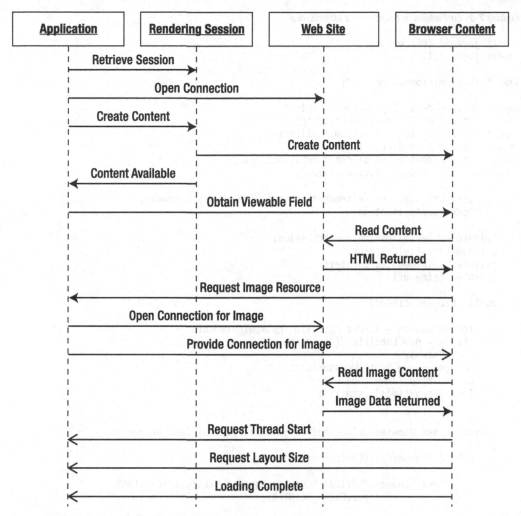

Figure 7-4. *Communicating with embedded browser components*

A Simple Example

In the most stripped-down form, all that you need to display an embedded browser field is to create the BrowserContent, hand it a connection to your web site, and minimally implement the RenderingApplication interface. Listing 7-2 shows a basic class that does just this by displaying the Google home page in the middle of your own screen. By default, the browser Field will fill the entire screen; since this is not what we want, we create a custom Manager that forces the browser to be only half as tall as the screen and slightly narrower. The StatusUpdater class is borrowed from the MediaGrabber app examples, and allows us to watch what is happening behind the scenes as the browser loads.

Listing 7-2. Embedding a Browser in a MainScreen

```java
import java.io.IOException;
import java.util.*;

import javax.microedition.io.*;

import net.rim.device.api.browser.field.*;
import net.rim.device.api.io.http.HttpHeaders;
import net.rim.device.api.system.Application;
import net.rim.device.api.ui.*;
import net.rim.device.api.ui.component.LabelField;
import net.rim.device.api.ui.container.*;

public class BrowserScreen extends MainScreen implements Runnable,
        RenderingApplication
{
    private RenderingSession renderSession;
    private LabelField status;
    private StatusUpdater updater;
    private String url;

    public BrowserScreen()
    {
        renderSession = RenderingSession.getNewInstance();
        status = new LabelField("Loading...");
        add(status);
        updater = new StatusUpdater(status);
        url = "http://www.google.com";
        (new Thread(this)).start();
    }

    private class BrowserFieldContainer extends VerticalFieldManager
    {
        public BrowserFieldContainer()
        {
            super(Manager.VERTICAL_SCROLL | Manager.VERTICAL_SCROLLBAR
                    | Manager.FIELD_HCENTER);
        }

        public void sublayout(int maxWidth, int maxHeight)
        {
            int width = BrowserScreen.this.getWidth();
            int height = BrowserScreen.this.getHeight();
            super.sublayout((int) (width * .9), height / 2);
        }
    }

    public void run()
    {
        HttpConnection conn = null;
        try
        {
            conn = (HttpConnection) Connector.open(url);
            updater.sendDelayedMessage("Connection opened");
```

```
            BrowserContent browserContent = renderSession.getBrowserContent(
                    conn, this, null);
            if (browserContent != null)
            {
                Field field = browserContent.getDisplayableContent();
                if (field != null)
                {
                    synchronized (Application.getEventLock())
                    {
                        deleteAll();
                        add(status);
                        add(new LabelField("Your search starts here."));
                        BrowserFieldContainer container =
                            new BrowserFieldContainer();
                        container.add(field);
                        add(container);
                        add(new LabelField("Don't forget to tip the service!"));
                    }
                }
                browserContent.finishLoading();
            }
        }
        catch (Exception e)
        {
            updater.sendDelayedMessage(e.getMessage());
        }
        finally
        {
            try
            {
                if (conn != null)
                {
                    conn.close();
                }
            }
            catch (Exception e)
            {
            }
        }
    }

    public Object eventOccurred(Event event)
    {
        updater.sendDelayedMessage("Handle event " + event.getUID() + " for "
                + event.getSourceURL());
        return null;
    }

    public int getAvailableHeight(BrowserContent browserContent)
    {
        return getHeight() / 2;
    }

    public int getAvailableWidth(BrowserContent browserContent)
    {
```

```
        return (int) (getWidth() * .9);
    }

    public String getHTTPCookie(String url)
    {
        return null;
    }

    public int getHistoryPosition(BrowserContent browserContent)
    {
        return 0;
    }

    public HttpConnection getResource(RequestedResource resource,
            BrowserContent referrer)
    {
        return null;
    }

    public void invokeRunnable(Runnable runnable)
    {
        (new Thread(runnable)).start();
    }

}
```

Tip: `Application.getEventLock()` is a static method useful in situations when you are working in a non-UI thread and want to update some UI elements before continuing to process in your separate thread. It is more compact and efficient than using `Application.invokeLater()` followed by creating and starting a new `Thread`.

If you create a simple app that pushes this screen and run the example, you will notice that the Google page partially loads, but, as Figure 7-5 shows, no images are displayed. Furthermore, if you try to click any links or type in a search, nothing will happen. Clearly, there is more to be done. On the positive side, everything just works from a UI perspective. If you are using a trackball-based device, you'll see that links automatically take focus as you scroll across them, and you can type in the embedded search field by highlighting it. On a touch-based device, links highlight as you touch them, and you can scroll the field by dragging your finger around.

Figure 7-5. A very simple browser field

A Fuller Example

The previous code shows the very bottom end of browser integration: useful for a static web page with no images or links, but not much else. On the other extreme, you could create a fully functioning web browser app by fully implementing all RenderingApplication methods. Most apps will fall somewhere between these two extremes, based on what features they want to provide. In this particular case, Google would be much more useful if it showed images and allowed you to follow links.

The first enhancement to look at is getResource(). The browser will invoke this method when it wants to obtain something else in the process of rendering a page, typically something like an image. You fulfill this request by providing an HttpConnection to the requested content. The interface allows you to do this in one of two ways. If a

BrowserContent referrer isn't provided, you must synchronously create this HttpConnection and return it. Otherwise, you may return null from this method (as we are doing) and kick off an asynchronous resource fetch (which we are not). You notify the referrer once the resource is available. You have seen something like this when viewing a web page on your browser: the initial page will display first, and then images will pop in as they become available.

First, let's write a helper method that creates an HttpConnection for a given URL and set of HTTP headers. The headers will be helpful as they contain information that the web server may require, such as what types of content we can accept. We open the requested URL in the default read/write state, then scan through all the current headers and add them to the new connection. If any problems occur, we simply return null, which the BrowserContent will interpret as being unavailable. The helper method is shown below.

```
protected HttpConnection getResourceConnection(String url,
        HttpHeaders requestHeaders)
{
    HttpConnection connection = null;
    try
    {
        connection = (HttpConnection) Connector.open(url);
        if (requestHeaders != null)
        {
            Hashtable headers = requestHeaders.toHashtable();
            if (headers != null)
            {
                Enumeration names = headers.keys();
                while (names.hasMoreElements())
                {
                    String name = (String) names.nextElement();
                    String value = (String) headers.get(name);
                    connection.setRequestProperty(name, value);
                }
            }
        }
    }
    catch (IOException ioe)
    {
        updater.sendDelayedMessage(ioe.getMessage());
    }
    return connection;
}
```

With this in place, we can properly implement getResource(), as shown in the next example. We first need to check to make sure that the request is valid; because we don't implement any caching in the app, we return null if the browser asks for cached content. We then retrieve the requested content from the current thread or a new thread, honoring the requirements for this method.

```
public HttpConnection getResource(final RequestedResource resource,
        final BrowserContent referrer)
{
```

```
    if (resource == null || resource.isCacheOnly())
    {
        return null;
    }

    String url = resource.getUrl();

    if (url == null)
    {
        return null;
    }

    if (referrer == null)
    {
        return getResourceConnection(resource.getUrl(), resource
                .getRequestHeaders());
    }
    else
    {
        (new Thread()
        {
            public void run()
            {
                HttpConnection connection = getResourceConnection(resource
                        .getUrl(), resource.getRequestHeaders());
                resource.setHttpConnection(connection);
                referrer.resourceReady(resource);
            }
        }).start();
    }
    return null;
}
```

If you run the screen again, you will see that the Google image appears. Much better, but search still doesn't work. Fortunately, that is just a matter of handling the request for a new URL, as shown in the following code. When we receive that event, we rerun this screen's main thread entry point, which will replace whatever is currently showing with the newly requested URL.

```
public Object eventOccurred(Event event)
{
    if (event.getUID() == Event.EVENT_URL_REQUESTED)
    {
        UrlRequestedEvent urlRequestedEvent = (UrlRequestedEvent) event;
        url = urlRequestedEvent.getURL();
        (new Thread(this)).start();
    }
    updater.sendDelayedMessage("Handle event " + event.getUID() + " for "
            + event.getSourceURL());
    return null;
}
```

When you run this example, you will see that you can finally search, as shown in Figure 7-6. Depending on what site you are using and what kind of user experience you want, you can make many more enhancements. Consider the following.

- Support for posting form data.
- Only follow URLs to specific sites.
- Maintain history and allow back navigation.
- Support running scripts.

Figure 7-6. An embedded browser field that supports images and navigation

Embedding Your App in a Browser

So far, we've looked at how to make your app call out to a browser, and how to pull the browser into your app. Both of these cases require the user to be running your app in order to show web content. But wouldn't it be cool if you could control what was shown in the browser whenever the user opened it?

MIME Type Providers

The BlackBerry browser identifies all pieces of content it finds on the Web by their content MIME types. Some of these it knows how to handle itself, like text/html. For other pieces, like music, it must call out to other pieces of software in order to handle them. And, for some, it just doesn't know what to do with them.

This is where we come in. The BlackBerry browser is designed with a pluggable architecture. Any piece of software can register itself as a provider for a particular type of content. When the browser finds something it doesn't recognize, it will query the providers to see if they want to take it. If they say yes, the browser will give them the content data and a space in which to render it.

> **Note:** You are not allowed to hijack the browser by registering as a handler for built-in content types, only for new types. You should check to make sure that your desired type is available on your target platforms. When you open that piece of content without a Plug-in, you should see a message such as "The item you selected cannot be displayed. Do you wish to save the item?"

Any given provider can register however many MIME types it wants. However, for simplicity, it is usually best to write a separate provider for each content type, unless there is considerable overlap between them.

Writing a Plug-in

All browser Plug-ins must extend the BrowserContentProvider class. They must declare what MIME types they can accept by implementing two methods. getSupportedMimeTypes() indicates all the MIME types that this Plug-in can ever render, and controls whether the browser will consider it for a given piece of content. getAccept() indicates what MIME types this Plug-in can render right now, given the current configuration of the browser. This may be a smaller returned set than getSupportedMimeTypes(); for example, if the Plug-in requires JavaScript support, it can decline to handle content if JavaScript is disabled.

The bulk of the Plug-in is contained in the method getBrowserContent(). This is the other side of the BrowserContent that we saw in the previous section: here, we create a BrowserContent of our own that handles the rendering of provided content. We have access to the requesting capabilities that we previously saw in RenderingApplication if we need them to complete the rendering task. BrowserContentBaseImpl is a useful base class that defines most of the necessary behaviors of a BrowserContent. This class can be configured or subclassed as appropriate to show your content.

Browser content is fairly flexible: your Plug-in may be called to fill the entire screen if showing a single piece of content, or just a small region if embedded within a larger web page. The default behavior is usually acceptable, but you can exert more control over the visual behavior of the Plug-in by implementing the BrowserPageContext interface. The rendering process will invoke these methods to find out what the rendering requirements are. Most of these are currently unused; you should return the provided default values for future compatibility. If queried for DISPLAY_STYLE, you can return one or more of the style enumerations included in BrowserPageContext as a bit field.

Listing 7-3 shows how to create a custom browser Plug-in for viewing Java source files. To make it more interesting, you can compact the source files for easier viewing on a mobile phone. When you open a class file, you will see the fields and methods but not the definitions. You can handle two of the more common Java MIME types, text/x-java and text/x-java-source. When invoked to show one of these, open the input stream that contains the Java source, and then read it in byte-by-byte, determining whether to show or hide each part. To make the source more obvious, place the scrollbar on the left and fill the whole screen if it is available.

Listing 7-3. *A Browser Plug-in for Displaying Java Source Files in Compact Format*

```java
import java.io.*;

import javax.microedition.io.HttpConnection;

import net.rim.device.api.browser.field.*;
import net.rim.device.api.browser.plugin.*;
import net.rim.device.api.ui.component.RichTextField;

public class JavaViewer extends BrowserContentProvider implements
        BrowserPageContext
{
    String[] MIME_TYPES = new String[]
    { "text/x-java", "text/x-java-source" };

    public String[] getAccept(RenderingOptions context)
    {
        return MIME_TYPES;
    }

    public BrowserContent getBrowserContent(
            BrowserContentProviderContext context) throws RenderingException
    {
        if (context == null)
            throw new RenderingException("No context");
        BrowserContentBaseImpl browserContent = new BrowserContentBaseImpl(
                context.getHttpConnection().getURL(), null, context
                        .getRenderingApplication(), context
                        .getRenderingSession().getRenderingOptions(), context
                        .getFlags());
        RichTextField contentField = new RichTextField();
        String fileName = "";
        try
        {
            HttpConnection conn = context.getHttpConnection();
            InputStream in = conn.openInputStream();
            fileName = conn.getFile();
            int numBytes = in.available();
            StringBuffer builder = new StringBuffer(numBytes);
            int depth = 0;
```

```
            int read = 0;
            do
            {
                read = in.read();
                if (read != -1)
                {
                    if (read == '}')
                        --depth;
                    if (depth < 2)
                        builder.append((char) read);
                    if (read == '{')
                        ++depth;
                }
            } while (read != -1);
            String compressed = builder.toString();
            contentField.setText(compressed);
        }
        catch (IOException ioe)
        {
            throw new RenderingException("I/O Error: " + ioe.getMessage());
        }
        browserContent.setContent(contentField);
        browserContent.setTitle(fileName);
        browserContent.setBrowserPageContext(this);
        return browserContent;
    }

    public String[] getSupportedMimeTypes()
    {
        return MIME_TYPES;
    }

    public boolean getPropertyWithBooleanValue(int id, boolean defaultValue)
    {
        return defaultValue;
    }

    public int getPropertyWithIntValue(int id, int defaultValue)
    {
        if (id == BrowserPageContext.DISPLAY_STYLE)
            return BrowserPageContext.STYLE_VERTICAL_SCROLL_ON_LEFT
                    | BrowserPageContext.STYLE_SHOW_IN_FULL_SCREEN;
        return defaultValue;
    }

    public Object getPropertyWithObjectValue(int id, Object defaultValue)
    {
        return defaultValue;
    }
    public String getPropertyWithStringValue(int id, String defaultValue)
    {
        return defaultValue;
    }

}
```

Registering the Plug-in

One crucial step is still missing: registering the Plug-in with the browser. Use
BrowserContentProviderRegistry as shown in the following example in order to do the
registration.

```
BrowserContentProviderRegistry providerRegistry = BrowserContentProviderRegistry
        .getInstance();
if (providerRegistry != null)
{
    providerRegistry.register(new JavaViewer());
}
```

After this executes, any time you view a Java source file with the proper MIME type,
your Plug-in will automatically run and display the compressed source, as shown in
Figure 7-7. This is true even if your application is no longer running.

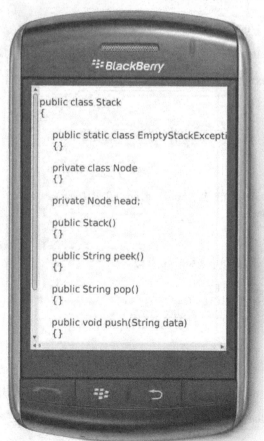

Figure 7-7. *A custom browser Plug-in displays a Java source file*

Tip: To test this, you will need to find a web server that attaches the correct MIME type to .java source files. Most online examples will serve these in "text/plain" for easier viewing. If you have access to a Linux box, you can easily install Apache 2, which has appropriate MIME defaults. Publish the Java file on your server, then visit the file from a desktop web browser. If your server is properly configured, you will probably be prompted to download the file, which will be identified as having a Java file type.

If you are running a web server on your local machine, remember that you cannot use the IP address "127.0.0.1" or "localhost" within the BlackBerry simulator; these addresses are assumed to refer to the simulator itself, not your machine. Instead, use an appropriate network address like "192.168.0.1" or "10.10.10.1". Also, make sure you are using a BlackBerry browser that can view pages within your local network. Try pressing the Menu key, then Options, then Browser Configuration. The Browser should be set to Wi-Fi, or a branded Wi-Fi name such as Hotspot Browser. Using the Internet Browser or other browser communicates with a gateway outside your local network, making those network IP addresses inaccessible.

However, there is a significant catch: you can only register a Plug-in once. If you try to register it again, an exception will be thrown and you may see an error such as "A browser content provider for text/x-java MIME type has already been registered with the browser." BrowserContentProviderRegistry doesn't provide any methods to remove a loaded Plug-in, or to determine what Plug-ins are already registered, so you cannot make your registration conditional. How can you safely register the Plug-in within your app? The answer is that you don't. In Chapter 1, you saw that it is possible to write a library that automatically runs on startup. You can stick the registration code in there and be confident that it will only execute once. As a bonus, the Plug-in will be ready to go from the moment the phone boots, even if the user never runs your app.

App: Friend Tracker

In Chapter 6, you saw how to piggyback on the existing contacts database in order to keep track of how many times you have shared media with each contact. It's an interesting piece of data, but currently there isn't any way to view it without opening up the address book. You can write a browser Plug-in that will run whenever the user views an appropriate piece of content in the Browser.

MIME Configuration

Before you start writing code, you'll need to decide how to deliver contact information that will integrate with your media-player app. Names starting with x- are available for use, and it makes sense to take advantage of existing VCard content, so define the new type text/x-vcard-media to hold this content. Because you invented this content type, there will not be a clash with any built-in types on the browser. If you have access to a web server, configure it to serve this MIME type. In Apache2, you can do this by adding the following to `mime.conf`, which instructs the web server to send .vcf2 files with the proper type and a content encoding of UTF-8. You will need to restart the web server after making any changes.

```
AddType text/x-vcard-media .vcf2
AddCharset UTF-8 .vcf2
```

Now you can create a sample vCard or two and upload them to the server. Many mail programs will allow you to export a contact's information in a .vcf or .vCard file. If you open it in a text editor, you should see something like the following. Change the file extension to .vcf2 and upload to your server.

```
BEGIN:VCARD
VERSION:2.1
N:Norton;Joshua
TITLE:Emperor
TEL;WORK;VOICE:(415) 555-0133
TEL;HOME;VOICE:(415) 555-0144
EMAIL;PREF;INTERNET:emperor.norton@sf.example.com
END:VCARD
```

If you access the .vcf2 file from within the BlackBerry browser, you will see an error message stating that the item cannot be displayed. The path is clear, and now you can write your Plug-in.

Creating the Plug-in Library

Open your existing MediaGrabber Eclipse workspace, or create a new one and import the current version of MediaGrabber. You won't actually be touching the MediaGrabber code, but you will want to ensure that MediaGrabber and the Plug-in are deployed together.

Create a new BlackBerry project. Name it "Friend Tracker," give it the Library type, set it to run on startup, and make sure it's always activated. The "Always make project active" option can be found on the General tab in BlackBerry Project Properties.

The actual Plug-in looks similar to the compressed Java source viewer you wrote previously. Create a new Java source file called `FriendViewer` that extends the `BrowserContentProvider` class. Formatting for the friend tracker is not important, so you can omit the `BrowserPageContext` methods. You can make free use of the PIM interfaces you learned in Chapter 6 to import vCard data, search for matching contacts, and extract interesting fields. For simplicity's sake, display text describing the user's level of interaction with the provided contact; a more elaborate Plug-in might also include graphical elements like a check mark, highlighted text, and so on. Listing 7-4 contains the entire Plug-in.

Listing 7-4. A Plug-in to Display a Web Contact's MediaGrabber Metadata

```java
package com.apress.king.mediagrabber;

import java.io.*;
import java.util.Enumeration;

import javax.microedition.io.HttpConnection;
import javax.microedition.pim.*;

import net.rim.blackberry.api.pdap.BlackBerryContact;
import net.rim.device.api.browser.field.*;
import net.rim.device.api.browser.plugin.*;
import net.rim.device.api.ui.component.RichTextField;
import net.rim.device.api.ui.container.VerticalFieldManager;

public class FriendViewer extends BrowserContentProvider
{
    String[] MIME_TYPE = new String[]
    { "text/x-vcard-media" };

    public String[] getAccept(RenderingOptions context)
    {
        return MIME_TYPE;
    }

    public BrowserContent getBrowserContent(
            BrowserContentProviderContext context) throws RenderingException
    {
        if (context == null)
            throw new RenderingException("No context");
        BrowserContentBaseImpl browserContent = new BrowserContentBaseImpl(
                context.getHttpConnection().getURL(), null, context
                        .getRenderingApplication(), context
                        .getRenderingSession().getRenderingOptions(), context
                        .getFlags());
        VerticalFieldManager manager = new VerticalFieldManager();
        RichTextField contentField = new RichTextField(
                RichTextField.USE_TEXT_WIDTH);
        manager.add(contentField);
        browserContent.setContent(manager);
        String email = "";
        try
        {
            HttpConnection conn = context.getHttpConnection();
            InputStream in = conn.openInputStream();
            // Remove network encoding by reading in to a memory stream.
            byte[] bytes = new byte[in.available()];
            in.read(bytes);
            ByteArrayInputStream bais = new ByteArrayInputStream(bytes);
            PIM pim = PIM.getInstance();
            PIMItem[] items = pim.fromSerialFormat(bais, "UTF-8");
            if (items == null || items.length == 0)
            {
```

```
                        contentField.setText("No contact found.");
                }
                else
                {
                    Contact friend = (Contact) items[0];
                    ContactList contacts = (ContactList) pim.openPIMList(
                            PIM.CONTACT_LIST, PIM.READ_ONLY);
                    // See if we know this person, based on their email address.
                    if (friend.countValues(Contact.EMAIL) == 0)
                    {
                        contentField.setText("No email found.");
                    }
                    else
                    {
                        email = friend.getString(Contact.EMAIL, 0);
                        Contact template = contacts.createContact();
                        template.addString(Contact.EMAIL, PIMItem.ATTR_NONE, email);
                        Enumeration matches = contacts.items(template);
                        if (!matches.hasMoreElements())
                        {
                            contentField.setText(email
                                    + " isn't in your address book.");
                        }
                        else
                        {
                            Contact match = (Contact) matches.nextElement();
                            if (match.countValues(BlackBerryContact.USER4) == 0)
                            {
                                contentField.setText("You haven't sent " + email
                                        + " any media yet!");
                            }
                            else
                            {
                                String sentString = match.getString(
                                        BlackBerryContact.USER4, 0);
                                contentField.setText("You have sent " + email + " "
                                        + sentString + " media files so far.");
                            }
                        }
                    }
                }
            }
            catch (Exception e)
            {
                throw new RenderingException("Error: " + e.getMessage());
            }
            browserContent.setTitle(email);
            return browserContent;
        }

        public String[] getSupportedMimeTypes()
        {
            return MIME_TYPE;
        }
    }
```

The last piece to write is the Plug-in loader, shown in Listing 7-5. Because the FriendTracker project is a library set to run on start-up, the libMain method will be called every time the phone boots. Claim the MIME type right away so it is immediately available.

Listing 7-5. Plug-in Registration

```
package com.apress.king.mediagrabber;

import net.rim.device.api.browser.plugin.BrowserContentProviderRegistry;

public class FriendTrackerLoader
{
    public static void libMain(String[] args)
    {
        BrowserContentProviderRegistry registry = BrowserContentProviderRegistry
                .getInstance();
        registry.register(new FriendViewer());
    }
}
```

Running the App

Run in the simulator first. You should be able to open the .vcf2 file you uploaded previously and view the appropriate text, as shown in Figure 7-8. If the browser still complains that it cannot display the file, double-check that the MIME types are correctly set on both the Plug-in and the web server, and that the Plug-in was activated and loaded on the simulator. You should be able to set a breakpoint within the libMain() method and see it hit as the simulator starts.

Figure 7-8. *Web content intercepted an interpreted with MediaGrabber data*

When loading the app on your BlackBerry device, first make sure that you generate an ALX file for the FriendTracker project, and sign both of them. You will need to load both ALX files in the Desktop Manager. (Since the MediaTracker project hasn't changed, if it is already loaded on your device, you can just load the FriendTracker.) When you visit the .vcf2 file in the device browser, you should once again see an appropriate message.

This seems to be working well so long as FriendTracker is installed, but, if a new user who did not have MediaGrabber visited that file, they would just see the unfriendly browser error message, with no instructions on how to solve the problem. Because of this, you should put custom content behind appropriate web page interfaces. You might write a simple HTML page with instructions such as "Click here to view Joshua Norton's public profile. If it doesn't load, you need to install FriendTracker: click here to get it today!" Another option is to embed the .vcf2 file within an iframe or other partitioned area. In these cases, the content will still render within the frame if the user has the Plug-in installed, and a blank space will appear if they do not. This allows you to attach appropriate messaging—"If you don't see the public profile, install FriendTracker here"—without requiring an extra click for the users who already have the proper content installed.

> **Caution:** Unfortunately, the BlackBerry browser does not update its HTTP accept headers with Plug-in content MIME types. If it did, your web server could easily determine whether the Plug-in was installed and serve up appropriate content depending on whether it was present or not.

WANT MORE?

There's a lot that you can do in a web browser window. So far, the app is presenting a proof of concept that demonstrates how to hook in to other sources of data to render custom content. You can do a lot more with this idea, including the following.

- Display the vCard's name, address, and other PIM fields.

- Automatically import vCards for contacts not already in the user's address book.

- Keep track of how many times a vCard has been viewed in another of the extended BlackBerry user fields. Update the MediaGrabber app so every time you send it to a contact it displays how often you have viewed them in FriendTracker and how many pieces of media you have sent them.

Of course, you aren't constrained to using a vCard. Many apps will define their own custom data types; you might also want to experiment with options for exporting and viewing other friends' online media files.

Excelsior

The Web is still the killer app. This is as true for mobile devices today as it was for desktop computers a decade ago. More and more people are turning to the Internet while on the go to find out information, connect with people, and entertain themselves. That's where the users are, and that's where you want to be too.

You have learned the relative merits of browser development *vs.* app development, and seen that, while both have their uses, app development offers much more power. You don't need to choose one or the other, though. BlackBerry has a very flexible system that allows you to launch a browser from within your app, embed browser content within an app screen, or even allow your app to run when the user views certain web pages. All of these techniques help bring your app closer to where users place their time and attention, making it yet more accessible and irresistible.

We have seen many options for integrating with the device's major built-in applications. BlackBerry devices also offer frameworks that allow apps to define custom behaviors, making them more accessible to other developers and more attractive to users. Chapter 8 will examine ways to complete your integration with the device.

Chapter 8

Digging in Deep

This chapter completes the tour of device integration by looking at various ways to tie into the device at a deeper level. These range from simple tasks, such as assigning attractive icons to your app, to more complex ones, such as providing a programming interface that other developers can use to invoke your app. When complete, you will have mastered most of the significant interfaces available for advanced BlackBerry development.

A Content Handling System

In Chapter 3, we briefly looked at the Content Handler API as a tool for launching media files in the native media player. However, the content handler system is far more versatile and powerful than just a media player. This complex yet extremely useful set of interfaces allows the creation and use of almost any functionality imaginable.

The Content Handling Philosophy

Back when Java ME was first developed, mobile devices could barely handle running a single app at a time, let alone multiple apps. The early promoters championed the advantages of bringing the Java virtual machine sandbox to the mobile space: rogue apps could not infect users' phones with viruses, and buggy apps could not crash and prevent you from placing calls. The entire purpose of Java ME was to enable simple, compact applications that could run with minimal resources in an isolated environment.

As the capabilities of mobile phones grow ever closer to those of desktop computers, this architecture has grown increasingly antiquated. Java ME phones now struggle against the richer multitasking operating systems found in smart phones. One major shortcoming of the original Java ME design is the inability to launch one application from another application. Again, this was sensible back in the 1990s when multitasking was beyond the physical capabilities of the device. However, there are many situations where one would like to take advantage of existing app functionality. If a photo-viewing application already exists on the device, it would be far better to launch that app to show your photos rather than reimplementing the capability within a new app and significantly increasing the app binary size.

Allowing the invocation of external apps is not as simple as it would first seem, though. How would you know whether the user has the other app installed? What would you do if they later deleted the other app? How can you handle upgrades, where one version behaves slightly differently from the other? And how do you avoid a proliferation of incompatible APIs for every new app?

Enter JSR 211. The Content Handler API (CHAPI) seeks to resolve all these tensions by establishing a framework for communication between apps. CHAPI's philosophy encompasses several desires.

- Request/Response Framework: Requesting apps should be able to ask for resources or for tasks, and receive information when the request is complete.

- Loose Coupling: Apps should not need to know exactly which app is servicing their request so long as it is capable of handling it.

- Seamless Transition: The device should automatically pass control between requesting and servicing apps, bringing each to the foreground or background as needed. The user should never need to manually exit one app and start another in order to complete a request.

- Enable Discovery: Apps should be able to learn which handlers are available to service desired requests and obtain basic information about them, such as their names.

- Expandable: New apps should be installable to provide additional capabilities, and apps should be able to initiate such installation.

- Support Delegation: An app servicing a request should be able to enlist the assistance of other apps to complete its task.

RIM has embraced this platform, using it to allow communication with built-in BlackBerry applications and between third-party apps. It is available on all devices with software version 4.3 or higher.

The Content Handling Architecture

Think of content handling as a client-server application. The client wants to accomplish a task, such as purchasing extra credits for a game, or acquire a resource, such as searching for a file. The client expresses its desire with a class called Invocation. The invocation combines several elements.

- A verb, such as "Edit", "Open", or "Print"

- A target, such as "http://example.com/credits.do" or "file:///SDCard/BlackBerry/Music/NationalAnthem.mp3"

- Optional extra parameters or data

Note: The terms client and server strictly refer to the request/response system of communication. Unlike a typical client/server application, no network communication is involved. In this chapter, I use the terms server and handler interchangeably.

The Registry class is used by the client to find whether any content handlers are available to service the request and to actually issue the request. Once the Registry receives the Invocation, it checks to see what appropriate content handlers exist to handle it. The Registry then instructs the device AMS to deliver the Invocation. Because the client and the server are separate applications running in different processes, the AMS will first need to create a new Java process if the app is not already running, then serialize the Invocation and copy it into the server app's memory. Figure 8-1 illustrates how this system works at a high level; note that the client and the server do not directly interact with one another, nor do they technically share the same Invocation instance.

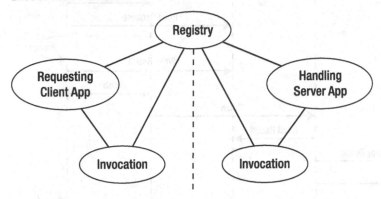

Figure 8-1. *A client/server view of CHAPI*

Server apps use the Registry to express their interest in handling certain types of content. Apps can register by content type, such as "audio/mpeg", by extension, such as ".mp3", or both. In some circumstances one app can specify which particular app should service the request. We will see examples covering all these invocations later in the chapter.

When a server receives a request, it will be started if it is not already running, and then it has the opportunity to dequeue the Invocation. If multiple invocations are pending, it can handle them one at a time, or spawn multiple threads to process them simultaneously. The server app has its own copy of the Invocation to work with; typically, it will examine the details of the request, try to fulfill the request, store any return information that might be available, and then notify the device about the success or failure of the operation.

After processing is complete, the device AMS will copy the modified Invocation instance back across the address space boundary into the client application. The client can choose to receive a notification that the request was executed, and can retrieve any information that was retrieved. Figure 8-2 shows one potential flow between client and server CHAPI applications.

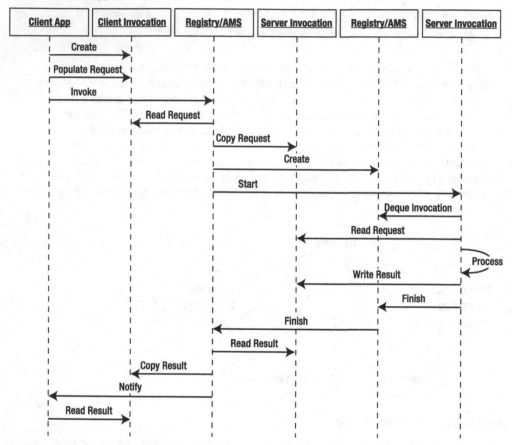

Figure 8-2. The life of a CHAPI request

The Major Players

Many classes are involved in smoothly fulfilling a content handling request. Some are only used by the client, others only by the server, and some by both. However, it is helpful to have a rough understanding of what each component does so you can anticipate what other apps might do.

Invocation

The data for a particular request is embedded within the Invocation. An Invocation's primary responsibility is to hold information that can be used to locate an appropriate handler. The Invocation is serialized to communicate between the client and the server app.

Locating Hints

Because multiple content handlers may be present on the device, the Invocation can provide multiple levels of hints and information to help locate the best candidate.

Each content handler must have a unique ID. These IDs are *guaranteed* to be unique: the BlackBerry will refuse to install or register a new application if it tries to claim a content handler ID that is already in use. Typically, developers name their IDs as they would fully qualified Java class names in order to distinguish between different authors; for example, if I were to write an image database, I might provide the content handler ID com.apress.king.imagestore. If you know the ID for a particular content handler you want to use, you can provide it to the Invocation. This takes priority over the other locating hints, and instructs the AMS to use this particular provider.

Ideally, a client application shouldn't actually care what server component is servicing the request. As with the "Software as a Service" model, components should be swappable after deployment without any client changes necessary. Therefore, the MIME content type determines most CHAPI handling. Any string is valid here; a component may register for a well-known content type, such as "text/html", or an invented one, such as "application/vnd.king.mediagrabber". The content type is the preferred method for finding providers if the handler ID is not provided, and all content handlers that have registered for that type will be considered.

In some cases, a client app may know that it needs to handle a particular piece of content, but not know exactly what type the content is. For example, a browsing application may locate a link for "http://example.com/card.vcf2". Absent any other information, a content handler will be selected by searching for components that can handle the .vcf2 suffix. Alternately, after the client app sets the URL of a piece of content on the Invocation, it can call Invocation.findType(). This causes the platform to locate the provided content and try to determine its type; this may be provided by the web server if the content is at an http:// link, or by the device if it is on the filesystem. After retrieving the type, this method automatically sets it on the Invocation, as if you had called Invocation.setType().

Actions

The various hints described so far are all nouns, describing the type, the target, or the desired handler. An Invocation can also specify a verb, the action to take. Content handlers can define actions using any string they want, such as "purchase". However, several standard actions are defined within the ContentHandler class, and their use is preferred over creating new actions. The defined actions are listed in Table 8-1.

Table 8-1. *Content Handler Actions*

Action	Value	Definition
ACTION_EDIT	"edit"	Modify the content
ACTION_EXECUTE	"execute"	Run the content

Table 8-1. Content Handler Actions (continued)

Action	Value	Definition
ACTION_INSTALL	"install"	Install the content onto this device
ACTION_NEW	"new"	Create new content
ACTION_OPEN	"open"	Open the content
ACTION_PRINT	"print"	Print the content
ACTION_SAVE	"save"	Save the content
ACTION_SELECT	"select"	Select from this content and return the value. This usually involves the user making an on-screen choice.
ACTION_SEND	"send"	Send the content off the device
ACTION_STOP	"stop"	Cease processing a previously provided piece of content

Content handlers must be able to provide the requested action. If an action is provided in the Invocation, only handlers that have registered for that action will be invoked. If the action is null, only the hints are considered, and the action will be ignored.

Parameters

Some content requests may only need a hint and an action to execute. If you provide a type of "audio/amr" and an action of "new", that may be enough information to communicate that you want the user to record a new audio file. In other cases, you may need to provide additional information. If you provide a URL of "file:///SDCard/BlackBerry/game.dat" and a type of "edit", the handling application will probably need more data to edit the file properly.

Invocation supports two methods of providing extra data. First, you can use Invocation.setArgs() to provide a String array. This allows the handler to receive arbitrary parameters on startup, similar to the traditional Java entry point's "public static void main(String[] args)" parameters. Different BlackBerry devices and software versions may have different limitations on the arguments; however, all devices are guaranteed to support at least 10 arguments with a total of at least 8192 characters. None of the arguments can be null.

The second option is to pass binary data. Invocation.setData() accepts a byte array, which can be interpreted however the handling application wants. Binary data might include a custom form of compact parameters, some extra data necessary to complete the request, etc.

Both arguments and data may be provided in the same Invocation. However, the device is only required to support a total of 16384 bytes of parameters. For every character that is included in the arguments, 2 bytes fewer space is available for binary data. Keep in mind that all parameters must be serialized and processed by the server application, so passing long chunks of data will slow down processing. If you have large pieces of data that need to be provided, such as large images or sound files, it will generally be more efficient for the client application to store that data to a temporary location on the file system and then pass the location in the Invocation, rather than try to stuff all the data within the Invocation itself.

Invocation Life Cycle

An Invocation always exists within a particular state. All states are listed as static fields within the Invocation class.

- INIT: The Invocation has been created.

- WAITING: It has been dispatched to an appropriate handler.

- ACTIVE: The handler has dequeued the request.

- HOLD: The handler must chain the request forward to another handler.

- ERROR: The handler exited without finishing service of the request.

- INITIATED: The handler cannot complete processing the request, but has started doing so.

- CANCELLED: The handler has ceased processing the request, possibly due to a second "stop" request.

- OK: The handler has successfully completed the request.

As noted previously, every logical Invocation will occupy two instances, one in the client application and one in the server application. Each follows a slightly different life cycle. Figure 8-3 shows an Invocation initially being created with the status INIT. It remains in this state while the client populates it. Once the Registry receives an Invocation and dispatches it, the status is changed to WAITING. After the server application has finished processing, the status will be one of INITIATED, OK, CANCELLED, or ERROR.

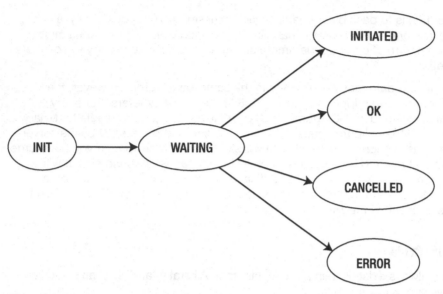

Figure 8-3. Client Invocation life cycle

The server application first sees the Invocation after it has been delivered, with an initial status of ACTIVE. The server retains ownership of the Invocation and can keep it in the ACTIVE state as long as it takes to process. Most apps will continue processing until they complete the request, in which case they set an OK value. Certain apps may support cancellation, which is indicated by going into the CANCELLED state. INITIATED should generally be avoided. After a request has entered the INITIATED state, it cannot later be set to OK, so out-of-band communication would be necessary to communicate the final disposition back to the invoking app.

If a server app needs to invoke another app to continue the request, it becomes a client itself. The original request will be set to the HOLD state while the new request is being handled. After the response comes back, the original request re-enters the ACTIVE state.

Note that the server app cannot place an Invocation into the ERROR state; this state is reserved for use by the AMS. However, you can easily imagine many reasons why a request might fail to complete: bad arguments from the client, a network error, running out of filesystem space. How, then, does the server communicate the error back to the client? The simplest way is for the server app to exit without providing a response; this sends the ERROR state back to the client, but provides no additional information about the cause of the error. A better way is to set the state to OK, but provide additional data that the client can read to determine whether the request succeeded or failed. In this sense, "OK" means "I'm done" rather than "Everything went fine." Figure 8-4 shows the complete Invocation life cycle within the server app.

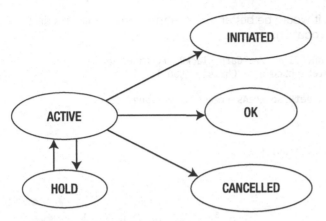

Figure 8-4. *Server Invocation life cycle*

In the same way that the client could set arguments or data in its request, the server can do the same. When it first receives the Invocation, it will see the arguments and data that were included in the request. It can set its own arguments and data using the same methods. After the request is finished, those values are copied back over to the client app, which can pull them out for examination. Of course, any changes made to arguments or data after a request is invoked or finished will not be updated in the other app.

There are no standards in place for formatting arguments and data. If you are writing a content handling app for other developers, you should clearly document any return parameters. If you are writing a client app, inspect the documentation to make sure you are handling all possible return values; if no documentation is available, print out the responses you get back so you can see what they are, and update your code to handle them appropriately. You might see extended status information, such as `"Status:ERROR file not found"`; returned content, such as `"file:///SDCard/BlackBerry/tmp/output.amr"`; or tracking data, such as `"RequestID=7238497"`.

Examples

The simplest type of Invocation that can still be handled only has a URL.

```
Invocation request = new Invocation("http://www.eff.org/");
```

If you want to make sure that one particular content handler processes your request, specify it in the ID, along with any other information necessary for it to service the request.

```
Invocation request2 = new Invocation();
request2.setID("com.apress.king.imagestore");
request2.setType("image/tif");
request2.setAction(ContentHandler.ACTION_PRINT);
```

You can provide extended parameters to the server app by setting arguments, data, or both. The following example updates a high score with a new name and player icon. The icon is presumed to be tiny; if not, it would be better to place the icon on the disk and only pass the file location in the Invocation.

```
Invocation request3 = new Invocation("file:///SDCard/BlackBerry/game1.dat");
String[] args = new String[]{"UpdateHighScore", "Chris", "500"};
request3.setArgs(args);
InputStream iconStream = getClass().getResourceAsStream("player.png");
byte[] iconData = null;
try
{
    iconData = new byte[iconStream.available()];
    iconStream.read(iconData);
}
catch (Exception e) {}
request3.setData(iconData);
```

ActionNameMap

If a handler provides a very narrow function, like updating a high-score counter, then choice is not very important: the app only does one thing, and can do it without user intervention. Sometimes, though, you may have multiple apps that can all handle the same type of request, such as playing a music file. In other cases, you might have a single handler that provides multiple actions, such as a high-score manager that can update, delete, display, or upload the current high scores. In both situations, the client app may not know exactly which handler or action to use.

The best solution is to present the available options to the user and allow them to select which one to use. Fortunately, CHAPI includes support for internationalization within its framework, and the most successful content handlers will support multiple languages. When apps register as handlers, they can provide locale-specific strings that describe the handler and all their actions.

These locale-specific strings are contained within an ActionNameMap instance. This essentially provides a two-way hashtable that allows you to map between actions (such as "open") and locale-specific action names (such as "Abra"), and between the locale-specific name and the corresponding action. Each ActionNameMap contains the mappings for one particular locale.

You can construct an ActionNameMap by providing matching arrays of actions and their associated names for a particular locale, as shown in the next example.

```
String[] actions = new String[]{"upload", ContentHandler.ACTION_EDIT};
String[] names = new String[]{"Upload to Server", "Update Data"};
ActionNameMap map = new ActionNameMap(actions, names, "en-US");
```

Later, when a program is looking for appropriate names to display, it will pass in a desired locale string, such as "en-GB" for Great Britain English. CHAPI will check to see if names have been defined for that locale; if not, it will strip off the characters after and including the last "-" and search again—in this case, for "en". The process repeats until a match is found or all options are exhausted. Because of this, it is a good idea to provide a basic language code, such as "en", that can be used as a default if a client app wants a country code that is not available.

Server applications may create ActionNameMap objects to advertise their capabilities. Client applications may obtain them to display available capabilities. Once a client has an ActionNameMap, it can look up the corresponding match for each name or action.

```
String localizedName = map.getActionName("upload");
String uploadAction = map.getAction("Update Data");
```

Alternately, an app may choose to iterate through all available actions and expose them all. The next example demonstrates how you could create a set of BlackBerry menu items for all available actions. Each will display a locale-appropriate name in the menu, but use the correct action when selected.

```
int size = map.size();
for (int i = 0; i < size; ++i)
{
    String name = map.getActionName(i);
    final String action = map.getAction(i);
    MenuItem item = new MenuItem(name, 0, 0){
        public void run()
        {
            // Process "action" here.
        }
    };
}
```

ContentHandler

As discussed in the previous section, client apps will sometimes want to obtain more information about their available options for processing a particular request. If they aren't satisfied with simply firing it off and trusting it will be done, they can obtain more information about available handler apps by querying available ContentHandler classes. The ContentHandler isn't actually an instance of the servicing application; rather, it holds descriptive information about the app.

- getAppName() retrieves the displayable name of the app.

- getAuthority() is supposed to report what authority has verified the identity of this application. On other MIDP Java ME devices, it will report the subject of the certificate used to sign the app, or null if the app is unsigned. For BlackBerry, however, this always returns null, even for the built-in media handler.

- getID() retrieves the handler's unique ID.

- getVersion() reports the handler's installed app version number. This can be useful if future versions of the app include more functionality.

More detailed information can be acquired about this handler's capabilities. Actions (such as "open"), suffixes (such as ".mp3"), and types (such as "audio/mpeg") can all be retrieved in two ways.

- By index. You can first find the count, as in `handler.getSuffixCount()`, and then loop through the items, as in `handler.getSuffix(i)`.

- By name. You can quickly determine whether a particular item is supported with a call such as `handler.hasSuffix(".mp3")`.

Finally, each `ContentHandler` contains actions and action names. You have multiple options for looking up this information.

- Use `getActionNameMap()` to get the `ActionNameMap` for the current device locale. As noted above, this will search for the best locale match.

- Use `getActionNameMap(String locale)` to retrieve a particular locale's information. This is useful if you allow switching languages within the app. Again, the best match will be retrieved.

- All mappings can be retrieved by calling `getActionNameMapCount()` and then iterating through the index with `getActionNameMap(int)`.

- If you only care about the actions and not the displayable names, use `getActionCount()` and `getAction()`.

> **Note:** You can obtain a `ContentHandler` instance from the `Registry`, as described later in this chapter.

The following snippet of code retrieves the name of a handler and then checks whether it supports executing content. If it does, the app will check for all the content types it handles, adding each one as a viewable element on a screen.

```
String appName = handler.getAppName();
if (handler.hasAction(ContentHandler.ACTION_EXECUTE))
{
    int typeCount = handler.getTypeCount();
    for (int i = 0; i < typeCount; ++i)
    {
        screen.add(new LabelField(appName + ":" + handler.getType(i)));
    }
}
```

ContentHandlerServer

`ContentHandler` is a client-facing description of handler capabilities. `ContentHandlerServer` is the server-facing class that can be used to retrieve pending requests, mark the status of completed requests, and query for information about its own capabilities and access.

A handler app can retrieve pending requests in one of two ways. By calling ContentHandlerServer.getRequest(), the handler app can directly receive an Invocation. This is useful if you know that a request is waiting, or if you prefer to process incoming requests serially within a separate thread. The method takes a boolean: if true, the method will block until an Invocation is received; if false, the method can return null if no Invocation is immediately available. The following example shows a handler application first checking to see if an Invocation is present. If not, it will spawn a thread that will continually loop and process all future incoming Invocation objects.

```
public void checkForRequest(final ContentHandlerServer server)
{
    Invocation pendingRequest = server.getRequest(false);
    if (pendingRequest != null)
    {
        // Process this request immediately.
    }
    else
    {
        (new Thread()
        {
            public void run()
            {
                while (true)
                {
                    Invocation incoming = server.getRequest(true);
                    if (incoming != null)
                    {
                        // Process invocation here.
                    }
                }
            }
        }).start();
    }
}
```

If a thread is blocking on getRequest(), another thread can call cancelGetRequest(). This forces the first thread to exit the method with a return value of null, even if it was waiting until an Invocation became available.

CHAPI also offers a non-blocking callback method. ContentHandlerServer.setListener() allows the handler app to register a listener that will be asynchronously notified of any future available requests. Each ContentHandlerServer can only support a single listener at a time. The registered listener will receive all notifications until setListener() is called again with a value of null. This system is useful when you want to handle all incoming requests as they become available. The next example shows how to define and register a simple listener.

```
private class PrintRequestListener implements RequestListener
{
    public void invocationRequestNotify(ContentHandlerServer queue)
    {
        Invocation incoming = queue.getRequest(true);
        // Process request here.
    }
}
public void registerForRequests(ContentHandlerServer server)
{
    server.setListener(new PrintRequestListener());
}
```

A handler might want to restrict access to only a particular set of invoking apps or certain other handlers. ContentHandlerServer provides methods to check whether a particular app ID is allowed access to this app, and to check all supported IDs. Access checks are performed by searching for matching prefixes. For example, if I write a handler that grants access to the ID "com.apress.king", then access is also granted to "com.apress.king.mediagrabber" and "com.apress.king.imagestore". If no access IDs are defined, all access is allowed. The next example shows how to verify whether a particular incoming Invocation has appropriate access; if not, we print out debugging information showing what does have access.

```
public void invocationRequestNotify(ContentHandlerServer queue)
{
    Invocation incoming = queue.getRequest(true);
    String source = incoming.getInvokingID();
    if (queue.isAccessAllowed(source))
    {
        // Process the request
    }
    else
    {
        int count = queue.accessAllowedCount();
        System.out.println("Only the following IDs are allowed:");
        for (int i = 0; i < count; ++i)
        {
            System.out.println(queue.getAccessAllowed(i));
        }
    }
}
```

When a handler has completed all processing, it should first update the Invocation object it received with any return arguments or data, and then call ContentHandlerServer.finish(). The completed Invocation should be provided, along with a final status of OK, CANCELLED, or INITIATED. This method prompts CHAPI to reserialize the Invocation and return it to the requesting app.

Note: `ContentHandlerServer` extends from `ContentHandler`, so all `ContentHandler` methods can be called on it as well. This helps a server app introspect itself to check what capabilities it had declared.

Registry

The final and most complex major component in the CHAPI system is the `Registry`. `Registry` provides many capabilities to both the client and the server app, including registering handlers, searching for available handlers, and processing requests.

Client Use of Registry

The most important method is `Registry.invoke()`. This method accepts an `Invocation` and dispatches it to an appropriate content handler. It can throw a host of errors, including `ContentHandlerException` if no suitable handler is found; `SecurityException` if this app is not allowed to access that content; `IOException` if the content provided in the URL cannot be found, and so on. The method may take a relatively long time to complete; for example, if only an http URL was provided in the Invocation, the `Registry` will need to open a web connection to determine the content type before it can select an appropriate handler.

This method returns `true` if the calling app needs to exit in order for the handler to start, and `false` if it can continue running. All BlackBerry devices are good enough at multi-tasking that `false` is always returned here; however, if you plan to port your app to non-BlackBerry platforms in the future, you should check the return value and exit if requested.

The `Registry` is also where client apps can query for `ContentHandler` objects and otherwise query for available capabilities. Table 8-2 shows the available methods.

Table 8-2. Client-facing Registry Queries

Method name	Return type	Description
`findHandler(Invocation invocation)`	`ContentHandler[]`	Handlers that would be considered for this Invocation
`forAction(String action)`	`ContentHandler[]`	All handlers that support this action
`forID(String ID, boolean exact)`	`ContentHandler`	The handler with the requested ID. If "exact" is false, prefixes are allowed to be returned; for example, if `"com.apress.king.mediagrabber"` is requested, the handler for `"com.apress.king"` may be returned.

Table 8-2. *Client-facing Registry Queries (continued)*

Method name	Return type	Description
forSuffix(String suffix)	ContentHandler[]	All handlers that support this suffix
forType(String type)	ContentHandler[]	All handlers that support this type
getActions()	String[]	All actions from all registered handlers
getIDs()	String[]	All IDs from all registered handlers
getSuffixes()	String[]	All suffixes registered by all handlers
getTypes()	String[]	All types registered by all handlers

Once an Invocation is initiated, the client is permitted to simply let it run. If it wishes to learn the result, it can call Registry.setListener() and pass in a ResponseListener. This object will be notified whenever an Invocation has completed, whether successfully or with an error. It will receive notifications of all invocations until setListener() is called again with null.

At any point, the client can call Registry.getResponse() to receive a completed Invocation. Like ContentHandlerServer.getRequest(), you can pass true or false to this method depending on whether you wish to wait until an Invocation is available or not.

A Registry instance can be obtained by calling the static method Registry.getRegistry() and passing in the classname. The provided classname must be the name of a class in the currently running package.

The next example shows a potential helper method that processes a file selection request. It first checks the Registry to see whether a preferred handler is installed. If so, it will specify that handler's ID in the Invocation to ensure that it is used; otherwise, it will accept whatever default the Registry chooses. The app registers a listener that will be notified when the request succeeds or fails. In a real app, it would continue processing from this point, perhaps by reading in data from the selected file.

```
private void chooseHandler(Invocation toSend) throws ContentHandlerException, ↵
    IOException
{
    Registry registry = Registry.getRegistry(getClass().getName());
    ContentHandler[] candidates = registry.findHandler(toSend);
    for (int i = 0; i < candidates.length; ++i)
    {
        String id = candidates[i].getID();
        if (id.startsWith("com.apress.king"))
        {
            toSend.setID(id);
            break;
        }
    }
}
```

```
        registry.setListener(new FileSelectionListener());
        registry.invoke(toSend);
}
private class FileSelectionListener implements ResponseListener
{
    public void invocationResponseNotify(Registry registry)
    {
        Invocation response = registry.getResponse(true);
        if (response.getStatus() == Invocation.ERROR)
        {
            System.err.println("Invocation failed");
        }
        else if (response.getStatus() == Invocation.OK)
        {
            String fileName = response.getArgs()[0];
            System.out.println("Selected file " + fileName);
        }
    }
}
}
```

Server Use of Registry

A handler app has access to all the same Registry methods that a client has. It will generally ignore these, except in the special case of request chaining. If a handler needs to invoke another handler in order to complete an initial request, it will behave like a client to configure an Invocation and optionally select a specific ContentHandler ID. The server will then call a special version of invoke() that takes two Invocation arguments. The first is the new Invocation to be dispatched forward; the second is the original Invocation, which will be set to a status of HOLD until the new Invocation has completed. Alternately, if a handler decides that it doesn't want to handle the provided Invocation, it can call reinvoke(). This tells the Registry to pick another handler to process the request.

In most cases, however, server apps will ignore much of the Registry, and focus on a few particular methods. The static method Registry.getServer() returns an appropriate ContentHandlerServer for the caller. The handler must have previously registered with CHAPI, and the provided classname must be in the current application package.

Finally, the Registry offers a pair of methods to dynamically register and unregister a handler. Registration includes all of the various pieces of information previously listed for a ContentHandler.

- A classname: this must be in the current application package and a main application entry point, such as a MIDlet for a MIDP application, a UiApplication for CLDC UI, or a library class that defines libMain().

- An array of String types, such as "audio/amr".

- An array of String suffixes, such as ".amr".

- An array of String actions, such as "play" or ContentHandler. ACTION_OPEN.

- An array of ActionNameMap objects for locale-specific action name display.

- An application ID, such as "com.apress.king.imagestore".

- An array of Strings containing application IDs that are allowed access to this handler, such as "com.apress.king.mediagrabber".

Other than the classname, all arguments are optional; you may pass null for any of them, or an empty array for arrays. A class can choose to register the type ContentHandler.UNIVERSAL_TYPE, which indicates that it can consume any type of content.

If the ID is not specified, the Registry must provide a unique ID that is guaranteed not to collide with any other IDs. A MIDlet will receive an ID such as "Chris_King-Image_Provider-com.apress.king.imageprovider.ImageProvider"; a BlackBerry CLDC handler will receive an ID such as "null-null-ImageProvider"—not quite as useful, but, if you aren't specifying an ID, you probably don't care what it's called.

Once an ID has been registered, no other app can register with it. Furthermore, no IDs can be registered that match a prefix of that ID. For example, if you register "com.example.food.lunch", no one can register "com.example.food" or "com.example.food.lunch.pizza". Such attempts will fail with a ContentHandlerException.

After an app has been registered, the registration continues to be valid even after the app exits. If an Invocation is issued for the app, it will automatically be started by the BlackBerry if it is not already running. Therefore, apps that can register for content requests should check their ContentHandlerServer soon after starting up to see whether they were started specifically to handle a request.

The next example demonstrates a potential server use of the Registry class. This will attempt to register an application called SigningApp with CHAPI. If this succeeds and no exceptions are thrown, it then retrieves its own ContentHandlerServer, and spends the rest of this thread's life servicing incoming requests. Note that most of the parameters passed to the register() method are null; very few handlers will need to specify all parameters .

```
private void register() throws ContentHandlerException, ClassNotFoundException
{
    String className = SigningApp.class.getName();
    Registry registry = Registry.getRegistry(className);
    String[] types = new String[]{"text/plain", "text/html"};
    String[] actions = new String[]{ContentHandler.ACTION_SAVE, "sign"};
    registry.register(className, types, null, actions, null, null, null);
    ContentHandlerServer handler = registry.getServer(className);
    Invocation next = null;
    do
    {
        next = handler.getRequest(true);
        // Process next request here
    } while (next != null);
}
```

Static Registration

The previous example carries a certain risk with it: what happens if this code is never executed? If the user installs but doesn't launch the signing app, the next time someone tries to issue a CHAPI request to sign text/plain, nothing will happen. Similarly, if an application wants to register with a particular ID but finds that another application has registered first, it may be installed but in an unusable state.

Static registration solves both of these problems. When an application statically registers, it reserves its place in the CHAPI registry at install time, not when its code is executed. BlackBerry will refuse to install applications that statically register for unavailable IDs. Therefore, you can be guaranteed that, if your app is installed on a device, it has been properly registered.

> **Caution:** Static registration only applies if the user is installing the application over the air (OTA). It will not take effect when directly installed to a device or simulator, which is likely how you will be debugging. You can combine static and dynamic registration to ensure you are registered no matter how the app is loaded. However, it is up to you to keep both registration methods in sync if you make any changes.

You statically register an app by modifying the JAD file, which will be located in the same folder as your .project, .alx, and .cod files. I find it's easiest to modify this file using a text editor outside Eclipse. Static registration takes the form of a series of lines inserted into the JAD that duplicate the information you would pass to the register() method. You can register multiple handlers in the same JAD file by providing each with a unique number; the numbers start at 1 and go up as high as you like.

You can list up to four types of information for each handler you wish to register.

- MicroEdition-Handler-<n>: This is the only required registration entry. It defines the entry point and capabilities of this handler, and requires five additional pieces of information.

  - The name of the class that should be created to handle incoming requests.

  - Content types handled. This can be empty if none is provided, "*" to provide all, or a series of types separated by spaces.

  - Suffixes handled, using the same formatting rules as for content types.

  - Actions performed, using the same formatting rules as for content types.

  - Locale displays supported. Note that the handler will be available in all locales; this just advertises whether locale-specific action names are provided.

- `MicroEdition-Handler-<n>-ID`: The unique ID used to identify this content handler. If specified, the app can only be installed if no other app has previously registered this ID or a prefix or suffix of it. If not specified, the BlackBerry will generate a unique ID, guaranteed not to clash.

- `MicroEdition-Handler-<n>-Access`: A space-separated list of all application and handler IDs that are permitted to access this handler. If not specified, all are permitted.

- `MicroEdition-Handler-<n>-<locale>`: Each locale specified in MicroEdition-Handler-<n> should have a corresponding locale entry. Each locale entry should contain one displayable text for every action defined. Texts should be separated by commas.

A sample static registration is shown below. This application provides two content handlers at two separate entry points. The first one is most complex: it can save any of several image formats, but only accepts requests from two package IDs. It supports displaying in English or German. The second handler is much simpler: it will edit the image store with a watermark provided in a plain text file. This second handler can be invoked by anyone, and apparently should not be presented to the user because no displayable text is provided.

```
MicroEdition-Handler-1: com.apress.king.imagestore.ImageStore, image/png↵
    image/jpeg image/bmp, .png .jpg .jpeg .bmp, save, en-US de
MicroEdition-Handler-1-ID: com.apress.king.imagestore
MicroEdition-Handler-1-Access: com.apress.king com.apress.rischpater
MicroEdition-Handler-1-en-US: Save Picture
MicroEdition-Handler-1-de: Bild Speichern
MicroEdition-Handler-2: com.apress.king.imagestore.Watermarker, text/plain, ,↵
    edit,
```

In most cases, you should statically register your application. That said, dynamic registration is sometimes easier during development, especially if you expect to frequently modify your handler settings.

Installing Handlers

In the course of issuing a request, you may realize that no handlers are available to service the request, but, so long as you know where at least one handler is located on the Internet, you can bring it down to the device. Simply create a fresh Invocation with the URL of the JAD file to install, and then execute the invocation, as in the following example.

```
Invocation install = new Invocation("http://example.com/ImageStore.jad");
Registry.getRegistry(getClass().getName()).invoke(install);
```

Even though you initiate the install, the user will still need to confirm it. Figure 8-5 shows the prompt screen, which is the same form that is used when installing an application from the browser.

Figure 8-5. *Installing a new content handler via CHAPI*

Built-in Handlers

Every BlackBerry device with software version 4.3.0 or higher will have at least one content handler available. BlackBerry provides a built-in content handler that can open a huge variety of media types. The specific set will vary depending on the device and software version, but it generally can handle more than 50 content types and nearly 100 content suffixes. It includes support for all types of media, pictures, and even HTML documents.

To directly reference this built-in handler, you can use the ID defined in `BlackBerryContentHandler.ID_MEDIA_CONTENT_HANDLER`. By providing this ID with no other parameters, the Invocation will open the native Media application.

Starting with device software version 4.7.0, you can also use one of the following arguments to control the initial landing screen when the Invocation is handled. All are defined in `BlackBerryContentHandler`.

- MEDIA_ARGUMENT_VIEW_MEDIA: Opens top-level media screen.

- MEDIA_ARGUMENT_VIEW_MUSIC: View music library.

- MEDIA_ARGUMENT_VIEW_PICTURES: View the photo library.

- MEDIA_ARGUMENT_VIEW_PLAYLISTS: Display the set of playlists.

- MEDIA_ARGUMENT_VIEW_RINGTONES: View all installed ringtones.

- MEDIA_ARGUMENT_VIEW_VIDEOS: View video library.

- MEDIA_ARGUMENT_VIEW_VOICENOTES: View voice notes.

The next example will cause the voice notes application to display.

```
Invocation media = new Invocation();
media.setID(BlackBerryContentHandler.ID_MEDIA_CONTENT_HANDLER);
media.setArgs(new String[]{BlackBerryContentHandler.↵
MEDIA_ARGUMENT_VIEW_VOICENOTES});
Registry.getRegistry(getClass().getName()).invoke(media);
```

Iconic

Up until now, no matter how cool MediaGrabber has become, the icon still looks dull. The default icon varies depending on your BlackBerry model, but generally looks like a simple blank terminal. The icon is the first thing any user will see of your app, and making a good first impression is important—you should pick something that makes people want to check out your app.

Design Notes

What makes a good icon is a subjective decision, but you should try to think of something that fulfills most of the following criteria.

- Legible: People should instantly recognize the icon.

- Relevant: A racecar is a great icon for a racing game, not so great for a word-processing app.

- Attractive: BlackBerry devices tend to have high resolutions, so your icon should be as detailed as other icons on the device.

- Transparent: In almost all cases, you will want to use a transparent background for a nicer look.

Ultimately, of course, the decision is yours. If you are a great artist, or know someone who is, try coming up with a variety of designs and see which one looks the best.

Technical Notes

For the best look, your icon size should exactly match the maximum icon size for that device. Unfortunately, icon size is dependent on the user's current theme, so, even if you know what device you are installed on, there may be multiple available sizes. Table 8-3 shows the supported icon sizes for the default themes on some of the most popular BlackBerry models.

Table 8-3. *Default Icon Sizes*

Device Model	Icon Width	Icon Height
7100	60	55
Pearl 8100	60	55
Pearl Flip	46	46
Curve 8300	53	48
8350i	52	52
Curve 8520	52	52
8700	53	48
8800	53	48
Curve 8900	80	80
Bold	80	80
Storm	73	73
Tour 9630	80	80

Providing an icon larger than the theme's supported size will have different effects depending on the device software version. If the software is older than 4.2, the icon will be cropped—that is, only the upper left part of the icon will display. On higher software versions, the image will be scaled down to fit, *without* maintaining the aspect ratio. For example, on a Curve 8300 with software version 4.5, if your provided icon is 106 pixels wide by 48 pixels tall, the icon will be horizontally squashed to make it fit within the 53×48 size. On the other hand, if you provide an icon whose size is smaller than the maximum, it will be left alone on device software versions before 4.6. For example, if you provide a 25×25 icon for an 8800 running software version 4.5, it will display as 25×25 pixels. On software versions 4.6 or later, if the provided icon is less than 25% smaller than the preferred size, it will be left as is; otherwise, it will be scaled to fit. So, on the Bold, a 75×75 icon will display as 75×75 pixels, while a 40×40 icon will be scaled up to 80×80.

Why should you care? Frankly, because scaled icons generally look really bad. There isn't a lot of detail available in an icon anyway, and any sort of distortion can quickly make an icon unattractive or illegible. This isn't a large problem for a personal application, but can have a serious impact on the perceived quality of a commercial app.

Icons can be provided in GIF, JPEG, or PNG format; PNG is usually the best choice. Color icons may be used for monochrome BlackBerry devices; however, monochrome icons may look better than those converted from color by the BlackBerry. Icons have a limited file size; if they exceed the limit, your application will fail to build.

Caution: Excessive icon sizes are one of several cases where a deep error may be reported within the BlackBerry Builder Console but does not stop the deployment of the application. If your changes don't seem to be available in the simulator or the device, carefully check the builder output to make sure that everything is building properly.

Providing an Icon

In the simplest case, you will just provide a basic default icon to display on the home screen or the Downloads/Applications folder. Follow these steps to assign an icon.

1. Right-click the project name in Eclipse and select Properties.

2. Open BlackBerry Project Properties.

3. Select the Resources tab.

4. Click Add under the Icon files section.

5. Navigate to the image you wish to add and select it.

Note: Even though you can add multiple icons here, only the first one will be used for your application.

Rollover Icons

You may notice that some icons change their appearance when you highlight them. This is especially pronounced on devices like the BlackBerry Curve: folders pop open, notes spring out, and browsers change colors. Why should only native apps get this cool effect? Fortunately, you can add your own rollover icon.

This process is easiest if you are using device software version 4.7 or later. Simply follow the instructions in "Providing an Icon" above, but update Focus icon files instead of Icon files.

Caution: This option displays for all software versions, but will only be used by versions 4.7 or later. It has no effect on earlier versions.

For software versions 4.1 through 4.6, you can use the method HomeScreen.setRolloverIcon(). This comes in three flavors: one to set the current application's icon, another to set the icon for another entry point in the same application, and a final one (added in software version 4.7) that lets you set the rollover icon for any application. All three take a Bitmap that provides the rollover image to display. The actual code, shown below, is quite simple.

```
Bitmap icon = Bitmap.getBitmapResource("rollover.png");
HomeScreen.setRolloverIcon(icon);
```

However, there's a catch: the code needs to execute first. By the time your app executes, the user must have already rolled over the icon, which rather defeats the point of a rollover icon.

You can solve this problem by setting your application to automatically run at start-up. You will then have two application entry points: one that automatically executes on start-up with no arguments, and another that executes with an argument when the user selects your icon. Follow these steps to set up your project appropriately.

1. Right-click your main project (such as MediaGrabber) in Eclipse and select Properties.

2. Open BlackBerry Project Properties.

3. Select the Application tab.

4. Check "Auto-run on startup" (to make the app run on boot) and "System module" (to keep this entry point from displaying in the main menu), and then click OK.

5. In Eclipse, click File, New, then Other. . .

6. Select BlackBerry Project and click Next.

7. Provide an application name (such as "MediaGrabberAlternate") and click Finish.

8. Open the new project's BlackBerry Project Properties and select the Application tab.

9. Change the Project type to "Alternate CLDC Application Entry Point".

10. If your workspace contains multiple BlackBerry projects, select the main project from the drop-down menu under the Project type.

11. Provide a simple but unique string in the box labeled "Argument passed to static public void main(String[] args)", such as "launch".

12. Leave the rest of the options at their default and press OK to exit.

Now your application's `main` method will be called twice: once when the phone boots, and again when the user selects it from the main menu. The following code shows how to set a rollover icon for a crossword puzzle app. Note that we specify an index of 1; this is because the default of index 0 refers to the auto-start entry point, which no longer has an icon to display.

```
public static void main(String[] args)
{
    if (args != null && args.length > 0 && args[0].equals("launch"))
    {
        CrosswordPuzzler puzzler = new CrosswordPuzzler();
        puzzler.enterEventDispatcher();
    }
    else
    {
        Bitmap rollover = Bitmap.getBitmapResource("explodingPuzzle.png");
        HomeScreen.setRolloverIcon(rollover, 1);
    }
}
```

Caution: Device software version 4.1 contains a bug that can cause an IllegalArgumentException when calling `setRolloverIcon()`. If you need to support this version, you can work around the problem by waiting until the device has finished starting up (by checking `ApplicationManager.inStartup()`) and only setting the icon once it is complete.

You must define a main application icon before you can set a rollover icon; otherwise the default icons will continue to show for both the focused and the nonfocused states.

Changing Icons

Sooner or later, you will need to wrestle with a troubling issue: how do you support multiple versions of your app that run on different devices? As you'll see, there are two major schools of thought on this: some people prefer to write a single version of the app that is capable of running on any BlackBerry, while others prefer to create a slightly different version of it for each device. Assume for the moment that you follow the first path. You would want to have a single application that displays the best icon, no matter whether it is running on a Curve, a Pearl, or a Bold.

Even if you create a custom version of your application for each of these devices, you still need to deal with the situation where the user has selected a new theme that has a different icon size from the default. Ideally, you would like to update your icon to minimize the effects of scaling.

The HomeScreen class offers additional methods that help with this problem. updateIcon() behaves like setRolloverIcon(), but it updates the main nonselected version of your icon instead of the rollover version. Additionally, etPreferredIconWidth() and getPreferredIconHeight() inform you of the best sizes for the current theme. You can even call getActiveThemeName() if you would like to show different icons depending on the selected theme—for example, you might prefer to use different colors to achieve the best contrast with the background.

The following code examines the current preferred icon width, then selects the best matching icon based on that. This example could be expanded to deal with any supported size. As with the previous rollover example, it would be best to place this within the application's main function.

```
Bitmap icon = null;
Bitmap rollover = null;
int width = HomeScreen.getPreferredIconWidth();
if (width <= 46)
{
    icon = Bitmap.getBitmapResource("icon_46x46");
    rollover = Bitmap.getBitmapResource("rollover_46x46");
}
else if (width <= 53)
{
    icon = Bitmap.getBitmapResource("icon_53x48");
    rollover = Bitmap.getBitmapResource("rollover_53x48");
}
else if (width <= 80)
{
    icon = Bitmap.getBitmapResource("icon_80x80");
    rollover = Bitmap.getBitmapResource("rollover_80x80");
}
HomeScreen.setRolloverIcon(rollover);
HomeScreen.updateIcon(icon);
```

Setting Icon Position

BlackBerry devices have a pretty major shortcoming: they do not provide any real organization for installed apps. Everything gets dumped onto the Home screen or a particular folder, without separation between Games, Tools, Productivity, etc. There are currently no settings to change this. However, you can control the relative position of an icon by following these steps.

1. Right-click your main project (such as MediaGrabber) in Eclipse and select Properties.

2. Open BlackBerry Project Properties.

3. Select the Application tab.

4. Enter a value for the "Home screen position" box.

Value 1 is the highest position in the list, 255 is the lowest, and all numbers in between are placed in descending order; 0 indicates no particular preference. In practice, most developers set 1 here in an attempt to increase the visibility of their app; less often, they will pick 255 to avoid having it lost in the middle.

Users can always manually adjust the position of an icon. When this happens, it permanently overrides the application's requested position.

Icon positions are most likely to be useful if you wish to group a suite of applications together. For example, if you are releasing a set of office applications (document editing, spreadsheets, presentations, etc.), you might assign positions 126, 127, and 128. This should ensure that, without any user intervention, all of your applications will be grouped together on the screen.

Native Menus

You already know how to define a custom menu for your application. What's really cool, though, is adding a new item to an existing BlackBerry menu. Virtually every menu on the device can be customized, including the browser, phone, and address book menus.

Defining Native Menu Options

Instead of a standard MenuItem, define these native menu entries with the special ApplicationMenuItem class. To do this, you must provide three pieces of information.

- In the constructor, an integer value indicating where this menu item should be located. As with the MenuItem class, lower values indicate higher placement; unlike MenuItem, there are not separate numbers for ordinal and priority.

- A toString() method that provides text to display for this menu item. If you wish to internationalize this string, you must do so yourself.

- A run() method that will execute when the user selects this menu item. Depending on the type of menu, it may receive an Object describing the context. For example, a TextMessage would be provided from the SMS editor's menu. You can do whatever you want within the run() method, whether it's starting another application, doing file or network operations, or displaying simple UI.

The next example shows a custom menu item that could be added to the Calendar application. When you create, edit, or view a meeting within the native Calendar, you can select from the menu to order pizza for that meeting. This example sets a ToDo reminder for yourself; it could also send an email request to your caterer, or start up the phone to call your favorite delivery place.

```
private class PizzaMenuItem extends ApplicationMenuItem
{
    public PizzaMenuItem()
```

```
    {
        // Pizza is the most important thing.
        super(0);
    }
    public Object run(Object context)
    {
        if (context == null || !(context instanceof Event))
            return null;
        try
        {
            Event event = (Event) context;
            if (event.countValues(Event.SUMMARY) > 0)
            {
                String name = event.getString(Event.SUMMARY, 0);
                ToDoList todos = (ToDoList) PIM.getInstance().openPIMList(↩
                    PIM.TODO_LIST, PIM.WRITE_ONLY);
                ToDo task = todos.createToDo();
                task.addString(ToDo.SUMMARY, PIMItem.ATTR_NONE,↩
                    "Order pizza for " + name);
                task.commit();
                Dialog.alert("Pizza Reminder Created");
                return null;
            }
        }
        catch (Exception e)
        {
            e.printStackTrace();
        }
        Dialog.alert("Couldn't create pizza reminder");
        return null;
    }
    public String toString()
    {
        return "Order Pizza";
    }
}
```

Inserting into the Native Menu

BlackBerry offers an almost absurd number of menus that can be modified. Table 8-4 shows everything that is supported, along with the object that is provided as a context when the item executes. All names are defined in the `ApplicationMenuItemRepository` class.

Table 8-4. Native Application Menu Items

Name	Displays In	Context Parameter Type
MENUITEM_ADDRESSBOOK_LIST	Address book in list mode	Contact
MENUITEM_ADDRESSCARD_EDIT	Open address book contact in edit mode	Contact
MENUITEM_ADDRESSCARD_VIEW	Open address book contact in view mode	Contact

Table 8-4. Native Application Menu Items (continued)

Name	Displays In	Context Parameter Type
MENUITEM_ALARM	Alarm app	N/A
MENUITEM_BROWSER	Browser	N/A
MENUITEM_CALENDAR	Calendar in view mode	Event
MENUITEM_CALENDAR_EVENT	Calendar event in view or edit modes	Event
MENUITEM_CAMERA_PREVIEW	Camera preview	String (contains image file location)
MENUITEM_EMAIL_EDIT	Email open in edit mode	Message
MENUITEM_EMAIL_VIEW	Email open in view mode	Message
MENUITEM_FILE_EXPLORER	File explorer running	String (contains file location)
MENUITEM_FILE_EXPLORER_BROWSE	File explorer open in browse mode	String (contains file location)
MENUITEM_FILE_EXPLORER_ITEM	Open item in file explorer	String (contains file location)
MENUITEM_GROUPADDRESS_EDIT	Group address entry in Contacts app open for edit	N/A
MENUITEM_GROUPADDRESS_VIEW	Group address entry in Contacts app open for viewing	N/A
MENUITEM_MAPS	Maps app	MapView
MENUITEM_MEMO_EDIT	Individual memo open for editing	BlackBerryMemo
MENUITEM_MEMO_LIST	List of memos	BlackBerryMemo
MENUITEM_MEMO_VIEW	Individual memo open for viewing	BlackBerryMemo
MENUITEM_MESSAGE_LIST	List of messages	Message, TextMessage, or MultipartMessage

Table 8-4. *Native Application Menu Items (continued)*

Name	Displays In	Context Parameter Type
MENUITEM_MMS_EDIT	MMS open for edit	MultipartMessage
MENUITEM_MMS_VIEW	MMS open for viewing	MultipartMessage
MENUITEM_MUSIC_SERVICE_ITEM	Music section of Media app	N/A
MENUITEM_PHONE	Phone (dialer) app	N/A
MENUITEM_PHONELOG_VIEW	Call log	PhoneLog
MENUITEM_SEARCH	Search window	N/A
MENUITEM_SMS_EDIT	SMS open for edit	TextMessage
MENUITEM_SMS_VIEW	SMS open for view	TextMessage
MENUITEM_SYSTEM	Any menu	Parameter type for this particular menu
MENUITEM_TASK_EDIT	Individual task open for editing	ToDo
MENUITEM_TASK_LIST	List of tasks	ToDo
MENUITEM_VIDEO_RECORDER	Video recorder	String (contains file location)
MENUITEM_VIDEO_SERVICE_ITEM	Video section of Media app	N/A

You may optionally add your app's ApplicationDescriptor when adding a custom menu item. This will cause your app to start when the item is selected. The filesystem and maps items require you to provide the ApplicationDescriptor. In the case of filesystem menu items, you can optionally pass a String context item that defines the MIME type that this menu item handles. For example, if you provide "text/plain", your menu will display if a .txt file is selected, but not for any other type of file.

Use ApplicationMenuItemRepository.addMenuItem() to insert new items into a native menu, and ApplicationMenuItemRepository.removeMenuItem() to remove a previously added item. The following snippet adds our previously defined pizza menu to the Calendar app.

```
ApplicationMenuItemRepository repo =
    ApplicationMenuItemRepository.getInstance();
repo.addMenuItem(ApplicationMenuItemRepository.MENUITEM_CALENDAR_EVENT,
    new PizzaMenuItem());
```

As you learned when looking at rollover icons, the main problem with this system is that you cannot insert this code into a menu until your app executes, whereas what you really want is to add the menu item before it executes. As with icons, the solution is to add the custom menu items within an auto-start application or library so you have a chance to run your code when the device powers on.

App: Enter from Anywhere

Up until now, every time you have run MediaGrabber you have needed to locate the icon first and select it. We will use the tools discussed in this chapter to enable launching MediaGrabber from native device menus or any third-party application. We'll also take this opportunity to add some custom icons for the app.

Adding CHAPI Handling

MediaGrabber mainly focuses on capturing and sending media. For now, let us look at exposing the sending functions to other applications.

Static Registration

Find the MediaGrabber.jad file, which will be located in the same directory as your .project file. Open it with your preferred text editor and insert the following lines anywhere in the file:

```
MicroEdition-Handler-1: com.apress.king.mediagrabber.MediaGrabber, image/png↵
    image/jpeg audio/amr audio/pcm audio/mpeg, .png .jpg .jpeg .amr .pcm .mp3,↵
    send, en
MicroEdition-Handler-1-ID: com.apress.king.mediagrabber
MicroEdition-Handler-1-en: Send Encrypted Via MediaGrabber
```

The first line says which class should be started when a request is received, lists the MIME types and suffixes that it can handle, describes the action it provides, and declares support for English language display. The second line provides a unique ID so other apps can specify whether they wish to invoke us directly. The final line shows a human-readable description of what our action does.

> **Note:** The JAD file automatically gets rebuilt every time you modify the project. Fortunately, the builder is smart enough to leave your modifications in place even when it changes other things. If you are using source control, you probably do want to check in the JAD file if you make modifications, but be prepared for frequent changes.

Listening for and Handling Requests

We use CHAPI to add new access to MediaGrabber, not to modify its behavior. Therefore, we only need to change `MediaGrabber.java`, the main application entry point. We will do the following:

- Add dynamic registration so we can use CHAPI when debugging in the simulator or cable-loading MediaGrabber.

- Add an alternate entry point to ensure that we register on app boot.

- As long as we're creating an alternate entry point, use it to set a rollover icon as well.

- When we receive a request, grab information about the file to send from the Invocation, and then move directly to the SendingScreen, skipping past the standard media capture prompts.

To get started, follow the instructions in the Rollover Icons section to change MediaGrabber into an auto-start system application and add a new alternate entry point called MediaGrabberAlternate. Find an icon that you like and set it as the application icon file in MediaGrabberAlternate. Find another icon, preferably of the same size and quality, and add it to MediaGrabber's "src" folder.

Now you are ready to update the main MediaGrabber file. Listing 8-1 contains the new file. Substitute your rollover icon name for rollover.png, or remove this line if you don't wish to use a rollover.

Listing 8-1. Adding CHAPI and Rollover Icon Support to MediaGrabber

```java
package com.apress.king.mediagrabber;

import java.io.InputStream;

import javax.microedition.content.*;
import javax.microedition.io.Connector;
import javax.microedition.io.file.FileConnection;
import javax.microedition.pim.Contact;

import net.rim.blackberry.api.homescreen.HomeScreen;
import net.rim.blackberry.api.menuitem.*;
import net.rim.blackberry.api.pdap.BlackBerryContact;
import net.rim.device.api.system.Bitmap;
import net.rim.device.api.system.RuntimeStore;
import net.rim.device.api.ui.UiApplication;
import net.rim.device.api.ui.component.Dialog;

public class MediaGrabber extends UiApplication implements RequestListener
{
    private Invocation pending;
    private ContentHandlerServer server;

    private static final String CHAPI_ID = "com.apress.king.mediagrabber";
    private static final String[] MIME_TYPES = new String[]
    { "image/png", "image/jpeg", "audio/amr-wb", "audio/amr", "audio/pcm",
```

```java
            "audio/mpeg" };
    private static final String[] SUFFIXES = new String[]
    { ".png", ".jpg", ".jpeg", ".amr", ".pcm", ".mp3" };

    public MediaGrabber()
    {
        String className = MediaGrabber.class.getName();
        try
        {
            verifyRegistration();
            server = Registry.getServer(className);
            pending = server.getRequest(false);
            server.setListener(this);
        }
        catch (Exception e)
        {
            System.err.println("Error checking CHAPI: " + e.getMessage());
            e.printStackTrace();
        }
    }

    public static void main(String[] args)
    {
        MediaGrabber grabber = new MediaGrabber();
        if (args != null && args.length > 0 && args[0].equals("launch"))
        {
            grabber.pushScreen(new ChoicesScreen());
            grabber.enterEventDispatcher();
        }
        else if (grabber.pending != null)
        {
            // Started via CHAPI. Show our UI.
            grabber.processRequest();
            grabber.requestForeground();
            grabber.enterEventDispatcher();
        }
        else
        {
            // Startup execution.
            try
            {
                Bitmap rollover = Bitmap.getBitmapResource("rollover.png");
                HomeScreen.setRolloverIcon(rollover, 1);
            }
            catch (Throwable t)
            {
                t.printStackTrace();
            }
        }
    }

    private void verifyRegistration()
    {
        String className = MediaGrabber.class.getName();
        Registry registry = Registry.getRegistry(className);
```

```
        ContentHandler registered = registry.forID(CHAPI_ID, true);
        if (registered != null)
        {
            return;
        }
        // Wasn't registered before, so do it now.
        String[] actions = new String[]
        { ContentHandler.ACTION_SEND };
        String[] actionNames = new String[]
        { "Send Encrypted Via MediaGrabber" };
        ActionNameMap[] maps = new ActionNameMap[]
        { new ActionNameMap(actions, actionNames, "en") };
        try
        {
            registry.register(className, MIME_TYPES, SUFFIXES, actions, maps,
                CHAPI_ID, null);
        }
        catch (Exception e)
        {
            System.err.println("Could not register for " + CHAPI_ID + ": "
                    + e.getMessage());
            e.printStackTrace();
        }
    }

    private void processRequest()
    {
        FileConnection file = null;
        InputStream is = null;
        try
        {
            String filename = null;
            String type = null;
            synchronized (this)
            {
                filename = pending.getURL();
                type = pending.getType();
            }
            if (filename != null && type != null)
            {
                file = (FileConnection) Connector.open(filename);
                is = file.openInputStream();
                byte[] data = new byte[is.available()];
                is.read(data);
                SendingScreen sending = new SendingScreen(type, filename
                        .substring(filename.lastIndexOf('/') + 1),
                        "Sent to you by CHAPI", data, true);
                pushScreen(sending);
            }
            else
            {
                pushScreen(new ChoicesScreen());
            }
            server.finish(pending, Invocation.OK);
        }
```

```
            catch (Exception e)
            {
                System.out.println("Could not send file: " + e.getMessage());
                e.printStackTrace();
            }
            finally
            {
                try
                {
                    if (file != null)
                        file.close();
                    if (is != null)
                        is.close();
                }
                catch (Exception e)
                {
                }
            }
        }

    public synchronized void invocationRequestNotify(
            ContentHandlerServer handler)
    {
        pending = handler.getRequest(false);
        if (pending != null)
        {
            processRequest();
        }
    }
}
```

As you can see, there are now three situations in which the MediaGrabber may be launched. The standard case is when the user selects it directly, which you can recognize by the "launch" parameter. The second case is when it is launched via CHAPI, in which case a CHAPI Invocation will be waiting when you start up. Here, the application starts, but does so in the already-configured SendingScreen if provided with a file to send. Finally, it can be started on device boot, in which case you simply register for CHAPI, set the rollover icon, and then exit. You need only register for CHAPI if you don't already have a CHAPI entry.

Note that you do register for incoming CHAPI messages. This allows the application to deal with requests if it is already running when a new request comes in. This would occur if, for example, the user backgrounded this app and then issued a request from another app. Some basic synchronization is used to make sure that the Invocation doesn't change while you are reading values from it.

Running with CHAPI

Believe it or not, just by making these changes within MediaGrabber, you may already have modified the capabilities of native applications. If you have access to a simulator or device with software version 4.7 or later, try taking a picture or navigating to a media file. Press the Menu key. Scroll around. There's the new command! RIM has rewritten most of its native apps to check for CHAPI registration and add all matches it finds. Figure 8-6 shows what this looks like on the Storm.

Figure 8-6. *Native apps exposing third-party CHAPI apps*

Tip: The simplest way to explore the filesystem is to open the Media app, press the BlackBerry Menu key, and then select Explore.

Once you select the link, MediaGrabber will launch into the sending screen, where you can enter a recipient and send as normal.

More Native Menu Integration

On older device software versions, you don't automatically see CHAPI items listed, but you can still add your own items. You are not restricted to CHAPI operations, either: you can run any sort of arbitrary code that you like.

To make something useful for both older and newer phones, add a new option to the Address Book app labeled "Verify Media Shared." This will check the contact to see if it has previously received any media from the MediaGrabber app. If not, it will offer to open MediaGrabber in its normal mode to send some media. Listing 8-2 shows the complete menu option class, which can be included within MediaGrabber as an inner class.

Listing 8-2. *A Custom Menu Item to Display in the Contacts Menu*

```java
private static class CheckContactMenuItem extends ApplicationMenuItem
{
    private Registry registry;

    public CheckContactMenuItem()
    {
        super(0);
        registry = Registry.getRegistry(getClass().getName());
    }

    public Object run(Object context)
    {
        if (context == null || !(context instanceof Contact))
            return null;
        try
        {
            Contact contact = (Contact) context;
            if (contact.countValues(BlackBerryContact.USER4) > 0)
            {
                // We've sent them media before.
                Dialog.inform("You have shared media with them.");
            }
            else
            {
                // Give a chance to select some media.
                int choice = Dialog.ask(Dialog.D_YES_NO,
                    "No sharing yet. Would you like to send media?");
                if (choice == Dialog.YES)
                {
                    Invocation request = new Invocation();
                    request.setID(CHAPI_ID);
                    registry.invoke(request);
                }
            }
        }
        catch (Exception e)
        {
            e.printStackTrace();
        }
        return null;
    }

    public String toString()
    {
```

```
        return "Verify Media Shared";
    }
}
```

The logical place to add a custom menu item is in the same startup code that we created for the rollover icon. However, the BlackBerry will occasionally start MediaGrabber even after boot, which could result in the same menu item being added multiple times. To guard against this situation, we use the `RuntimeStore` to check if the item has previously been added to the native menu, and only insert it if it has not. The device clears out the `RuntimeStore` every time the device reboots, which is also when it removes all custom menu items. The following code can be inserted below the rollover icon assignment in order to register the custom menu item.

```
RuntimeStore store = RuntimeStore.getRuntimeStore();
long menuItemID = 0×65fad834642a5345L;
if (store.get(menuItemID) == null)
{
    CheckContactMenuItem item = new CheckContactMenuItem();
    ApplicationMenuItemRepository repo =
        ApplicationMenuItemRepository.getInstance();
    repo.addMenuItem(ApplicationMenuItemRepository.
        MENUITEM_ADDRESSBOOK_LIST, item);
    store.put(menuItemID, item);
}
```

The next time you run the app, you will see the "Verify Media Shared" option within the address book app. Selecting this item will show the appropriate dialog, and allow you to enter the main MediaGrabber screen if you haven't previously shared media.

WANT MORE?

CHAPI offers plenty of possibilities, both as a producer and as a consumer. Consider these options to further enhance MediaGrabber's inter-process cooperation.

- Create multiple entry points into MediaGrabber, such as one for sending unencrypted files.

- Experiment with adding support for multiple languages. Try switching the active language on your device and see if the menu item labels change.

- If using a recent device, use CHAPI to call out from MediaGrabber into other native applications using the BlackBerryContentHandler arguments.

- Create a new, stand-alone application in a new workspace that uses CHAPI to start MediaGrabber. For example, it could download a media file from the Internet, and then use MediaGrabber to send it to your friends.

If you know someone else who is learning BlackBerry development, try splitting these tasks between you. It is great practice to create and expose APIs to other developers, and a more realistic look at how real applications are designed, developed, released, and used.

Excelsior

When two applications share responsibilities and features, the result is more than the sum of its parts. Imagine a world where you couldn't print images you found on the Internet, or where you couldn't attach files to your email. The more applications that can touch and share data with one another, the more useful and compelling they become.

In this chapter, you have learned how to take advantage of multiplicative utility in your own apps. You can tap a wealth of features already designed by RIM when you use their hooks to add features to your app. And, in the other direction, you can make your app far more useful to your users if you create an API that allows other developers to use you. If five other apps all use your app, you have just become even more indispensable, without even needing to write those five new apps.

This level of deep integration blurs the lines between a built-in app and an installed app. When your app is displaying as an option in the Contacts menu, and showing a custom rollover icon, and getting opened from other apps, it becomes almost indistinguishable from the apps that came pre-installed on the BlackBerry.

You have now mastered the critical aspects of making powerful, useful, integrated apps. The next goal is to get those apps onto as many devices as possible, operating as smoothly as you can. Part 3 will show you how to make sure your apps can be used by as many people as possible.

Part 3

Going Pro

Don't be selfish. Now that you can write an interesting and powerful BlackBerry app, you should share it with as many people as you can. Whether you send it to a few friends for fun, or sell it to hordes of eager consumers, people will appreciate your effort and achievement.

However, there can be a world of difference between writing an app that runs well on your personal phone and one that runs smoothly on everyone's phone. You don't want to deal with frustrated customers, confused managers, or sniping competitors. You especially don't want to take ten times as long making your app run on ten devices as you did on the first one. This final section of the book tackles the tricky problem of scaling up. Anticipate security problems before they arise, port your app to a variety of languages and devices, and make building multiple versions easier than before. These techniques won't just improve your work; they will also let you be more generous with the results.

Chapter 9

RIM Security

Few topics trip up BlackBerry developers more than the RIM security model. It can be extremely frustrating to take an app that works perfectly in the simulator and find that it won't even start on a handset; or, worse, one that passes all your internal testing, but exhibits strange behavior in the field. Such problems are often the result of occasionally arcane security rules. Some of them you can bend, some you can break, and others you must live with: in all cases, though, just understanding them will allow you to make better decisions. This chapter examines the most important features of BlackBerry device security and how they affect your applications.

The Ownership Question

Who owns your BlackBerry?

At first, that may seem like a foolish question: "I do, of course." After all, you carry it with you, it's got your phone number, and it shows your name on it.

However, actual possession is not quite as straightforward as it may seem at first. If you got your BlackBerry from an employer, then, despite the fact that you carry the device, they are the ones who really own it: they paid for it, they run the network it connects with, and they are responsible for the behavior of the devices. A business has an interest in the ongoing use of BlackBerry devices. They may not want you to upload 3 gigabytes of video files onto the corporate intranet, make phone calls to 1-900 numbers, or install virus-ridden software. When people do these things, they don't only affect their own devices, but they also create financial and administrative headaches for their employers.

Even if you got your BlackBerry for a personal mobile phone account, the ownership question might not be quite as simple as you might think. If, like most Americans, you got your BlackBerry as part of a two-year contract, you might have only paid $100 or so instead of a list price of $700 or higher. Your mobile carrier will have subsidized the remaining cost to Research in Motion (RIM) to entice you as a customer. In return, you are expected to continue with them as a loyal customer for multiple years. What happens if you renege on your contract after a month and walk away with your new BlackBerry? You could argue that, having violated the contract, the phone company is the one who really "owns" it: they paid for the majority of it, and set the terms under which you could have it. The company might not want you to switch to another company and continue using the BlackBerry.

Understanding the intricacies of BlackBerry ownership helps to illuminate many of the topics addressed later in this chapter. As consumers, we tend to feel a certain right to things we own. Once we have paid for something, we expect to continue using it without interference: we should be able to install the software we want, run it when we want for as long as we want, browse to the web sites we want to visit, and so on. Because BlackBerry devices often have complicated ownership, though, your desires might clash with those of other stakeholders. Where there is a dispute, the "real" owner of the device usually comes out on top.

Security Policies: "You Can't Do That!"

The 900lb-gorilla of the security model is the security policy. Inviolate and determined, the policy acts as the ultimate enforcer, providing the final word on what is and is not allowed on a particular device.

Background

BlackBerry devices started life as corporate connectivity devices, only available to businesspeople who needed them to keep in contact when away from their offices. As discussed in "The Ownership Question" section, despite the fact that each individual person carries a particular BlackBerry, the devices are actually owned by the company, and the company has a strong interest in ensuring that the devices behave appropriately on the network.

Strong, secure IT policies provide one of RIM's strongest selling points. Unlike other smart-phone platforms such as Windows Mobile, RIM devices can be securely locked down with particular rules about their behavior. These rules are contained within a particular file called the security policy, often named policy.bin. This file is loaded into the BlackBerry at a very low level: you cannot find it by browsing the filesystem, and you cannot copy over or remove it. The device reads in this policy when first starting up, and, once it is loaded, nothing can change the rules.

Actual policies will vary tremendously. If you buy a phone through a wireless carrier, it will likely come with a very permissive policy that allows you to do almost anything. After all, the carrier wants you to use your device and be a satisfied customer. Some companies similarly run an open system. Most corporations, however, will place at least some restrictions on the use of their devices, and others will be locked down so tightly that they are completely unusable other than for a few specifically allowed actions.

IT Policy Examples

Administrators have access to a wealth of different IT policy settings. These can be configured differently to apply to individuals, to groups of users, or to an entire organization. For instance, an administrator may grant herself and a handful of power users very open IT policies, provide developers with policies that will not limit their network usage, and send a standard restrictive policy to everyone else. A few of the many available policy settings are listed below, focusing on the settings most likely to interfere with your applications or your development. Many disable or enable particular features, while others allow administrators to configure particular settings such as visible text or URLs.

Device Security Policy Examples

Disable BlackBerry Messenger

Disable Forwarding Contacts

Control Bluetooth Power Range

Allow Outgoing Calls on Bluetooth

Allow Application Download via Browser

Allow Wi-Fi Browser

Disable JavaScript in Browser

Enable HTML Tables in Browser

Enable Style Sheets

Disable Photo Camera

Disable Video Camera

Public-Private Key Generation Algorithm

Users Must Confirm Before Sending SMS, MMS, email, or PIN Message

Disable MMS

Set Owner Information

Enable PIN Messaging

Allow SMS Messaging

Default Browser

Browser Home Page Address

Home Page Address is Read-Only

Automatically Download Email Attachments

Display Prompt when Downloading Images

Disable Rich Text/HTML Email

Duration to Keep Received Messages

Prepend Disclaimer to Outgoing Email Messages

Restrict Incoming Calls

Restrict Outgoing Calls

Allow Browser

Allow Phone

Disable BlackBerry Maps

Report GPS Location to Enterprise Server

Force Memory Cleaner

Disable Wireless Synchronization for Calendar, Memos, etc.

Allow External Non-Enterprise Connections

Allow Internal Enterprise Connections

Allow Resetting Idle Timer

Allow Screen Shot Capture

Allow Split Pipe Connections

Allow Apps to Use Persistent Store

Allow Apps to Use Serial, USB, and IrDA Ports

Disable Cut/Copy/Paste

Disable External Memory Media Card

Disable Photo Sharing Apps

Disable Social Networking Apps

Disable USB Mass Storage

Disable Installing Unsigned Apps

External File System Encryption Level

Firewall Block Incoming Messages

Firewall Whitelist Addresses

Password Required for Application Download

Allow Other Browser Services

Allow Other Calendar Services

Allow Public IM Services

Set Local Area Code

TCP APN/Username/Password

TLS Support

Allow VOIP

Enable VPN

VPN Username/Password/DNS

Disallow Rollback to Previous Software Version

Disable Wi-Fi

Caution: Split Pipe can be a particularly frustrating setting. Most applications will either attempt to connect through an enterprise MDS connection or through a device-side TCP connection. If an application attempts to open both types of connections, it is said to have a split-pipe. This can cause security concerns: for example, a malicious app might open a connection to the corporate network, collect data from internal servers, and then open a connection to a hacker's web server and upload sensitive data. The split-pipe IT policy forbids this happening: if an app has ever attempted to open an MDS connection before (even if it failed), it is forbidden from attempting to open a public connection. If this happens, you should first change your app to make sure that it only attempts to open either MDS (deviceside=false) or public (deviceside=true) connections. Wipe the affected device by removing all software via the BlackBerry Desktop Manager and then reload all software.

In addition to these general settings, administrators can also configure a set of application control policy rules. These provide more fine-grained controls that specifically apply to third-party applications that are installed by users. Some of the more important ones are listed below.

Application Control Policy Examples

Allow Internal Network Connections

Allow External Network Connections

Allow Local Connections

Modify Device Settings

Reset Security Timer

Set Applications as Mandatory, Optional, or Forbidden

Access to Browser Filter API

Access to Email API

Access to Event Injection

Access to File API

Access to GPS API

Access to Local Key Store (Crypto)

Access to Interprocess Communication API

Access to Media API

Access to Phone API

Access to Module Management API

Access to Media Recording APIs (Microphone, Video, and Screen)

Access to Serial Port/Bluetooth API

Access to Wi-Fi API

List of Domains with Browser Filter Support

List of Permitted External Domains

List of Permitted Internal Domains

Pushing Policies

So how do policies get loaded? A default policy will be in place when you first obtain your device. For most people, this will stay the same for as long as they continue to own the BlackBerry.

If a BlackBerry device connects to a corporate BES network, though, the administrator has the option of pushing down a new IT policy. This will replace whatever policy was previously loaded on the device. Even if the policy was somehow changed since the last time it connected to the network, that change will be undone the next time it connects.

Policies can be loaded via the BlackBerry Desktop Manager. This is not an option you will see in the menu when you connect your device; rather, the policy will be automatically and silently sent to the phone. There is no indication provided when this occurs, but you may notice different behavior later on.

Beware of eBay

This is a good place to comment on one of the common traps that new developers fall into. BlackBerry devices can be expensive, and there is a strong temptation to purchase them second-hand at a substantial discount. Sometimes this leads to good results, but be aware of what you might be getting into.

Many of the devices for sale online, especially those sold by individuals through sites like Craigslist and eBay, were once corporate devices that connected to company networks. The devices might have been replaced with newer models, or an employee might have been allowed to keep her BlackBerry when leaving, or decided to just keep the BlackBerry anyway. These models might be fully functioning and able to make calls, send and receive text messages, and perhaps even be compatible with multiple carriers. However, if they ever were part of a company network, odds are very high that they still have an IT policy installed.

If you get one of these devices, everything might seem fine at first: you will be allowed to use it as you would any other device, and hopefully also load applications. However, you might notice mysterious problems as you use it more. Certain Java API calls might simply fail. You might see annoying security prompts that you are not allowed to permanently dismiss. Maybe the application simply will stop running.

In one sense, this can actually be considered a useful problem to have. After all, there are plenty of real users out there with IT policies on their devices, and if you know how their devices will behave you can better anticipate the problems they might encounter. Still, having a device with a restrictive security policy can kill your productivity and massively slow down development.

What's the solution? If you can afford it, it's safest to buy your BlackBerry devices new. Otherwise, try to contact the seller and get a clearer picture of what this particular device did before. If it was bought new by an individual for a personal wireless account, it will probably be fine. If it has been bought and sold multiple times and was most recently on a corporate network, you might want to avoid it, or at least ask for a return if it proves to carry a policy.

Replacing an Old Policy

If you get stuck with a restrictive IT policy, you might have a couple of options. If you are on a corporate BES network, or have access to one, you can ask the administrator to create an open IT policy for your device to use. This might or might not be successful. Administrators have much larger responsibilities than your individual development, and might not want to have loose policies floating around.

There are also some online tools available that claim to remove IT policies. In reality, nothing actually removes a policy; the best that can happen is that it replaces the existing policy with a more permissive one. Use such tools at your own risk. The updated policy you receive might not be much better than the one you got rid of.

Finally, keep in mind that, even if you do replace an old policy, updated policies will still be pushed to the device every time you connect to a corporate network. Because of this, you might want to avoid using an individual BlackBerry as both a development device and as part of a secure company network. It's more expensive to get two devices, but over the long run you will more than make up for the cost with your increased productivity.

What Can You Do?

Your development device aside, you must decide if and how you want to handle devices with security policies that interfere with the running of your app.

In one sense, there's nothing you *can* do. Applications execute in a sandbox, and the security policy is far beyond the reach of that sandbox. Your app cannot replace the IT policy, cannot disable it, and cannot even pre-emptively determine whether or not a restrictive policy is installed.

You should first consider the potential audience for your app, the likelihood that users will have restrictive IT policies, and the impact of those policies on your app. If you are writing an app for yourself or a small group of people, and know that nobody has special IT policies, you're done—nothing to worry about.

If you are writing an app for your company's use, or that will be used in one particular corporation, you should coordinate with the BlackBerry administrator. Early on define what your app will need to do, focusing on aspects like network usage and data access, and communicate those needs to the administrator. If a policy needs to change, she will have the authority to get it done. If the policy cannot change, you need to find out as soon as possible so you can change the scope of your app or get authority from higher levels of management to make the change.

If you are writing an app for general public consumption, you're in a relatively tricky spot. Most commercial apps are sold through BlackBerry App World, carrier stores, or independent smartphone stores. The majority of these buyers will have clean devices and no issues. A minority will be using secondhand phones or devices they got from work, and a subsection of those users will be unable to run all but the simplest apps. You can consider several possible responses.

- Buyer Beware: If possible, warn users ahead of time about what your app does, and clearly state that, if their device cannot function properly, it's their problem, not yours.

- Good Neighbor: If users complain that your app is unusable, appease them by offering a refund. This works best if your app contains a server component so you can track individual users. You won't need to advertise this method, and complaints should be rare enough that this will be the exception.

- Graceful Degradation: Depending on your app design and features, you may be able to continue operating even if the security policy blocks some functions. For example, if an offline game connects to a server for a shared high-score counter, your users should still be able to play even if the app cannot connect to the server.

- Over-communicate: Include plenty of warnings and help within your application advising the user about what your app is doing and what their options are if stuff isn't working.

Again, at the end of the day, you are powerless to fix any problems that your users encounter that stem from strong IT policies. The best you can do is be aware of the problem, realize how it may affect your app, evaluate the severity of impact on your users, and plan ahead of time how you wish to handle the problem.

User Permissions: "May I Do This?"

Let's assume that a user's company is fine with everything your app does, or that the user does not belong to a company with an IT policy. This removes one significant barrier from your application's proper functioning, but is not the end of the story. In addition to IT policies, which protect the interests of the corporation, BlackBerry devices also support user permissions, which protect the interests of the individual.

Many users share concerns similar to those faced by large corporations. If a user is on a data plan that bills them per kilobyte sent or received, she will get quite unhappy if an application uploads several megabytes of data without her knowledge. If a user is concerned about her privacy, she won't want an application to take photos and record her GPS location, and email that information to someone.

Therefore, within the confines of the IT policy, each BlackBerry device also offers a flexible set of user permissions that are applied to installed applications. These are initially set to certain default values, which can be defined by the organization or the manufacturer. Users can later fine-tune them in a variety of situations.

Setting User Permissions on OTA Installs

When someone installs an application over the air by loading a JAD file in his browser, he will be given the choice to set individual application permissions as part of the download. If he selects this option, he will be greeted with a prompt similar to that shown in Figure 9-1. You cannot control the text in this prompt, nor can you control what permissions are shown on the following screen. However, you can include instructions about what the user should do on an HTML landing page before directing them to the JAD. For example, you could include a statement such as, "This app must access the Internet in order to function properly. On the following screen, please set application permissions and verify that the Internet permission is set to Allow."

Figure 9-1. Setting individual permissions

When the user starts setting application permissions, she will see a variety of settings. The specific choices will vary depending on the device model and the software version loaded. Choices are organized into three broad groups.

1. Connections: These concern data entering or leaving the device.

2. Interactions: These control the app's access to low-level device functions.

3. User Data: These describe the ability to read or write persistent data.

Each group should be set to "Allow", "Custom", or "Deny". If you'd like to modify a group's settings for this app, click the current setting and select a new value from the drop-down menu. This allows you to quickly grant an app all permissions, or to turn off broad areas of concern.

In many cases you will want to exert more fine-grained control. Press the BlackBerry Menu key and select "Expand" to view all the sub-options under a particular group. This allows you to make more detailed decisions. For instance, you might want to allow an app access to the USB port and Wi-Fi, but forbid access to GPS. Each individual permission can be assigned one of three settings.

1. Allow: Always permit the app to do this.

2. Prompt: Display a message each time the app attempts to do this. (You can later permanently dismiss this prompt.)

3. Deny: Never allow the app to do this.

> **Note:** Certain low-level permissions, such as Interprocess Communication and Keystroke Injection, only offer the "Allow" and "Deny" settings. This is because these actions are usually initiated by libraries, background threads, or other components without a user interface, and so it is awkward to display a prompt when they run.

Figure 9-2 shows a user modifying the default permissions for the MediaGrabber app. This device was configured to disallow recording, which will seriously hinder the usefulness of the app. If changed to "Allow", recording will always work; if "Prompt", the user will still need to click through a message the next time they try to start recording.

Figure 9-2. *Changing a specific permission*

Default Permissions

Every phone comes with a default set of permissions. These are applied to applications that you install through a cable, and are also set as the permissions for OTA installed apps if the user doesn't choose to set the application permissions.

To set the global user permissions on your device, follow these steps.

1. Open Options.

2. Open Advanced Options.

3. Open Applications.

4. Press the BlackBerry Menu Key.

5. Select Edit Default Permissions.

Within this next screen, you can select and modify permissions as you would for an OTA download. The changes that you make will be applied to all applications installed in the future. If you'd like to apply them to all previously installed applications, press the BlackBerry menu key and then select "Apply Defaults to All".

Specific Application Settings

If you cable-load or download an application and later realize that it does not have the proper permissions, you can modify the permissions to what you want.

1. Open Options.

2. Open Advanced Options.

3. Open Applications.

4. Highlight the application name.

5. Press the BlackBerry Menu Key.

6. Select Edit Permissions.

Once again, you can customize the individual permissions here. Don't forget to save the changes once you are done. You may need to exit and restart the app for the changes to take effect.

Programmatic Control

So far, we have been looking at user permissions from the user's perspective. As you have seen, the person who installs your app can exert a great deal of control over the app's behavior. This can lead to serious problems within your app, though. If you require an Internet connection to run, and cannot open that connection, then the app is effectively broken.

In older versions of BlackBerry device software, there is no good solution to this problem. The best you can do is detect when a problem has occurred and display an error screen to the user describing what they must do to solve the problem. Some people will be reluctant to modify their device settings, and others might get lost while navigating the menus, and as a result your app stays broken.

ApplicationPermissions

Fortunately, starting with device software version 4.2.1, RIM has offered developers an API that allows insight into the user's current permissions settings. Since you know what resources your app needs to function, you can inspect the current settings and display a message if they are wrong. Even better, you can ask the user to change them.

RIM does not allow an app to force its permissions preferences upon the user. This would defeat the whole point of user-controlled permissions, and allow malicious apps a clear shot at whatever they wanted. RIM's solution is fairly elegant: your app can describe the specific permissions it wants, and then the BlackBerry will ask the user to confirm the changes.

Of course, the user may decide that she does not want to give you all the permissions you ask for. Your app can examine the permissions again and decide how it wants to proceed. If you simply cannot function, you may exit the app or continue asking for permissions. Otherwise, continue running normally, perhaps warning the user about what degradation she will see.

9-1 shows the permissions that are available to query and change. All are defined in the `ApplicationPermissions` class.

Table 9-1. Application Permissions

Name	Allows	Added	Deprecated
PERMISSION_APPLICATION_MANAGEMENT	Install or delete other applications	4.6	
PERMISSION_BLUETOOTH	Send and receive data via Bluetooth and access Bluetooth profiles	4.2.1	
PERMISSION_BROWSER_FILTER	Register a filter with the web browser	4.2.1	
PERMISSION_CHANGE_DEVICE_SETTINGS	Change configuration and user settings	4.2.1	4.6, use PERMISSION_DEVICE_SETTINGS
PERMISSION_CODE_MODULE_MANAGEMENT	Install or delete other applications	4.2.1	4.6, use PERMISSION_APPLICATION_MANAGEMENT
PERMISSION_CROSS_APPLICATION_COMMUNICATION	Share data and messages with other apps	4.6	
PERMISSION_DEVICE_SETTINGS	Change configuration and user settings	4.6	

Table 9-1. *Application Permissions (continued)*

Name	Allows	Added	Deprecated
PERMISSION_DISPLAY_LOCKED	Draw on top of the device lock screen	5.0	
PERMISSION_EMAIL	Send and read email	4.2.1	
PERMISSION_EVENT_INJECTOR	Simulate user events	4.2.1	4.6, use PERMISSION_INPUT_SIMULATION
PERMISSION_EXTERNAL_CONNECTIONS	Connect to the Internet	4.2.1	4.6, use PERMISSION_INTERNET
PERMISSION_FILE_API	Read and write files	4.2.1	
PERMISSION_HANDHELD_KEYSTORE	Access locally stored crypto keys	4.2.1	4.6, use PERMISSION_SECURITY_DATA
PERMISSION_IDLE_TIMER	Reset security timer to prevent the device from locking	4.2.1	
PERMISSION_INPUT_SIMULATION	Simulate user events	4.6	
PERMISSION_INTER_PROCESS_COMMUNICATION	Share data and messages with other apps	4.3	4.6, use PERMISSION_CROSS_APPLICATION_COMMUNICATION
PERMISSION_INTERNAL_CONNECTIONS	Connect to corporate MDS network	4.2.1	4.6, use PERMISSION_SERVER_NETWORK
PERMISSION_INTERNET	Connect to the Internet	4.6	
PERMISSION_KEYSTORE_MEDIUM_SECURITY	Access locally stored medium-strength crypto keys	4.2.1	4.6, no replacement
PERMISSION_LOCAL_CONNECTIONS	Connect through USB or the serial port	4.2.1	4.6, use PERMISSION_USB
PERMISSION_LOCATION_API	Access GPS and other LBS resources	4.2.1	4.6, use PERMISSION_LOCATION_DATA

Table 9-1. Application Permissions (continued)

Name	Allows	Added	Deprecated
PERMISSION_LOCATION_DATA	Access GPS and other LBS resources	4.6	
PERMISSION_MEDIA	Access and modify media files	4.3	
PERMISSION_ORGANIZER_DATA	Access data from calendar, contacts, tasks, and memos	4.6	
PERMISSION_PHONE	Make voice calls, receive voice calls, read phone logs	4.2.1	
PERMISSION_PIM	Access data from calendar, contacts, tasks, and memos	4.2.1	4.6, use PERMISSION_ORGANIZER_DATA
PERMISSION_RECORDING	Access microphone, camera, or screen capture	4.6	
PERMISSION_SCREEN_CAPTURE	Capture screenshots	4.3	4.6, use PERMISSION_RECORDING
PERMISSION_SECURITY_DATA	Access locally stored crypto keys	4.6	
PERMISSION_SERVER_NETWORK	Connect to corporate MDS network	4.6	
PERMISSION_THEME_DATA	Provide themes	4.2.1	4.6, use PERMISSION_THEMES
PERMISSION_THEMES	Provide themes	4.6	
PERMISSION_USB	Connect through USB	4.6	
PERMISSION_WIFI	Make Wi-Fi connections and collect data about Wi-Fi configuration	4.3	

ApplicationPermissionsManager

ApplicationPermissions contains information about the permissions set on an application. ApplicationPermissionsManager allows you to retrieve the current permissions, query the setting of a particular permission, or ask for more permissions.

Checking Permissions

If you want to find out whether a particular permission is set, use one of the versions of ApplicationPermissionsManager.getPermission(). You must provide one of the permissions from
Table 9-1. You will get back the current setting.

- ApplicationPermissions.VALUE_ALLOW means access is granted.

- ApplicationPermissions.VALUE_PROMPT means access will be permitted if the user confirms.

- ApplicationPermissions.VALUE_DENY means access is forbidden.

The following snippet demonstrates how you can check to see whether a permission is properly set before starting a potentially restricted operation.

```
ApplicationPermissionsManager permissions = ⏎
    ApplicationPermissionsManager.getInstance();
int currentSetting = permissions.getPermission(⏎
    ApplicationPermissions.PERMISSION_FILE_API);
if (currentSetting == ApplicationPermissions.VALUE_ALLOW)
{
    // We can access the file here.
}
```

You can optionally provide two extra arguments to getPermission(). If the permission deals with accessing a network, like ApplicationPermissions.PERMISSION_INTERNET, it's possible that a domain-specific permission may be in effect. For example, a user might ordinarily set connections to "Prompt", but allow all connections to www.google.com. You can pass in the domain you plan to connect to learn what its setting is, as shown in the following example.

```
int domainSpecificSetting = permissions.getPermission(⏎
    ApplicationPermissions.PERMISSION_SERVER_NETWORK, "securesite.example.com");
```

Starting with device software version 4.7, you can also provide a boolean indicating whether to ignore the current setting of the firewall. Firewalls are discussed in more detail later in this chapter; for now, be aware that unless you specify true here, ApplicationPermissionsManager will allow the firewall setting to override the actual permission that the user has set. You generally do want to take the firewall into account, since you likely care most about the actual behavior for a request you would make and not just what is shown on the permissions screen. Only set true here if you need to know the actual underlying setting.

To retrieve *all* the permissions set for an app, use getApplicationPermissions(). This allows you to more compactly check multiple permissions settings at once, as the following example shows.

```
ApplicationPermissions current = permissions.getApplicationPermissions();
if (current.getPermission(ApplicationPermissions.PERMISSION_INPUT_SIMULATION)
        != ApplicationPermissions.VALUE_ALLOW || current.getPermission(
            ApplicationPermissions.PERMISSION_IDLE_TIMER) !=
                ApplicationPermissions.VALUE_ALLOW)
{
    // Deal with lack of permissions.
}
```

Changing Permissions

To request greater permissions, first construct an ApplicationPermissions object that contains your desired settings. Everything you include will be displayed to the user as a prompt, regardless of the current setting; you can include all of your required permissions to communicate all your app needs, or only those permissions which are not currently granted so the user doesn't have to review as many. All requested permissions will be requested as VALUE_ALLOW; you cannot request the user to grant you VALUE_PROMPT or VALUE_DENY permissions.

After your ApplicationPermissions are configured, issue a request to ApplicationPermissionsManager.invokePermissionsRequest(). This is a synchronous blocking call: your app will suspend while the user reviews your request. By the time it returns, the user has completed his selections. You can inspect the return value to see what he chose: true means all your requests were granted, false means at least one was set to "Prompt" or "Deny". The next example requests a set of permissions that are necessary to run a particular app.

```
ApplicationPermissions requested = new ApplicationPermissions();
requested.addPermission(ApplicationPermissions.PERMISSION_LOCATION_DATA);
requested.addPermission(ApplicationPermissions.PERMISSION_INTERNET);
requested.addPermission(ApplicationPermissions.PERMISSION_FILE_API);
if (permissions.invokePermissionsRequest(requested))
{
    // Granted, continue running the app.
}
else
{
    // Denied, show an error and exit.
}
```

Note: The permissions dialog is generated by the operating system, not your app, and so you can invoke a permissions request from a library or other invisible component.

Keep in mind that, even when your app really wants certain permissions, the user may not be able to grant them if his IT policy forbids it. Avoid haranguing users for things beyond their control. If you like, you can check ApplicationPermissionsManager. getMaxAllowable() to find the most permissive possible setting for a particular permission. It might be that the IT policy demands a setting of at least "Prompt" for Internet connections, so, if it's already set to "Prompt", you can't get anything better.

Give Me a Reason

As a strange sort of parallel to application permissions, a particular set of APIs generate their own warning when accessed. Starting with device software version 4.2.1, if you call one of the following methods and the "Device Settings Modification" permission is set to "Prompt", the user will see a message such as, "The application MyFlashlight is attempting to change device settings."

APIs with Customized Prompts

ApplicationDescriptor.setPowerOnBehavior

ApplicationManager.lockSystem

ApplicationManager.requestForeground

ApplicationManager.requestForegroundForConsole

ApplicationManager.setCurrentPowerOnBehavior

ApplicationManager.unlockSystem

Backlight.enable

Backlight.setBrightness

Backlight.setTimeout

Device.requestPowerOff

Device.requestStorageMode

Display.setContrast

Device.setDateTime

EventLogger.clearLog

EventLogger.setMinimumLevel

Keypad.setMode

Locale.setDefaultInputForSystem

MIMETypeAssociations.registerMIMETypeMapping

MIMETypeAssociations.registerType

Radio.activateWAFs

Radio.deactivateWAFs

The user can allow or deny this access, and also has the option of suppressing future requests. What's especially unusual about this set of APIs is that you can provide some custom text that will display as part of the permissions prompt. You do this by implementing the ReasonProvider method and invoking ApplicationPermissionsManager. addReasonProvider(), as shown in the next example.

```
ApplicationPermissionsManager mgr = ApplicationPermissionsManager.getInstance();
mgr.addReasonProvider(ApplicationDescriptor.currentApplicationDescriptor(),
        new ReasonProvider(){
    public String getMessage(int permissionID)
    {
        if (permissionID ==
            ApplicationPermissions.PERMISSION_CHANGE_DEVICE_SETTINGS)
        {
            return "I need to change device settings to keep the screen on.";
        }
        return "Please allow this access for full app functionality";
    }});
Backlight.setTimeout(255);
```

After you set a reason provider and invoke one of the restricted methods, the user will see a link labeled "Details from the vendor. . ." as part of the application permissions window. If she clicks this link, she will see your custom message.

As you can see, the specific permission ID is passed as a parameter to your ReasonProvider, and you can select an appropriate message depending on the permission. This would make much more sense if ReasonProvider was invoked for other permissions requests. As it is, this class has very limited utility. In practice, it is much better to simply ask for permissions to be granted prior to invoking sensitive APIs rather than to display some custom text buried within a prompt. If you'd like to communicate with the user, do it before invoking the permissions request.

Firewall: "Don't Go There"

You are probably already familiar with the concept of a firewall from your own personal computer or company network. A firewall is a piece of software, typically integrated with the operating system, which applies a set of rules to all incoming and outgoing connections. Figure 9-3 illustrates some typical behavior from an active BlackBerry firewall.

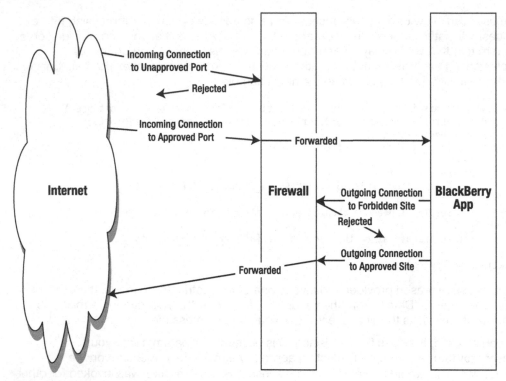

Figure 9-3. *A BlackBerry firewall*

Firewall Actions

Any time the device receives an incoming request, it checks to see whether that request is permitted. The rules might call for blocking certain ports, or only permitting connections from certain approved IP addresses, ranges, or domains. If the request is approved, and an application is listening on that port, it will receive the incoming data. If the request is denied, the data will not be provided. In both cases, the firewall is invisible to the application: if you get data, it looks just the same whether it passed through a firewall or not; if you don't get data, it's as though it was never sent.

Similar rules apply on outgoing connections, although here your app does get a little more visibility into the presence of a firewall. At the moment the app tries to open a connection, the firewall will check to see whether to permit the connection. This decision will be made based on a combination of factors: the permissions granted to the requesting app, the domain being accessed, the port number used, and the transport protocol type. The request will either succeed or fail.

On BlackBerry devices, the firewall can have more subtle effects as well. The firewall might prevent certain file operations, prevent certain dialogs from displaying, or interfere with app installation.

Firewall Settings

To view and modify your firewall, follow these steps.

1. Open Options.

2. Select Security Options.

3. Select Firewall.

The firewall can be enabled or disabled from this screen. If your IT policy mandates use of a firewall, you may see a lock icon here, which indicates that it cannot be modified. Otherwise, simply tab the current Status setting to switch between Enabled and Disabled.

The firewall also allows you to block certain types of incoming messages, such as SMS text messages or PIN messages. You can choose to allow messages from everyone in your contacts or only specific addresses. If you select specific addresses, you can press the BlackBerry Menu key to configure the exceptions; this takes you to a new screen where you can enter the approved senders.

Firewall Effects

Many users aren't aware that they have a firewall. The firewall silently grants or denies permissions. If the firewall is disabled, it doesn't even interfere with any operations.

However, one common use of the firewall is to warn users about app actions. The standard firewall prompt will show a message such as, "The application SearchCrawler has requested a http connection to www.google.com." Users can allow or deny the request. They also can check options like "Do not ask for http" or "Do not ask for http to www.google.com."

While the prompt displays, app execution will be frozen. Once the user has dealt with the prompt, the operation will return or an exception will be thrown. You cannot influence the text that is displayed in this firewall prompt or provide a default setting.

If the user selects an option like "Do not ask again," they will never again see the prompt in this app unless they later reinstall the application or modify the firewall settings. If the prompt is for accessing a particular domain, they may need to reapprove accesses to later domains.

> **Tip:** If the firewall is set to prompt, your app's execution will cease at the moment it attempts to open a connection. This allows the BlackBerry to display a modal security prompt that allows the user to grant or deny permission. However, if the connection was made from the app's main UI thread, the BlackBerry might not be able to draw the modal dialog and the app will freeze. To avoid this problem, follow the best practice of always making connections from another thread.

Even if the firewall is disabled, firewall-style prompts will still display for unsigned applications. Such applications are presumed to be less trusted than signed apps, so they are held to a higher level of scrutiny.

Dealing with the Firewall

Unfortunately, the BlackBerry API does not offer developers a good way to deal with the firewall. You cannot query it to determine whether it is enabled, and you cannot request it to be disabled for your app or globally. If you wish to influence the firewall setting, your best option is to provide the user with instructions on how to manually modify the firewall.

> **Tip:** If your app will be running in a corporate network, you can ask a new firewall setting to be pushed to your app's users.

As discussed in the "User Permissions" section, ApplicationPermissionsManager. getPermission() takes the firewall settings into effect. This does provide a useful way to determine ahead of time whether a network operation will succeed or fail. You can use an alternate version of getPermission() that lets you ignore the firewall setting. If you learn that an Internet connection to a particular domain is set to deny, but ignoring the firewall is set to allow, then you know that the firewall is responsible for the narrower permissions.

Firewalls can be frustrating for users and developers, as they require extra clicking that interrupts the flow of the app. There isn't much that you can do about this, so just advise your users of the situation and describe what steps they can take to mitigate it. On the plus side, most BlackBerry users who do have firewalls are very accustomed to seeing these prompts, and after a while become used to automatically granting new apps safe passage through the firewall.

MIDlet Permissions: "I Will Do These Things"

If you write MIDlets, you are used to requesting permissions in your JAD and MANIFEST.MF files. The Java ME MIDlet security model requires applications to pre-emptively declare what sensitive APIs they will be using. Users can view these permissions before they choose to download and install an app.

Adding MIDlet Permissions

Permissions are provided on a single line with the name MIDlet-Permissions. The following example shows an app requesting permissions to open secure and unsecure web URLs.

```
MIDlet-Permissions: javax.microedition.io.Connector.http, ↵
    javax.microedition.io.Connector.https
```

Alternately, you can specify some or all of your permissions with `MIDlet-Permissions-Opt`. These are optional permissions that your application requests but does not require. If the user does not grant these permissions, the application will still install, but the affected operations will fail at runtime. This is useful if optional program features require MIDlet permissions, such as a recipe app with options to email recipes to yourself.

A variety of permissions are available for use; some of the most common are shown in Table 9-2. There is no limit on the number of permissions you can request.

Table 9-2. *MIDlet Permissions*

Name	Description
`javax.microedition.content.ContentHandler`	Use CHAPI
`javax.microedition.io.Connector.datagram`	Send UDP datagrams
`javax.microedition.io.Connector.datagramreceive`	Receive UDP datagrams
`javax.microedition.io.Connector.file.read`	Read filesystem
`javax.microedition.io.Connector.file.write`	Create and write files
`javax.microedition.io.Connector.http`	Open HTTP connections
`javax.microedition.io.Connector.https`	Open secure HTTPS connections
`javax.microedition.io.Connector.mms`	Open MMS connections for sending or receiving
`javax.microedition.io.Connector.sms`	Open SMS connections for sending or receiving
`javax.microedition.io.Connector.socket`	Open socket connection
`javax.microedition.io.Connector.ssl`	Open secure (SSL or TLS) socket connection
`javax.microedition.io.PushRegistry`	Automatically start application when push events are received
`javax.microedition.location.Location`	Access GPS/LBS location
`javax.microedition.media.control.RecordControl`	Record audio
`javax.microedition.media.control.VideoControl.getSnapshot`	Record snapshots
`javax.microedition.pim.ContactList.read`	Read contacts
`javax.microedition.pim.ContactList.write`	Create or modify contacts

Table 9-2. MIDlet Permissions (continued)

Name	Description
javax.microedition.pim.EventList.read	Read calendar
javax.microedition.pim.EventList.write	Create or edit calendar events
javax.microedition.pim.ToDoList.read	Read tasks
javax.microedition.pim.ToDoList.write	Create or edit tasks
javax.wireless.messaging.mms.receive	Receive MMS messages
javax.wireless.messaging.mms.send	Send MMS messages
javax.wireless.messaging.sms.receive	Receive SMS messages
javax.wireless.messaging.sms.send	Send SMS messages

Add MIDlet permissions by editing your application's JAD file. RIM's application compiler automatically modifies this file each time the app builds, but it recognizes the permissions setting and will leave it alone.

MIDlet Permissions and BlackBerry

RIM did not invent MIDlet permissions, but rather it inherited them from the existing Java ME standard. As such, they behave a little strangely, and do not exactly fit the expectations of either Java ME or BlackBerry developers.

Recognize that these permissions are just one piece of the security puzzle, and a tiny piece at that. Veteran Java ME developers who are new to BlackBerry are sometimes confused why a file connection operation would fail with a security exception when they had explicitly declared that their app requires the file connection API. As you have seen, this is because BlackBerry devices first and foremost look to the security policy settings, and after that to the user permissions, before allowing any sensitive API access. When you request MIDlet permissions, you are asking for permissions from the Java ME environment, but the lower-level BlackBerry environment still has the authority to deny your request. As such, MIDlet permissions are entirely superseded by application permissions: setting them has no effect, and, even if you do not set them, the operations will still be permitted so long as the proper application permissions are set.

The bottom line: If you are making MIDlets and intend to run them on nonBlackBerry devices, include permissions. If not, don't bother.

Application Signing: "Do I Know You?"

What's the deal with signing? Unlike several other phone platforms, signing a BlackBerry application is quite cheap, and you are permitted to sign an effectively limitless number of apps. You might wonder what the usefulness is.

Identity Establishment

The most important factor in application signing is to establish authorship. Every set of code signing keys is unique, and every code signing request verifies that you are the person who originally ordered the keys.

Unlike some other certificate-style operations, RIM doesn't actually perform a background check or physically verify your identity. Still, it does recognize you as an individual entity, and, because your apps are signed with your keys, it knows who wrote a given app.

Code Signing Impacts

Almost nobody will ever have a serious problem with application signing. Still, by setting up the system the way they have, RIM has gained certain abilities.

- They can monitor the APIs used by individuals. This allows them to, for example, deny cryptographic API use to people in certain geographic regions.

- Because signatures are provided by a remote server, in extreme cases, RIM could revoke a set of code signing keys, for example, if a developer was discovered writing virus software.

If an app is not signed, it is missing this audit trail. As a result, the application is less trusted and will be treated differently from signed apps.

- All restricted APIs will fail to execute. This includes items like the application manager, email messages, the persistent object store, and many more.

- Certain operations will always result in a user prompt requiring their approval before proceeding. These operations include network I/O and filesystem access.

Signing only has an impact when running on an actual BlackBerry device; the simulator does not need signatures and will not behave any differently if an app has been signed.

App: Ask for Permissions

MediaGrabber exercises a wide range of functions. This also means it crosses a lot of boundaries and requires a large set of permissions to function properly. You won't notice any problems while running in the emulator, but, once you start running it on devices, you may run across some things that don't work properly: maybe the audio recording doesn't start, or the file isn't saved, or you can't invoke it via CHAPI.

Fortunately, by using knowledge from this chapter, you can help mitigate these problems. When the app starts up, check if you have the permissions necessary to run. If so, proceed as normal. If not, ask the user to grant you the proper permissions, and refuse to start unless you get them.

The Version Problem

When studying Table 9-1, you probably noticed that a host of new permissions were added in device software version 4.6, and many old ones were deprecated. Therefore, the permissions to ask for will vary depending on what version of the software you plan on using.

You will shortly be shown strategies to deal with these kinds of versioning problems. In the meantime, let's divide the targets into two groups: one for software after 4.3 but before 4.6, and another for everything from 4.6 onward.

Checking and Requesting Permissions: The Old Way

Listing 9-1 shows a helper method that checks the current application permissions. If it sees that any of them are not set to "Allow", it will ask the user to grant those permissions. This method uses only APIs and fields that are defined in software versions 4.3 and later.

Listing 9-1. Checking and Requesting Required MediaGrabber Permissions

```
private boolean checkPermissions_4_3()
{
    ApplicationPermissionsManager manager = ApplicationPermissionsManager
            .getInstance();
    ApplicationPermissions current = manager.getApplicationPermissions();

    int email = ApplicationPermissions.PERMISSION_EMAIL;
    int interProcess =
        ApplicationPermissions.PERMISSION_INTER_PROCESS_COMMUNICATION;
    int file = ApplicationPermissions.PERMISSION_FILE_API;
    int media = ApplicationPermissions.PERMISSION_MEDIA;
    int pim = ApplicationPermissions.PERMISSION_PIM;
    int screenCapture = ApplicationPermissions.PERMISSION_SCREEN_CAPTURE;
    int allow = ApplicationPermissions.VALUE_ALLOW;

    if (current.getPermission(email) != allow
            || current.getPermission(interProcess) != allow
            || current.getPermission(file) != allow
            || current.getPermission(media) != allow
            || current.getPermission(pim) != allow
            || current.getPermission(screenCapture) != allow)
    {
```

```
        ApplicationPermissions updated = new ApplicationPermissions();
        updated.addPermission(email);
        updated.addPermission(interProcess);
        updated.addPermission(file);
        updated.addPermission(media);
        updated.addPermission(pim);
        updated.addPermission(screenCapture);
        return manager.invokePermissionsRequest(updated);
    }
    return true;
}
```

> **Note:** I assigned the permission names to local variables simply to make the code more legible on the printed page. In a real app, you would likely just refer to the `ApplicationPermissions` fields directly.

This just shows one of a few potential ways to make the request. You could check for and request each permission individually; this would be annoying, but possibly more elegant to code. An even better solution would be to check all permissions, but only ask for the permissions that are not already granted. This is less likely to intimidate the user, who may be more likely to accept the change if he sees that you're only asking for permission to record than he would be if you ask for a half-dozen permissions at once.

Checking and Requesting Permissions: The New Way

You can use the previous method in more recent devices because the APIs are still available. However, if you're like me, you won't like looking at those deprecation warnings. You can easily convert this method to use only nondeprecated APIs by making the following substitutions.

```
int email = ApplicationPermissions.PERMISSION_EMAIL;
int interProcess = ↵
    ApplicationPermissions.PERMISSION_CROSS_APPLICATION_COMMUNICATION;
int file = ApplicationPermissions.PERMISSION_FILE_API;
int media = ApplicationPermissions.PERMISSION_MEDIA;
int pim = ApplicationPermissions.PERMISSION_ORGANIZER_DATA;
int screenCapture = ApplicationPermissions.PERMISSION_RECORDING;
int allow = ApplicationPermissions.VALUE_ALLOW;
```

You might find even more fine-grained differences between versions. Some permissions were added in device software version 4.2.1, others in 4.3, others in 4.6, and more will surely be added in future versions. To make sure you can compile for each version, you may need to make slightly different versions of the class. Fortunately, permissions tend to be added along with the corresponding functions: if a permission is not defined, it probably means the associated feature is not available on that device.

Plugging In

Where do you want to invoke your checkPermissions() method? This is a tough call. The best place to locate it is within your constructor: because MediaGrabber checks for CHAPI registration right away, and CHAPI is guarded by an application permission, it would be nice to check that you have permissions before doing anything else. However, because MediaGrabber is an auto-start application, it will start running automatically on boot-up, as well as whenever it receives CHAPI requests. Users may get confused or annoyed if they see permissions windows popping up, seemingly without any cause.

As a compromise, I have decided to call the method after the user directly launches MediaGrabber from the icon, as shown in the following code. At this point, the user knows what app is running and is more likely to grant permissions. In practice, most users will run the app directly shortly after installing it. And, once we get the permissions we want, they will still be set the way we want even after the device reboots.

```
public static void main(String[] args)
{
    MediaGrabber grabber = new MediaGrabber();
    if (args != null && args.length > 0 && args[0].equals("launch"))
    {
        if (grabber.checkPermissions_4_3())
        {
            grabber.pushScreen(new ChoicesScreen());
            grabber.enterEventDispatcher();
        }
    }
    // Remaining startup cases handled below.
}
```

Because MediaGrabber is ultimately an entertainment application, this approach makes sense. If your app is designed to provide more low-level capabilities or doesn't contain a UI component, you'll probably want to ask for permissions almost immediately.

Running the App

Adding permissions checks won't have any impact at all on the simulator, where everything is always permitted. The impact on the device may be different based on the particular handset you are using. If you have previously always been able to run MediaGrabber with no problems or annoyances, odds are high that you already had all the permissions you need, and so the permissions request will never display. For most developers, though, you will see the prompt display the first time you launch the new version of MediaGrabber on the device.

Experiment with granting or denying permissions to see how it affects the app's behavior. If you have previously set all permissions, you can continue testing by changing some back to Deny or Prompt, as previously described in the "Application Permissions" section of this chapter.

WANT MORE?

As you have seen, there is only a limited amount of code available to control security features. However, your use of that code and accurate information about application and device security will make your app look truly professional. Consider making these additional enhancements.

- Delay permissions requests until they are necessary. You may never need to ask for email permission if the user never sends the media they record.

- Check the highest level of permission that a user can grant instead of always requiring "Allow". If corporate users install MediaGrabber and have a restrictive IT policy, they may not be able to change permissions no matter how often you ask.

- Consider allowing the user to continue running even without the requested permissions. This may cause problems later on, so display a warning.

Requesting permissions is a little like a dance between yourself, the user, and BlackBerry. Like any dance with three partners, it is a little awkward. Applications that handle themselves with grace stand out from the field.

Excelsior

You probably know more than you ever wanted to know about how application security works on RIM. Although the details occasionally seem arcane, they are absolutely critical to creating smoothly functioning apps and developing an app distribution strategy. You wouldn't want to embarrass yourself with a huge release, only to find out that the app doesn't even run for many of your users.

The fundamental point to keep in mind when thinking about device security is that your needs as an application developer are subordinate to other stakeholders' needs. The carrier wants the network to function smoothly, the company wants their information to remain secure, the user wants their privacy protected, governments want to control the export of security software, and so on. Navigating these often conflicting desires can feel like a negotiation. Simply recognizing the complexity of the situation places you ahead of the curve.

Fortunately, there's more to do than just complain about tight security. APIs do exist that allow you to query most permissions settings, and you can use these to try to free your app from some of its constraints. Even when the app is on a device that simply refuses to run, at least you can communicate the reason to the user and describe what they could do to fix it, even if that solution involves buying a new phone.

Toward the end of this chapter, we took our first close look at the problems that crop up when you try to use an API that has changed across different software versions. This is only the tip of the iceberg: if you are a successful developer who wants to release your app across the widest possible range of devices, software versions, countries, and languages, you will need to come to grips with the challenges of porting. The next chapter will introduce you to these challenges and discuss ways to help resolve them.

Chapter **10**

Porting Your App

It's easy to make assumptions when you start programming for BlackBerry. You probably have a single device that you're looking at, and any time you have questions about how BlackBerry devices handle something, you can simply check to see what the device does. The picture grows far more complicated after you have written your app and start making it available to other devices. Suddenly, you must deal with different keyboards, varying screen sizes, unavailable APIs, different carrier Internet settings, and more. Navigating this can be a nightmare. Or it can be exhilarating. This chapter will discuss the major items to keep in mind as you write and port your app, and, by considering them from early on, you can cut down on the grindwork of rewrites and focus on the joy of bringing your app to everyone.

Understanding Hardware Differences

It's sometimes hard to believe that BlackBerry smartphones were first released in 2002. Since that time, the sheer number of devices has exploded, along with the set of capabilities they offer. To a large degree, this has been driven by RIM's increasing push from the business market into the consumer market. For the most part companies are happy giving everyone the same device, but when it comes to private wireless subscribers, everyone seems to want a phone that is uniquely theirs.

Processors

Mobile phones have more detailed CPU requirements than computers or other devices. In order to minimize costs and power consumption, modern phones usually combine general-purpose computing and cellular operations onto a single chip. RIM uses specialized chips from a variety of manufacturers to achieve their goals for performance and costs. Depending on the device model, the chip may come from Intel, ARM, or Qualcomm. Qualcomm chips are most common on CDMA devices such as those used on the Verizon and Sprint networks.

Each chip will have its own MHz clock speed. The latest devices are capable of over 600MHz, while older devices operate at far slower speeds. As with PC chips, though, the megahertz tell only part of the story. Your app's speed will vary a great deal depending on how it uses the display, the filesystem, and the network, and a processor that is efficient at doing these things may run your app more quickly even if it has a lower MHz rating.

> **Caution:** Don't assume that MHz always refers to clock speed. MHz is also used to describe wireless frequency ranges. A "800/1900 MHz" device describes the radio frequencies at which it can operate, not two different processor speeds.

Processor speeds are most important for games and for computationally complex applications, particularly scientific and graphical apps. Because apps are written in Java, you do not have access to as many tricks as you might have when compiling native code such as C. It's a good idea to create an early, rough version of your app and then try to run it on all the devices you are considering to judge whether the processor speeds will cause an issue. If an app runs a little slowly, you can probably find ways to make it acceptable. If it runs unbearably slowly, you may need to skip that device, drastically rewrite the app, or consider profiling and dropping features that slow it down.

Radios

Different BlackBerry devices are designed to work with different wireless technologies. These technologies restrict the carriers that a phone can use, and also can create subtle differences in seemingly unrelated behavior.

GSM

Worldwide, Global System for Mobile (GSM) is a dominant technology. GSM phones are distinctive for including Subscriber Identity Module (SIM) cards. A SIM card carries your information as a wireless subscriber, independent of the phone you are using. You can freely move a SIM card between multiple GSM devices and continue to make calls on your wireless account.

In the US, many GSM devices are locked by the carrier. A locked device will only connect to that particular carrier; you can give it to another subscriber, but not to the customer of a competing carrier.

GSM devices generally have very good battery life.

GSM generally describes the voice-calling features of a mobile network. Data networks are also available to GSM users.

- GPRS offers fairly slow speeds of roughly 50–100 kilobits per second.
- EDGE is a superset of GPRS and has been fairly deployed. Many different versions of EDGE are available with widely varying speeds, including more than 200 kbit/s.

■ UMTS is the newest and fastest data network with theoretical speeds above 20 megabits per second. Like EDGE, there are many flavors of UMTS, and ongoing work will continue improving it. UMTS requires different radio and tower technologies than standard GSM. It is available in most major cities to 3G subscribers, and will likely continue spreading.

CDMA

Code Division Multiple Access (CDMA) is common in North America. CDMA describes an alternate algorithm for supporting a large number of simultaneous conversations within a relatively narrow frequency spectrum. CDMA was developed by Qualcomm, who has continued advancing it through multiple iterations.

Unlike GSM devices, CDMA devices are usually tied to a particular subscriber. If you wish to trade devices, you will need to contact your wireless carrier to do so.

CDMA devices often offer slightly better voice quality and fewer dropped calls, at a cost of lower battery life.

As with GSM, several data networks have evolved in parallel with CDMA as the technology matures.

■ 1xRTT usually has a maximum transfer speed of about 144 kbit/s.

■ Evolution Data Optimized (EV-DO) offers faster speeds with maximums above 3 mbit/s.

A related technology, WCDMA, also shares some characteristics with GSM and is most common in Japan.

CDMA devices run on top of different chipsets from GSM devices, and so they actually require a different operating system. This can lead to some nonintuitive situations; for example, a Curve 8320 and Curve 8330 look identical, but they will run at different speeds, and they handle SMS messages differently.

Dual Band

In recent years, interest in so-called *world phones* has increased. These phones tackle the challenges met by people who travel overseas and find that they are no longer able to make calls.

As a solution, these BlackBerry devices actually contain multiple radios: one that operates along the GSM networks, and another that uses CDMA. Each radio will have the characteristics that you would expect from a phone that only supported that radio.

In the United States, BlackBerry world phones are sometimes locked so they will only connect to CDMA networks in the United States and to GSM elsewhere.

iDEN

iDEN was developed by Motorola and is best known in the United States for its use by Sprint/Nextel. iDEN supports the Push-to-Talk feature, which makes mobile phones behave more like walkie-talkies. It has borrowed several features from GSM, including the use of SIM cards.

Again, iDEN phones use a different chipset with different capabilities, and so they behave differently from similar GSM or CDMA models. The most striking difference is their different treatment of BES networks. As you may know, you can specify that a connection should be made using the client-side TCP stack by appending ";deviceside=true" to the end of a URL, and specify an MDS network connection by appending ";deviceside=false". On most models, if you do not specify either option, the BlackBerry will first try to make the connection with MDS, and, if MDS is unavailable, it will fall back to TCP. However, on iDEN devices, the device will attempt to open a TCP connection by default.

Wi-Fi

Many modern BlackBerry devices include a Wi-Fi antenna in addition to a standard mobile antenna. This allows users to connect to a Wi-Fi access point instead of or in addition to a cellular tower.

Wi-Fi is most common on GSM devices; even many recent CDMA devices do not include Wi-Fi.

Wi-Fi is a completely separate interface from the mobile interface, so if you wish to make a connection over Wi-Fi you must explicitly do so by specifying ";interface=wifi" in a URL connection string. You can use APIs to determine whether a particular device has Wi-Fi and is connected to a network.

External Memory Storage

All recent BlackBerry models include support for MicroSD cards, and some of the very newest support MicroSDHC. By inserting these cards, users can drastically expand the amount of storage available on the device. If your application will be storing large files, it should definitely place them on the SD card if available.

Most newly purchased devices come with a card, and users can later purchase replacements with larger capacity if desired. The maximum capacity varies depending on the device model and the operating system version.

Memory storage should have a minimal effect on your porting efforts, but do be aware that very old devices do not have external storage available, and users might have removed their cards from newer devices. Try to avoid blindly writing out to the SD card: a more polished app will first check if the card is available by checking FileSystemRegistry.listRoots(). If unavailable, the app should fall back on writing to internal storage or display a friendly error message asking the user to run the app again with a valid card inserted.

Keyboard

In order to support different form factors, RIM has created several different types of keyboards for use in its phones.

Keyboard Profiles

BlackBerry devices made their reputation by offering full QWERTY keyboards, similar to those found in Figure 10-1, at a time when other phones almost universally used awkward 12-key multi-tap text entry. The QWERTY keyboard lets you directly enter every letter of the alphabet by pressing a single key, and allows access to common special characters through use of an ALT key. A hardware SYM key offers more unusual characters. Slightly different QWERTY keyboards can be found on different models, adding or removing particular nonletter keys.

Figure 10-1. A BlackBerry with a QWERTY keyboard

Later, RIM released a new keyboard technology dubbed SureType. A SureType keyboard is more compressed than a full QWERTY keyboard, and displays multiple letters on each key, as shown in Figure 10-2. The SureType software examines the letters you have pressed and tries to guess what word you meant to enter. For example, if you type 112318, it will assume you mean to type "return", since that is the only English word that can be constructed out of the possible letters. SureType will enter the text "return" and also display a pop-up window that lists other possible words; you can select one of these by scrolling and clicking the one you want. This technology is similar to those found on more traditional phone designs, such as iTap and T9.

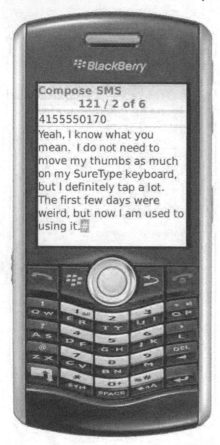

Figure 10-2. *A BlackBerry with a SureType keyboard*

When using a SureType keyboard, you can also enable Multitap mode. This makes the keyboard behave more like a traditional multi-tap phone keypad that cycles through the available letters when you press each key. To enter an "e" you would press 1 once; to enter "r" press 1 twice. To type "return" in Multitap mode, you would type "11 (pause) 1231188".

Touch-screen BlackBerry devices such as the Storm do not have a physical keyboard at all. Instead, they can display one of several virtual "soft" keyboards. This can allow more flexibility and comfort to a user. For example, a full QWERTY keyboard might display when the phone is in landscape mode (held horizontally), but a SureType keyboard might display when the phone is in portrait mode (held vertically). A number-only version can display when dialing a phone number or entering a PIN. Users generally have the option to show or hide the keyboard in order to manage the amount of visible space shown.

Detecting Keyboards

The Keypad API allows you to detect at runtime what keyboard is present on the device. Call Keypad.getHardwareLayout() to return one of the enumerations found in Table 10-1.

Table 10-1. BlackBerry Keyboards

Name	Description	Mode	Hardware Series	OS availability	Physical?
HW_LAYOUT_32	38-key keyboard	QWERTY	87xx	4.1	Yes
HW_LAYOUT_39	39-key keyboard	QWERTY	88xx	4.3	Yes
HW_LAYOUT_LEGACY	30-key keyboard	QWERTY	57xx, 58xx	4.1	Yes
HW_LAYOUT_PHONE	34 keys with phone keyboard layout	QWERTY	65xx, 67xx, 72xx, 75xx, and 77xx	4.1	Yes
HW_LAYOUT_REDUCED	23-key keyboard	SureType	71xx	4.1	Yes
HW_LAYOUT_REDUCED_24	24-key keyboard	SureType	81xx	4.2	Yes
HW_LAYOUT_TOUCHSCREEN_12	12-key phone-style keyboard	Dial pad	95xx	4.7	No
HW_LAYOUT_TOUCHSCREEN_24	24-key keyboard	SureType	95xx	4.7	No
HW_LAYOUT_TOUCHSCREEN_29	29-key keyboard	QWERTY	95xx	4.7	No

> **Note:** Starting with device software version 5.0, many of the HW_LAYOUT_TOUCHSCREEN keyboards also have special versions for particular languages, such as HW_LAYOUT_TOUCHSCREEN_12A for 12-key Arabic and HW_LAYOUT_TOUCHSCREEN_35J for Kana Kapanese.

For most physical keyboards, the hardware layout directly corresponds to the physical device. On touch-screen devices, this allows you to determine which virtual keyboard is currently displaying.

In some cases, you won't care about the specific keyboard that is being used, but rather whether a specific key is available. You can use the following static Keypad methods to make this determination.

- hasCurrencyKey() shows whether there is a dedicated key for entering currency symbols.

- hasSendEndKeys() indicates whether the device has dedicated keys for starting and ending phone calls.

- isOnKeypad(char ch) allows you to check whether a specific character is available on this keyboard.

- isValidKeyCode(int code) checks if the provided key code exists for this keyboard.

Changing Keyboards

On touch-screen devices, you can use the VirtualKeyboard class to determine whether the keyboard is displaying, and also to force it to hide or show.

isSupported() returns a boolean that describes whether the device supports virtual keyboards. If not, the other methods will have no effect.

setVisibility() allows you to specify whether the keyboard should display when this application's context has focus. VirtualKeyboard supports the following modes.

- HIDE: The keyboard should be hidden at the next opportunity. Afterward, it will automatically be shown or hidden as normal.

- HIDE_FORCE: The keyboard should always be hidden.

- IGNORE: Keep track of keyboard visibility, but do not automatically show or hide it.

- RESTORE: Return keyboard to its previously saved state.

- SHOW: Display the keyboard at the next opportunity. Afterward, it will automatically be shown or hidden as normal.

- SHOW_FORCE: Always show the keyboard.

getVisibility() will return the currently set keyboard visibility state.

VirtualKeyboard can only be used by BlackBerry CLDC applications. If developing a MIDlet, you have access to VirtualKeyboardControl, which provides similar methods for querying, showing, and hiding the virtual keyboard. You can obtain a VirtualKeyboardControl by creating a BlackBerryCanvas or BlackBerryGameCanvas and retrieving the virtual keyboard from getControl() or getControls().

Porting Impact

If you are developing business or productivity apps that mainly involve text entry, you may be able to ignore the keyboard issue altogether. The native BlackBerry text entry fields are well integrated with keyboard behavior, automatically handling QWERTY or SureType keys, so no extra effort is necessary on your part.

However, if you are developing a game or have a highly customized nonBlackBerry user interface, keyboards are much more likely to be an issue. For example, you might control a game by pressing four buttons, but those four buttons might not exist on all devices.

You can use the methods described in this section to dynamically query the phone and determine what the keyboard layout is like, and then make an appropriate decision about how to handle incoming key events. Setting up such a system can take some effort, but in the long run it will be much more efficient than creating a new version of your app for every keyboard type.

If you support touch-screen devices, carefully consider the user experience. If you write a game that is entirely touch-based, you might want to forcibly hide the keyboard so the full screen is always available for play. If your game supports a high-score name entry, you might want to show the keyboard on that screen while hiding it everywhere else.

Hardware Features

Every device has some sort of CPU, radio, and keyboard. However, only some devices have cameras, and only some have GPS. If your app requires these features, or optionally supports them, you will need to determine whether they are present on the device.

Determining by Model Number

Even before you install the app, you should be able to determine the phone's capabilities by looking at the device model number. This can be very useful if you have a web page that allows users to click through their phone before they download your app.

BlackBerry devices have four-digit model numbers, such as 8120 or 9530. The first two digits are the *series* number. These identify broad families of devices, which often share a similar marketing name. For example, the 8300, 8310, 8320, 8330, and 8350i are all part of the 8300 series and are known as BlackBerry Curve. All devices in a particular series share the same form factor and physical characteristics. For example, all BlackBerry Curve devices have a QWERTY keyboard, a trackball, and a 2-megapixel camera.

The final two digits for modern BlackBerry devices complete the *model* number, and identify what radio technologies are available on the device. Radios include both the cellular technology and also Wi-Fi and GPS.

- xx00: GSM
- xx10: GSM with GPS
- xx20: GSM with Wi-Fi
- xx30: CDMA
- xx50: CDMA with Wi-Fi
- xx50i: iDEN

For example, the 8120, 8320, and 8820 all look different, but each is a GSM-compatible device with Wi-Fi capabilities.

The model-number naming scheme can be inconsistent at times, particularly on older models, so you should verify with your particular device early in a project if you are depending on the presence of certain capabilities.

Determining by API

Several methods can be used to determine a device's identity or capabilities at runtime.

- `DeviceInfo.getDeviceName()` reports the model number of the device, with an optional suffix describing the radio type.

- `DeviceInfo.hasCamera()` reports whether a camera is physically present on the device. This does not necessarily mean that your app will have access to it.

- `DeviceInfo.getTotalFlashSize()` reports the maximum storage capacity of the flash filesystem.

- `WLANInfo.getWLANState()` reports whether the device is connected to Wi-Fi.

- `RadioInfo.getNetworkType()` reports the cellular network technology, which may be `NETWORK_802_11`, `NETWORK_CDMA`, `NETWORK_GPRS`, `NETWORK_IDEN`, or `NETWORK_UMTS`.

- `LocationProvider.getState()` reports the GPS state, which will be `OUT_OF_SERVICE` if GPS is not present, and either `AVAILABLE` or `TEMPORARILY_UNAVAILABLE` if the phone has GPS.

Porting Impact

If your app requires certain hardware capabilities to function, you should start communicating this fact well before the user downloads the app. It's frustrating to find that something doesn't work, and even worse if someone has paid for it.

You might consider releasing different versions of your app for different devices, based on whether or not they support particular features. For example, you might make a version of MediaGrabber that omits camera support for devices like the 8800 that do not include a camera. This would slightly decrease the size of the app, and could prevent confusion if you clearly state that the app does not support taking pictures.

To some extent, though, MediaGrabber already does a good job of examining device capabilities by checking the presence of recording options when building its options menu. Many developers will prefer to go this route. In such cases, the best strategy is usually to check for supported device statistics when the app first starts. Depending on what you find, you can enable or disable particular app features, and also display messages to users if you want to advise them of what they may be missing out on.

Screen Sizes

Possibly the most important difference between BlackBerry devices, the screen resolution will determine what art assets are available for use, what size of sprites to create, how much text you can fit on a screen without wrapping, and so on.

You can generally reuse an application's design between two different BlackBerry devices that share the same screen resolution. If the resolutions are different, you should decide whether a redesign is necessary. The BlackBerry CLDC UI components generally adjust well to multiple screen sizes so long as you stick to simple organizations like the VerticalFieldManager. However, elaborate user interfaces that look great on one screen size may be illegible on another.

In addition, touch-screen devices can be rotated into either portrait or landscape mode. Here too, so long as you stick to common UI designs, your app will probably function well in both orientations. Otherwise, you have a few options.

- Lock the screen into a particular orientation. You can do this by calling `Ui.getUiEngineInstance().setAcceptableDirections()`, passing in one of the direction orientations from the `net.rim.device.api.system.Display` class, such as `Display.DIRECTION_LANDSCAPE` or `Display.DIRECTION_PORTRAIT`.

- Detect the device orientation by calling `Display.getOrientation()`. This will return one of the enumerated direction values listed above. Then, display an appropriate UI for that orientation. You might need to switch to another UI if the user rotates while on the same screen.

Some common BlackBerry devices and their screen resolutions are shown in Table 10-2.

Table 10-2. *Screen resolutions*

Device Series	Horizontal Pixels	Vertical Pixels	Rotates?
71xx/81xx	240	260	No
82xx	240	320	No
83xx/87xx/88xx	320	240	No
89xx/96xx	480	360	No
90xx	480	320	No
95xx	360	480	Yes

Understanding OS Differences

Hardware capabilities are locked in stone. If your device doesn't have a camera, it won't ever have a camera. The OS, though, is much more fluid, and can evolve over time. Because your software runs on top of the OS, you must carefully note the OS availability and features as you port to different phones.

OS Availability and Updates

BlackBerry can be the gift that keeps on giving. RIM has traditionally released updated versions for every BlackBerry device. Sometimes these are patches that fix bugs and improve performances; other times, they add significant new features.

Updates are released by RIM, but will be approved by the wireless carrier or enterprise prior to being made available to end-users. Updates from wireless carriers are optional, and can either be installed through the BlackBerry Desktop Manager or over the air. Enterprises have the option of pushing out forced updates to newer software versions.

BlackBerry has a far higher proportion of power users than most phones, and it is not uncommon for people to seek out and install unapproved device updates in hopes of getting better features or performance. The BlackBerry toolset allows a user to later downgrade to a previous software version, so there is little risk in doing so.

Determining the Version

You can find a device's current software version by clicking Options and then About. The current OS software version will display towards the top, followed by the Platform version. Both these versions can change as part of an update.

At runtime, you can find the version by calling DeviceInfo.getSoftwareVersion(). When parsing this string, remember the four-part format of the version number; you cannot simply cast it to a double and compare to a desired version. Instead, examine each numbered section individually to find what the version is.

If you are hosting application downloads or help on your own web server, you can inspect the HTTP headers to see what version a phone is using. This is typically contained in the `User-Agent` header, which generally will have a value similar to `"BlackBerry9530/4.7.0.148 Profile/MIDP-2.0 Configuration/CLDC-1.1 VendorID/105"`.

> **Caution:** The BlackBerry browser includes options to masquerade as Firefox or Internet Explorer. If the user has selected one of these options, the User-Agent string will be replaced with a fake version. Also, users may be using a third-party browser such as Opera Mini.

Version Effects

OS versions are listed in a four-part version number. The first two parts describe the major feature set, the third number is the minor feature set, and the final number describes the patch version. For example, an upgrade from 4.7.0.122 to 4.7.0.148 will fix bugs but not change behavior. However, an upgrade from 4.2.1.130 to 4.5.0.110 will significantly affect the device's capabilities.

The OS version has a direct correlation to API availability. Throughout this book, I have occasionally made note of certain features becoming available in particular OS versions. The terms operating system and device software are often used interchangeably. Patch numbers have no impact on API behavior.

As described in Chapter 9, the OS version can also impact the default permissions. Certain operations that used to work in prior versions of the OS may not initially function due to more restrictive permissions settings.

Porting Impact

From your perspective, the single most important impact of the OS version is program compatibility. RIM devices are backwards compatible; that is, a program that runs on the 4.2 version of software will also run on the 4.5 version. However, they are not forwards compatible. You cannot run a program designed for newer software on older software.

> **Note:** Compatibility is generally determined by API usage, not the actual compiler. If you compile an app using the 4.5 version of the BlackBerry JDE, but only use APIs from version 4.2, the app can run on a 4.2 handset.

This leads to a quandary in writing portable software. You cannot write something like the following pseudocode; the mere existence of an API is what makes a program incompatible, not the moment you call it.

```
if (softwareVersion >= requiredVersion)
{
    callFutureAPI();
}
```

You have a few strategies available to deal with this problem.

The Lowest Common Denominator

Early on, determine the oldest BlackBerry software version that you must support. Write the app using this version of the BlackBerry JDE, only using APIs from this version or earlier.

You will still need to test your app on multiple versions; even though your app will run on all future devices, certain aspects may behave differently. If you find discrepancies, you can test the device software version at run-time and behave appropriately depending on the version.

- Pros: This is the simplest approach. At the end of the project, you will have a single version of the app that runs on everything you want.

- Cons: Your app may be missing out on useful features from future versions. This could lead to a disadvantage if your app has competitors.

Multiple Builds

Suppose you have an app that uses the network a lot. It would be really nice to use the Wi-Fi connection if it is available. Coding good Wi-Fi support is very difficult in OS versions prior to 4.3. However, many of your users never upgraded to 4.3.

In this scenario, you might consider making two different versions of your app, one with Wi-Fi support and one without. This will ensure that your app gets the widest possible usage, and that each user can get the most out of their app.

If you take this approach, I highly recommend putting all OS-specific code in a few particular files or packages, rather than scattering them throughout your app. This will make it much easier to maintain two versions of the software in parallel, since you can share the majority of the code between both versions.

- Pros: This offers a high reach and a high level of performance.

- Cons: This is the most complicated approach. If you support multiple OS levels, the complexity of your source control and build systems can rapidly explode.

Mandate Change

Your app simply might not make sense if a particular API feature is not available. Or perhaps the app would run on a previous OS version, but would offer a very poor experience. As long as you are willing to accept the consequences, it's perfectly acceptable for you to mandate a particular OS version and require users to have at least that version installed in order to use your app.

As mentioned previously, BlackBerry users have a far easier job than most phone owners when it comes to upgrading their operating system. If a newer version of device software is available, odds are that many users have already upgraded to it, and, if your app is sufficiently compelling, you may convince the remainder to take the plunge.

- Pros: You only need to maintain a single version of your app. It offers a superior product.

- Cons: Provides the smallest potential user base. It may alienate users who cannot upgrade their devices or do not wish to do so. The latest operating systems are not available for older devices.

Understanding Language Differences

Once you write a great app, you can get a large audience. In order to get the largest audience, though, you cannot confine yourself to one particular language or one particular country. BlackBerry has a significant global presence, and only a fraction of those users live in your nation.

If you try to add multi-language support to multi-device and multi-OS support, you can enter a nightmare where any little change needs to be copied and tested on dozens or even hundreds of possible combinations. Fortunately, RIM offers a decent set of tools to support localizing your app for different markets.

Localization Overview

The terms localization, internationalization, and i18n are often used interchangeably to describe the process of translating a product into a different form for different markets. Translation is an important part of this process; you probably would not choose to use a Greek-language app if you could not read Greek, and likewise a Greek speaker would probably not choose to use an English-language app if they couldn't read English.

Localization goes deeper than simple translation. Different cultural groups have different associations with images and sounds that you should keep in mind as you develop your app. For example, many Americans would look at a red octagon and assume that it means "Stop." However, many Chinese users would not have that same association, which could lead to confusion and frustration. Part of localization is to make appropriate substitutions, or, even better, to avoid ambiguity in the first place.

As noted previously in this book, a locale is described as a two-character language code combined with an optional country code. English words can be spelled differently in the

United States than they are in Great Britain, so you can choose to provide different words for the "en-US" locale than you would for "en-GB". In some cases, you might only offer a single "en" locale that would be applied to all English-speaking users. Similarly, English and French are both official languages in Canada, so a Canadian user might select between "en-CA" and "fr-CA".

Adding Multi-Language Support

A fair amount of effort is required to internationalize your app, but it will save you far more time and grief later on.

Defining Resource Files

Follow these steps to add support for internationalized text to your app.

1. Click "File", "New", "Other...", "BlackBerry Projects", "BlackBerry Resource File".

2. Navigate to the package where your app is located. If your app uses multiple packages, I recommend selecting the highest-level common package.

3. Give the file the same name as your app, with an extension of .rrh. For example, if your app is named BonjourWorld, name it BonjourWorld.rrh.

> **Note:** rrh stands for Resource Header. This "header" file is similar to a header file in C or C++.

4. Observe that two files were created in your selected package with extensions .rrh and .rrc. rrc stands for Resource Content.

5. If you'd like to add support for other languages now, repeat steps 1–3, but this time append the language code to the app name and add the .rrc extension. For example, to create a US English language file, create BonjourWorld_en_US.rrc; to create a generic English language file, create BonjourWorld_en.rrc.

6. Double-click the .rrh file to open it. You should see a grid similar to that shown in Figure 10-3.

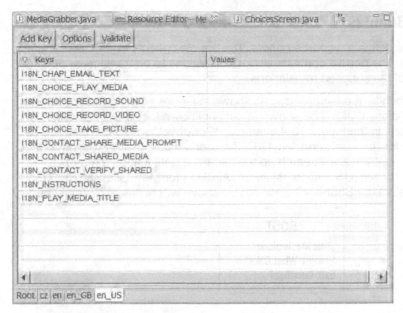

Figure 10-3. *Localizing an application*

7. Click "Add Key". Enter the name of your localized resource.

> **Tip:** I prefer to prefix my keys with the string "I18N_" to make them easier to find with Eclipse's auto-complete feature. Try to pick descriptive key names that indicate the meaning or role of the text instead of its default value. For example, use I18N_INITIAL_GREETING rather than I18N_WELCOME_TO_MY_APP.

8. Repeat step 7 for all the text you wish to internationalize in your app.

9. Provide a default translation for every key listed. You will probably use your native language for this, or text provided by a designer.

10. For each language that you added previously, a tab will display at the bottom of your translation window. You can provide translations for all of these now, or leave them alone until later on.

11. Save the resource file. If you have not configured Eclipse to build automatically, right-click on your BlackBerry application project and select "Build Project".

Behind the scenes, the BlackBerry Plug-in will generate a Java interface file that contains all the keys you defined. You can now add this text into your source files instead of using hard-coded literal strings.

Understanding Bundles

A set of resource files define a *resource bundle*. The bundle collects together a set of localizable resources. The bundle contains all possible values to be translated, identified by their key, and all of the supplied translations.

The locales within a bundle are hierarchical, as shown in Figure 10-4. At the root level are the default translations that will be shown for any unknown locale or for locales that do not override the key. In the Figure 10-4 example, "Goodbye!" would be provided as the "Exit" translation for "fr", "en", and "en_GB". If a user's locale is not present or does not contain a desired key, Java will search up the hierarchy until it finds a match. Therefore, the "Title" for "en_US" will translate as "Airplane for Me". Likewise, the "Exit" for "cs_CZ" will translate as "Sbohem!" since "cs" is above where "cs_CZ" would be.

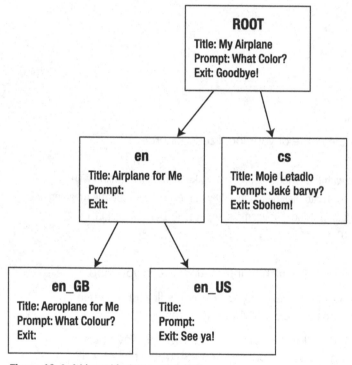

Figure 10-4. A hierarchical resource bundle

This system has the advantage of reducing the total amount of data required for complete translations. For example, most US and UK translations will probably be the same. Rather than duplicate the same texts for both locales, you can define all the common elements in "en", and only override the cases where you need to use a variant spelling.

Adding Resources to Java Classes

Modify your class declaration to implement the generated resource file. The file will have the same name as your app with the word Resource added to the end, as in the following example.

```
public class BonjourWorld extends UiApplication implements BonjourWorldResource
```

To make it more convenient to access translated text, include a `static ResourceBundle` member in your class that loads the bundle. By implementing the resource file, you gain access to the `BUNDLE_ID` and the `BUNDLE_NAME` that uniquely identify this resource bundle. I like to use a short name here, as shown below, since it cuts down on typing if a lot of text must be translated.

```
static ResourceBundle r = ResourceBundle.getBundle(BUNDLE_ID, BUNDLE_NAME);
```

Now, all that's left is the actual translation. Any place where you would ordinarily use a `String`, you can look up the proper translation from the `ResourceBundle`. Your resource interface provides all the keys you added as integer enumerations. If you follow a consistent naming scheme, you can type the prefix (like "I18N") and then select the proper key from the drop-down selection box. A sample localization is shown below.

```
add(new LabelField(r.getString(I18N_PROMPT)));
```

When this line executes, Java will check to see what the current locale is. It will then check the bundle for a match, walking up the hierarchy tree if necessary. Once it finds the best match, it returns the `String`, which is then handled by the program as though you entered it literally.

Testing Languages

The BlackBerry device simulators tend to be a little skimpy in language support. Depending on your device, you may only have access to US English and UK English. You can still use these languages to verify the correct functioning of your localization effort.

To switch your language, open Options and then the Language menu. Of course, these may have different names depending on the current language setting of the device. UK English uses "Localisation" instead of "Language." In the Language screen, you can select the language or dialect you wish to use from the drop-down menu.

> **Note:** You may need to close and restart your application in order to test a new language setting. You can completely close the application by pressing Menu and then Close.

Many more languages are usually available for the device, although it requires a little effort to get them. Each language has its own dictionary, menus, and other resources, so unnecessary languages are typically removed as part of the initial Setup Wizard. You can check for available languages following the same steps you took on the simulator. To load additional languages, follow these steps.

1. Download a recent version of BlackBerry device software from your wireless provider or your enterprise and install it on your PC.

2. Open the BlackBerry Desktop Manager.

3. Select Application Loader and then Add/Remove Applications.

4. Select the checkboxes for languages you wish to load. You may also choose to remove languages here.

5. Select "Next" and follow the prompts to load the languages.

After your phone reboots, the new languages will be available for testing.

Managing Resource Bundles

Using a single resource bundle is a no-brainer for a simple app with a single class file. Most real-world apps, though, will contain substantially more. Depending on your needs, there are several strategies you can consider.

One Bundle, Many Implementors

You can follow the steps given above, changing all your class files that contain localizable resources so that they each implement the same generated bundle interface.

- Pros: This approach simplifies translation efforts; because all your strings are located in a single .rrc file, none will be overlooked. This approach also requires the smallest amount of typing, since you can directly reference all the resource keys within each class.

- Cons: If you have a large number of resource keys, it can become confusing to keep them all straight. This approach will slightly increase the size of your final executable, especially if you have a large number of class files.

One Bundle, Single Implementor

You can follow the steps given above to implement the generated bundle in a single class. Give the ResourceBundle member public, protected, or package visibility. Other classes can then access translations through the implementing class, as in the example below.

```
String translated = BonjourWorld.r.getString(BonjourWorld.I18N_HELP);
```

This approach has the same pros and cons listed above, except that the size of the final executable will be slightly smaller, and a bit more typing is required.

Multiple Bundles

If you prefer, you can create multiple .rrh files, each of which will generate its own bundle. Each class can then choose which bundle class to implement, or even implement multiple bundles.

- Pros: You can easily group together the localizable resources for a particular screen or area of the program. Implementation is usually easy, as you have only a small set of key options for each class and little extra typing.

- Cons: It can be difficult to track the resource files, making it easier to overlook particular translations. This approach will generally create larger executables than the previous two.

Other Localization Concerns

Once you understand the basics of translation, you will be well prepared to handle other localization needs that your app may require.

Dealing with Images

Although the resource files are oriented toward text translation of words and phrases, you can also use them for images and other nontext resources. Imagine creating a key called I18N_IMAGE_ALERT_ICON. The default English value for this key might be "/YellowExclamation.png", while the Chinese value might be "/ChAlert.png". You can then use code like that shown below to display the proper image for the user's locale.

```
String alertPath = r.getString(I18N_IMAGE_ALERT_ICON);
Bitmap alert = Bitmap.getBitmapResource(alertPath);
```

This approach works best if your app only has a few images, all relatively small. Otherwise, supporting multiple images for many locales can quickly increase your app's size. In those cases, you might consider the following options.

- Place the resources in separate library COD files for each language. Users can choose to load the languages that they need, and not take up space for unnecessary languages.

- Do not place images in your app at all. Instead, store them on a server, and have the app download them as needed. This will make the app a bit slower and use more network resources, but also gives you more flexibility if you later decide to change images.

Locale-aware Formatting

Different languages and countries have more differences than just their words. They also use different conventions for displaying dates (such as 5/30/10 or 30/5/10), numbers (such as 13,500.42 or 13.500,42), plural forms, and subject-verb-object placement. If your app programmatically generates such text, translating words will not suffice when localizing to a new country.

Java ME has traditionally lacked good support for such localization, forcing developers to create their own solutions or build custom versions of their apps for each locale. More recently, JSR 238 with the `javax.microedition.global` package has begun to offer a more standard way to treat some of these tasks. However, BlackBerry has included many familiar classes from Java SE and Java EE that provide powerful and fairly simple tools for flexible localization. These classes, which were originally located in `java.text` or `java.util`, can all be found in `net.rim.device.api.i18n`. Some of the most useful are listed below.

- `SimpleDateFormat` lets you format and parse an abstract time representation, provided by `Calendar`, into a natural style for a given locale. Despite the name, it is very flexible, offering strings of varying length (such as "6/10/10" as opposed to "June 10th, 2010") and structure (such as "15:00" as opposed to "3 o'clock PM").

- `MessageFormat` allows you to define flexible string constructions that can be dynamically built with varying data at a later time. For example, a `MessageFormat` for a particular locale might have the pattern "Only {0} more shopping {1} until Guy Fawkes Day!" You could then format this pattern with the variables 1 and "day", or with 10 and "days". In another language, the order of the words would likely change, but the appropriate variables would be inserted into the {0} and {1} fields.

Dynamic Localization

In almost all cases, your app should use the current device locale setting. However, certain apps might allow the user to choose their own locale. For example, a city travel guide might include an option to switch languages so you could hand your phone to a native speaker and have them pick out a restaurant for you. Switching locales within the app can also make it easier to test the display of different languages without needing to exit the app and switch device languages. To change the locale, retrieve the `Locale` you want to use, and then pass it to `setDefault()`. Locales can be retrieved by name or from an enumeration. The two examples below are equivalent.

```
Locale.setDefault(Locale.get("cs"));
Locale.setDefault(Locale.get(Locale.LOCALE_cs));
```

Porting Impact

You should think early on about whether your app will require localization. If you're confident that its use will be so narrow that localization is unnecessary, ignore it. Otherwise, the earlier you start addressing localization, the more easily it will go.

If you are working from a specification, you might know before you start coding exactly what text will be used by the app. This is the best situation to be in: you can define all your strings even before you start writing code, inserting the keys in the app as you write it.

If you don't know the text up front, create a blank resource bundle at the start of your project. As you write your app, create keys for any user-visible text you create. Provide a default translation in your native language; don't worry about other languages for now. Once the app is done, you can pass off the keys to a translator to get the necessary translations. More likely, your app will initially be released with only your native language supported, but, once you have demand from other countries or languages, you'll be able to meet their needs almost instantly.

In practice, most programs (including MediaGrabber) start off with hard-coded String literals. Towards the end of the project, or even after release, someone will go through the source code to find all visible text and convert it to using resource bundles. This approach requires the greatest total effort, but it does mean that the initial stages of the project can be more legible than they would be with resource keys.

While designing the visual look of your app, keep localization needs in mind. The length of text will probably change drastically depending on the language used; going from English to German will greatly increase the text length, while going from English to Japanese may shrink it. As such, text might flow to multiple lines or be cut off. Design your UI flexibly so you can accommodate these changes.

Avoid including text within your images: for example, don't include the word "Stop" in a stop-sign graphic. Doing this would force you to create a new image for every language, which takes up much more space than creating new text. Instead, consider creating blank versions of your images, and then drawing text on top of the images at run-time. Even better, pick images that are self-explanatory, or place labels outside the image.

Try to be culturally sensitive. Images, sounds, and phrases that are innocent or funny in one culture might be very offensive in another. Avoid using casual speech, idiomatic phrases, and dialect. This doesn't mean that your app shouldn't have personality, but, if your app uses language too narrowly, it won't make a good impression on foreign users.

Understanding Platform Differences

Apps used to be a sideshow; now they can take center stage. Consumers and businesses increasingly base their phone purchase decisions on what applications are available. If you write a great app, people will hear about it, and you may soon hear a clamor from other users to support them. Other smartphone platforms such as Android, Windows Mobile, and iPhone should have the power to run any app that would run on BlackBerry; feature phone platforms like Java ME and BREW may need to be evaluated to determine whether they can handle your app.

Porting to another platform is an order of magnitude more difficult than porting to another BlackBerry. However, by following some basic tips, you can make this process less painful.

Forget Porting the UI

Each phone platform has its own UI toolkit, and each is incompatible with everything else. Good programmers have learned the importance of reusing code, and will try to take advantage of the UI code they have already written. Don't. The effort involved in translating between platforms is usually greater than that required to rewrite the UI from scratch. Additionally, by using a phone's native UI, your application is more likely to look and feel like the native apps that the phone's users are accustomed to.

Functionally Divide the App

Taking a chunk of code and translating it to a new platform can be an overwhelming, frustrating process. Instead, follow good object-oriented design techniques. Divide your application into components. Where possible, cleanly separate concerns through strategies like the Model-View-Controller paradigm. Diagram your app's structure, and ensure it makes sense.

You will then be able to translate individual components, a far simpler task. You should be able to test each individual component prior to finishing the entire app. For example, if your app contains networking operations, pull those operations into a separate networking component and write unit tests to verify that you receive the same data on each platform.

Some components, like those that contain pure business logic, should be fairly straightforward to port; you will just need to translate them into a new programming language. On the other hand, components that contain a lot of platform-specific functionality such as user interface or persistent storage will require more substantial changes. Be prepared to spend extra time making these changes and testing to ensure they work.

Identify Language Reuse Opportunities

Java ME and Android both use versions of Java. You may be able to reuse nonUI code between these platforms. If so, consider creating a separate JAR project that contains your application engine, business logic, or other generic Java code.

Be aware, though, that many Java APIs are not shared between these platforms. For example, none of the `javax.microedition` packages is available on Android. Conversely, Android is based on a later version of Java, so many of its basic Java APIs are not available for BlackBerry.

Back to the Drawing Board

Many apps that are ported to multiple platforms fall into the trap of the lowest common denominator. If you only support the features present on every platform, you miss out on many opportunities for taking advantage of the unique advantages each phone has to offer.

You shouldn't re-create your app for every individual phone—that would take far too much effort for far too little return. But do take a fresh look whenever you are considering moving to a new platform. It may be an opportunity to do something new, fun, and interesting, instead of the drudgery of a boring port.

App: Localized Text

MediaGrabber's simple UI can be run on a wide variety of devices without requiring changes to the code. By using the CLDC UI framework, the same code works fine on touch-screen and QWERTY devices. Throughout the book, I have been careful to test for feature support within the app, so no extra work is required to support the presence or absence of a camera or other piece of hardware.

MediaGrabber does make use of APIs from version 4.5, but none from later OS versions. It seems reasonable to require 4.5 as a minimum version as most of the consumer-oriented BlackBerry devices have at least this version available.

Throughout this book, I have been happily putting hard-coded strings into the MediaGrabber source. This makes the samples easier to read and understand (assuming English is your native language), but, as you have seen in this chapter, it also limits the potential audience for the app.

Fortunately, there are still a manageable number of classes to work with. While a fair amount of code is required to internationalize the app, it's a very simple process.

Create the Resource Files

Following the steps given in the section "Adding Multi-Language Support," create a new resource header file called MediaGrabber.rrh. Provide .rrc files for each language you would like to support. I have chosen to use "_en", "_en_US", "_en_GB", and "_cs", but you can include any other language you would like to see.

Create keys for all visible strings in MediaGrabber and copy the existing string values into the default MediaGrabber.rrc file. You can either do this in the Eclipse grid editing window, or directly edit the .rrc file by hand if you prefer. If you edit the .rrc file outside of Eclipse, you might need to refresh or restart Eclipse for the changes to be recognized.

A partial set of the English translations are shown in Listing 10-1, covering the main MediaGrabber class file as well as the initial UI from ChoicesScreen.

***Listing 10-1.** Initial Default Translations for MediaGrabber*

```
I18N_CHAPI_EMAIL_TEXT#0="Sent to you by CHAPI";
I18N_CHOICE_PLAY_MEDIA#0="Play Media";
I18N_CHOICE_RECORD_SOUND#0="Record Sound";
I18N_CHOICE_RECORD_VIDEO#0="Record Video";
I18N_CHOICE_TAKE_PICTURE#0="Take a Picture";
I18N_CONTACT_SHARED_MEDIA#0="You have shared media with them.";
I18N_CONTACT_SHARE_MEDIA_PROMPT#0="No sharing yet. ↵
Would you like to send media?";
```

```
I18N_CONTACT_VERIFY_SHARED#0="Verify Media Shared";
I18N_INSTRUCTIONS#0="Please enter a location, ↵
then select a choice from the menu.";
I18N_PLAY_MEDIA_TITLE#0="Playing {0}";
I18N_PROMPT_LOCATION#0="Location:";
```

Notice the {0} at the bottom. This indicates a place where we will want to dynamically construct the final displayable string based on other variables.

Provide any translations you like at this point. The initial Czech translations are shown in Listing 10-2. Notice that Unicode characters are supported by simply entering "\uXXXX". You can also copy and paste Unicode characters directly into the Eclipse editing window. Unicode support allows you to port to any locale, including traditionally difficult ones like Chinese and Arabic.

Listing 10-2. Initial Czech Translations for MediaGrabber

```
I18N_CHAPI_EMAIL_TEXT#0="Zasláno na Vá\u0161 CHAPI";
I18N_CHOICE_RECORD_SOUND#0="Záznam zvuku";
I18N_CHOICE_RECORD_VIDEO#0="Video záznam";
I18N_CHOICE_TAKE_PICTURE#0="Vyfotografovat";
I18N_CONTACT_SHARED_MEDIA#0="Máte sdílená média.";
I18N_CONTACT_SHARE_MEDIA_PROMPT#0="Dosud \u017Eádné sdílení. Chcete poslat média?";
I18N_CONTACT_VERIFY_SHARED#0="Ov\u011B\u0159te Media Sdílená";
I18N_INSTRUCTIONS#0="Prosím, zadejte umíst\u011Bní, vyberte volbu z menu.";
I18N_PLAY_MEDIA_TITLE#0="Hra {0}";
I18N_PROMPT_LOCATION#0="Poloha:";
```

> **Tip:** Most of the above translations come from Google Translate. However, translations by native speakers are always superior to those generated by a machine, which can have a difficult time capturing nuances or determining different parts of speech. If you are creating a commercial app, hire a professional translator. If you are releasing a free or open-source app, you can often find volunteers who will do a good job. When using volunteers, it's a good idea to get input from multiple sources so you can determine the best and most common translations.

Modify Source

For the most part, the changes to MediaGrabber are very straightforward. Simply follow the instructions in "Adding Multi-Language Support" to make each file implement `MediaGrabberResource`, obtain a `ResourceBundle`, and look up strings dynamically.

One wrinkle occurs when it comes to building up strings that include variables. Here, you want to define a pattern in your translation file, with placeholders defined with a numbered sequence like {0}, {1}, and so on. Then, instead of manually concatenating strings, use the `MessageFormat` class to apply the variables to your translated pattern. Listing 10-3 contains the complete internationalized class for ChoicesScreen. Note the new code in LaunchPlayer near the bottom, which will create a string like "Playing file:///SDCard/BlackBerry/Music/captured.amr" that is localized for the user's language.

Listing 10-3. Localized Version of ChoicesScreen

```
package com.apress.king.mediagrabber;

import net.rim.device.api.i18n.*;
import net.rim.device.api.ui.*;
import net.rim.device.api.ui.component.*;
import net.rim.device.api.ui.container.MainScreen;

public class ChoicesScreen extends MainScreen implements MediaGrabberResource
{
    private static ResourceBundle r = ResourceBundle.getBundle(BUNDLE_ID,
            BUNDLE_NAME);

    private BasicEditField location = new BasicEditField(r
            .getString(I18N_PROMPT_LOCATION), "file:///SDCard/BlackBerry", 100,
            Field.FIELD_VCENTER | BasicEditField.FILTER_URL);
    private MenuItem audioItem = new MenuItem(r
            .getString(MediaGrabber.I18N_CHOICE_RECORD_SOUND), 0, 0)
    {
        public void run()
        {
            launchRecorder(RecordingScreen.RECORD_AUDIO);
        }
    };
    private MenuItem pictureItem = new MenuItem(r
            .getString(MediaGrabber.I18N_CHOICE_TAKE_PICTURE), 0, 0)
    {
        public void run()
        {
            launchRecorder(RecordingScreen.RECORD_PICTURE);
        }
    };
    private MenuItem videoItem = new MenuItem(r
            .getString(MediaGrabber.I18N_CHOICE_RECORD_VIDEO), 0, 0)
    {
        public void run()
        {
            launchRecorder(RecordingScreen.RECORD_VIDEO);
        }
    };
    private MenuItem launchVideoItem = new MenuItem(r
            .getString(MediaGrabber.I18N_CHOICE_PLAY_MEDIA), 0, 0)
    {
        public void run()
        {
            launchPlayer();
        }
    };

    public ChoicesScreen()
    {
        setTitle("MediaGrabber");
        add(new LabelField(r.getString(MediaGrabber.I18N_INSTRUCTIONS)));
        add(location);
```

```java
    }

    public void close()
    {
        location.setDirty(false);
        super.close();
    }

    public void makeMenu(Menu menu, int instance)
    {
        if (instance == Menu.INSTANCE_DEFAULT)
        {
            String property = System.getProperty("supports.audio.capture");
            if (property != null && property.equals("true"))
            {
                menu.add(audioItem);
            }
            property = System.getProperty("video.snapshot.encodings");
            if (property != null && property.length() > 0)
            {
                menu.add(pictureItem);
            }
            property = System.getProperty("supports.video.capture");
            if (property != null && property.equals("true"))
            {
                menu.add(videoItem);
            }
            menu.add(launchVideoItem);
        }

        super.makeMenu(menu, instance);
    }

    private void launchRecorder(int type)
    {
        String directory = location.getText();
        RecordingScreen screen = new RecordingScreen(type, directory);
        UiApplication.getUiApplication().pushScreen(screen);
    }

    private void launchPlayer()
    {
        String url = location.getText();
        String pattern = r.getString(MediaGrabber.I18N_PLAY_MEDIA_TITLE);
        MessageFormat format = new MessageFormat("");
        format.setLocale(Locale.getDefaultForSystem());
        Object[] arguments = new String[] { url };
        format.applyPattern(pattern);
        String formatted = format.format(arguments);
        PlayingScreen screen = new PlayingScreen(url, formatted);
        UiApplication.getUiApplication().pushScreen(screen);
    }
```

```
public boolean onSavePrompt()
{
    return true;
}
}
```

The other localized classes can be found online. They follow the same technique shown here. If your app includes a large number of dynamically constructed strings, you should create a helper method that manages the `MessageFormat` operations to cut down on repeated code.

Testing Localization

Depending on your simulator, you can probably switch between US English and UK English, or two other language variants. As such, it's good to define at least these languages so you can verify that you are localizing correctly in the simulator.

When you are ready to test on the device, load MediaGrabber and start changing languages. Try to keep track of what the Language menu is called in each new language so you can find it again. Navigating the native BlackBerry menus can be tricky—for example, the permissions prompt will display in the new language, so you may need to hunt a bit for the "Save" option. You should see your localized text display in the new languages you have defined.

If possible, you will want to send the translated version to a native speaker. They will be able to let you know if any of the text needs to change. They can also quickly identify problems that might not be obvious to you, such as text being truncated or diacritical marks missing.

WANT MORE?

Porting can be a pain, but it's a good pain. If you're interested in porting it means that you have made a good impression on your initial target market and are looking to expand. Here are some other things you can try with MediaGrabber to get more practice.

- Include still more languages. If you know a native speaker for a language you do not speak, work with them to translate the app. This is very valuable experience and will help you learn how to manage translation efforts.
- Include menu options on the Choices screen for switching between supported languages within the app.
- If you have a BlackBerry with older software on it, try creating a new version of MediaGrabber that will run on it.
- Try running MediaGrabber on a variety of BlackBerry form factors, including QWERTY devices, touch-screen devices, and SureType devices. Are you happy with the experience? If not, think about ways you could change the app so it performs better on those devices.

The good news is, after your first couple of experiences with porting, you will start automatically thinking about it when you start a new project. Making smart decisions about your program's structure early on will ease the development process and turn the porting process into a pleasant afterthought rather than a chaotic scramble.

Excelsior

Porting gets too little respect. Without porting, each app would only run on a tiny fraction of phones. Without efficient porting, the amount of time spent getting an app to run on a new phone can approach the amount of time writing the app in the first place.

As you have seen in this chapter, the secret is to start thinking about porting before you write your first line of code. Early decisions can make an app far more difficult to port later on. Spend some time with a sheet of paper or a whiteboard and ask some fundamental questions. On what devices does the app need to run? Will it need to run on more later on? Can I force people to use a particular phone or OS version? Do I only want English-speaking Americans to use my app? Get input from your management or users if possible.

Then, as you construct your app, always keep the future in mind. Even if you are just writing for a particular device and language now, write flexibly so that the same code can be used to support other types of users. If you can, test with different configurations as you develop so you can verify that your code does adapt as planned.

If all goes well, your app will be a roaring success. Then you can spend an afternoon translating text and dropping in new image files, rather than weeks or months struggling with a labyrinth of hard-coded values. You will reach every market while your competitors are still lacing up their boots.

Once you're reaching a market this big, it's time to make sure you can handle it. Sooner or later, you'll want to consider how to best run your engineering process, including generating builds, delivering updates, and managing multiple versions. The next chapter will look at how to best build apps.

Chapter 11

Advanced Build Techniques

Whether you're running a one-person programming shop or belong to a multinational corporation, building and maintaining software will be an integral part of your BlackBerry experience. You saw in Chapter 10 how applications can grow more complicated as you increase the number and variety of users you target. This chapter looks at the other side of the problem: how you can manage your project and keep it under control.

Things that worked very well when you first started, such as using Eclipse to build an app and the Desktop Manager to load it onto a phone, become unfeasible once your app is running on a dozen different phone models. You will learn the techniques to scale up your development so you can handle the trials that come with success.

Moving Beyond Eclipse

I love Eclipse. I've used every major IDE, as well as old-school Unix editors and tools, and I feel more productive in Eclipse than I do anywhere else. That said, while Eclipse is a great resource for development, it's not a great tool for managing a large number of builds. For that, you will need to look elsewhere.

The Command Line

Behind the scenes, the BlackBerry Plug-in for Eclipse wraps some existing tools that have been around for much longer. Like RIM's proprietary JDE stand-alone IDE, the Plug-in calls out to these tools to handle the real work of building your app.

rapc

rapc is the core compiler that transforms your Java source files and other resources into a BlackBerry executable. rapc has an executable, `rapc.exe`, that mainly controls access to the JAR, `rapc.jar`.

Operations

You can study the use of rapc by examining the Eclipse build output window. Typically, it will run on all source files under a particular tree. This process runs through several operations.

- Initialization: Check to make sure that the passed arguments are correct and all required files have been provided.

- Compilation: All source files are run through a compatible Java compiler. If a compiled JAR file is provided, this stage is skipped.

- Verification: Inspect the resulting bytecode. Report any warnings or errors.

- Obfuscation: Remove any unused classes or methods.

- Create CODs: BlackBerry phones actually deal with small sections of code, referred to as sibling COD modules, which are typically 64kb or smaller in size. rapc will divide the application among all the sibling CODs (such as "MyApp.cod", "MyApp-1.cod", "MyApp-2.cod", etc.) and then zip them up into MyApp.cod.

- Modify JAD: BlackBerry-specific fields will be added to the JAD file. These include descriptions of the sibling COD modules, SHA1 checksums, and other fields.

Arguments

You can directly call rapc.exe yourself. The command has the following form.

```
rapc.exe {parameters} {Source files, compiled .class files, or compiled JAR file}
```

Note: Unfortunately, rapc does not support wildcards. If you wish to supply multiple files, you must list each one.

rapc isn't very well documented. The most important parameters are shown below.

- `import={paths}`: Specifies the location of `net_rim_api.jar` and any other required libraries.

- `codename={name}`: Provides the application name.

- `-midlet`: Indicates that this application is a MIDlet.

- -quiet: Suppress some messages.
- -verbose: Show all messages.
- jad={file}: Provides the input JAD file to use. This same file will be modified with the final JAD contents.

A typical use of rapc may look like the following.

```
C:\dev\ide\eclipse_34\plugins\net.rim.eide.componentpack4.7.0_4.7.0.46\↵
    components\bin\rapc.exe -import="C:\dev\ide\eclipse_34\plugins\↵
    net.rim.eide.componentpack4.7.0_4.7.0.46\components\lib\net_rim_api.jar"↵
    BonjourWorld.java BonjourWorld.rrh BonjourWorld.rrc
```

SignatureTool

Eclipse also wraps the important SignatureTool program, which contacts the BlackBerry signing servers and applies signatures to your compiled program. As with rapc, you can directly interact with SignatureTool through the command line.

> **Note:** Refer to Chapter 1 for more information on using SignatureTool with multiple software versions, as well as how to install signing keys.

You can run SignatureTool on a compiled BlackBerry program with the following command line.

```
{Path to JDE installation directory}\bin\SignatureTool.jar {Cod Name}.cod
```

The parameters include the following options.

- -r {Directory}: Recursively search a directory for COD files to sign.
- -f {File}: Read the COD files to sign from the provided file.
- -d: Delete the file passed with the -f command.
- -a: Automatically request signatures.
- -p {Password}: Password for code signing requests.
- -s: Show statistics about signatures requested and received.
- -c: Close the window after successfully requesting signatures.
- -C: Always close window after requesting signatures.

Build Environments

Armed with knowledge of how the BlackBerry toolchain works, you can set up automated builds. These will greatly increase your productivity. Rather than needing to open Eclipse, navigate to a particular project workspace, switch to the proper version of the BlackBerry Plug-in, then click on the options to build and sign, you can simply double-click a build file, or wait for an automated build server to incorporate your changes.

Build Options

You can use any tool that is capable of running a command-line argument and passing parameters: that is to say, pretty much any build tool ever. If you belong to an organization that already has a build system in place, it will be worth the effort to adapt the BlackBerry build process to fit that system. If you are working from a blank slate, you can consider the following.

Batch Files

Really, a build script is just a couple of executable commands. You could simply type those commands into a .bat file, place it in the folder with your source code, then double-click it any time you wanted to do a build. The batch file might look like the following.

```
set FILES=BonjourWorld.java BonjourWorld.rrh BonjourWorld.rrc
set JDE_PATH=C:\dev\ide\eclipse_34\plugins\↵
    net.rim.eide.componentpack4.7.0_4.7.0.46\components\
%JDE_PATH%\bin\rapc.exe -import="%JDE_PATH%\lib\net_rim_api.jar" %FILES%
%JDE_PATH%\bin\SignatureTool.jar MediaGrabber.cod
```

> **Caution:** Whenever you are dealing with automated builds, be careful about what JDE version you reference. Remember Chapter 10's rules about forwards and backwards compatibility.

Ant Scripts

Ant is the most popular build scripting option for Java programmers today. A full description of Ant is beyond the scope of this book; essentially, it divides a build into a set of targets and tasks, each with parameters that can control their behavior. Therefore, you can write a generic Ant build file to compile any of your projects, and use different parameters to control the specific project to build.

You can directly call out to the rapc tool by using Ant's <exec> task. However, consider looking at the useful and free BlackBerry Ant Tools package, also known as bb-ant-tools. This useful set of Ant tasks is not officially sanctioned by RIM, but has been widely adopted by developers. Prior to the release of the BlackBerry Plug-in for Eclipse, many people used bb-ant-tools to develop BlackBerry programs within Eclipse.

bb-ant-tools contains tasks for nearly every BlackBerry-specific task you can imagine.

- ■ <rapc> will run rapc to generate your executable. It has a large number of options, including choices for setting the application location, icon, etc.

- `<sigtool>` will start the signature request process. All command line arguments are supported here, including the option to automatically supply a password.

- `<alx>` packages together a release with a valid ALX file and all the associated COD files. This is useful when preparing a cable-load version.

- `<jadtool>` will patch up a JAD file by adding information for all the COD files. This is useful when preparing an OTA version.

One of the best things about bb-ant-tools is its cross-platform support. You will still need a Windows machine to install the tools, but you can copy the JDE installation to a Linux or Mac machine and then use bb-ant-tools to perform the actual builds.

Makefiles

Many in-house build systems rely on makefiles. While not as elegant as Ant, make has a long history and supports powerful command-line expressions.

If you plan to use makefiles, consider defining a BlackBerry rule to build the .cod target. This rule can then in turn use other rules for running rapc, signing, and performing any other required build steps. Your BlackBerry rule can be invoked as part of the standard build cycle, which may include steps for documentation, publishing, or other important tasks.

Versioning Strategies

One of the most important BlackBerry properties you can define is the version number of the app. The BlackBerry uses the version number to determine whether a user needs an upgrade. However, versioning goes far beyond picking a unique version number. Before you decide your app needs a new version, you will need to decide how to make that version available to your users.

Version Numbers

Like Java MIDlets, BlackBerry applications come with a three-part version number: you can define two or three version numbers, each separated by a dot, each with a value between 0 and 99. So 1.0.3, 4.2, and 0.99.0 are all valid numbers; 2, 1.125, and 4.1.3.2 are not.

The first two numbers are known as the *major* and the *minor* version numbers. The optional third number is called the *patch* version. By convention, a version with a different patch number will contain bug fixes but no new features; a minor version change means that new features are available; and a major version number change indicates significant changes that include a break in program compatibility.

For example, imagine that you release an app that lets college students register for their courses. Your first version might be 1.0. Later, you let students add their reviews of professors and classes. This change would be released as version 1.1. You might find that some reviews aren't formatted properly; you fix this bug and issue an update as version 1.1.1. Then the college changes its course scheduling software, meaning your app no longer works with the new system. You could then make the necessary changes and release version 2.0.

A switch from a lower version to a higher version number is called an *upgrade*. BlackBerry also supports switching from a higher version to a lower version, which is a *downgrade*. You may also choose to install a new copy with the same version number. This is useful during development, because it may not be practical to create a new version number with every build change, but it could be confusing to your users. Any time you release a new version of your app, it should have a higher version number.

> **Note:** If you change the application name or the vendor name, it will be considered a different application and won't replace the previous version. So, if the name changes from CollegeBuddy to MyRegistrar, a user who upgraded to MyRegistrar will actually have both apps. As long as the name and vendor remain the same, installing a new version will replace the older version.

Distribution Options

Once you have built a new version of the app with a new version number, you must decide how to make it available to your users. You can choose between several options.

- Cable load: Send the updated app to the user's PC. You can do this through any mechanism you like: send them an email with the new version attached, instruct them to visit a web site where they can download it, and so on. If the downloaded .alx file is placed in the same location as the original .alx, the user will automatically be prompted to install the updated version the next time they view the applications within BlackBerry Desktop Manager. Otherwise, they can browse to the updated file within the desktop manager and select it. In general, you must use a higher version number or the Desktop Manager will resist installing the update.

- OTA: Place the JAD file and the sibling COD modules on a web server. Configure the JAD files to have a MIME type of `text/vnd.sun.j2me.app-descriptor` and the COD files to a MIME type of `application/vnd.rim.cod`. Direct the user to visit the JAD file with their BlackBerry web browser. They will be prompted to download and install the new app.

- Store: Recent versions of BlackBerry App World will notify users within the store if a previously purchased application has a new version available. Other stores may offer this feature as well; check to see if they support it.

- In-app updates: BlackBerry's CodeModuleManager API allows one application to install another application. If you have a suite of applications, you could have one app check for updates for another application, then download and install them. This approach allows you to provide your own user interface on the device to manage updates, rather than relying on the BlackBerry browser.

- Push: If your app is running in a BES environment, the administrator can forcibly send a new version of the app to all affected phones.

You also must decide how to let users know when a new version is available. Even if you are using an application store to deliver your updates, keep in mind that some people may frequently use your app but only rarely launch the store, so otherwise they may not be aware of updates.

- Poll: Your app can connect to a server you control to check for the latest version number. If it finds an update, alert the user within the app. This works best when the user can complete the update on the device, either OTA through the browser or within the app.

- Push: If you have access to the user's email address or similar information, you can send him notifications when new versions are available. This approach works best if the update must be completed on the desktop.

You will generally have the most successful upgrades if you deliver updates through the same channel that originally installed the app. If you initially distributed the app OTA, use OTA for updates; if you used a PC-based application to download the app, use that same app to download the latest versions.

Where's My Data?

Nearly every interesting app will make some use of persistent storage. Whether saving games, user preferences, or downloaded art, persistent storage enhances apps by providing more convenient and increasing speed.

Persistence also leads to potential problems, though. Different versions of the app may store data in different formats, leading to potential problems if the user updates.

Files

BlackBerry does not have any logic that associates files to applications. Your app can write to any directory and read from any directory that it wants. When the app is deleted or upgraded, all existing files will remain in place.

This has a few ramifications. First, if you store actual program data in files, you will be responsible for maintaining your own versioning system. For example, you might tag the start of each file with the version number of the file format. This way, when future versions of the app try to read those files, they can quickly determine whether the files are compatible, and either translate or delete them if the file format has changed. Second, if you store media files like images or sounds, you can keep them in place and safely reuse on newer app versions. However, if you have a larger number of media files, they will still be taking up space after the user deletes your app; this may annoy some people. To be a good citizen on the phone, offer a choice within your app to clean up any such files. Users can run this option before deleting your app and return to a blank slate.

RMS

BlackBerry borrows the Record Management System from Java ME. This provides a very convenient way to store sets of records, such as recent news headlines or restaurant details. Records are stored as raw byte streams, without any version number or ordering.

Unlike files, RMS records are tied to a particular application. If you delete an app, all its RMS records will automatically be removed. When you install an upgraded version, the RMS records will remain in place and the new version will be able to read the old data. If a user updates OTA through the web browser, she will be able to choose whether or not to retain the old RMS data.

Few applications actually want to deal with raw bytes, so typically an app will serialize and deserialize to translate between the RMS record data and some sort of object. For example, you might define plain Java classes like NewsStory or RestaurantInfo and define methods to create these objects from byte arrays. So long as the class structure remains exactly the same, you can reuse the data across different app versions. However, odds are high that the record format will need to change at some point to support later application features. In order to future-proof your record storage, you should always tag the beginning of an RMS record with the version number. Future versions of the app can inspect this value first and decide how to handle the data that follows.

> **Tip:** The version number of your record can be different from the version of your app. Maybe app versions 1.0, 1.3, and 2.0 all use the same record structure; if so, the records can share version number 1. If you later change the structure, such as adding a "Byline" field to the NewsStory class as part of your changes to app version 2.1, you would increase the RMS record version number to 2.

BlackBerry Persistent Storage

The `PersistentStore` and `PersistentObject` classes provide the capability to save application data. Unlike RMS, BlackBerry persistent storage is object-based rather than byte-based. This allows for more flexible and elegant coding.

You store persistent objects based on a provided key. However, BlackBerry also tracks persisted objects by the application that created them. If an application is later removed, BlackBerry automatically deletes all persistent objects that are no longer accessible on the device.

BlackBerry tries to detect the compatibility of persisted objects. If you load a new version of the application that has the exact same class structure for the persisted objects, the previous data will probably be maintained. On the other hand, if the data in a class changes or its structure is significantly altered (for example, by adding, removing, or reordering many methods), the old data will be automatically removed when the new version is installed. Therefore, you should avoid relying on BlackBerry persistent storage for data that you will need to access in future versions of the app. Look at this as a convenience to speed program operation, not as a reliable storage system.

Debugging and Logging

Applications have bugs. It's a fact of life. Pretending that your app is perfect won't make the problem go away, but only makes its bugs more difficult to squash. In order to quickly detect bugs and determine the root cause, developers often rely upon logging and debug information placed within their apps.

This leads to a quandary. Ideally, you would like to place debugging features in your app so you can quickly and conveniently debug any problems that come up. However, you probably don't want end-users to have access to the program's inner workings. This often leads developers to create separate "debug" and "release" versions of their application. This in turn has problems, as it means that the version a developer uses for testing isn't exactly the same as the version that people are actually using. Few things are more frustrating than finding a bug in the release version, which you cannot debug, which does not appear in the debug version.

Capturing Logging

The most primitive method of debugging is to make your program print out information about what it's doing. While low-tech, it can also be perfect. If the phone is not able to connect to the network, and when you hook it up to the logger you see the message "ERROR: Permission not set to open connection," you have cut an hour-long debugging session down to a few minutes.

BlackBerry makes it easy to get logging information. Simply connect the device to your PC with a USB cable, start Eclipse, and start debugging the BlackBerry device. Even if you do not have access to the source code or .debug files, you will be able to watch the output window to view all the messages that are generated by the BlackBerry. These include messages from the running application, as well as more inscrutable messages from the BlackBerry operating system.

So, what gets written to the BlackBerry logger? Anything that you send to System.out or System.err. It can be a good idea to include plenty of logging information as your write your app, particularly for areas that you suspect might fail at some point.

> **Tip:** Stack trace information also gets printed to the log. However, most exceptions will not produce a useful stack trace. If you want to see the full trace information in the log, you must catch the Throwable instead of an Exception subclass. Don't blame me, I didn't create this system.

Visual Logging

Sometimes it's nice to actually see what's happening on the device itself, without needing to hook it up to a PC. This is especially useful if someone else is testing the app and you want more information about a problem that occurred. You can capture relevant information yourself, and then direct that information to an onscreen element. We have used this approach with StatusUpdater in MediaGrabber to get more detailed information about exceptions that occurred.

You can even take this idea one step further and create a full-blown logging screen within your app. Rather than directing logging information to System.out, store it within your app or in a log file. Your debugging screen can then read through this information on demand and display a detailed log of everything the app has done.

On or Off?

You can follow several strategies to address the problem of providing a useful debugging environment without giving users or competitors overly detailed looks into the app's functions.

- Bifurcate: Create two versions of the application, one with debugging compiled in and another without. If you use a preprocessor as part of your build process, you can use it to automatically strip out logging calls. Alternately, you could create a proxy logging method like Log.writeLog(), then provide different versions of the Log class for debug and release builds. The debug build would write to standard out or your internal log, while the release build does nothing.

■ App property: You can include a special JAD property in your application that controls whether or not to display the log. If this property is set, Log.writeLog() would create logging information; if the property is unset, it would do nothing. The advantage of this approach is that you only need to build the application binary once, and the same code is loaded on both testing and user devices; the only difference is the run-time check for whether logging is enabled.

■ Secret code: Similar to the previous strategy, you can have a flag within your application that controls whether or not to display debugging information. You can toggle this flag by entering a secret code, following a particular sequence, or otherwise performing some unusual action within the app. What is really nice about this approach is that, even if a bug occurs on an actual released version, you can ask the affected user to enter the code and report the logging information to you. The disadvantage is that the secret code will eventually leak out, and once it does your logging information will no longer be safe from competitors.

Data Collection

Even if you can look at logging information, it may be awkward and difficult to parse. It's much easier to deal with detailed log files on the PC than it is on a handset.

Therefore, consider including some error reporting capabilities within your app. For example, you might include a menu option that reads "Send report to developer." If a user selects this item, the app will collect all the current logging information that it has collected, place it in an email, and send it to you. This way, if a user runs into a problem with their application, they can help you solve it by providing more insight into what the app is doing.

Consider combining this approach with the "Secret code" strategy. You might not want to receive reports from thousands of curious users, but it's nice to have the option for cases where things have gone seriously wrong.

Other Build Issues

No two people or organizations will settle on the exact same process for building and releasing their applications. You may encounter several other issues and ideas when preparing your builds.

Obfuscation

Java ME developers often rely on obfuscators such as Proguard to optimize their code. Obfuscators have several effects. First, true to their name, they conceal the workings of an application by renaming classes, variables, and method names; therefore, even if someone decompiles an application, he will find it difficult to understand. More importantly than the decompilation part, though, obfuscators also remove unused sections of code. If an obfuscator determines that a method can never be called, or a class will never be instantiated, it will strip out the affected code. For mobile platforms that have a limited amount of space available for applications, such savings can prove crucial.

As noted above, rapc includes an obfuscation stage that will strip out unused code. In addition, because the COD file format is proprietary and unique to RIM devices, it cannot be reverse-engineered with the same ease that Java ME JAR files can. We have previously seen that you can open a COD file in a hex editor to view program information, but, currently, no true decompiler exists for the COD format.

Because of these aspects, you can generally omit obfuscation from your build process. However, there are times when Proguard offers more aggressive obfuscation settings or more fine-tuning than the automatic behavior you get from rapc. If you feel that your application is still too large, you may choose to add a third-party obfuscator to your process. In this case, you would probably follow these steps.

1.   Compile your source using the RIM tools; a JAR file will be produced as part of this process.

2.   Extract the JAR contents to another directory.

3.   Run an obfuscator on the resulting files.

4.   Run RIM's preverify.exe command (found in the bin directory) on the obfuscated files.

5.   Pass the preverified files to rapc for the final transformation into a COD.

> **Caution:** If you do not use rapc to preverify and compile your source files, you can encounter unusual and frustrating errors such as the dreaded Stack Map message when launching your app. Pay careful attention to your Java compiler version, obfuscation settings, and especially any messages generated by rapc. You may need to tweak your settings to get the right results.

Packaging OTA Installs

You have already seen how to configure a web server to deliver BlackBerry applications directly to a phone via its web browser. This approach works great for simple applications with a single module. However, if an application contains multiple parts, such as related applications in a suite or a set of libraries, the user must individually download and install each module. This is a tedious and error-prone approach.

Fortunately, you can short-circuit this problem by referencing all required COD modules within the JAD file. The user then sees a single application that he is downloading, but behind the scenes all other required apps will be installed as well.

If you are using bb-ant-tools to generate OTA deployments, you can easily get this behavior by using the `<jadtool>` task with multiple COD files. Otherwise, you might need to collate the JAD information yourself. First, build each project separately. Open the JAD files. You'll notice that the COD information inside includes text like the following.

```
RIM-COD-Module-Dependencies: net_rim_cldc,net_rim_os,net_rim_bb_framework_api,↵
    net_rim_bbapi_menuitem,net_rim_pdap,net_rim_crypto_1,net_rim_crypto_3,↵
    net_rim_bbapi_mailv2
RIM-MIDlet-Flags-1: 1
RIM-MIDlet-Flags-2: 0
RIM-COD-URL-9: MediaGrabber-9.cod
RIM-COD-Size-9: 49972
RIM-COD-SHA1-9: a4 75 3d 10 c9 93 e6 49 b0 05 80 96 39 03 42 0f 12 ff 69 9d
RIM-COD-URL-10: MediaGrabber-10.cod
RIM-COD-Size-10: 49976
RIM-COD-SHA1-10: 87 b5 20 cb c5 7e 29 10 4c 8e c6 2a 4d fa 90 11 8f 1d 70 87
```

You can take all the `RIM-COD-*` lines in the other JAD files and merge them into the first JAD file. You will need to increment the COD file numbers. For example, if the first JAD file goes up to `RIM-COD-URL-13`, then you would import the next JAD file's `RIM-COD-URL-1` as `RIM-COD-URL-14`. You might also need to edit the `RIM-COD-Module-Dependencies` so it contains the dependencies of each individual project. Finally, any `RIM-MIDlet-Flags` or `RIM-Library-Flags` must be moved over into the main JAD file. Again, you should renumber so that the imported modules start one number higher than the highest number.

You can edit a JAD file by hand, and this approach will be fine if you create OTA releases very infrequently. Otherwise, look into creating a basic script to handle the JAD file collation process. Python, perl, and sed are all good candidates. If you don't know any text processing scripting languages, this is a great excuse to learn.

Packaging ALX Installs

As with OTA installation, a cable load install is more likely to succeed if all the required code modules can be sent as part of a single operation. You can use bb-ant-tools to easily generate an ALX file that contains multiple COD components. Or you can simply edit the ALX file yourself. The following code shows a simple ALX file that includes both an application and a library as part of the install.

```
<loader version="1.0">
    <application id="MediaGrabber">
        <name>MediaGrabber</name>
        <description>All media everywhere</description>
        <version>1.0.0</version>
        <vendor>Apress</vendor>
        <copyright>Copyright (c) 2009 Apress</copyright>
        <fileset Java="1.39">
            <directory ></directory>
            <files >
                MediaGrabber.cod
                FriendTracker.cod
```

```
                </files>
            </fileset>
        </application>
    </loader>
```

App: Logging, Building, and Updating

You will make a trio of changes to MediaGrabber: two for your own convenience, and one for your users' convenience. None of these uses advanced APIs or esoteric techniques, but all are very practical and lead to smoother development and use.

Adding a Logger

You already collect information about almost everything interesting that occurs in your app within the StatusUpdater class. You can easily extend this class to hold that logging information in memory, and provide a way to get access to it. This can be useful if you see that something has gone wrong but the onscreen messages have already been replaced.

Listing 11-1 shows the changes to StatusUpdater. To maintain a single unified log that captures the use of all individual instances, use a single static instance of a Vector that holds the old log messages.

Listing 11-1. StatusUpdater with Stored Logging

```
package com.apress.king.mediagrabber;

import java.util.*;

import net.rim.device.api.ui.UiApplication;
import net.rim.device.api.ui.component.LabelField;

public class StatusUpdater implements Runnable
{
    private LabelField status;
    private String message;
    private UiApplication app;
    private static Vector messages = new Vector();

    public StatusUpdater(LabelField status)
    {
        this.status = status;
        app = UiApplication.getUiApplication();
    }

    public void sendDelayedMessage(String message)
    {
        messages.addElement(message);
        this.message = message;
        app.invokeLater(this);
    }
```

```
public static String getLog()
{
    StringBuffer result = new StringBuffer();
    Enumeration lines = messages.elements();
    while (lines.hasMoreElements())
    {
        String line = (String) lines.nextElement();
        result.append(line);
        result.append("\n");
    }
    return result.toString();
}

public void run()
{
    status.setText(message);
}
}
```

You'll invoke this code soon. For now, recognize that this captures almost every Throwable that can occur within the program because of the way you have already set up your error handling. On a successful run of the application, very little logging information will be generated. Failures will be retained until the application is unloaded. Of course, this could be enhanced to support multiple log severity levels and other useful items.

Build Script

Even if you don't have GNU make or Apache Ant installed, you can whip together a quick and dirty build script using Notepad or another basic text editing program. Use the build script in Listing 11-2 to generate a new application without requiring Eclipse to be open. You can modify the variables at the top of the script with the location of your BlackBerry component package, signing password, and so on.

Listing 11-2. Build Batch File

```
set JDE_PATH=C:\dev\ide\eclipse_34\plugins\↵
    net.rim.eide.componentpack4.7.0_4.7.0.46\components\
set PASSWORD=swordfish
set FILES=MediaGrabber.java ChoicesScreen.java PlayingScreen.java↵
    RecordingScreen.java SendingScreen.java StatusUpdater.java MediaGrabber.rrh↵
    MediaGrabber.rrc MediaGrabber_cs.rrc MediaGrabber_en.rrc↵
    MediaGrabber_en_GB.rrc MediaGrabber_en_US.rrc
set SOURCEPATH=src\com\apress\king\mediagrabber
set STARTDIR="%CD%"
cd %SOURCEPATH%
%JDE_PATH%\bin\rapc.exe -import="%JDE_PATH%\lib\net_rim_api.jar" %FILES%
%JDE_PATH%\bin\SignatureTool.jar -a -p %PASSWORD% -c MediaGrabber.cod
copy MediaGrabber.cod %STARTDIR%
cd %STARTDIR%
```

Updates

If you have access to a web server, you can place the MediaGrabber JAD file and the unzipped sibling COD files on a publicly accessible directory. Then, direct MediaGrabber to open a browser to the JAD location to check for an update. You can do this using the Browser. Listing 11-3 shows the changes to ChoicesScreen that add a new menu item to perform the update. You can also create a menu item that captures information from the logger, and then sends it via email using our existing SendingScreen class.

Listing 11-3. Adding Logging and Updates to MediaGrabber Choices

```
public class ChoicesScreen extends MainScreen implements MediaGrabberResource
{
// ...
    private MenuItem sendLogItem = new MenuItem("Send Log", 0x10000, 0)
    {
        public void run()
        {
            String message = StatusUpdater.getLog();
            SendingScreen sending = new SendingScreen("text/plain", "log.txt",
                    "Log attached", message.getBytes(), false);
            UiApplication.getUiApplication().pushScreen(sending);
        }
    };
    private MenuItem updateItem = new MenuItem("Get Latest Version", 0x20000, 0)
    {
        public void run()
        {
            String url = "http://www.example.com/MediaGrabber.jad";
            Browser.getDefaultSession().displayPage(url);
        }
    };
// ...
    public void makeMenu(Menu menu, int instance)
    {
        if (instance == Menu.INSTANCE_DEFAULT)
        {
            String property = System.getProperty("supports.audio.capture");
            if (property != null && property.equals("true"))
            {
                menu.add(audioItem);
            }
            property = System.getProperty("video.snapshot.encodings");
            if (property != null && property.length() > 0)
            {
                menu.add(pictureItem);
            }
            property = System.getProperty("supports.video.capture");
            if (property != null && property.equals("true"))
            {
                menu.add(videoItem);
            }
            menu.add(launchVideoItem);
            menu.add(sendLogItem);
```

```
            menu.add(updateItem);
        }

        super.makeMenu(menu, instance);
    }
// ...
}
```

Excelsior

Even though the build chapter comes at the end of the book, it holds great importance. Even the smallest developer will appreciate the convenience of a powerful build system when she starts releasing multiple versions of her application. You will probably spend some time tweaking your builds to find a process that works well for you. Once you understand how the tools work and the implications of upgrading, you can mix and match techniques until you find the best possible fit.

You have now encountered the tools and strategies that you can use to elevate your app from a good idea up to a professional piece of software. This has been a great journey, but it does not need to be the end. A truly successful developer will always be learning more, staying ahead of the curve and learning to look down the road at what comes next. The conclusion will describe some of the best resources available to maintain a top-notch grasp of BlackBerry software development.

Chapter 12

Conclusion

You've reached the top! Congratulations—by learning the advanced BlackBerry APIs, discovering how to integrate with the phone's built-in applications, and discovering the tools to create polished and efficient professional apps, you have earned the right to call yourself an advanced BlackBerry developer.

That said, there is still plenty to learn and even more to do out there. While this book has laid a broad foundation, it's up to you to build something on top of it. This section shares a few final thoughts on how to maintain an eager, up-to-date mindset towards BlackBerry development.

Parting Shots

During my time writing BlackBerry apps, I have stumbled across several useful tips. I have tried to work most of them into the text of this book; here are a few final ones that did not fit anywhere else.

- Older simulators: The strength of the BlackBerry simulator also serves as its curse: because it accurately reproduces the entire operating system, the simulator takes a long time to launch and "boot up." Different versions of the simulator can have noticeably different launch times. If you use an older version of the simulator that is still compatible with your app, you can save a great deal of time over the hundreds of times that you launch the simulator.

- WTK: As a more extreme version of the above, if you are developing MIDlets, consider using Sun's Wireless Toolkit (WTK) for the bulk of your development. This emulator is much more lightweight than the RIM emulator, albeit less representative of the actual device. If your app uses BlackBerry APIs, you can develop the bulk of your application with the WTK, and then switch to the BlackBerry simulator when you need to test RIM-specific code.

- Clean slate: The simulator folder contains a file called `clean.bat`. Whenever the simulator seems to be behaving strangely, try running this file. It will place the simulator back into its original state, removing any changes you have made.

- Not clean enough: The Eclipse Plug-in includes options for erasing simulator files. At the time of writing, these are pretty unreliable, particularly for extra simulators you have downloaded. It might be necessary to navigate to the simulator directory yourself and manually delete the modules you have loaded.

- Too many changes: Any time you switch the JDE Component Package you are using, be sure to also change the MDS simulator version and clean the simulators. Otherwise, even if your application runs, you may encounter strange networking errors or other problems. Also, clean and rebuild your project until no errors occur.

- Source control: RIM's Eclipse tools do not always work well with source control metadata files; in particular, it can get confused with Subversion files that look similar to resource files. These are often transient errors, and a fresh build will fix the problem. If it grows too annoying, consider exporting your source control files to a clean directory, running Eclipse with those files, and then copying back when you are ready to check back in.

Resources

The single most valuable skill you can learn is how to find additional information. I've found the following resources to be especially useful. When you're facing an unusual BlackBerry bug or want to learn how to do something new, check these first.

- The BlackBerry Technical Solution Center at `www.blackberry.com/btsc/`. The Developer Knowledge Base articles are particularly useful. They tend to be very specific, describing how something works or how to accomplish a particular task. Articles are updated as new versions of software are released, so check back periodically for more information.

- The official BlackBerry Java developer forums are a sub-forum found at `supportforums.blackberry.com/rim/`. RIM runs one of the best forums of any mobile software platform; I really wish other companies would follow their lead. RIM employees frequent the boards and offer authoritative answers on particular issues and questions. There are many talented private contributors who gain kudos with their helpful input. If you run across a problem, odds are high that someone else has already stumbled across it and solved it on these forums.

- Unofficial BlackBerry developer forum at www.blackberryforums.com/developer-forum/. Prior to the launch of the official RIM forums, this was the main go-to place for technical questions. They have grown much quieter since the official forums launched, but a good amount of historical information about prior software versions can be found here.

- Sample code: Unfortunately, the BlackBerry Plug-in for Eclipse does not come with any program samples. However, the RIM JDE and the JDE Component Package both include samples along with the development tools. You can download and install these from RIM's web site. Look for the samples folder under the installation directory. The samples are very comprehensive, well organized, and provide good insight into how to successfully use particular APIs.

- BlackBerry Developer Newsletter: You can sign up for this newsletter at any time. While the technical information is not very dense, it's a great way to keep abreast of ongoing changes within RIM.

Note: URLs can change frequently, but the names tend to stay constant, so a quick search on RIM's web site or your favorite search engine is the best way to locate these.

Summit

Have fun! Write code! The more you practice and the more you build stuff, the more you will learn. Every new project brings new opportunities with it, and there's no substitute for hands-on experience.

Feel free to continue tweaking MediaGrabber; you may have some new ideas about how to make it more powerful or useful to you. If so, go for it! Or, while reading this book, you might have come up with a cool app idea on your own. Great! The wonderful thing about BlackBerry development is its combination of a powerful platform, low barrier to entry, and immediate impact. If you write a good app and put it out where everyone can see it, you will be noticed.

Keep in mind that everything changes. Future versions of the platform will come along, offering still more features and capabilities. Keep your eyes open, find out what's new, and calculate what would be useful. At the same time, hold on to the essentials. Now that you have mastered the key aspects of BlackBerry software development, you should be able to incorporate new information without losing sight of the critical elements of an application.

The journey never stops. Keep climbing a little higher—you never know what sight awaits you over the crest.

Codec Support

Chapter 3 discussed how BlackBerry devices offer a range of codecs to play back audio and video content. This appendix provides some more details on codec support for a range of popular BlackBerry devices. Please see Table A-1 for this information. Notes applying to each device/codec combination follow the table.

Table A-1. *Devices and Their Supported Codecs*

Device Model	Container	Codecs	Notes
Bold 9700	MP4/M4A/3GP/MOV	H.264	(1)(2)
		H.263	(2)(8)
		MPEG4	(2)(6)(22)
		AAC-LC/AAC+/eAAC+	(2)(6)
		AMR-NB	(2)
	AVI	MPEG4	(2)(22)
		MP3	
	ASF/WMA/WMV	Windows Media Video 9	(5)
		Windows Media Audio 9 Standard/Professional	(2)
		Windows Media 10 Standard/Professional	(2)

Table A-1. *Devices and Their Supported Codecs (continued)*

Device Model	Container	Codecs	Notes
	MP3	MP3	
Tour 9630, Storm 2 9520, Storm 2 9550	MP4/M4A/3GP/3GP2	H.264	(1)(2)(6)
		H.263	(2)(3)
		MPEG4	(2)(4)
		AAC-LC/AAC+/eAAC+	(2)(6)
		AMR-NB	(2)
		QCELP EVRC	
	AVI	MPEG4	(2)(4)
		MP3	
	ASF/WMA/WMV	Windows Media Video 9	(5)
		Windows Media Audio 9	(2)
		Windows Media 10 Standard/Professional	(2)
	MP3	MP3	
Storm 9500/9530	MP4/M4A/3GP/3GP2	H.264	(1)(2)(6)
		H.263	(2)(3)
		MPEG4	(2)(4)
		AAC-LC/AAC+/eAAC+	(2)(6)
		AMR-NB	(2)
		QCELP EVRC	

Table A-1. Devices and Their Supported Codecs (continued)

Device Model	Container	Codecs	Notes
	AVI	MPEG4	(2)(4)
		MP3	
	ASF/WMA/WMV	Windows Media Video 9	(5)
		Windows Media Audio 9	(2)
		Windows Media 10 Standard/Professional	(2)
	MP3	MP3	
Bold 9000	MP4/M4A/3GP/MOV	H.264	(2) (11)
		H.263	(2)(8)
		MPEG4	(2)(6)(12)
		AAC-LC/AAC+/eAAC+	(2)(6)
		AMR-NB	(2)
	AVI	MPEG4	(2)(11)
		MP3	
	ASF/WMA/WMV	Windows Media Video 9	(13)
		Windows Media Audio 9 Standard/Professional	
		Windows Media 10 Standard/Professional	
	MP3	MP3	
Curve 8900, 8520	MP4/M4A/3GP/MOV	H.264	(2) (7)

Table A-1. *Devices and Their Supported Codecs (continued)*

Device Model	Container	Codecs	Notes
		H.263	(2)(8)
		MPEG4	(2)(6)(9)
		AAC-LC/AAC+/eAAC+	(2)(6)
		AMR-NB	(2)
	AVI	MPEG4	(2)(9)
		MP3	
	ASF/WMA/WMV	Windows Media Video 9	(10)
		Windows Media Audio 9	
		Windows Media 10 Standard/Professional	
	MP3	MP3	
Curve 8330, 8830	MP4/M4A/3GP/MOV	H.263	(2) (8)
		MPEG4	(2) (6) (19)
		AAC-LC/AAC+/eAAC+	(2)(6)
		AMR-NB	(2)
	ASF/WMA/WMV	Windows Media Video 9	(21)
		Windows Media Audio 9 Standard/Professional	
		Windows Media 10 Standard/Professional	
	MP3	MP3	

Table A-1. *Devices and Their Supported Codecs (continued)*

Device Model	Container	Codecs	Notes
Curve 8300, 8310, 8320, 8350i, 8800, 8820	MP4/M4A/3GP/MOV	H.263	(2) (8)
		MPEG4	(2) (15) (19)
		AAC-LC/AAC+/eAAC+	(2)(15)
		AMR-NB	(2)
	AVI	MPEG4	(2)(18)(20)
		MP3	(16)(18)
	ASF/WMA/WMV	Windows Media Video 9	(21)
		Windows Media Audio 9 Standard/Professional	
		Windows Media 10 Standard/Professional	
	MP3	MP3	
Pearl 8130	MP4/3GP	H.263	(2) (8)
		MPEG4	(2) (6) (14)
		AAC-LC/AAC+/eAAC+	(2)(6)
		AMR-NB	(2)
	ASF/WMA/WMV	Windows Media Video 9	(17)
		Windows Media Audio 9 Standard/Professional	
		Windows Media 10 Standard/Professional	

Table A-1. *Devices and Their Supported Codecs (continued)*

Device Model	Container	Codecs	Notes
	MP3	MP3	
Pearl 8100, 8110, 8120, 8220	MP4/M4A/3GP/MOV	H.263	(2) (8)
		MPEG4	(2)(14)(15)
		AAC-LC/AAC+/eAAC+	(2)(15)
		AMR-NB	(2)
	AVI	MPEG4	(2)(16)(18)
		MP3	(18)
	ASF/WMA/WMV	Windows Media Video 9	(17)
		Windows Media Audio 9 Standard/Professional	
		Windows Media 10 Standard/Professional	
	MP3	MP3	

Notes

(1)   Baseline Profile. 480×360 resolution. Up to 2Mbps, 30fps.

(2)   Supports RTSP streaming with device software 4.3 or later.

(3)   Profile 0 and 3, Level 30. 480×360 resolution. Up to 2Mbps, 30fps.

(4)   Simple Profile, Level 3. 480×360 resolution. Up to 2Mbps, 30fps.

(5)   WMV3 Simple Profile. 480×360 resolution. 30fps.

(6)   Recommended format for local playback.

(7)   Baseline Profile. 480×360 resolution. Up to 1.5Mbps, 24fps.

(8)   Profile 0 and 3, Level 45.

(9)   Simple/Advance Simple Profiles. 480×360 resolution. Up to 1.5Mbps, 24fps.

(10) WMV3 Simple Profile, Main Profile. 480×360 resolution. 24fps.

(11) Baseline Profile. 480×320 resolution. Up to 1.5Mbps, 24fps.

(12) Simple/Advance Simple Profiles. 480×320 resolution. Up to 1.5Mbps, 24fps.

(13) WMV3 Simple Profile, Main Profile. 480×320 resolution. 24fps.

(14) Simple Profile. 240x320 resolution. Up to 768kbps, 24fps.

(15) Recommended format for local playback for device software version 4.5 or higher.

(16) Simple/Advance Simple Profiles. 240×320 resolution. Up to 768kbps, 24fps.

(17) WMV3 Simple Profile. 240×320 resolution. 24fps.

(18) Recommended format for local playback for device software version 4.2 or 4.3.

(19) Simple Profile. 320×240 resolution. Up to 768kbps, 24fps.

(20) Simple/Advance Simple Profiles. 320×240 resolution. Up to 768kbps, 24fps.

(21) WMV3 Simple Profile. 320×240 resolution. 24fps.

(22) Simple/Advance Simple Profiles. 480×360 resolution. Up to 2Mbps, 30fps.

Index

D

K

L

O

P